NUTRITION AND HEALTH AMONG INDIAN TRIBES

With Special Reference to Eastern India

NUTRITION AND HEALTH AMONG INDIAN TRIBES

With Special Reference to Eastern India

Editors
Jyoti Ratan Ghosh
Jaydip Sen

SERIALS PUBLICATIONS PVT. LTD.
New Delhi

Editors
Jyoti Ratan Ghosh
Jaydip Sen

ISBN: 978-93-91844-00-4

Printed in India
SERIALS PUBLICATIONS PVT. LTD.
4830/24, Prahlad Street, Ansari Road, Darya ganj,
New Delhi-110002 (India)
Phone : 23245225, 23259207, 23272135
E-mail: serials@mail.com

CONTENTS

ACKNOWLEDGEMENTS

The editors would like to acknowledge the help of all the persons involved in the process of compiling and publishing this book, more specifically, to the authors. Without their support, this book would not have become a reality.

The editors would like to thank each and every author for their valuable contributions. Our sincere gratitude goes to the authors who contributed their valuable time and research expertise to this book.

The editors also wish to thank Professor S. P. Singh for writing the Foreword for the book.

The editors also wish to thank the publishing team who helped us so much and for publishing this book.

FOREWORD

Indian tribes are not only socially marginalized but also live under extreme hardships. Due to the loss of forest cover, expansion of agriculture and mining, the already limited resources of these tribes have been shrinking very fast. This has led to extreme poverty and loss of jobs resulting in poor health and nutrition of Indian tribes. The present edited volume by Dr. Jyoti Ratan Ghosh and Prof. Jaydip Sen precisely addresses this problem by compiling a number of socio-biological studies on Indian tribes. They have invited research workers from 20 different institutes to contribute their findings on tribal health and nutrition. In spite of the fact that Government of India has launched numerous schemes for the betterment of Indian tribes, their situation still remains far from satisfactory. These studies highlight and focus on the assessment of health, health care delivery system, various nutritional deficiencies, undernutrition, over nutrition and obesity and the intricate relationship between nutrition and child growth in the Indian tribal scenario. The findings presented in this volume have documented the latest situation of Indian tribes, how far have they improved their plight and where they stand now. For the purpose of the readers, the information about this volume is being explained thematically under four different sections.

The first section of studies is about 'Evaluation of the healthcare delivery system in India with special reference to Indian tribes'. The second section has compiled research on 'The health of Indian tribes and various factors responsible for ill health and disease'. The third section has highlighted the 'Nutritional assessment and various factors impacting it'. The last section consists of studies regarding 'The growth and development of children and adolescents and various factors affecting it especially the nutritional ones and the consequences of such interactions'.

In the first section, evaluation of health care delivery system in India with special reference to Indian tribes has been done by 4 different teams. Banerjee and her colleagues have used NFHS-4 data from East India and found an alarming number of tribal women not receiving TT vaccination during their pregnancy. The states of West

Bengal and Odisha provided much better health care than Jharkhand and Bihar. Middle income and rich wealth index categories of women had better access to the healthcare system. They found that enhancement of education among tribal women was very necessary for availing the healthcare. Dash Sharma analyzed different reports on tribal health and found that the root causes of overall poor health status of Jharkhand, which has a huge tribal population, are poverty, social deprivation, low literacy rate, especially among females and structural inequalities in terms of class, caste and sex. According to Kameih and Kshatriya, maternal age, husband's positive attitude and women's education are significant predictors of receiving antenatal care services among the Lamkang tribe of Chandel district, Manipur. Another paper by Panigrahi and Mohanta has pointed out that health ecology and its impact on healthcare delivery services for the tribal people of Odisha is very important and that the state should focus on this for a functionally better healthcare system.

The second section includes 6 papers on 'The health of Indian tribes, and various factors responsible for ill health and disease'. The first paper by Chakraborty is about the Lepchas, an indigenous community of Darjeeling and Sikkim Himalayas. They have a unique tangible knowledge of natural biotic resources which they use to cure illnesses with tribal belief systems. They carry forward this knowledge from generation to generation. Chatterjee and Majumdar focused their attention on the health of the elderly especially how the social relationships ensure their wellbeing. The moral values and social ethos regarding the status of elderly in the family and the community among these tribes often channelizes the energy and attention of younger generations to keep their elders healthy by providing healthcare. The relationship of poverty and health of Particularly Vulnerable Tribal Group (PVTG) of the Asur community of Jharkhand India was investigated by Ghosal and Raul. Their livelihood depends on small farming and daily wage earning. Being very poor they generally cannot access the healthcare delivery services. Not only does this affect their health but their poor status is responsible for their undernutrition as well. However, they do not consider their condition as miserable due to their social and psychological pressure. The study by Mahato includes tribal people of Santhal, Oraon, Munda, Birhor, Bedia and Ho of Jharkhand. The health status of these groups is affected by numerous factors such as alcoholism and drug addiction, belief system, indigenous health practices, occupation pattern and poor economy, deforestation, education and lack of awareness, migration, mining and involuntary displacement besides nutrition. Sengupta and colleagues have pointed out the importance of Chronic Pain (CP) which affects a huge proportion of Santals and Lodhas of West Bengal. They have found an information-deficit situation on CP which incapacitates the public health system resulting in unavailability of appropriate facilities and reluctance of physicians to address CP. The question of how much socio-cultural and demographic factors affect Post-partum Amenorrhea (PPA) among the Mishing Tribe of Assam has been investigated by Sharma. Although Post-partum Amenorrhea is primarily biologically controlled yet the findings of the study suggest a significant association of duration of breastfeeding, birth order, family type and the survival status of the preceding child with PPA.

The third section throws light on the importance of 'Nutritional assessment and various factors impacting it in 7 different papers. Bose and Sen highlighted the importance of zinc as a trace nutritional element which has a significant role in biochemical processes of the body. Zinc deficiency from the viewpoint of nutrition among humans has generally been neglected and the authors discuss the biomarkers used, the supplementations, and interventions approach to lower the rate of zinc deficiency with special reference to tribal groups. Anemia being widespread has been investigated by Goswami who found that among tribal populations of West Bengal, about 60% people suffer from anemia. Abnormal hemoglobin variants were responsible in about 15% of anemic patients, and of these patients, nearly half (50%) had associated nutritional deficiencies as well. Jami and Limbu reported findings on Lotha Naga, a tribal community of Nagaland, about their nutritional status from anthropometric measurements using WHO recommendations. There is an emerging trend of over nutrition even among tribal communities, thereby calling for increased research and awareness initiatives on these aspects, especially among those communities transitioning to an urban setting. The paper of Nayak and Sreegiri reported BMI from anthropometric measurements and found thinness in 18% of tribal women of Visakhapatnam district. Pallor was observed among 61% of the women. Women from families with continuous earnings and debt free condition had BMI above 18.5. One fifth of the study population were at risk of further nutritional deficiency. In another paper, these authors have studied the dietary habits of these tribal women and observed that 33% of women were taking less calories and 40% of them were taking less proteins than their RDA requirements. In the next paper, Bharali and colleagues tried to determine the relationship between maternal nutritional status and physical growth measures of tribal children (<5 years).

They found significant association and effect of mothers' nutritional status and anthropometric measures with children's physical growth variables. Mandal and Mitra in the next chapter tried to evaluate the nutritional status by both prevalence of thinness (low BMI for age) and obesity among primary school children. Mandal and Mitra found that some of the primary school children were over nourished but the occurrence of undernutrition as a whole measured by thinness was very high which could affect the growth and development of these children.

The fourth section of this volume consists of 3 studies regarding growth and development of children and adolescents and various factors affecting it especially the nutritional ones and the consequences of such interactions'. Basumatary and Begum reported that cardio-metabolic risk is considerably much higher in Wancho living in hills than the Wancho of the plains of Arunachal Pradesh and Assam. The hill Wancho lives in a much difficult and challenging terrain doing moderate to vigorous physical activity every day. This is found to be positively associated with central obesity defined cardio-metabolic risk. Body physique and nutritional status of Mising population of Assam was assessed by Lohe and Ghosh who found that Heath-Carter somatotype characteristic of mesomorphy dominates over the other two somatotype components in males, whereas mesomorphy and endomorphy were found to be co-dominant in females. Gender emerged as one of the most influential determinant of all the three components of physique in both males and females whereas age group significantly influenced nutritional status as judged from BMI. The chapter by Saha and colleagues reported age at menarche in relation to nutritional status among school going Chakma tribal girls aged 10-18 years from North, Unokoti, Dhalai and South District of Tripura. Socio-economic conditions and family size exert great influences on age at menarche. Nutritional status is better in post-menarcheal girls than in pre-menarcheal girls.

The book is a treasure house of findings on tribal situation in India in terms of social and biological issues. It is a document worthy of consideration as a social audit on the performance of administration in particular and society in general, about how far they have succeeded in improving the plight of Indian tribes. The book would be useful to students and researchers who will get first hand information tribal situation, Governmental agencies involved in tribal uplift, social organizations committed to tribal cause and to all those who as fellow Indians want to see the tribal people marching ahead. This volume by Dr. Jyoti Ratan Ghosh and Prof. Jaydip Sen is highly recommended to the students and researchers and it deserves a prominent place in various libraries. The editors and the authors of various papers have done a commendable job by compiling the findings and doing research on tribal situation in India and deserve my appreciation.

Professor S. P. Singh, Ph.D.
Editor-in-Chief, Human Biology Review
Former Dean, Faculty of Life Sciences,
Punjabi University, Patiala, India -147002

PREFACE

India has the second largest concentration of tribal communities in the world followed by Africa. According to 2011 census, there are 104,281,034 persons of scheduled tribes in India, comprising 8.6% of the total population. However, these tribal communities cannot be clubbed together as one homogeneous group, because they populate in widely varying ecological and climatic conditions throughout the country. Moreover, they are endogamous group with rich cultural and poor socio-economic background. They have their own healthcare system associated with a strong religious belief and practice.

The health status of any community is influenced by a number of factors including socio-economy, culture, demography, education and politics. Health is an essential aspect of human development and also a vital component for the well being of the mankind. But, the health status of tribals is poor and this is poorest in primitive tribes. Being the poorest and most marginalized groups in India, tribal peoples experience extreme levels of health deprivation. They lag behind the national average on several vital health indicators, with women and children being the most vulnerable. This is mainly because of their isolation and remoteness. Thus, the health status of tribal communities in India is in need of special attention. In this book scholars tried to explore nutritional and health status of tribal people from different perspectives.

In the first chapter Banerjee and others et al demonstrated the effect of socio-economic and demographic factors in the utilization of maternal healthcare services among tribal women of East India using NFHS-4 data. They found that better maternal healthcare services among tribal women were more concentrated with middle and richer wealth index categories than women belong to the poor wealth index category. They also demonstrated that enhancement of education among tribal women was very necessary.

In the next chapter Dash Sharma discussed the health and health-care situation in Jharkhand, a highly mineral rich State of eastern India.

In the third chapter Kameih and Kshatriya examined the determinants of antenatal care utilization among Lamkang tribe of Chandel District, Manipur and found that factors such as maternal age, positive husband's attitude and women's education are the significant predictors of receiving antenatal care services among Lamkang tribe of Chandel district, Manipur.

In chapter four, Panigrahi and Mohanta tries to justify the fact that in spite of the inclusive development approach adopted by different stakeholders, the state of Odisha is yet to consider health ecology and its impact on health services delivery for the tribal people as productive tool while the scheduled areas are yet to be considered as human endowment for a healthy growth of Odisha.

The next chapter by Chakraborty is an outcome of empirical research work conducted in various Lepcha villages in Darjeeling district and west and north districts of Sikkim in various phases from 2007-2010. The study shows that the Lepchas, an indigenous community of Darjeeling and Sikkim Himalayas and being an inhabitant to nature with their tangible knowledge utilizes the natural biotic resources in one hand and prefer to undertake therapy by means of belief system to identify illness causation and its cure.

The sixth chapter by Chatterjee and Majumdar addresses the conceptual underpinnings of various aspects of social wellbeing constructed in the context of tribal elderly. The findings from this inquiry may provide new insights capable of strengthening policies for the welfare of the elderly tribal people of the country.

Next, Ghosal and Raul's chapter primarily focuses on the poverty and health and tried to understand how they inter-related among vulnerable (PVTG) Asur community of Jharkhand.

Mahato in the next chapter tried to explore the decisive factors causing health problems among tribal people of Jharkhand. The study reveals that it is not merely the nutritious food and diseases that affects their health but there are other factors like alcoholism, drug addiction, belief system, indigenous health practices, occupation pattern, poor economy, deforestation, education, lack of awareness, migration, mining and involuntary displacement.

Sengupta and others in the ninth chapter discussed on maladies of elderly belonging to tribal communities of Santal and Lodha of West Bengal and suffering from various forms of chronic pain. The article strongly suggests for tribal-specific information, chronic pain addressal mechanism from primary healthcare level, public health campaigns to raise awareness, and structural changes to prioritise chronic pain as an essential healthcare intervention.

An analysis of covariates of post-partum amenorrhoea among the Mishing tribe of Assam by Sharma in tenth chapter shows that duration of breastfeeding, birth order, family type and the survival status of the preceding child are significantly associated with post-partum amenorrhoea.

In the eleventh chapter Bose and Sen highlights the importance, recommended dietary allowances, effect, the targeted group including the tribal health about zinc, and its deficiency in India. The paper also discusses the biomarkers used, the supplementations, and interventions approach to lower the rate of zinc deficiency.

In the twelveth chapter Goswami tried to assess the magnitude of nutritional anemia among tribals of North Bengal and found that iron and folic acid deficiency played an important role in it.

Jami and Limbu in the thirteenth chapter highlight the nutritional status of the Lotha Naga, a tribal community of Nagaland, Northeast India. The study shows that there is an emerging trend of overnutrition even among tribal communities.

Nayak and Sreegiri in the next chapter discussed about the nutritional status of tribal women in Visakhapatnam district of Andhra Pradesh. The study shows that one fifth of the study population were at risk of further nutritional deficiency.

In chapter 15, Nayak and Sreegiri examined dietary habits of tribal women in Visakhapatnam district of Andhra Pradesh and found that one third of women were consuming less than 80% RDA of energy and two fifths of women were consuming protein less than 80% RDA.

Next, Singh and others studied the relationship between maternal nutritional status and physical growth measures of tribal children (<5 years) of Arunachal Pradesh. Northeast India the study shows significant association and effect of mothers' nutritional status and anthropometric measures with children's physical growth variables. Thus, appropriate interventions by improving the maternal nutritional status are important and could have the significant role to improve the physical growth/undernutrition in preschool children.

Mandal and Mitra in the next chapter tried to evaluate the nutritional status of the primary school children and demonstrated that the occurrence of undernutrition as a whole measured by thinness was very high among the school children.

In the next chapter, Basumatary and Begum tried to assess how different physical activity levels of adult hill and plain Wancho impact on cardio-metabolic risk defined by central obesity. The study concludes that among the hill Wancho, cardio-metabolic risk is considerably much higher than plain Wancho. The hill Wancho are living in a much difficult terrain doing moderate to vigorous physical activity every day. This is found to be positively associated with central obesity defined cardio-metabolic risk. They are relatively more at risk than the plain Wancho, who despite sharing the same ethnicity and culture are geographically and ecologically living in a less challenging environment.

Next, Lohe and Ghosh tried to determine the association between somatotype characteristics and nutritional status among adult Mising males and females. They found that Mising males were muscular, whereas Mising females were mostly muscular-fatty in their physique with both showing overweight and/or obesity in their nutritional status.

The study on nutritional status and age at menarche of Chakma tribal girls of Tripura by Sil and others shows that nutritional status is better in post-menarcheal girls than pre-menarcheal girls.

We sincerely acknowledge all contributing authors for their valuable contribution, because their expertise and insights will be very helpful to the interested readers as well as researchers working on nutritional and health status of tribal people.

Jyoti Ratan Ghosh
Jaydip Sen
Editors

SECTION I

Chapter One

MATERNAL HEALTH CARE SERVICES OF TRIBAL WOMEN OF EASTERN REGION STATES OF INDIA

SREEPARNA BANERJEE, SHIMUL ROY, SUBIR BISWAS, MANORANJAN PAL AND PREMANANDA BHARATI

ABSTRACT

The present study tried to understand the effects of socio-economic and demographic factors in the utilization of maternal health care services among tribal women of East India using NFHS-4 data. The present study considered only tribal women, who conceived the baby within the last five years. All the study women were married and the age range was 15-49 years. The total sample size consisted of 8296 of ever-married women. For maternal health care services, six measures were examined, namely antenatal visit, postnatal check-ups, TT vaccination, place of delivery, use of the contraceptive method, and family planning. The present study was comparative and ex-post-facto research. Descriptive statistics, Pearson chi-square test and binary regression were used to understand maternal health care services by different socio-economic and demographic attributes. The present study revealed that in most of the cases no significant differences were found between maternal health care services and socio-economic and demographic variables among tribal women of East India. The majority of tribal women did not take TT vaccination during their pregnancy which is very alarming. The study concluded that maternal health care services in West Bengal and Odisha was much better than Jharkhand and Bihar. No significant difference found between residential pattern (rural-urban) and maternal health care services in the

Eastern region. Better maternal health care services among tribal women were more concentrated with middle and richer wealth index categories than women belong to poor wealth index category. The present study also concluded that enhancement of education among tribal women was very necessary.

Keywords: *Antenatal care, postnatal care, titinus, place of delevary, family planning, contraceptive, socio-economic and demographic factors.*

Introduction

"A moment of unimaginable joy is what a mother feels when a newborn is placed on her arms – a joy every mother should have the right to experience. But for many pregnant women in India this memory will never come to be, the moment of birth is often frightening (UNICEF India, 2020)." The above sentence was used as the introductory sentence of UNICEF India's maternal health page. It appropriately summarizes the maternal health care situation in India.

Maternal health care services are very important for the health and well being of mothers and children (Chopra et al., 2018). Every year, more than half a million women die due to complications during pregnancy and childbirth (Ray et al., 2018; Ghosh, 2020). The majority of maternal deaths associated with pregnancy and childbirth are a direct or indirect result of improper/absence of routine and/or emergency maternal health care (Sinha and Chattopadhyay, 2016). Many of these deaths can be avoided if proper maternal health care service can be provided during pregnancy and childbirth (Neeta et al., 2018).

One of the major public health challenges globally is to provide maternal health care to every woman (Yadav et al., 2020). But the maternal healthcare situation in most developing countries is not even promising (Prusty et al., 2015). The gap between developed and developing countries in maternal deaths is still very high (Ali and Chauhan, 2020). Though, India showed remarkable progress in lowering the Maternal Mortality Ratio in the last 3 decades (Paul and Chouhan, 2020), Maternal Mortality Ratio still remains very high (Ministry of Health and Family Welfare, 2010). India contributes a large number of maternal deaths (Chakrabory and Bhattacharjee, 2017), only second to Nigeria (Singh et al., 2019). Annual maternal deaths in India was 32000 in 2015, which was reduced to 30000 in

2017. It simply means that every 20 minutes a mother is dying due to pregnancy or childbirth-related issues in India (UNICEF, 2020). Most developing countries could not provide maternal healthcare services (Arokiasamy and Pradhan, 2013). Unavailability/ inaccessibility to health care services prevented many from getting maternal healthcare services in India (Joshi et al., 2016). Even more troubling was the rural-urban disparity in maternal health care services (Sharma and Mukherjee, 2014).

The lower health status of tribes is a global problem, but not as bad as in India. In high-income countries the life expectancy of indigenous people is more than 70 years. Infant mortality is less than ten, even in Thailand, it is 6.6, wherein India it is 74 (The Expert Committee on Tribal Health, 2018). The above report also mentioned that despite the huge diversity and heterogeneous nature, Indian tribal people share one commonality and that is they have poorer health indicators, a greater burden of morbidity and mortality, and very limited access to health care services. Many studies suggested poorer maternal health care services among tribal women (Adhikari et al., 2016; Contractor et al., 2018; Pandey et al., 2018; Sengupta, 2019).

Many other studies have been conducted in different parts of India to understand maternal health care services (Chandhiok et al., 2005; Mavalankar et al., 2009; Mohanty, 2012; Mojumdar, 2015), especially among tribal women (Mumbare and Rege, 2011; Jose et al., 2014; Dehury, 2016).

Objectives

The present study aimed to investigate the maternal health care services in tribal women in thestates of Eastern region of India, namely West Bengal, Odisha, Jharkhand and Bihar. The present study also tried to understand the effect of socio-economic and demographic factors towards utilization of maternal health care services in different states of Eastern region of India.

Methodology

The study area included Eastern States/zones of India. The Eastern zone included the state of Bihar, Jharkhand, West Bengal and Odisha. The present study considered only tribal women of East India, who conceived baby within the last five years. All the studied women were married and in the age range was 15-49 years. The total sample size consisted of 8296 tribal women. In the present study, maternal health care services included antenatal visit (at least 3 visits during their last pregnancy in health care centers), postnatal care (care received from health professionals within two months of delivery) and tetanus toxoid (TT) vaccination (at least two tetanus vaccination during pregnancy). Here delivery place was broadly classified as Institutional and Home delivery. The modern method of contraceptive use included male and female sterilizations, injectable, intra-uterine devices (IUDs/PPIUDs), contraceptive pills, implants, female and male condoms, diaphragm, foam/jelly, the standard day's methods, the lactational method, and emergency contraception. Women were divided into two groups according to their family planning involvements. The group "jointly with husband" referred to those women who alone or jointly with husband took family planning (FP) decisions. The other group comprised of those women who didn't have any decision-making rights. Different socio-economic and demographic indicators like educational attainment, occupation of the respondent, wealth Index, age, residential pattern were also included in the study to understand their influence on maternal health care services. The present study was based on the unit level data extracted from National Family Health Survey (NFHS-4) conducted by IIPS during 2015-16. NFHS 4 provided various socio-economic, demographic information that helped to capture maternal health care services in East India. It was a comparative as well as ex-post-facto research. Categorical binary logistic regressions were done to show the effect of socio-economic and demographic factors on maternal health care services. Dependent variables were taken as binary. Each of the maternal health care services was coded as '1' if the woman received the complete dose, else it was coded as '0'. For antenatal visit, the complete dose referred to 'at least 3 visit', in which case it was coded as '1' or else '0'). Similarly, other health care services were given codes '1' or '0' according to the service was respectively given or not given. Thus the code '1' was given for at least 2 tetanus injections during pregnancy, for institutional delivery and for Post-natal check-up. The code was given as 0 for the corresponding service not given. Again modern contraceptive method was coded as '1' and traditional as '0', the decision on family planning taken jointly with husband was coded as '1', else '0'. Statistical analysis was done using the statistical software package SPSS (version: 18.0) and $p<0.01$ and $p<0.05$ were considered as statistically significant. (Pearson chi-square test was performed to understand differences in maternal health care services in different states in East India.)

Results

Table 1 presents the percentage distribution of tribal women aged 15-49 years by their socio-economic and demographic attributes like age, educational attainments, respondent's working status, residential pattern and wealth Index. The study revealed that about 34.7 percent of tribal women were aged 25-29 years followed by 20-24 years (30.0%), 30-34 years (19.2%), 35-39 years (8.0%), 15-19 years (4.0%), 40-44 years (2.9%) and 45-49 years (1.3%). The study revealed that majority of tribal women was not working (75.7%). Only 24.3 percent of tribal women were working. More than 50 percent of tribal women had no formal education. In Eastern region of India, 14.1 percent and 29.3 percent of tribal women had completed their primary and secondary education respectively. Only 1.9 percent of tribal women got higher education. The present study highlighted that more than 90 percent of tribal women resided in rural area. Only 8.1 percent of tribal women settled in urban area. The study pointed out that more than 89 percent of tribal women had poor wealth index, 7 percent of tribal women belonged to middle wealth index category and only 3.8 percent of tribal women belonged to richer wealth index category.

Table 1: Percentage distribution of tribal women (15-49 years) by their socio-economic and demographic attributes

Socio-economic and demographic variables	Number of tribal women (%)
Age (Years)	
15-19	331 (4.0)
20-24	2487 (30.0)
25-29	2879 (34.7)
30-34	1593 (19.2)
35-39	664 (8.0)
40-44	237 (2.9)
45-49	105 (1.3)
Working status	
Not working	1089 (75.7)
Working	350 (24.3)
Educational attainment	
No	4542 (54.7)
Primary	1166 (14.1)
Secondary	2432 (29.3)
Higher	156 (1.9)
Residence	
Rural	7625 (91.9)
Urban	671 (8.1)
Wealth Index	
Poor	7395 (89.1)
Middle	584 (7.0)
Rich	317 (3.8)

Table 2 showed the maternal health care services among tribal women of East India. The study revealed that West Bengal and Odisha had better maternal health care services than Jharkhand and Bihar. Complete antenatal visit was the highest in West Bengal (82.6%), which was followed by Odisha (78.9%). The percentages were much low in Jharkhand (39.6%) and Bihar (22.7%). The highest percentage of post-natal care was observed among tribal women of Odisha (83.7%) followed by West Bengal (75.5%). Less than 50 percent of tribal women got post-natal care in Jharkhand and Bihar, which showed very unsatisfactory result. The highest percentage of Institutional delivery was found in West Bengal and Odisha, followed by Bihar and Jharkhand. The present study revealed that less that 30 percent of tribal women of East India took TT vaccination during pregnancy. Only 22.5 percent of tribal women from Bihar took TT vaccination, which was followed by Jharkhand (16.4%), West Bengal (12.8%) and Odisha (10.7%). Pearson chi-square test revealed that maternal health care services were significantly different among the states of East India.

Table 2: Percentage distribution of maternal health care of tribal women of East India

East Indian States	antenatal visit		χ^2	Postnatal care		χ^2	Place of delivery		χ^2	TT Vaccination		χ^2
	No	Com plete		No	Yes		Institutional	Home		Complete	No	
Bihar	420 (77.3)	123 (22.7)	1207.517**	338 (62.2)	205 (37.8)	999.003**	466 (55.9)	368 (44.1)	443.708**	122 (22.5)	421 (77.5)	67.949**
West Bengal	61 (17.4)	290 (82.6)		86 (24.5)	265 (75.5)		341 (78.6)	93 (21.4)		45 (12.8)	306 (87.2)	
Jharkhand	1606 (60.4)	1051 (39.6)		1428 (53.7)	1229 (46.3)		1786 (50.3)	1767 (49.7)		435 (16.4)	2222 (83.6)	
Odisha	584 (21.4)	2145 (78.6)		443 (16.3)	2282 (83.7)		2526 (72.9)	941 (27.1)		293 (10.7)	2436 (89.3)	
Total	2671 (42.5)	3609 (57.5)		2295 (36.6)	3981 (63.4)		5119 (61.8)	3169 (38.2)		895 (14.3)	5385 (85.7)	

Table 3 depicted that tribal women of East India preferred to take joint decision regarding family planning. The highest percentages of tribal women, who preferred to take joint decision with husbands,were from the state of Jharkhand (91.6%), which was followed by West Bengal (90.0%), Odisha (88.9%) and Bihar (78.2%). The study also revealed that less than 30 percent of women depended on other family members regarding family planning decisions. Less than 60 percent of tribal women in Eastern region had no idea about the use of contraceptive method. The worst performing states were Jharkhand (18.2%) and Bihar (9.8%) in case of use of contraceptive method. West Bengal (59.7%) and Odisha (52.0%) performed little better, though the result was not upto the mark. The Pearson chi-square revealed a significant difference in family planning and contraceptive use among tribal women of different states of eastern region.

Table 3: Percentage distribution of use of family planning and contraceptive methods in Eastern States

East Indian States	Family Planning		χ^2	Contraceptive method used		χ^2
	Jointly	Others		Yes	No	
Bihar	61 (78.2)	17 (21.8)	14.193**	82 (9.8)	752 (90.2)	1248.087**
West Bengal	233 (90.0)	26 (10.0)		259 (59.7)	175 (40.3)	
Jharkhand	592 (91.6)	54 (8.4)		645 (18.2)	2908 (81.8)	
Odisha	1591 (88.9)	199 (11.1)		1806 (52.0)	1669 (48.0)	
Total	2483 (89.3)	296 (10.7)		2792 (33.7)	5504 (66.3)	

Table 4 tried to show the effect of socio-economic and demographic factors on maternal health care services through regression analysis. The study revealed that in tribal community working women were more likely to visit for antenatal care (1.056 times), post-natal care (1.130 times), use contraceptive method (1.206 times) than not working women, though no significant associations were found between maternal health care services and working status of the respondents. Education played a vital role in women's life. The study revealed that maternal health care services also improved with the increase of education level among tribal women, except in few cases. Secondary educated women were 1.467 times more likely to visit for antenatal care than women with no formal education and it was significant. Primary (1.569 times) and secondary (1.429 times) educated women were more likely to take postnatal care than women having no formal education and the result was statistically significant. The study also showed that increase in educational level among tribal women lead to significant increase institutional delivery. No significant association were found between educational attainment and TT vaccination. But the study showed that increase in education level influenced awareness regarding TT vaccination. Primary and secondary educated women were more likely to use contraceptive method than women with no education and the result was significant. The study depicted that tribal women of East India had no significant association between education and family planning. In tribal community as the age increased women were less likely to visit for antenatal care, though no significant association was found except in the age group 40-44 years. Women aged 20-24 years were 1.795 times more likely to take post-natal care than women aged 15-19 years and the result was statistically significant. Women in the age groups 40-44 years (0.756 times) and 45-49 years (0.613) were less likely to take post-natal care than women in the age group 15-19 years, though the result was not significant.

Table 4: Effects of socio-economic and demographic variables on safe motherhood through regression analysis (Dependent variable: no or incomplete=0, complete= 1)

Socio-eco and socio-demo	Antenatal Exp (B)	Post Exp (B)	Insti Exp (B)	TT vaccination EXP (B)	Contraceptive Exp (B)	Family Planning Exp (B)
Respondents' Occupation						
Not working®						
Working	1.056	1.130	0.730	0.955	1.206	0.658
Education						
No®						
Primary	1.123	1.569*	2.157**	1.042	1.440*	0.511
Secondary	1.467*	1.429*	2.733**	1.506	1.551**	0.506*
Higher	1.728	1.581	17.006**	4.935	1.016	0.739
Age						
15-19®						
20-24	0.741	1.795*	0.932	0.920	0.888	1.103
25-29	0.636	1.474	0.673	1.037	1.338	1.297
30-34	0.536	1.173	0.570	0.783	1.411	1.004

35-39	0.689	1.356	0.514*	0.504	1.539	0.802
40-44	0.236**	0.756	0.455	0.675	1.811	0.592
45-49	0.769	0.613	0.261	0.280	1.416	0.375
Residence						
Rural						
Urban	1.232	1.457	1.281	1.547	1.109	2.479
Wealth Index						
Poor						
Middle	1.869*	1.361	1.726*	1.320	1.700*	0.694
Rich	1.735	1.222	4.191**	0.926	1.265	1.273
Constant	1.928	1.061	1.564	0.955	0.315	10.791
Ethnicity						
Non tribal®						
Tribal	0.732**	0.948	1.580**	1.051**	0.895**	0.999
Constant	1.351	1.735	1.615	6.017	0.507	8.389

*: p<.05, **: p<.01, Dependent variable: no or incomplete=0, complete= 1

The study revealed that as the age increased tribal women of East India were less likely to go for Institutional delivery. In particular there was significant difference among women between the age groups 15-19 years and 35-39 years. No significant association were found between ages of women and TT vaccination, use of contraceptive method and family planning. The present study also revealed that residential pattern had no significant influence in maternal health care. In most of the cases wealth index showed no significant association with maternal health care services among tribal women of East India. The study revealed that women with better wealth Index were more likely to visit for antenatal care than women with poor wealth index. However, the result was not significant except women belonging to the middle wealth index category. No significant association was observed between wealth index and post natal care, but the result showed that women with better wealth index were more likely to take post natal care. Women belonging to middle and rich wealth index were 1.726 times and 4.191 times more likely to prefer institutional delivery than women belonging to poor wealth index. TT vaccination showed no significant association with wealth Index. Women, who belonged to middle wealth index (1.700 times) were more likely to prefer the use contraceptive method than women, who belonged to poor wealth index and the result was significant at 1 percent level. No significant association was found between wealth index and family planning. The present study also revealed that there was a significant association between tribal, non-tribals and maternal health care services except family planning.

Discussion

In India, the National Health Services have often neglected the tribal community, especially the tribal women. Socio-economic, demographic factors contributed to the low health status of underprivileged group. Cultural factors and taboo might also play a role (Maiti et al., 2005).The present study revealed that majority of women belonged to the age 25-29 years. More than 70 percent of tribal women were not working. The present study depicted that 54.7 percent of tribal women had no formal education in their life time. Around 14.1 percent and 29.3 percent of tribal women were primary and secondary educated. Only few women got higher education. More than 90 percent of tribal women resided in rural area. Only 8.1 percent of tribal women resided in urban area. As expected, more than 85 percent of tribal women belonged to poor wealth index category. Seven percent of tribal women belonged to middle wealth index category and only 3.8 percent of women belonged to richer wealth index group. The study depicted that utilization of maternal health care services (antenatal care, post-natal care, Institutional delivery, TT vaccination, family planning, use of contraceptive method) were higher in West Bengal and Odisha followed by Jharkhand and Bihar. An impressive study of Maiti et al. (2005) highlighted that socio-economic, demographic as well as health status of the tribal women were very unsatisfactory. The present study pointed out that working women were more likely to take better maternal health care services than not working women but the result was not significant. Desai and Jain (1994) revealed that working women had more knowledge about pregnancy and are more likely to utilize maternal health care services. Shah (2011) depicted that working women had negative impact on utilization of maternal health care services. In general, tribal women were found mostly working as agricultural labor or construction labor and hence were less likely to visit health care services (Desai and Jain, 1994). Education played a pivotal role in women's life. The study revealed that women with better education were more likely to take antenatal visit, post-natal care, prefer to delivering at an institution, take TT vaccination, use contraceptive method, have family planning than women with no formal education or illiterate and the result was significant except in few cases. Navaneetham and Dhrmalingam (2002), highlighted that respondent's literacy is an important predictor for utilization of maternal health care services. Women's age was also an important factor towards utilization of maternal health care services. As the age of a women increased, women were less likely to have maternal health care services. Women in the age group 40-44 years were 0.236 times less likely to have antenatal visit than women in the age group15-19 years and the result was statistically significant. Women in the age group 20-24 years were

1.795 times more likely to take post-natal care than women in the age group 15-19 years and the result was significant at 5 percent level. As the age increased, women were less likely to prefer institutional delivery compared to the lowest age group 15-19 years, but the result was not statistically significant except in the age group 35-39 years. No significant association was found between TT vaccination and women's age. But the study revealed that as age increased, less percentages of women prefered to take TT vaccination. No significant relation was found between women's age and contraceptive method and family planning. We found that residential pattern among tribal women was not an important factor towards utilization of maternal health care services in Eastern region. The present study also revealed that women with better wealth Index preferred better maternal health care service. Women belonging to middle wealth index were more likely to visit for antenatal care. No significant relation was found between wealth index and post-natal care. Women belonging to middle and richer wealth index groups were more likely to prefer delivering at an institution. Women in middle wealth index group were 1.320 time more likely to take TT vaccination, though the result was not significant. Women belonging to middle wealth index group were more likely to use contraceptive method than women belonging to poor wealth index group. No significant influence of wealth index on family planning was found. The present study revealed statistically significant differences between ethnicity and utilization of maternal health care services. Tribal women were less likely to visit for antenatal care, take post natal care, use of contraceptive method and family planning. Many studies showed that exposure of mass media promoted better maternal health care service among women (Retherford and Mishra, 1997; Rao et al., 1998).

We can thus conclude from the study that maternal health care services were not same across the states in the East region of India. West Bengal and Odisha performed better in terms of maternal health care services than Jharkhand and Bihar. Women's educational attainment was an important predictor for the utilization of maternal health care services in East India. Illiterate women or women with no formal education were less likely to use maternal health care services. The study of Wolfe et al. (1988) claimed that relation between women education and health care behaviour may not be due to education, but also due to women's childhood background for which education plays an important role. Non-earning women were less likely to use maternal health care services than earningwomen. The utilization of maternal health care services was very least among tribal women and it could create a long term impact on health and well being of the tribal community.

Significance of the study

The present study helped us to understand how the socio-economic and demographic attributes influenced utilization of maternal health care services among tribal women of Eastern India. The study tried to find the invention programmes that were needed towards better utilization of maternal health care services among tribal women. The study will provide us the knowledge of maternal health care services in different states of Eastern India.

Limitation of the study

The present study was based on secondary data. The data was not collected for the same purpose as the original researcher had in mind. So the analysis was limited to the use of already collected variables.

References

Adhikari T, Sahu D, Nair S, Saha KB, Sharma RK, Pandey A. 2016. Factors associated with utilization of antenatal care services among tribal women: A study of selected states. *Indian Journal of Medical Research.* 144: 58-66.

Ali B, Chauhan S. 2020. Inewualities in the utilization of maternal health care in rural India: Evidences from National Family Health Survey III & IV. *BMC Public Health.* 20:1-13.

Arokiasamy P, Pradhan J. 2013. *Maternal health care in India: access and demand determinants.* Primary Health care Research and Development. Cambridge University Press. Doi: 10.1017/S1463423612000552.

Chakrabory A, Bhattacharjee D. 2017. Maternal Health: Which States are more Caring?. *Demography India.* 46: 82-96.

Chandhiok N, Dhillon BS, Kambo I, Saxena NC. 2005. Determinants of antenatal care utilization in rural areas of India: A cross-sectional study from 28 districts (An ICMR task force study). *The Journal of Obstetrics and Gynecology of India.* 56: 47-52.

Chopra D, Jauhari N, Dhungana H. 2018. A study of Utilization of Maternal Health Services and Gactors Influencing the Utilization in Urban Slums of Lucknow. *International Journal of Medicial Science and Public health.* 8: 77-81.

Contractor SQ, Das A, Dasgupta J, Belle SV 2018. Beyond the template: the needs of tribal women and their experiences with maternity services in Odisha, India. *International Journal for Equity in Health.* 17: 1-13.

Dehury RK.. 2016. Maternal health services in the tribal community of

Balasore district, Odissa: Challenges and implications. *BMG Glob Health*. 1: A2-A43.

Desai S, Jain D. 1994. Maternal employment and changes in family dynamics: The social context of women's work in rural south India. *Population and Development Review* 20: 115–136.

Ghosh A. 2020. Inewuality in maternal health-care services and safe delivery in eastern India. *WHO South-East Asia Journal of Public Health*. 4: 54-61.

Jose JA, Sarkar S, Kumar SG, Kar SS. 2014. Utilization of maternal health-care services by tribal women in Kerala. *Journal of Natural Science, Biology and Medicine*. 5: 144-147.

Joshi P, Mahalingam G, Sorte DY. 2016. Factors influencing utilization of maternal and child health services among the postnatal mothers in hilly region. *International Journal of Research in Medical Sciences*. 4: 2170-2176.

Maiti S, Unisa S, Agrawal PK. 2005. Health Care and Health Among Tribal Women in Jharkhand: A situational Analysis. *Studies of Tribes and Tribals*. 2: 37-46.

Maternal Health Division. 2010. *Guidelines for Antenatal care and skilled attendance at birth by ANMs/LHVs/SNs*. Ministry of Health and Family Welfare, Government of India.

Mavalankar DV, Vora KS, Ramani KV, Raman P, Sharma B, Upadhyaya M. 2009. Maternal Health in Gujrat, India: A Case Study. *Journal of Health, Population and Nutrition*. 2: 235-248.

Mohanty SK.. 2012. Multiple Deprivations and Maternal Care in India. *International Perspectives on Sexual and Reproductive Health*. 38: 6-14.

Mojumdar SK. 2015. Trends in Maternal care utilization in urban India: A temporal analysis. *Environment and Urbanization ASIA*. 6: 212-224.

Mumbare SS, Rege R 2011. Ante natal care services utilization, delivery practices and factors affecting them in tribal area of North Maharashtra. *Indian Journal of Community Medicine*. 36: 287-290.

Navaneetham K, Dharmalingam A. 2002. Utilization of maternal health care services in Southern India. *Social Science and Medicine*. 55: 1849-1869.

Neeta PN, Sameena ARB, Suresh CM, Goud G, Bharat, Sajjan, Chetana S. 2018. Assessment of utilization of maternal health care services in rural field practice areas of VIMS, Ballari. *Internaltional Jouranl of Community Medicine and Public Health*. 5: 170-176.

Pandey VV, Singh SK, Kumar A. 2018. Study on Reproductive and Maternal Health care Services among Tribes: Research for Tribe Development in Jharkhand. *International Journal of Pediatrics and Neonatal Health*. 2: 67-78.

Paul P, Chouhan P. 2020. Socio-demographic factors influencing utilization of maternal health care services in India. *Clinical Epidemiology and Global Health.* 8: 666-670.

Prusty RK, Gouda J, Pradhan MR. 2015. Inequality in the utilization of maternal healthcare services in Odisha, India. *International Journal of Population Research.* Article Id. 531485, 1-10.

Rao KV, Mishra VK, Retherford RD. 1998. *Effects of exposure to mass media on knowledge and use of oral rehydration therapy for childhood diarrhea in India.* National Family Health Survey Subject Report No.10. Mumbai: International Institute for Population Sciences and Honolulu: East West Center Program on Population.

Ray S, Bhandari P, Prasad JBJ. 2018. Utilization pattern and associated factors of maternal health care services in Haryana, India: a study based on district level household survey data. *International Journal of Reproduction, Contraception, Obstetrics and Gynecology.* 7: 1154-1163.

Retherford, RD, Mishra VK. 1997. *Media exposure increases contraceptive use.* National Family Health Survey Bulletin August, 7. Mumbai: International Institute for Population Sciences and Honolulu: East-West Center Program on Population.

Sengupta A. 2019. Maternal health in underserved tribal India. *Sexual and Reproductive Health Matters.* 27: 304-306.

Shah R. 2011. socio-economic correlates of utilization of maternal health services by tribal women in India. *Canadian Studies in Population.* 38: 83-98.

Sharma C, Mukherjee K. 2014. Maternal healthcare Providers in Uttar Pradesh, India: How to position informal practitioners within the system?. *Journal of Family and Reproductive Health.* 8: 183-188.

Singh R, Neogi SB, Hazra A, Irani L, Ruducha J, Ahmad D, Kumar S, Mann N, Mavalankar D. 2019. Utilization of maternal health services and its determinants: a cross-sectional study among women in rural Uttar Pradesh, India. *Journal of Health, Population and Nutrition.* 38: 1-12.

Sinha A, Chattopadhyay A. 2016. Utilization of maternal and child health care services in North and South India: does spousal violence matter?. *International Journal of Population Studies.* 2: 107-122.

The Expert Committee on Tribal Health. 2018. *Tribal Health in India: Bridging the Gap and a Roadmap for the Future, Executive summary and recommendations.* Ministry of Health and Family Welfare and Ministry of Tribal Affairs, Government of India. 1-36.

UNICEF India. 2020. *Maternal health.* Retrived from: https://www.unicef.org/india/what-we-do/maternal-health, on: 8.9.2020.

Wolfe BL, Behrman JR, Deolalikar AB. 1988. Nutrients: Impacts and

Determinants. *The World Bank Economics Review*. 2:299-320.

Yadav AK, Sahni B, Jena PK, Kumar D, Bala K. 2020. Trends, differentials, and social determinants of maternal health care services utilization in rural India: An analysis from polled data. *Women's Health Reports*. 1: 179-189.

Chapter Two

HEALTH, HEALTH CARE AND DEVELOPMENT IN INDIA

PARAMANANDA DASH SHARMA

ABSTRACT

The wide spread poverty, illiteracy, malnutrition, non-availability of safe drinking water and unhygienic living conditions and poor maternal and child health services, have been reported in several studies as the possible contributing factors for the dismal health conditions prevailing among the tribal communities in India. Extensive studies have had been done by anthropologists on the status of health and nutrition among the numerous tribes and castes of India. The present author would limit his discussion to the health and healthcare situation in Jharkhand, a highly mineral rich State where 26 per cent were tribals as per the census decade 1981, which was at that time under the State of Bihar. An overview of the population, health and social development scenario of Jharkhand was presented by UNFPA advisor Dr Almas Ali of Planning Commission and Dr B. P. Thiagarajan of Population Foundation of India. The report says that the root cause of overall poor health status of Jharkhand is poverty, social deprivation, low literacy rate, especially among females, and structural inequalities in terms of class, caste and sex. Dismal and very dreary picture is prevailing in the State of Jharkhand in the public health workforce and health infrastructure. This very grim situation prevails even after more than a decade of Jharkhand formation particularly in rural areas, in tribal villages. Health care in public sector shows much inadequacy and indifference. The doctor population ratio in India is 1:1456 against the WHO recommendation of 1:1000. In hospitals, care ethics is greatly involved with patient-doctor interaction. Care ethics would urge physicians to perceive the patient as social being and not a deceased body. It would be interesting to see if younger anthropologists take up some issues of public health and health care system and explore these through anthropological insights in rural health centers.

Keywords: *Health, health care, development*

HEALTH AND *SWASTHYA*

Health is a multidimensional phenomenon. In many developing countries more girls than boys die between the age-group of 1 to 4 years. In most developing countries, death rates for girls are higher than boys, indicting the socio-cultural patterns that discriminate against women. Young girls may not get the same health care and nutrition as young boys.

Most of the measures used to indicate the health status of a society are in terms of mortality rates. But this does not and cannot adequately reflect health status of the living. The need is for suitable measures of morbidity that would help understand the relative incidence and effects of different types of illness, the demographic and geographic pattern of their incidence and their sensitivity to various socio-economic factors like income levels, cultural basis / habits and occupation.

Good health is difficult to define, but it is certainly more than just the absence of disease. The widely accepted definition of health is that given by World Health Organization (1948): “Health is a state of complete physical, mental and social well-being and not merely an absence of disease or infirmity.” Some argue health cannot be defined as a ‘state’. It must be seen as a process of continuous adjustment to changing demands of living and of the changing meaning we give to life. It is a dynamic concept.

Osho in one of his meditation discourse (Osho International Foundation, *www.osho.com*) to his Western disciples had said, ‘health is only understood from the innermost being of man where his soul is’. The English word ‘health’ is not the same as the Hindi word ‘*Swasthya*’. Health is derived from the word healing, illness is associated with it. Health means healed — one has recovered from illness. '*Swasthya*' does not mean that. '*Swasthya*' means one who has settled within oneself. One who has reached to the deepest point in oneself. And from this concept of '*Swasthya*' the dimensional models of health developed in stages.

Five dimensional model of health can be presented in a pentagonal figure, which includes: physical, social, emotional, intellectual, and spiritual dimensions. Now with it a sixth dimension has been added, the environmental dimension: which includes — external surroundings (habitat, occupation etc.) and internal (individual's internal structure, genetics). Thus it can be seen as a condition of quality of the human organism expressing the adequate functioning of the organism in given conditions, genetic and environmental.

'Many of us now realise we face the collapse of our life support systems', thus said Mr George Manbiot an iconic environmental writer, conservationist and a campaigner. His reply to the question, 'Does the pandemic offer us lessons in terms of the environment?' His answer was, "Yes, one of the lessons it offers us is that people can change their lives when they must do so. So often, we have been told that people would never accept the changes required to prevent the climate breakdown. But the changes we need to make in order to alter environmental outcomes are actually much less severe than the changes we are making now to prevent the pandemic from spreading" (Manbiot, 2020, *Times of India*, *Kolkata*, July 11, 2020, Times Evoke). Forests are part of humanity's life support system. Trees are vital for humanity, yet deforestation is rampant. Forests absorb green house gases, stop soil erosion and limit harmful zoonotic diseases.

The survival of all living beings in a fundamental sense depends on three basic life-supporting materials, namely air, water and food. These basic materials supply the body with chemical substances – the nutrients – in food and water to make it possible for the body to carry on all its metabolic functions such as growth and repair, regulation of physiological functions and energy metabolism. In fact, food conveys many meanings and helps us meet a number of personal, social, economic and cultural needs. Since the highest priority of all basic needs is physiological survival, and different nutrients of food meet the physiological demands of man, so the people define food as that substance which nourishes the body and ensures survival.

Poverty, Illiteracy and Malnutrition

The wide spread poverty, illiteracy, malnutrition, non-availability of safe drinking water and unhygienic living conditions and poor maternal and child health services, have been reported in several studies as the possible contributing factors for the dismal health conditions prevailing among the tribal communities in India. About 40 percent of the world's undernourished children and 35 percent of the low birth-weight babies are from India. It has been found that certain states in India like Madhya Pradesh, Odisha, Rajasthan, Gujarat, Assam and in some other areas, certain diseases like goitre, yaws, malaria and guinea-worm are endemic (Government of India, 1989). Primitive Tribal Groups (PTGs) of India, now formally designated as 'Particularly Vulnerable Tribal Groups (PVTGs) have special health problems because of their ignorance, unhygienic conditions, lack of health education and non-availability of health care facilities in their habitation areas. Extensive studies have had been done by anthropologists on the status of health and nutrition among the numerous tribes and castes of India. The study list on nutrition status of the tribes and castes populations of India runs in several hundreds, since the Twelfth Dr. B. C. Guha Memorial Lecture was delivered by Dr. P. N. Sen Gupta at the 62nd Session of the Indian Science Congress Association, held at Delhi University on January 4, 1975. Dr. P. N. Sen Gupta was the nutrition officer of the UN Food and Agricultural Organization. At the time of delivering the Twelfth Dr. B. C. Guha Memorial Lecture, Dr. P. N. Sen Gupta had already retired from the service of FAO. Dr. Sen Gupta's lecture topic was on 'Nutrition and National Development', where he had greatly stressed the importance of nutrition as an integral part in the national plans for economic development in India, raising broadly several issues which are directly involved in the problem.

In 2012, a World Bank report stated that India had the largest number of poor people. "India was the home to the largest number of poor in 2012, but its poverty rate is one of the lowest among those countries with the largest number of poor people." According to the report released on Monday (*Hindustan Times, Ranchi,* Tuesday, October 06, 2015) the number of people living in extreme poverty around the world is likely to fall as the long sustained reduction in poverty is moving the world closer to the historic goal of ending poverty by 2030.

Poverty line is an income threshold below which families are considered poor. Different countries have different methods defining threshold income, depending on the level of socio-economic conditions. In 2014 the Prime Minister's Economic Advisory Council Chairman, Mr C. Rangarajan considered that 29.5 percent of India's

1.2 billion people lived in poverty in 2011-12. The Rangarajan panel considered people on less than Rs. 32 a day in rural areas, and Rs. 47 a day in urban areas are poor. The erstwhile Planning Commission estimated number of poor people in India based on Tendulker Committee's methodology which showed that 21.9 percent of India's population lives below the poverty line. The panel headed by Tendulkar fixed the poverty line at an income threshold of Rs. 27.2 a day in rural areas, and Rs. 33.3 a day in cities (Dash Sharma, 2017).

"World Bank (1994, p.9) recognized that poverty is not only a problem of low income; rather it is a muliti-dimensional problem that includes low access to opportunities for developing human capital and to education. As UNDP (1996, p. 27) commented, income poverty is only a part of the picture. Just as human development encompasses aspects of life much broader than income, so poverty should be seen as having many dimensions and accordingly developed the concept of human poverty. It observed that human poverty is more than income poverty: it is denial of choices and opportunities for a living a tolerable life" (UNDP, 1997, p. 2) (*cf.* Singh, *et al.*, 2012:2).

Relative incidence of poverty across occupation groups reveals that poverty is more severe among agricultural labourers followed by non-agricultural labourers; self-employed in non-agriculture sector; self-employed in agriculture and allied activities, and others, as salaried jobs. Except for Andhra Pradesh and Kerala, relative incidence of poverty is highest among agricultural labourers (Kumar and Sharma, 2005).

There are controversies on threshold line for defining the poor in India. While in nutrition and health status estimation controversies are usually not arising as these are based on biological measurements and clinical assessments, and is free from political interference. It is not so while defining threshold line economically.

Nutrition is a Process

The Council of Food and Nutrition (USA, 1963) defines nutrition as "the science of food, the nutrients and other substances therein, their action, interaction and balance in relation to health and disease and the process by which the organism ingests, transports, utilizes and executes food substances. In addition, nutrition must be concerned with social, economic, cultural and psychological implication of food and eating.

The first part of the definition addresses the functioning of bio-physiological system of the body as an index of optimal health, while we find, the second part of the definition lays emphasis on the nutritional processes that relate to social and cultural condition, economic background, dietary habits, attitude and belief towards food, nature of physical activity and so on.

Nutritional Status in India

In a country like ours malnutrition with a high incidence of infection is a major health problem. Malnutrition is the significant underlying factor for high incidence of infant and child mortality, growth retardation and reduced mental efficiency. The worst victims of malnutrition are not only the economically vulnerable segments of the society but more particularly, the biologically vulnerable groups like infants, pre-school children, expectant mothers and lactating mothers. All these proximate causes are ultimately linked to a host of underlying factors, specifically poverty and ignorance being the most significant determinants.

Thus malnutrition and poverty are closely linked and consequently, an attack on poverty will affect the severity and extent of malnutrition. It is also true that affluent families also suffer from malnutrition as the recent studies indicate. Malnutrition can be characterized by both overnutrition and undernutrition. The former is defined as excessive intake of energy and/or macronutrients. Importantly, both overnutrition and undernutrition are associated with a range of poor health conditions. Underweight can contribute to poor infant health, and can lead to delayed physical and mental development in children, while on the other hand obesity is a main risk factor for chronic diseases such as hypertension, cardiovascular disease, type-2 diabetes, and some types of cancers. It has been suggested that an obesogenic environment is considered to be a major promoting factor in such cases. On one hand, the prevalence of undernutrition still remains a serious public health issue in the developing countries, while in on the other side we find the prevalence of overweight-obesity is increasing substantially. This coexistence of underweight and overweight (i.e., double burden malnutrition) is now becoming a matter of concern in public health. This aspect has been extensively studied by Mondal, *et al.* (2018) in the Indian context. Underweight and overweight can occur in close proximity and these conditions may coexist at national, community, and household levels. Several research studies have reported that co-existence of malnutrition is increasing at a high rate, and that double burden exists in India at the individual level, household level, population/community level and country level (Mondal *et al.*, 2018).

There is a general agreement that the health status of the tribal population in India is very poor and many scholars have tried to establish this with the help of morbidity, mortality and health statistics (Basu, 1986, 1996; Rizvi, 1986; Roy Burman, 1986; Bardhan *et al.*, 1989; Swain *et al.*, 1990; Ghoshmaulik and Karmahapatra, 1995; Bhattaccharya, 1995, 2009a,b; NNMB, 2000; Bulliyya, 2003; Bhattacharya, Haque and Biswas, 2006; Mitra and Sahu, 2006; Gangopadhyay, 2006; and many others). The low health status of the tribal community in general is closely linked with factors such as their poverty, illiteracy, lack of infrastructure facilities for medical care in the area where they inhabit (see Kalla and Joshi, 2004; Pathak, Sinha *et al.*, 2008; Dash Sharma and Chatterjee, 2013).

Dash Sharma (2004) had reported on the 'Nutrition and health among the tribes of India', an exhaustive study dealing with measures, methods and assessment, and classification of health status among the tribes of Jharkhand, Odisha, Madhya Pradesh and West Bengal. It had two objectives, one academic and the other administrative. Why the government is failing? Dash Sharma had concluded at that time, "Extensive investigations have been done by anthropologists on diet surveys and nutritional anthropometry which have contributed significantly in the understanding of the nutritional status of the tribal populations of India who are living in different ecological set up which in many ways differ from the general population of the country. The paper reflects the nutritional status of some of the tribal groups with particular reference to the states of Jharkhand (part of Bihar), Odisha, Madhya Pradesh (including Chhattisgarh of the present), and West Bengal. Most of the tribes mentioned in the paper (Dash Sharma, 2004:95) namely, Abujhmaria, Asur, Korwa, Sauria Paharia, Birhor, Kamar, Hill Korwa, Bondo, Toto, Juangs and Kharwar are primitives tribes (now called Particularly Vulnerably Tribal Groups) of India, excepting the Santhals (Santals), Ho, and the Oraons, who are settled agricultural tribal populations" (p. 95). One thing clearly emanates from this general review that there is an alarming state of malnutrition among the tribes of India in general, and particularly among the vulnerable tribal groups (PVTGs) of India (Dash Sharma, 2006).

The present author would limit his discussion to the health and healthcare situation in Jharkhand, a highly mineral rich State where 26 per cent were tribals as per the census decade 1981, which was at that time under the State of Bihar. The State of Jharkhand was created after bifurcating Bihar, a long cherished dream of the tribals of the area which came to reality on 15th November 2000, for which they struggled hard tenaciously through peaceful agitation for about sixty long years. Formation of the State of Jharkhand had happened only under a non-Congress government at the Centre. The political history of Jharkhand movement has been presented by Dash Sharma (2018) in his book titled *Mundas and Their Country: A Century After.*

The nutritional goal of any country would be to provide adequate nutrition and health support to its population so that they attain their full genetic potential in growth and development. Malnutrition in children in the tropics is important not only because it is common but also because it highlights important relationships between infection, immunity and nutrition which are of universal application. All malnourished children show reduced growth and muscle protein deficiency. Two 'polar' types of protein energy malnutrition (PEM) are recognised, they are Marasmus and Kwashiorkor, but many children have a mixed clinical picture (Cowen and Heap, 1993:259).

Marasmus occurs in infants aged under 1 year when maternal milk supply is interrupted by death or illness, and in older children in time of famine. The child has clearly lost muscle and subcutaneous fat. The skin is dry and wrinkled and there is no peripheral oedema. The hair is thin and dry. Body temperature is low. The child looks anxious but moves less than normal and may be hungry, but vomit any foods offered. Such children are susceptible to diarrhoeal and respiratory infections, trachoma ad vitamin A deficiency.

Children with kwashiorkor are usually aged 18 months to 4 years and have been weaned from the mother's breast. Muscle loss occurs but subcutaneous fat is preserved, and there is obvious peripheral oedema. The hair is dry, straight and depigmented. The skin is scaly and glistening, peeling and hyperpigmented, especially on the legs. The abdomen is distended and the liver enlarged. The child is fractious and irritable and often has diarrhoea. Clinical vitamin A deficiency may be present.

Children with mixed 'marasmic kwashiorkor' have a varied picture with muscle loss, oedema and damaged skin (Cowen and Heap, 1993). The diagnosis of the malnutrition syndromes is primarily clinical. Anthropometric documentation is essential for the individual child and for the study of the community. Body weight on a centile chart is a measure of current nutritional status, allowing for the presence of oedema; body length or height indicates previous progress in growth. Children with kwashiorkor have low serum albumin, potassium, zinc, magnesium and calcium levels and low blood sugar, and may be anaemic with defective blood clotting.

Fortunately India is not having children suffering from marasmic or kwashiorkor cases as is often reported from some African countries. There may be a few cases that have been reported sporadically from some inaccessible interior rural areas at familial level due to various socio-economic reasons. But it is not locally alarming being only sporadic, and when media report such critical news help reach privately through NGOs or through government agencies to the suffering family/families. However, general malnutrition exists in India among the children of school going age coming from families with poor socio-economic background living in towns and cities and in rural areas. Malnutrition exists alarmingly among children living in slums in the fringe of the big towns. Several hundreds of research reports are available on Indian tribes and castes populations on the status of health and nutrition published by several Indian University Departments of Anthropology, Anthropological Survey of India, and Government Health Departments and other health related research institutes in India.

Recently encouraging news on the nutritional status has appeared in the media that has been reported by United Nations. The report says, "The number of undernourished people in India has declined from 60 million, from 21.7 percent of the population in 2004-06 to 14 percent in 2017-19, according to a UN report". The State of Food Security and Nutrition in the World Report, released on Monday (*Times of India, Kolkata*, and Wednesday, July 15, 2020) said there were less stunted children but more obese adults in India. The report is prepared jointly by the Food and Agricultural Organization of the United Nations (FAO), the International Fund for Agricultural Development (IFAD), the United Nations Children's Fund (Unicef), the UN World Food Programme (WFP), and the World Health Organization (WHO).

Health Infrastructure in Jharkhand

The wide spread poverty, illiteracy, malnutrition, non-availability of safe drinking water and unhygienic living conditions and poor maternal and child health services have been reported in several studies as the possible contributing factors for the dismal health conditions prevailing among many tribal and caste communities in different regions of India. Apart from poverty and illiteracy of the people this dismal situation in the health sector particularly in the rural areas and interior villages is greatly due to mismanaged planning health infrastructure programmes of the State government agencies.

Let us discuss what happened in Jharkhand. Prevention of

childhood malnutrition in a community depends on:

1. Adequate community food supply;
2. Education of mothers in the use of nutritious foods which are cheap and available in their village community; and
3. Primary health care programmes including monitoring of child development, treatment of or immunization against common infections, provision of vitamin A supplement.

Let me present the situation of childhood malnutrition and the state of health infrastructure that prevailed in Bihar and in Jharkhand when it was established in the year 2000.

In the decades 80s and 90s in India, prevention of childhood malnutrition was almost non-existent because of the extremely inadequate infrastructure facilities for health care in rural India, and the people were much poorer and there were no adequate food supplies in interior villages, parents were illiterate, and primary health centres were non-existent in the villages.

Report of the facts and figures about the existing health care infrastructure in the State of Jharkhand during the year 2003 showed an 'unhealthy figures'. According to the government of India guidelines there should be 7260 health sub-centres in rural areas at that time but there are only 4462. The situation was more pathetic in areas where a large number of sub-centres were non-existent. It makes painful reading of the annual report published by the undivided Bihar that from 1990 to 2000 not a single new sub-centre was set up anywhere in the entire State. The 'unhealthy figures' reported in *Hindustan Times*, HT Ranchi Live (Saturday, October 11, 2003) was as follows:

Health Centres	Should be	Is	Gap
Health Sub-Centre	7260	4462	2798
Primary Health Centre	561	193	368
Community Centres	211	37	174
Sub-Division Hospitals	35	16	19
Hospital Posts	1740	0	0

The Chief Minister and Health Minister of Jharkhand had assured to revamp the health sector in rural areas of Jharkhand by the year 2007. But hardly any noticeable change was observed in the year 2007. This is the situation prevailing in a highly concentrated tribal population of the State of Jharkhand. We can presume that the situation is not much better in other rural areas of the various States of India where there is large concentration of tribal groups.

An overview of the population, health and social development scenario of Jharkhand was presented by UNFPA advisor Dr. Almas Ali and Dr. B.P. Thiagarajan of Population Foundation of India. The report says that the root cause of overall poor health status of Jharkhand is poverty — both income and human related, social deprivation, low literacy rate, especially among females, and structural inequalities in terms of class, caste and sex. The report gives the nutritional status of Jharkhand as follows (State-Level Advocacy Conference on Population Stabilization, Health and Social Development, held at Ranchi on 18 November 2003):

1 in 9 children dies in the first year of life;

1 in 3 dies in the first year of life;

Girls are more likely to be stunted and boys wasted;

54% children under 3 years are underweight, 49% stunted and 25% wasted;

Just 26% children aged 6-9 months receive breast milk and mushy food;

Only 6.5% children is fully vaccinated;

32% children was never vaccinated;

2 out of 5 women are undernourished;

Anaemia in young children is 70%;

Anaemia in women is as high as 72.5%;

40% women has chronic energy deficiency.

This shock presentation had other bad news: All the 31 scheduled tribes including the nine primitive tribes, are severely disadvantaged. In comparison to other states the situation is very poor in terms of infrastructure for personal hygiene, sanitation, water supply, education — especially among the females and the number of girls schools, employment, health consciousness and also availability, affordability and accessibility of the health services.

Malnutrition is the single most important risk factor for spread of diseases in Jharkhand. About 54 percent of children up to 3 years of age are underweight, 49 per cent are with stunted growth, while 25 percent are wasted and 70 percent suffer from anaemia. The ratio of children suffering from malnutrition is higher in rural areas and among the disadvantaged groups particularly scheduled tribes. Based on body mass index 41 percent women are undernourished and 73 per cent have some degree of anaemia. Only 56 per cent of household in the State used iodised salt at recommended levels. This was the report by CARE (a prominent NGO in Jharkhand) and the report specified that malnutrition among scheduled castes and scheduled tribes in the State is highest in the country. Almost in all the health and nutrition indictors right from immunisation to check up of pregnant women, Jharkhand is far below the national average. The report further observed "Reason for existing plight is multi-dimensional. People in the State are largely rural based and are even oblivious of the fact and even lack awareness about health behaviour. The concept of immunising the children against deadly diseases is yet to catch up. The lack of knowledge and adherence to traditional practices of healing hinder their belief to accept modern medicines." (Report by CARE; *Hindustan Times*, Ranchi Live, February 3, 2004).

Let us see the comment of Dr N. C. Saxena, who was heading the 'hunger panel' which appeared in the local media at Ranchi (*Sunday, Hindustan Times, Ranchi, News*, March 31, 2004).

"Dr N. C. Saxena, who was appointed by the Supreme Court to review the hunger situation, met the Governor Sri Ved Prakash Marwah, on Saturday (13th) and apprised him of the status of the various programmes in the State. Despite clear cut orders of the Supreme Court to provide 300-500 additional calories and 10-25 grams of proteins to the children, adolescent girls and breast-feeding mothers respectively, food is not reaching the hungry masses in this State, he reported to have told the Governor during his 45 minutes long meeting." He said, 'the State has failed to comply with the orders of the Supreme Court, meant to ensure that the weaker sections of the society do not suffer from hunger and starvation' (Dash Sharma, 2008).

A report given by the Government of Jharkhand (2006) through its website of the Department of Health, Medical Education and family Welfare on the health facilities in Palamau district and the position of the manpower available in the health department of the district. The record and the figures show a grim picture of the health sector so far as the medical administrative system is concerned in Jharkhand. This has been discussed elaborately by Dash Sharma (2008).

So this is the situation in a tribal concentrated region like Jharkhand that was prevailing in the year 2004-2006. It may be assumed that the situation is not very different in other areas particularly in States of Madhya Pradesh, Chattisgarh, Odisha, where there is large concentration of the tribal groups.

Let us see what happened eight years later in the health care system of Jharkhand.

In the year 2012 National Health Systems Resource Centre published a report on *Jharkhand: Public Health Workforce Issues and Challenges*. Jharkhand has a population of 32.96 million, 28 percent of which are tribals (NHSRC, 2012). In an overview of Public Health Workforce report (NHSRC, 2012) present the statistics of the workforce and health infrastructure in its 24 districts through a table as follows:

Table 1: Public Health Workforce and Health Infrastructure in Jharkhand

<table>
<tr><th>Health Facilities</th><th>Present</th><th>Required</th></tr>
<tr><td>District Hospitals</td><td>21</td><td>24
(Required in East Singhbhum, Bokaro and Dhanbad)</td></tr>
<tr><td>Sub Divisional Hospitals</td><td>10</td><td rowspan="2">329
(If taken as one per lakh population)</td></tr>
<tr><td>Community Health Centers</td><td>188 (149 under construction)</td></tr>
<tr><td>Primary Health Centers</td><td>330</td><td>1684 (@ 1/20,000 population)</td></tr>
<tr><td>Sub Centers</td><td>3958</td><td>10968 (@1/3,000 population)</td></tr>
</table>

Source: NHSRC, 2012.

The Table 1 present the dismal and very dreary picture prevailing in the State of Jharkhand in the public health work force and health infrastructure. This very grim situation prevails even after more than a decade of Jharkhand formation particularly in rural areas, in tribal villages, as is evident from the figures given for the Primary Health Centers and Sub Centers reported by NHSRC. Primary Health Centers and Sub Centers are essential in rural areas and interior villages for the attention of primary and urgent medical care.

The health care workforce (inclusive of contractual) availability in the State of Jharkhand was as follows (NHSRC, 2012):

State	Auxiliary Nurse Midwife (ANM)	Staff Nurse	Lady Health Visitor (LHV)	Pharmacist	Laboratory Technician	X-Ray Technician	Medical Officers
Jharkhand	7347	634	125	361	456	109	1519

It may be noted that the report on Jharkhand showed that there was only 125 Lady Health Visitors (LHVs) who have to attend the rural villages of the 24 districts of Jharkhand. ANM who is the village level female health worker who is known as the first contact person between the community and the health services, and are regarded as the grass roots workers in the health care system are only 7347. Imagine this tiny number and the management system that it requires where Jharkhand has 24 districts, 260 blocks and 3260 villages out of which only 45% have access to electricity and while only 8484 are connected by roads.

The health care workforce in Jharkhand can broadly be classified into 3 categories: regular government employees; state contractual employees and NRHM contractual. Jharkhand Public Health HR Profile 2012 is as follows: Regular Appointment: 39 percent; State Contractual: 18 percent and NRHM Contractual: 43 percent. Thus we find regular government appointees are less than 40% the rest are contractual.

This contractual appointment has greatly impacting the health care system in Jharkhand. This situation is prevailing in many states of India, Jharkhand is not an exception.

To meet the Human Resources Gap in the public health facilities, the State of Jhaarkhand intends to increase annual intake in its 3 Medical Colleges (RIMS, Ranchi; MGM, Jamshedpur; PMCH, Dhanbad) and operationalize 7 more ANM Training Centers during 2012. NHSRC (2012) also reports that process is underway to set up new Medical Colleges by upgrading DH at Ranchi, Hazaribagh, Saraikela, Dumla and Daltonganj), to be made operational by 2015-2016.

The 'Current Bed Strength' for Ranchi (District Hospital) as reported in NHSRC (2012) was 50-60 (currently operational – renovation going on); and the 'Projected Bed Strength' is 500 for Ranchi under Public Private Partnership.

For the other four District Hospitals the 'Projected Bed Strength' is 300.

Now it is the year 2020, nothing has been flashed through the media, no inauguration ceremony by Mantri *ji*, so you can imagine what has happened.

Democracy is a game of number. Nine Chief Ministers and three times President's rule in a span of thirteen years in Jharkhand.

This reflects the unique political culture of the region. Development cannot take place when there is scrambling for the chair by the elected politicians. There is a general feeling among the people that something is missing in our Constitution (Dash Sharma, 2018).

But now I find that even an elected stable political party that formed a government and ruled a State uninterrupted for thirty-four long years for seven consecutive terms from 1977 to 2011, could not develop the infrastructure and health care facilities to the expectations of the people who voted the party to power, with the hope, that the people would be served better now by their elected representatives.

It only transpires and reflects that something is wrong with the elected representatives who govern us, not the Constitution.

The people's aspiration was that there will be more District hospitals, Community health centers, Primary health centers and Sub-centers in rural areas and the villages and they would be happy getting good health care facilities with increased health care workforce as government of their choice has come. But nothing much happened to make them happy. This they realized after many years. The power of the party and the time span the party had got to rule over the State could not deliver the goods to the people.

So now we realize that it is not the political power – the absolute majority of the single political party – the power the ruling party enjoys, and the time span it rules, for creating development initiatives and establishing development programmes, particularly the health care services, it is something else. It is the individual and his or her team that matters. If the leadership has the intention to carry on projects for the betterment of the common man and an urge to do good and to listen to their voices and take development initiatives for the people in right earnest, things would not have come to such a state as we see it now.

Human development depends on the quality of the leadership, not the political power.

Amartya Sen in many of his discussions had always stressed on education and health. In his recent book '*Bola Jay*' (Sen, 2020) which is a collection of his interviews, lectures and discussions, he had stressed that there exist great inequality and absence of facilities in education and health sector. If we have to compete with the developed countries, particularly China he stressed, we have to pay great attention to develop greatly these two sectors, health and education in India.

Beds Don't Treat Patients

Recently I read a very interesting and informative column titled "Beds Don't Treat Patients" that appeared in *Times of India, Kolkata* (July, 17, 2020),written by the renowned cardiac surgeon, Chairman and Founder, Narayana Health, Dr. Devi Shetty. He writes, "Thanks to the early lockdown by the government we got two month to prepare for the Covid onslaught. Today we are debating about exporting PPEs and ventilators, rather than struggling to import them a couple of months ago. Our attention should now shift towards reducing mortality especially in rural India."

What an admiring greatness this world-known cardiac surgeon of Bangalore has, we find, amidst his extreme busy schedule, he gets time to think about and feel concerned about reducing mortality in rural India. For the last seventy years our health ministers and health officers and officials have paid little attention to medical care in rural areas, though our politicians and *netas* gleefully express 'India lives in villages', when they move in search of votes.

Dr. Devi Shetty further writes, "To manage 1000 private and government hospitals with over 200 beds for a year we need at least 50,000 to 70,000 young MBBS doctors who, after internship have gained experience in medical ICU or surgical ICU or coronary care unit, accident and emergency rooms."

He then goes on discussing about "How to get 50,000 young trained specialist doctors for Covid ICUs?". And about requirement of other medical specialists, junior doctors, physician assistants in critical care unit, and nursing students, and what to do about when there is short supply of medical workforce. He suggests, "…the aim should be to create a large floating skilled workforce of doctors and nurses who can be deputed where Covid peaks, especially to protect rural India."

His model of 'floating skilled workforce of doctors' can be taken up where there is dearth of regular doctors in rural hospital centers. At least with such an approach a few precious lives of rural areas can be saved.

Government Hospital a Shambolic Structure

After knowing that 'beds don't treat patients' let us have a look at the hospital structure and the medical workforce of well-know government hospitals. The three government-run State hospitals of Jharkhand are sick. The buildings are falling that is what people say when they see great cracks on the walls of the rooms due to the utter neglect of the administration. Doctors, nurses, pharmacists and technicians are in short supply, despite the Medical Council of India warnings since 2004 to scale up the numbers. The Medical Council of India Team had reported many violations in the campus of the government-run Medical Colleges and Hospitals in Jharkhand. *Hindustan Times, Ranchi*, in April 2015, had reported in three-part series about the situation prevailing in the three big hospitals of Jharkhand, one each in Jamshedpur, Dhanbad and Ranchi.

Let us see the situation that prevailed in Ranchi, now the capital of Jharkhand. Rajendra Medical College and Hospital at Ranchi (popular as RMCH) was founded in 1965. Now it is also known as Rajendra Institute of Medical Sciences (RIMS), which was established on 15 August 2002 by upgrading the then RMCH, and is an institute of Ranchi University.

During the visit of the MCI team in April 2017 a media report appeared as follows (*Hindustan Times, Ranchi*, April 19, 2015): "Ranchi: Nicknamed 'the paradise' for ailing VVIPs, the state-run Rajendra Institute of Medical Sciences (RIMS) has been hitting the headlines for all the wrong reasons — politics, patient-doctor clashes and recurring violations of Medical Council of India (MCI) norms. This super speciality hospital of Jharkhand which came into existence in 2002, had witnessed five doctor-patient classes and three protest strikes by the doctors last year. The reason behind these classes and strikes had been the prevailing shortage of medical staff, leading to poor patient care and doctor-patient clashes." The media has reported on the situation in RIMS supported by several photographs showing — 'garbage outside the government doctors' quarters, broken ceiling of hostel building, patients rely on pedestal fans as all ACs are out of order in the BURNs Ward of RIMS'.

The then Health Minister Sri Ramachandra Chandra Chandravanshi had said to the media "It is true that the situation is poor. But efforts are being made to rectify it." What else the embarrassed minister can say.

The Chief Minister and Health Minister of Jharkhand had assured to revamp the health sector in rural areas of Jharkhand by the year 2007 (Dash Sharma, 2004). But not much has improved since then as we find the situation presented by the media to the public about the prevailing situations in the State-run hospitals. Another much embarrassing shocking news had appeared later, the health minister responsible to move forward and to renovate the health sector in Jharkhand, has been booked by the law authorities for money laundering charges (‘*Bhanu Pratap ki caroro ki sampatti attach*’, appeared in *Hindustan, Ranchi*, 27 March 2015).

With the new government of BJP that has taken over the reins of governance and administration from December end 2014, the hopes of the people have brightened as reflected in the comments that have appeared in the media. People waited to see what this government delivers to the people of Jharkhand in health sector in the coming years. People say some improvement have been made in the structure of the hospital, some additions and alterations etc as it usually happens when the reins of administration is taken over by a new government, but nothing more, nothing remarkable, they find.

The health care management system remains the same unless something happens which shakes and gives a shock to the common man, the general public of the region.

And that happened two years later. ‘Jharkhand Healthcare System in a Shocking State’ was reported by Savita on 27 September 2016, Ranchi (*https://medicaldialogues.in/jharkhand-healthcare-system-in-a-shocking-state,* accessed on 29.07.2020). The report says, “The shocking photograph of a mentally-challenged patient, Munni Devi , being served meals on the floor at a local hospital here has once again brought to the fore the dismal state of Jharkhand’s healthcare system — despite all the tall developmental talk by the state’s BJP government. When a newspaper carried the photograph, the Jharkhand High Court took *suo motu* cognizance, converted it into public interest litigation (PIL) and has now served notice on the state government.”

The hospital authorities are least concerned about the health care and health care ethics. Their insouciant attitude is worrisome for the sick patients and their relatives particularly those coming from rural areas for seeking hospital care. The authorities wake up when court intervenes.

Rakhi Ghoshal (Ghoshal, 2015) in her article titled ‘What ails India’s two-tiered healthcare system? A philosophical enquiry’ writes, “India’s two-tiered healthcare system (viz. the public and private sectors) has been suffering from various ailments, and each sector has been criticised for its own set of deficiencies.” Against this backdrop, her article explores whether there is any possible commonality between the two sectors, and she suggests that the ‘common logic’, or common ground, is the model of biomedical knowledge, which forms the foundation of both sectors.

Service for the Poor are Poorer Services

Ghoshal (2015) finds in her research (her article is a theoretical piece and stems from the doctoral work at Centre for the Study of Culture and Society), that, "the higher concentration of private health care ventures in urban and peri-urban areas is explained by the simple fact that such set-ups need to generate economic profit, and are consequently dependent on consumers who are willing and able to pay for it. Since it is the middle and upper classes which are the most compatible with this sector, most private institutions are located in areas populated by these classes. "The growing glamour of the private health care sector has led to the formation of a distinct class of patients – the affluent ill, with those outside this ambit constituting the class of the non-affluent or the poor ill."

The poor ill are also marked by their economic buying power, i.e. the *lack* of it. This allows them to access only the public health care sector, in which costs of treatment are subsidised by the state. However, the standards of care and service in public hospitals are usually abysmal, bearing out the well-known adage that "services for the poor are poor services". In India, the concept of "health care as service" has long fallen out of favour, and the state's role in providing basic curative and preventive care diminished significantly between the 1950s and 1990s (Zachariah *et al.*, 2010).

While the two health care sectors are distinct in terms of form, modality of disbursing services, and ideology of care, both have been criticised by dissatisfied patient groups, health rights and human rights activists, feminists and bioethicists (Ghoshal, 2015). .

Health Care in Public Sector: Indifference and Inadequacy

The doctor population ratio in India is 1:1456 against the WHO recommendation of 1:1000 (*https://www.deccanherald.com*Samiksha Goel, *DHNS, Bengaluru*, Jan., 31, 2020; accessed on 01.08.2020). The economic survey 2019-20 has released information regarding the medical infrastructure evincing a shortage of doctors in the country (DH *Deccanherald, Bangaluru*, Jan., 31, 2020). 'India has just one doctor for every 1700 people', thus stated Kumar AU (Kumar, 2013), in *Indian Express*[*Internet*] 2013 Sept.22.

Approximately only 20% of health care in India continues to be in the public domain even as it is accessed by more than half the country's population (Dutta, 2012). Ghosal has reported citing earlier studies that 'Medical students too are reportedly keener to undergo their undergraduate and residency training in government medical colleges (Thomas, 2009), because of the sheer volume and variety of cases from which they can learn. It has been found that medical professionals think of serving in the rural areas as a punishment and thus there is a general reluctance towards rural postings (Ghoshal, 2015; Kumar, 2013). It is due to this reluctance that the physician-patient ratio in rural areas is skewed, and the few doctors who do serve their postings get overburdened and overworked, resulting in early burnout (*cf.* Ghoshal, 2015). Luthra (2012) had stated that in public health care institutions, even basic medical and surgical items, such as essential medicines and sutures are in short supply and have to be purchased by the patient's family.

Kutty (2010) had stated, since these institutions are accessed mostly by poor patients, whose literacy levels are often low, providers commonly display minimum accountability towards them (Ghoshal, 2011), and patients themselves are intimidated by the sheer physical space of a hospital (Kutty, 2010).

Ghoshal (2011) further stated many health care providers believe that patients who come to public hospitals and receive subsidised treatment are being done a favour by the state, and such patients are perceived as learning material; consequently, issues such as respecting privacy, obtaining adequately informed consent, sharing details of the diagnosis and prognosis, and involving the patient in decision-making commonly take a backseat (Fochsen *et al.*,2006; Jesani, 2009; Kumar *et al.*, 2012; Ghoshal *et al.*, 2013). These various shortcomings, in combination, besides creating an atmosphere of extreme apathy, have also led to a precipitous fall in the quality of health care services in this sector (Dilip and Duggal, 2004; Sharma *et al.*, 2011; Gupta and Srinivasan, 2011).

People are governed by some set of moral principles, which is expressed by the word 'ethics'. Ethics involve great many things. In hospitals, care ethics is greatly involved with patient-doctor interaction. Care ethics is emotion-based virtues such as mercy, compassion, kindness, friendship, leniency, reconciliation and sensitivity. Care ethics is a philosophy of relationality and imagines the individual as determined by the social, economic, relational and cultural coordinates (Ghoshal, 2015). Care ethics with its emphasis on the component of care and relationality, seems to offer a conceptual gateway to re-think health care. Applied to the physician-patient relationship, care ethics would urge physicians to perceive of the patient as a social being and not just an asocial diseased body. Lakshmi Kutty (Kutty, 2010) enunciates the ways in which "a patient's subjectivity is determined by the axes of gender, caste, religion, poverty, desires and expectations."

Anthropologists have not shown much interest in the study of the prevailing public health care systems in India, its structure and function, which reflects the medical culture in India and a great regional variation. Using care ethics to define physician-patient relationship will open up an immense scope for situational studies and would thus help to understand the medical culture in the health care system. It would be interesting to see if younger anthropologists take up some issues of public health and health care system and explore these through anthropological insights in rural health centers.

References

Amartya S. 2020. *Bola Jay*. Ananda Publishers: Kolkata.

Bardhan A, SK Sinha, K Gopinath, AK Brahmbhatt. 1989. *A diagonostic study of factors responsible for lesser or no utilization of health facilities among the Bhills of Madhya Pradesh. PAC Report (mimeographed).* National Institute of Health and Family Welfare: New Delhi.

Basu J. 1986. *Genetic, socio-cultural and health-care among tribal groups of Jabalpur and Konta tehsils of Bastar district (Madhya Pradesh).* In: A. K. Kalla and K. S. Singh (eds.), *Anthropology, Development and Nation Building*, Concept Publishing Company: New Delhi. pp. 87-105.

Basu J. 1996. Need for action research for health development among tribal communities in India. *South Asian Anthropologist.* 17: 73-80.

Bhattacharya KK. 1995. Nutritional status of Oraons of Sunderban, West Bengal. *South Asian Anthropologist.* 16: 99-104.

Bhattacharya KK. 2009a. *Nutritional Status of Indian Population: Eastern Region* (ed.). Anthropological Survey of India: Kolkata.

Bhattacharya KK. 2009b. *Nutritional Status of Indian Population: North Western Region* (ed.). Anthropological Survey of India: Kolkata.

Bhattacharya KK, M Haque, TK Biswas. 2006. Nutritional status of two primitive tribes of Eastern India. In: P. Dash Sharma (ed.), *Anthropology of Primitive Tribes in India*, Serials Publications: New Delhi. Pp. 323-335.

Gandham B. 2003. Secular deterioration in nutritional status of young children: An alarming situation for the state of Orissa. *Man in India.* 83: 49-71.

Cowen GO, BJ Heap. 1993. *Clinical Tropical Medicine*, (First Edition). Chapman & Hall: London.

Dash Sharma P. 2004. *Nutrition and health among the tribes of India.* In: A. K. Kalla and P. C. Joshi (eds.), *Tribal Health and Medicines*, Concept Publishing Company: New Delhi. pp. 71-98.

Dash Sharma P. 2006. *Anthropology of Primitive Tribes in India* (edited). Serials Publications: New Delhi.

Dash Sharma P. 2008. *Bio-social and administrative dimensions of health care system in Jharkhand.* In: R. K. Pathak, A. K. Sinha, B. G. Banerjee, R. N. Vasishat and C. J. Edwin (eds.), *Bio-Social Issues in Health*, Northern-Book Centre: New Delhi. pp. 445-460.

Dash Sharma P. D Chatterjee. 2013. *Livelihood and Health: Issues and Process in Rural Development* (eds.). Serials Publications: New Delhi.

Dash Sharma P. 2017. On poverty and health infrastructure in Jharkhand. *North Bengal Anthropologist.* 5: 1-12.

Dash Sharma P. 2018. *Mundas and Their Country: A Century After.* Serials Publications: New Delhi.

Dilip TR, R. Duggal. 2004. Unmet need for public health-care services in Mumbai, India. *Asia-Pacific Population Journal, June* 2004.

Dutta N. 2012. What ails India's healthcare system? *The Health Site* [Internet].2012 Aug 18[cited 2014 Dec 20]. Available from *http://health.india.com/diseases-conditions/what-ails-indias-healthcare-system/*(*cf.* Ghoshal, 2015).

Fochsen G, K Deshpande, A Thorson. 2006. Power imbalance and consumerism in the doctor-patient relationship: Health care providers' experiences of patient encounters in a rural district in India. *Qual. Health Res.* 16: 1236-1251.

Shampa G. 2006. Nutritional status of Kamar of MadhyaPradesh. In: P. Dash Sharma (ed.), *Anthropology of Primitive Tribes in India*, Serials Publications: New Delhi. pp. 412-430.

Ghoshal R. 2011. 'Hands on learning' in medicine: Who benefits? *Economics and Political Weekly.* XLVI: 16-18.

Ghoshal R., N Madhiwalla, A Jesani, P Samant, V Badhwar, S Surve. 2013. The absent discourse of communication: Understanding ethics of provider–patient relationship in six hospitals in urban India. *J. Med. Ethics Hist. Med.*, 2013 Jan. 23(6):2 (*cf.* Ghoshal, 2015).

Ghoshal R. 2015. What ails India's two-tiered healthcare system? A philosophical inquiry. DOI:*https://doi.org/10.20529/IJME/2015.006* (accessed on 25.07.2020 *https://ijme.in/articles/ what-ails-indias-two-tiered-healthcare-system-a-philosophical-enquiry/?galley=html*)

Ghoshmaulik SK, RK Karmahapatra. 1995. Health situation of the Juangs of Orissa. *South Asian Anthropologist*, 16: 79-83.

Gupta N, S Srinivasan. 2011. Serial maternal deaths in a tertiary care hospital: Some questions. *Indian Journal of Medical Ethics.* 8: 70-72.

Jesani A. 2009. About student research and blanket consent from patients. *Indian Journal of Medical Ethics.* 6: 216-218.

Kalla AK, PC Joshi. 2004. *Tribal Health and Medicines* (eds.). Concept Publishing Company: New Delhi.

Kumar S, R Mohanraj, A Rose, MJ Paul, GThomas. 2012. How "informed" is informed consent? Findings from a study in South India. *Indian Journal of Medical Ethics.* 9: 180-186.

Kumar AU. 2013. India has just one doctor for every 1,700 people. *Indian Express* [Internet]. 2013 Sept 22 [cited 2014 Dec 20]. Available from: *http://www.newindianexpress.com/magazine/India-has-just-one-doctor-for-every-1700-people/2013/09/22/article1792010.ece*

Kutty L. 2010. The 'intractable' patient: managing context, illness, health care. In: A. Zachariah, R. Srivatsan, and S. Tharu (eds.), *Towards a Critical Medical Practice: Reflections on the Dilemmas of Medical Culture Today,* Orient Blackswan: Hyderabad. pp.226-245.

Luthra S. 2012. Healthcare in India: A call for innovative reform [an interview with Victoria Fan]. The *National Bureau of Asian Research* [Internet]. 2012 Dec 20. [cited 2014 Dec 21].Available from: http://www.nbr.org/research/activity.aspx?id=298(*cf.* Ghoshal, 2015).

Mitra N. Sahu. 2006. Nutritional status of Abujhmaria pre-school children. In: P. Dash Sharma (ed.), *Anthropology of Primitive Tribes in India,* Serials Publications: New Delhi. pp. 396-411.

Mandal N, K Bose, J Sen. 2018. *Malnutrition: A Double Burden,* (eds.), B. R. Publishing Corporation: Delhi.

NHSRC 2012. *Jharkhand: Public Health Workforce Issues and Challenges.* National Health Systems Resource Center, September 2012. *nhsrcindia.org* (accessed on 25.07.2012).

NNMB 2000. National Nutrition Monitoring Bureau (NNMB). *Diet and Nutritional Status of Tribal Populations.Report on First Repeat Surveys, Hyderabad, pp. 1-24.* National Institute of Nutrition: Hyderabad.

Pathak RK, AK Sinha, BG Banerjee, RN Vasishat, CJ Edwin. 2008. *Bio-Social Issues in Health* (eds.). Northern Boook Centre: New Delhi.

Rizvi SNH. 1986. Health practices of the Jaunsaries: A socio-cultural analysis. In: B. Chaudhuri (ed.), *Tribal Health: Socio-Cultural Dimensions,* Inter-India Publications: New Delhi. pp. 223-246.

Roy Burman BK. 1986. Morbidity and nutritional status of the scheduled tribes of India. In: B. Chaudhuri (ed.), *Tribal Health: Socio-Cultural Dimensions,* Inter-India Publications: New Delhi. pp. 85-98.

Singh KM, MS Meena, RK Singh, A Kumar, A Kumar. 2012. *Rural Poverty in Jharkhand, India: An Empirical Study Based on Panel Data.* ICAR-RCER, Patna. NCAP: New Delhi. (On line at *https:/mpra.ub.uni-munchen.de/45258. MPRA Paper No. 45258, posted 20 March 2013*)

Sharma A, G Anand. M Bahree. 2011. The ailing health of a growing nation. *The Wall Street Journal* [Internet].2011 July 30[cited 2014 Dec 21]. Available from: *http://online.wsj.com/news/articles/SB10001424053111903591104576466251010968520*

Swain S, SC Jena, P Singh. 1990. Morbidity status of Khond tribe of Phulbani (Orissa). In: B. Chaudhuri (ed.), *Cultural and Environmental Dimensions of Health*, pp. 177-191. Inter-India Publications: New Delhi.

Thomas V. 2009. Rural doctors – do we need a separate entity [editorial]? *Calicut Med. J.*, 7(4): e1.

Vijaya Kumar T, SSP Sharma. 2005. Economic reforms and rural poverty in India: Some emerging issues. In: C. Narashima Rao (ed.), *Rural Development in India: A Multi-Disciplinary An*alysis, Serials Publications: New Delhi. pp. 5-26.

Zachariah A, R Srivatsan, S Tharu 2010. *Towards a Critical Medical Practice: Reflections on the Dilemmas of Medical Culture Today (eds.)*, pp. 1-34. Orient Blackswan: Hyderabad (*cf.* Ghoshal, 2015).

Chapter Three

UTILIZATION OF ANTENATAL CARE SERVICES AMONG THE LAMKANG TRIBE OF MANIPUR

GANGAINA KAMEIH AND GAUTAM K. KSHATRIYA

ABSTRACT

Antenatal care(ANC) among pregnant women is one of the important factors in reducing maternal and child morbidity and mortality. Unfortunately, many women in developing countries do not receive the World Health Organization (WHO) recommended minimum of four antenatal visits. Therefore, the present study examined the determinants of antenatal care utilization among Lamkang tribe of Chandel District, Manipur. A community based cross sectional study was carried out in 200 Lamkangs women. Descriptive analysis was used to describe the number of respondents and percentages according to socio-demographic characteristics. Binary logistic regression analysis was applied between dependent variable and independent variables. ANC utilization was taken as dependent variable. The findings indicate that factors such as maternal age, positive husband's attitude and women's education are the significant predictors of receiving antenatal care services among Lamkang tribe of Chandel district, Manipur.

Keywords: *Antenatal care, Lamkang tribe, Manipur*

INTRODUCTION

Antenatal care (ANC) is defined as the care provided by skilled health-care professionals to pregnant women and adolescent girls in order to ensure the best health conditions for both mother and baby during pregnancy. One of the most important components of antenatal care is to offer information and advice to women about pregnancy related complications and possible curative measures for early detection and management of complications. Despite progress in some countries, maternal healthcare remains a major challenge to the global public health system, especially in developing countries where mortality rates is much higher than the developed countries. Women in developing regions face a lifetime risk of maternal death of 1 in 160, as compared with 1 in 3700 for women living in developed regions (WHO, 2014). It has also been documented that over 95% maternal deaths in India occur among women who have never had antenatal care check-up (Ronsmans and Graham, 2006). Proper ANC is one of the important ways in reducing maternal and child morbidity and mortality. There are many women who do not receive the World Health Organization (WHO) recommended minimum of four antenatal visits mostly in underdeveloped regions. The considerable variation in maternal and child health in the developing world is believed to be partly due to differences in the availability of and access to health services. An important contribution of the body of research to our understanding of utilization of maternal health services is that there is no universal explanation that applies to all places and times: the determinants of utilization of maternal health care services are not the same across socio-economic and cultural contexts (Navaneetham and Dharmalingam, 2001).

Although studies have been extensively done on antenatal care in most part of the globe, only few studies are from Manipur that also on different population (Mao, 2009) and on different topics (Laishram *et al.*, 2013; Maheo and Devi, 2018). Therefore, the present study was carried out with the objective of examining the determinants of antenatal care utilization among Lamkang tribe of Chandel District, Manipur.

The Lamkang tribe is one of the underdeveloped tribes in Manipur recognized by the Government of India in 1956. They are mainly concentrated in the south-eastern part of Manipur in the district of Chandel and they speak Lamkang dialect which belongs to the Tibeto-Burman group. The Lamkang people in the past were animistic. However, with the advent of Christianity in Lamkang in the early 1920s, these beliefs and practices started slowly vanishing. Today, 100 percent of Lamkang follow Christianity. Agriculture is the largest and primary mode of production. Both Jhum and wetland cultivation is practiced by the people. They cultivate varieties of vegetables and grow a number of fruit trees. Though restriction on food habits is not given much importance by the population in general, yet, women are expected to abstain from certain foods during pregnancy, lactation and other health problem. They also have food taboo for clans, presumptuous of causing serious health problems. Among the age group 15-49 in Chandel district, male and female literacy rate are found to be 95.9 percent and 75.3 percent respectively [NFHS-4 (2015-2016)].

Materials and Methods

A cross sectional study was conducted among Lamkang tribe residing in 10 rural villages of Chandel district, Manipur. At the first stage of sampling, all the villages were arranged according to the size of the population. Then, a sample of 10 villages namely Betuk, Kanpandaam, Paraolon, Lamrinkhuw, Aibuldaam, Deeringkhew, Charangching, Daampi, Mantripantha and Thamlapokpi were selected on the basis of PPS Sampling (Probability Proportional to the size of the population). At the second stage, 200 mothers (reproductive age groups between 15-49 years) who gave birth at least once in the last five years preceding the survey who are permanent residents of the study area were randomly selected from these 10 villages. An interview schedule was framed and tested before applying to the field. Proper consents were taken before starting the interview after making them understand the purpose and benefit of the study. Interviews were conducted in isolation in order to maintain privacy and confidentiality. The interview schedule includes socio-demographic profile and questions pertaining to ANC service utilization. Some of the doubted information were verified and confirmed from their spouse or elders of the family. Data collected were checked for completeness and consistency at the end of each day. Each schedule was entered in Ms-Excel data sheets. Descriptive analysis was used to describe the number of respondents and percentages according to socio-demographic characteristics.

Statistical analysis was performed using SPSS version 17.0. Binary logistic regression was applied between dependent variable and independent variables. ANC utilization was taken as dependent variable. Statistical significance was checked at 5 percent level of probability.

Results

Socio-demographic characteristics are presented in Table 2. The average age of the women was 35 years. Only 1 percent of the respondents were in the age group less than or equal to 19 followed by

27 percent, 34.5 percent and 37.5 percent in the age group 20-29, 30-39 and 40-49 respectively. Forty six (23%) of the Lamkang women were found to be illiterate andone hundred fifty four (77%) were found to be literate but among the literate women, seventy (35%) had received only primary education, sixty five (32.5%) up till tenth grade and only nineteen (9.5%) had received till graduation. Thirty two(17.9%) of the Lamkang husbands were found to be illiterate. Further, twenty seven (15.1%) of the Lamkang husbands had received till graduation. It indicates that overall, males were better educated than females. Majority of the women (53%) were engaged in seasonal workers such as conducting the household activities, handloom weaving, kitchen gardening etc. Fifty nine (32.9%) of the men were engaged in agriculture. Only ten (5%) and forty (22.4%)of the Lamkang women and men respectively were involved in government jobs. Overall, men were placed better in occupation than women. Majority (74%) of the people annual income was less than Rs.10000 in cash, which is independent of the various agricultural produce that they receive in kind. They are dependent on farm products and employment depending on their requirements and needs. Ninety eight (54.7%) of Lamkang women received positive support from their husbands with respect to ANC.

Characteristics of ANC services among Lamkangs mothers of Chandel district is presented in Table 1. It can be seen that 3.5 percent had major illness during pregnancy. Among the women included in the study 72 percent had attended at least one to three ANC services, 11 percent had attended four or more ANC service while 17 percent had none. Among one hundred sixty six mothers who had antenatal visit 89.2 percent received antenatal check-up from Government sectors and only 10 percent received from private sector. It was observed that only 11.5 percent women had taken IFA tablets more than 100 during the last pregnancy. One hundred forty (70%) of the women received two TT doses while 20.5 percent had received none. Out of thirty four women who deny ANC visits, 47.1 percent was due to non-availability of time. Home delivery is the most preferred by the Lamkangs women as it can be seen that 68 percent of the deliveries were conducted at home. Among the women who had home delivery, only 4 percent were conducted with the help of trained personal(doctor or nurse) while 3.5 percent and 60.5 percent were conducted by self and untrained birth attendant, friends or relatives respectively.

Socio-demographic determinants of ANC utilization among Lamkang mothers in Chandel district is presented in Table 2. In the present study, among one hundred sixty six women who had received antenatal care, about 39.2 percent of the mothers who are in the age group of 30-39 years had availed the highest number of ANC services (39.2%) than the other age groups. With regard to women's education, out of thirty four women who had never utilized ANC service, about 52.9% is found among the illiterate mothers and the utilization of ANC services increases with increase in level of educational attainment. Among one hundred and fifty Lamkangs husband who had utilized ANC services, the least (15.3%) is found among illiterate husbands. In both women and husbands, with regard to occupation, seasonal workers have the greater number who had never utilized the ANC services while government employees have the least number. Women who had annual income more than Rs. 10000 are found to be greater in utilizing the ANC service. Women whose husbands had positive attitude towards antenatal care are greater than women whose husbands had negative attitude towards ANC.

Table 1: Patterns of maternal health care utilization among Lamkangs mothers in Chandel district

Characteristics		Number	%
Major illness during pregnancy	Yes	7	3.5
	No	193	96.5
ANC attended	None	34	17.0
	Incomplete	144	72.0
	Complete	22	11.0
Place of antenatal check up (n=166)	Govt. sector	148	89.2
	Private sector	18	10.8
No. of IFA tablets taken	≤99	178	89.0
	≥100	22	11.0
TT doses received	Zero	41	20.5
	One	19	9.5
	Two	140	70.0
Reasons for denial of ANC visits (n=34)	Lack of Knowledge	12	35.3
	Non availability of time	16	47.1
	Not necessary	6	17.6
Place of last delivery	Home	136	68.0
	Govt. Hospital	43	21.5
	Private Hospital	21	10.5
Delivery conducted by	Untrained birth attendant, friends or relatives	121	60.5
	Self	7	3.5
	Doctors/Nurses	72	36.0

Table 2: Socio-demographic determinants of ANC utilization among Lamkangs mothers in Chandel District

Characteristics	Number	%	ANC utilization			
			Yes		No	
			Number	%	Number	%
Age group of women						
≤19 years	2	1.0	2	1.2	0	0.0
20-29 years	54	27.0	53	31.9	1	2.9
30-39 years	69	34.5	65	39.2	4	11.8
40-49 years	75	37.5	46	27.7	29	85.3
Women's Education						
Illiterate	46	23.0	28	16.9	18	52.9
Up till primary	70	35.0	57	34.3	13	38.2
Up till tenth grade	65	32.5	62	37.3	3	8.9
Up till graduation	19	9.5	19	11.5	0	0.0
Husband's Education						
Illiterate	32	17.9	23	15.3	9	31.0
Up till primary	61	34.1	46	30.7	15	51.7
Up till tenth grade	59	32.9	55	36.7	4	13.8
Up till graduation	27	15.1	26	17.3	1	3.5
Women's Occupation						
Government employees	10	5.0	10	6.0	0	0.0
Small business	17	8.5	15	9.0	2	5.9
Agriculturalists	67	33.5	54	32.5	13	38.2
Seasonal workers	106	53.0	87	52.5	19	55.9
Husband's Occupation						
Government employees	40	22.4	36	24.0	4	13.8
Small business	36	20.1	31	20.7	5	17.2
Agriculturalists	59	32.9	51	34.0	8	27.6
Seasonal workers	44	24.6	32	21.3	12	41.4
Annual Income (per person annually)						
Less than Rs.10000	148	74.0	120	72.3	28	82.4
More than Rs. 10000	52	26.0	46	27.7	6	17.6
Positive Husband's attitude						
Yes	98	54.7	89	59.3	9	31.0
No	81	45.3	61	40.7	20	69.0

Yes= more than 1 ANC visits irrespective of the number of TT and IFA tablets; No=no ANC visit

Table 3: Results of binary logistic regression analysis on the determinants of utilization of antenatal care in Lamkangs mothers of Chandel district

Variable	Odd ratios	SE	*p*
Age of women			
30-39 years	25.408	1.044	0.002
40-49 years	8.356	0.578	0.000
Positive husband's attitude	3.242	0.434	0.007
Women's education (literate)	0.300	0.445	0.007

Table 3 presents the results of binary logistic regression analysis for Lamkang women of Chandel district. It has been observed that age of the women, husband's attitude and women's education were found to be important predictors of receiving antenatal care. Although, there were no significant differences in the likelihood of receiving antenatal care among the age groups (category) ≤19 years and 20-29 years, it is an important predictor for women's age groups 30-39 years and 40-49 years as it is seen that 25 times and 8 times respectively was more likely to use antenatal care. Women whose husbands had positive attitude were 3 times more likely to use antenatal care compared to women whose husbands had negative attitude. Literate women were more likely to use antenatal care as compared to illiterate women.

Discussion

Antenatal care provides opportunities in management of pregnancy, detection and treatment of complications and promotion of good health to both women and babies. It also increases the chance of using skilled attendant at the time of birth and will decrease the chance of morbidity and mortality. However, women rarely perceive childbearing as problematic and do not seek help. Moreover, women in developing countries have other reasons for denying antenatal visit. Reasons such as non-availability of time, afford ability and lack of knowledge are also one of them. These affects the utilization of maternal health services in regions of the country where poverty and illiteracy are widespread. World Health Organization (WHO) recommends a minimum of four antenatal visits based on review of the effectiveness of different models of antenatal care. In the present study, only 11 percent of Lamkangs women received full antenatal care. Comparing with earlier reports from Manipur, Mao (2009) reported 13% had received full ANC in Senapati district and National Family Health Survey-4 (2015-2016) reported 16.1 percent had received full ANC in Chandel district, and these figures are consistent with the present study. However, the finding of these studies significantly differs with the result of the study carried out among Rongmeis women of Tameng long district which showed 46.6 percent attendance of complete ANC (Maheo and Devi, 2018).

Among thirty four women of Lamkangs who had never attended ANC visits, non-availability of time (47.1%) was the main reasons for denial of ANC visits, followed by lack of knowledge (35.3%) and feeling unnecessary (17.6%). In developing countries, most of the women spend more time on their multiple responsibilities for care of children, collecting water or fuel, cooking, cleaning and trade than on their own health (Abose *et al.*, 2010). Lamkangs women who are seasonal workers and agriculturalists also conduct handloom weaving, kitchen gardening etc. along with the above mention responsibilities. Hence, availability of time is very important so that priority on their antenatal health could be considered too.

Regarding determinants of ANC service utilization, the present study revealed that maternal age is significantly associated with ANC utilization. Mothers who are in the age groups 30-39 years and 40-49 years were more likely to utilize ANC service than women who are 29 years and younger. This finding is consistent with the study conducted in Southern Ethiopia (Abosse *et al.*, 2010) but it is contrast with the study conducted in Imphal East district of Manipur (Laishram *et al.*, 2013).

Positive husband attitude towards ANC was significantly related to antenatal care service utilization. This result is comparable with the study conducted in Southern Ethiopia (Abosse *et al.*, 2010). We have also found that women's literacy was an important predictor for the antenatal care service utilization. This result agrees with the findings from the studies conducted in Imphal East district of Manipur (Laishram *et al.*, 2013) and Southern Ethiopia (Abose *et al.*, 2010). Literate mothers were more likely to attend ANC than women who are illiterate unable to read and write. Several explanations have been advanced in the literature as to why educated mothers are more likely to use antenatal care services than uneducated mothers. Educated women may have a greater decision making power on health related matters and also attach a higher value to welfare and their health. Further, educated mothers will have more confidence in handling the officials and have the ability and willingness to travel outside the home to seek services (Caldwell, 1979; Caldwell *et al.*, 1983; Cleland and Van Ginneken, 1988).

Binary logistic regression indicates that factors such as maternal age, positive husband's attitude and women's education are the significant predictors of receiving antenatal care services among Lamkang tribe of Manipur.

Acknowledgements

We acknowledge the respondents for providing us the necessary information. We would also like to thank Department of Anthropology, University of Delhi for giving opportunity to conduct this study.

References

Abosse Z, Woldie M, Ololo S. 2010. Factors influencing antenatal care service utilization in hadiya zone. *Ethiopian Journal of Health Sciences*, 20(2).

Caldwell JC. 1979. Education as a factor in mortality decline an examination of Nigerian data. *Population Studies*.33: 395-413.

Caldwell JC, Reddy PH, Caldwell P. 1983. The social component of mortality decline: an investigation in South India employing alternative methodologies. *Population Studies*. 37: 185-205.

Cleland JG, Van Ginneken J K. 1988. Maternal education and child survival in developing countries: the search for pathways of influence. *Social science and medicine*. 27: 1357-1368.

Laishram J, Thounaojam UD, Panmei J, Mukhia S, Devi HS. 2013. Knowledge and practice of ante-natal care in an urban area. *Indian Medical Gazette*. 2013: 101-106.

Maheo LM, Devi AM. 2018. Maternal and child health care: astudy among the Rongmeis of Manipur, India. *International Journal of Humanities and Social Sciences*. 11: 2197-2202.

Mao LP. 2009. Factors associated with antenatal care in Senapati district, Manipur, India, 2008. M.A.E dissertation submitted at National Institute of Epidemiology (ICMR), Ayapakkam, Chennai.

National Family Health Survey-4 (2015-2016). District Fact Sheet Chandel Manipur.

Navaneetham K, Dharmalingam A. 2002.Utilization of maternal health care services in Southern India. *Social Science and Medicine*. 55: 1849-1869.

Ronsmans C, Graham WJ, Lancet Maternal Survival Series steering group. 2006. Maternal mortality: who, when, where, and why. *The Lancet*. 368: 1189-1200.

World Health Organization. 2014. Trends in Maternal Mortality: 1990 to 2013, http://www.who.int/reproductive health/publications/ monitoring/maternal-mortality-2013/en/

Chapter Four

IMPACT OF ECOLOGY ON HEALTH SERVICES DELIVERY: AN EMPIRIC NOTE FROM ODISHA

NILAKANTHA PANIGRAHI AND SEPHALI MOHANTA

ABSTRACT

Odisha is one of the States of India carrying largest tribal populations. The State has housed 62 tribal communities, who constitute around 22.08 percent of the total population living in 44.21 percent of the total State geographical areas. During last seven decades scheduled tribe communities and tribal dominated scheduled areas due to their backwardness have been specially treated and provided with various preferential welfare benefits both by government and non-government agencies. However, many of these communities and their habitations are deprived of getting quality services and became unreached due to various factors resulting in high backwardness among these communities, which is visible in terms of various health parameters like ANC and PNC coverage, institutional delivery, immunization coverage, undernutrition, IMR, MMR, age at marriage etc. This has impacted the qualitative growth of these communities and their inhabited regions. The plethora of literature so far available on health status of the tribal has attempted to study the micro health situations of tribal reflects a very dismal situation. With this premise the paper is based on the part findings of a research project carried out in Malkangiri district one of the most inaccessible tribal dominated districts of India. The paper tries to justify the fact that in spite of the inclusive development approach adopted by different stakeholders, the State is yet to consider health ecology and its impact on health services delivery for the tribal people as productive tool while the scheduled areas are yet to be considered as human endowment for a healthy growth of Odisha.

Keywords: *Scheduled area, health iInstitution, disease and treatment, RNTCP, ethnic healers.*

Introduction

World Health Organisation defines human health as a 'state of complete physical, mental and spiritual well-being and not merely the absence of disease and/or infirmity'. Human life is materially and socially productive and culturally meaningful if one is endowed with physical and mental well being. Humans everywhere transform the natural milieu of their habitat into a cultural milieu in so far as they modify their natural life to cultural one. The biological needs are common to all humans, and these are satisfied through cultural imperatives. Further, in traditional societies people continue to follow ethnic methods and depend on their ethnic healers, since modern medical facilities are yet to be made easily available to them. Non-availability of proper medical facilities in tribal dominated regions provides an opportunity to quacks and medical mafias to operate and thrive on the ignorance and helplessness of the tribal people. Historically it has been observed that the coping processes adopted by human being with their environment are both biological and cultural by nature. Gradually these biological and cultural forces became a kind of resource for human society is it rural and/or urban, tribal and/or non-tribal. The concept of health, disease, illness and sickness are inextricably intertwined with these social, cultural and economic factors, which are the product of and influenced by the well being of family members and on their access to resources. The socio-cultural factors more or less determine beliefs and practices related to health, disease and treatment. The social consequences of disease and illness though universal but are specific to the community in terms of their manifestations. The normative orientation of a community by and large determines the perceptions about the diseases, its symptoms and methods of treatment (Kroeger, 1983). Disease perceptions on the one hand and treatment and healing choices on the other are interdependent. Thus, discourse on the native perceptions and *emic* understanding regarding disease is a necessity in understanding folk therapeutic behaviour.

It is observed that, systematic investigation into folk system of disease classification has gained imperative consideration in Medical

Anthropological studies from the late 1960s. Such studies not only help in better understanding of folk therapeutic behaviour, but also explore ethno-medical care in a systematic manner. Most of the special health related service delivery programs are implemented from time to time for improving the accessibility of the target communities. Many times such programs do suffer due to the lack of adequate infrastructure base and lack of consideration of the socio-cultural factors of the communities which by and large influence the success and/or failure of a program.

The role of State in the health care service delivery system is of recent origin. Over the time due to various factors the State sponsored health care service delivery system is over-burdened and is unable to meet the health needs of the people. Though this has given away scope for the private sector to play effective role but in practice they have by and large confined to certain sections of the population and regions of the country. With the opening of scope of health services to the open market, the nature of treatment, cost factor and requirement of specialized skills has increased. This no doubt is an asset to the health delivery system of the country, but, accessing and ability to pay for such services by a larger section of the population seems to be at stake. In this situation the relevance of 'Human Capital School Approach' (Schultz, 1961) which attempted to measure the economic value of human being and gave the rationalities for 'investment in men', and treated human beings as a 'Productive Tool', which requires cost of repairing and maintenance of human capital is very important. Similarly, the relevance of 'Health Care Service' approach' by Kroeger (Ibid), which emphasizes the combined nature of supply and demand of health service providers needs to be looked into a more pragmatic way; since the inception of the State intervention in health sector, attempts are being made to establish a State controlled and/or ambulatory health service delivery system (Padhi and Mishra, 2002). High infant, child and maternal mortality and morbidity due to communicable diseases (Tuberculosis, malaria and respiratory infections), water borne diseases (cholera, gastro-enteritis, malnutrition, measles) and pregnancy related conditions, forced the state to look after the Primary Health Care (PHC) approach emphasizing both on preventive and promotional health care in a more pragmatic and integrated manner (Green, 1992).

In the early part of the 19th century one finds change of relation between sanitary conditions and health problems,. In the mid 19th century public health got a new face with the introduction of large scale immunization, curative and hospital based services which are popularly known as 'therapeutic phase'. The dominant thought was that good health is predominantly due to the result of medical interventions and hospital services which later on found wrong. The 1st quarter of the 20th century is popularly known as New Public Health Phase again emphasized on the 'preventive' and 'promotive' health initiatives for public health as a part of social sector development. It emphasized the wider scope of public health. The Alma Ata Declaration of 1978 committed the world to achieve 'Health for All by 2000 AD', made public health more integrated and holistic in its approach and coverage. For the first time the National Health Policy of 2001 in India thought of achieving good health in the general population by increasing the access rate into the public health system by way of decentralization, up gradation of infrastructure and thereby strengthening the capacity of the public health. For the first time it talked of equity aspect in terms of inter-regional, rural and urban divide, and economic classes. Certain goals were fixed with respect to different diseases and time. In addition to, emphasis was made to improve village level health care delivery system involving gram sabha, gram panchayats, and providing adequate health infrastructure and service contents of PHC.

It has been felt that the World Bank and World Health Organisation have played a major role in arguing in favour of minimizing public health expenditure. The introduction of 'user fees' for the public services remained as a condition for the free market in the health care sector (Mackintosh, 2003). The World Bank (1990) proposed that the public sector should only provide essential services as 'clinical packages' for the needy, and the government should open up the rest to open market. A market based approach to health not only drives up the cost of health care, but can also lead to lack of interest in the factors that make people ill. Concepts like 'good health' 'good physique' etc. are sold in the market. This sufficiently indicates that those who have access and paying capacity can only have access into these services and enjoy the fruits of development.

Odisha: The State

Odisha is one of the States of India carrying huge tribal population. The State has housed 62 tribal communities, who constitute around 22.08 percent of the total population living in 44.21 percent of the total State geographical area constitutionally declared as the scheduled area, which covers most of the districts except the coastal and few inland. Out of 314 CD blocks of Odisha, 118 (37.3%) blocks are covered under

Tribal Sub-Plan (Govt of Odisha, 2005). During last seven decades scheduled tribe communities and tribal dominated scheduled areas due to their backwardness have been specially treated and provided with various preferential welfare benefits both by government and non-government agencies. During the 11th Five Year Plan period attempts were also made for inclusion of these communities and their habitations for inclusive development. However, many of these communities and their habitations are deprived of getting quality services and became unreached due to various factors resulting in high backwardness among these communities, which is visible in terms of various health parameters like ANC and PNC coverage, institutional delivery, immunization coverage, undernutrition, IMR, MMR, age at marriage. This has impacted the qualitative growth of these communities and their inhabited regions. With this premise the paper is based on the findings of two empiric study carried out in two time periods in Malkangiri district one of the most inaccessible naxal infected tribal dominated districts of India. The paper tries to justify the fact that in spite of the inclusive development adopted by different stakeholders, the State is yet to consider health services for the tribal communities as a productive tool and the scheduled areas are yet to be considered as human endowments for a healthy growth of Odisha.

Objectives

Firstly, the paper with a brief theoretical understanding tries to identify the gaps in and barriers to health services among the tribal communities of Malkangiri district one of the geographically inaccessible, tribal dominated and naxal infected districts of India. It critically reflects the availability of various types and quality of health service institutions at various levels of district, study block and villages. Secondly, the paper tries to reflect the ecological dimensions influencing the perceptions of tribal on disease and curative measures. It also quantifies the status of health condition and health care service in study villages with respect to disease pattern, sources of treatment, status of Traditional Birth Attendant and Traditional Healers. Finally, the paper argues that an integrated community based decentralized health service approach can cover the unreached tribal population who are more or less living in geographically inaccessible regions, which is a part of the Eastern Ghat tracts of India. At the end the paper while concluding gives certain suggestions for improvement of health services delivery and access of the tribal people to appropriate benefits to maintain good health. The paper tries to justify the fact that the State is yet to consider the ecological dimensions as the productive tools and their tribal dominated regions as human endowments to influence the delivery of quality health services in Odisha.

Ecology, Medical Anthropology and Tribal Population

Medical anthropology is an inter-disciplinary field which studies "human health and disease, health care system and bio-cultural adaptation (McElroy, 1996). It is one of the latest and most developed areas of anthropology and applied anthropology (Charlottee, 1990), which emphasizes culture and society being organized around or influenced by the issues of health, health care and related issues. The term medical anthropology is in use since 1963 as a level for empirical research and theoretical production by anthropologists in social processes and cultural representation of health, illness and the nursing care practices (Scotch, 1963). Health care clinic personnel have failed to reach targeted populations due to their ignorance and lack of education on the target people because the native populations are largely guided by traditional belief, value orientations and cultural practices. Ethnography since 20th century has been a tool to seek knowledge in primary health care and rural medicine. Foster and Anderson (1978) viewed the development of medical anthropology is due to the interest of early physical anthropologists, ethnographic interest in primitive medicine, studies on psychiatric phenomenon and anthropological work in international health. Kroger dealt with the primitive medical beliefs and practices. Since 1940s anthropologist have been helping health care providers to understand cultural differences in health behaviors.

Anthropologists consider human population as biological as well as cultural entities. Human culture determines the responses of population towards environment and environmental problems along with the genetic and physiological problems. Adaptation of human beings with the changing environment brings changes and modifications in the larger political economy and socio-cultural system. The concept of adaptation was first applied by Alland (1970) in medical anthropology which for him takes place through genetic changes, physiological responses, cultural knowledge and practices and individual coping mechanisms. Such a concept is based on two premises that health is determined by environmental adaptation and occurrence of diseases is due to the equilibrium in the environment. Since the evolution of disease is determined by biological and socio cultural evolution of human population and of the society, it is understood that the development and epidemiological profile of different economic groups like forager, peasant, animal husbandry and industry varied due to their eco system, food pattern, domestication and pathogens. Therefore, medical ecologists study the food pattern, body growth and development, geographical hazards and injuries, demographic change over time in the isolated populations living in rigorous environment like high altitudes, the arctic and tropical forests (Thomas 1973; Chagan, 1992). Since 1980s research studies have given by biologists and medical anthropologists to seasonality and health in agricultural populations, environmental and cultural regulations of fertility, migration and change in health status, work productivity in under nourished and infected population. The political economy of health basically propounded popularly known as Marxist theory or dependency theory analyses the impact of global economy on local and national health and suggests that any intervention of policy and practices should be in accordance to the understanding of social production of illness and poverty within the larger dynamics of class interactions, colonialism and world economic system.

Methodology

The study was purposefully carried out in Malkangiri district and Kudumuluguma PHC of the district since both the regions are inaccessible and unreached by nature. In the cut off area of Kudumulugumma PHC seven villages in three clusters consisting of neighboring villages were selected in two health sectors of Jodambo and Janbai. The study adopted ethnographic Field Work approach and collected data through in-depth interviews, group interviews, life histories, illness stories and participant observation. The study also collected secondary data from District Medical Office, PHCs, Additional PHC, NGOs and related organisations. Along with the household survey in selected villages it also adopted in-depth interviews with the help of check lists from dhais i.e. Traditional Birth Attendants (TBAs), disharis or traditional healers, members of Panchayati Raj Institutions, Multi-Purpose Health Workers (both male and female) Anganwadi workers of Integrated Child Development Service (ICDS), DOT Providers, T.B. Patients, Medical Officers etc. The interviews were carried out with few selected role players found even beyond the study villages. Two types of separate and comparative analysis have been made on ethnic group and geographical unreachability which represents two different health sectors of Kudumuluguma P.H.C. The paper is based on the findings of two different studies first one carried out by the author in 2003-04 and the second revisit to assess the development in 2012 carried out after a gap of one decade of the first study.

Review of literature

The research findings of few anthropologists in India and more particularly in Odisha on health care practices of the tribal people, their access to outreach health services provided by the State agencies and quality of health services are highlighted. The study of Dalton (1872) and Bodding (1925) reflects the progress of the anthropological studies on relatively isolate populations in hills and forests of India. Majumdar's (1933) study among the Mundas highlighted the importance of 'Pahan' the religious headman in Munda village who worships the village deities on behalf of the entire village and exercises enormous authority in the decision making processes of the village relating to suffering due to diseases and treatment. Sarkar (1958), Ray Choudhury, et al. (1976) have emphasized the importance of understanding the social environment and cultural dimensions of health and diseases of the tribal population. Behura (2003) identified five basic categories of situations on which folk etiology in tribal communities are believed to be responsible for illness. They are (i) sorcery, (ii) breach of taboo, (iii) intrusion of disease object, (iv) intrusion of disease causing spirit, and (v) loss of soul.

From Odishan context couples of research studies are analyzed to understand the concept of health perceived by tribal communities and major constraints faced by different stakeholders while accessing the health services and/or while providing health services in tribal region. Pattnaik et al. (1980) has made an analysis on the health status and associated disease profile of the Bhuiyan tribe, their dietary habits, extent of malnutrition, belief regarding their diseases, traditional method of treatment and attitude towards the modern treatment. He found that the Bhuiyans with respect to their understanding on the concept of disease and treatment are largely guided by their age old cultural beliefs and practices. Sahu (1986) focused his study among the Oraons of Sundargarh district who have access to the modern health facilities available around Rourkela Steel Plant and those who are residing in remote rural areas where the modern health facility is a dream. He reported that Oraon when encounter any serious health disorder seek the services of modern medical practitioners in spite of unfavorable conditions. The change in the attitude and understanding of the Oraons is basically due the impact of Christianity, industrialization and their access to market. Basu's (1994) study shows that the Kutia Konds and Kharias of Odisha have developed strong magico-religious health care systems and they wish to survive and live in their own style. L.K Mahapatra (1994) viewed that the concept of health–as understood and believed by almost all the tribal societies- is a functional one and it is mostly non-clinical in nature. As per the author's view the health–in terms of the beliefs of most of the tribal's- is threatened not only by the evil spirit, including specialized disease resulting spirits, but also by persons emanating evil, mystical powers like evil eye, evil mouth and evil touch or witch craft. Basu (1994) examined the concept of health and pattern of health seeking behavior of the Muria, Madia, Bhattra and Halba tribal groups of Bastar district of Madhya Pradesh, primitive Kutia Kondhs of Phulbani district of Odisha and Dudh Kharias of Sundargarh district of Odisha. The poor health seeking behavior among the tribal populations, in general, can be attributed to their social and living conditions, poor economy, illiteracy, ignorance, superstitions etc. Ghoshmaulik et al. (1995) has examined and analyzed the health situation of the Juangs which is considered as a primitive tribal group of Odisha. He established the fact that this primitive tribe is more dependent on the traditional 'medicine man' rather than that of the government primary health centers.

Behura (2003) has emphasized the concept of human capital in relation to various health aspects with special reference to Odisha. Taking into account the indicators like infant mortality rate, under five mortality rate, institutional delivery and deliveries assisted by a health professional, he viewed that the health scenario of Odisha is not encouraging one. Patra (2007) has made an attempt to analyze the health care delivery system prevalent in Odisha, examined the issues of accessibility of the health services along with the financing aspects which influence the effective utilization of the health services. Dash et al. (2002) has delineated the concept of illness conceived by the "Dongria Kondh" of Raygada district of Odisha. They examined the classification of diseases, the medicinal and magical treatments adopted by Dongaria Kandhas, role of the specialists and etiology of the diseases. Shailabala (2007-08) while undertaking the health accounts of Odisha, sponsored by European Union, provided the health accounts matrix for the State. She has also concluded that health expenditure of Odisha is 4.45 percent of SDP of Odisha. The out pocket expenditure incurred by households was about 3/4th (72.73%), of total expenditure on health. The major share of expenditure of H&FW Department of the Government of Odisha goes to hospital and health administration. She also agreed that around 66 percent of the total health expenditure by households is for purchase of drugs and medicines. A look into various health strategies emphasis have been made from "curative to preventive" approach, from "urban to rural" from "privileged to under privileged" and from "vertical mass campaigns to a system of integrated health services" forming a component of overall social and economic development (Newill, 1975). Still the health policies so far adopted are yet to bring satisfactory results (Padhi and Mishra, 2002; Panigrahi, 2004, Acharya, 2011). However, most of these health policies have been lacking to consider certain human factors like values, attitudes, motivation and commitment by the health service providers.

Thus, the above literature reviews show that Tribal communities are by and large guided by their socio-cultural institutions which shape and reshape their understanding, adoption, and/or rejection pertaining to disease and treatment. Secondly, the health services delivered by the state agencies through health institutions in tribal region are inadequate, perform poor quality services, and unable to overcome the socio-psychological attitude of the tribal people. Thirdly, the State led health institutions and health functionaries are yet to respect to and/or recognise of the cultural practices of the tribal communities. Fourthly, the availability and accessibility to the health service provisions/facilities provided in tribal dominated region is neglected, but are equally important in the acceptance of modern health care facilities.

Profile of Malkangiri District: The Study Universe

Malkangiri predominantly a tribal district is situated in south Odisha. Consequent upon the bifurcation of Koraput district (undivided) into four districts, Malkangiri came into existence with effect from October 2, 1992. The total geographical area of the district is divided into three Tahasils and seven Community Development Blocks. The district has 878 inhabited villages distributed over 108 numbers of Gram Panchayats. The rural population of the district accounts to the tune of 93.79 percent. The sex ratio of the district is 996 per 1000 males, is above the state average of 972. The density of population per sq. km. is the second lowest (83), reflects that the population is very thinly distributed compared to other districts of the state. The geographical inaccessibility along with the thin distribution of population in the district many times creates physically unreached pockets and population (Census of India 2011). The predominant tribal communities of the district are the *Bondos, Koyas, Bhumias, Parojas, Kondhs, Gadabas, Didayis, Natias, Dharuas, and the Halvas* who maintain their distinct socio-cultural boundaries, which are reflected in dialects, dresses, customs, taboos, food pattern etc. The subsistence economy of the tribal people is largely contributed by forest, livestock and shifting cultivation. Many of these groups are in transitions, who have adopted other languages like Oriya and Telugu, their dress and ornaments. Tribal people ordinarily ascribe diseases to evil influence of different deities or to witchcraft. They propitiate the deities and take the services of imposter-doctors (known differently among tribes as *disari, bejius, gurumai, siras*) who pretend to counter the effects of black art. The district cannot be strictly called as healthy, for the fact that malaria is endemic almost everywhere. The major diseases observed in the district include Malaria, Gastro-intestinal like diarrhea, dysentery, pneumonia, yaws and respiratory diseases.

Kudumuluguma: The Study Block

Kudumulugumma is one of the seven C.D. Blocks of Malkangiri district. The geographical area of the block is almost equally divided by the reservoir of the Balimela dam project. Korkunda and Khairaput blocks of Malkangiri district and Andhra Pradesh (A.P.) the neighboring state surround the block. Kudumulugumma block is divided into 11 G.Ps. It is the third geographically largest block of the district which covers 569.56 sq. kms accommodates highest number of (252) inhabited villages and 9162 residential houses. The block is situated 52 kms away from district head quarter (Census of India 2011). The major tribal communities living in Kudumuluguma block are *Kondh, Paroja, Bonda, Didayi and Konda Dora,* who share a large portion of the total population. The establishment of residential colonies of Water Resource Development Department at Chitrakonda and Balimela has invited immigrants in subsequent periods, have substantially influenced the numerical strength of the tribals in the block. Balimela water reservoir physically separates the southern side of the block that covers six Gram Panchayats. Three Gram Panchayats named Jodambo, Panasput and Andarapalli are communicated only through reservoir by government launch based transport services, available from Chitrakonda and it takes 4 to 8 hours to reach different major places of cut-off area. The entire reservoir catchments area is full of different hills, which very often creates physical barriers for the movement of the motor launch. This has not only affected the communication networks within and to outside, but also creates physical communication problems for government departments to deliver their basic services in different gram panchayats of the block.

Physiography of the Study Villages

The study covered seven revenue villages distributed in two different health sectors of Kudumulugumma P.H.C. The two villages viz: Tarabeda and Janturai i.e the first cluster was selected under Jodambo Additional PHC. From Chitrakonda one has to take government launch service to cover around 40 Kms. (4 hours journey) to reach Palaspadar and from Palaspadar one has to cover a distance of 8 kms by walk which takes almost 4 hours to reach the villages. The hills stretched around both the villages influence the ecology, economy, inflow and outflow of various livelihood and development inputs. Kudumulugumma the block head quarter is situated at a distance of around 100 kms which is covered by 4 hours journey by walk, four hours journey by motor launch (the only mode of transport), and again one and half hour journey by road transport. The availability of launch service provided by Dam Project of the Water Resource Development Department is not regular due to frequent technical and non-technical problems. The second cluster of two villages selected under Janbai Subsidiary Health Center (SHC) is Khajurigumma and Karlamal. These villages are covered under Badapada gram-panchayat. Both the villages are situated at a distance of 2.5 kms and 4 kms from the Subsidiary Health Center at Janbai respectively which takes almost one hour to one and half hour by walk. Both the villages are equally covered with different hill systems. Recently in the year 2017 a flyover bridge links the island with the mainland. Kudumulugumma the block headquarters is located at a distance of 70 to 75 kms from both the villages (which takes 7 to 8 hours by walk, boat journey and public transport). The third cluster consists of three villages i.e. Lambasing, Banguru and Banguru Resettlement Colony-17. All these villages are linked by kutcha roads, which join the main road at a distance of 1 to 2 kms. The villages are covered under Janbai Subsidiary Health Center and are located at a distance of 12 kms physically separated by the water reservoir. In practice these villages are closer to Balimela Dam Project Hospital (BDPH) situated at Chitrakonda at a distance of 6 kms. The Banguru Resettlement Colony-17 was started by the Revenue Department during the year 1962-63. Different hills, forests and streams also surround the villages of this cluster which physically separates during the rain.

Ethnic Composition of Study Villages

The study in total covered 292 (90.11%) tribal households belonging to different ST groups. The villages are largely mono-ethnic by nature dominated by the tribal households. The Kondhs (32.64%) and *Parajas* (43.71%) dominates in all the cut off villages of both the health sectors, whereas, in third cluster the villages are multi-ethnic by nature. The Banguru resettlement colony-17 has more number of non-tribals. In Janbai health sector the share of tribals in village social composition tunes to 86.86 per cent, (205 HHs), In Jodambo health sector the percentage of tribal households in villages is 97.95 (87HH), whereas in Janbai health sector it include 99 Paraja HHs (41.94%), 69 *Kondh* (20.23%) HHs and 37 *Konda Dora* (15.67%) HHs. Jodambo health sector covers 47 *Paroja* (43.71%), and 40 *Kondha* (32.64%) households.

Impact of Mega-Power Projects in the Study Population and Area

Malkangiri district has witnessed two numbers of hydro power projects. In 1949 the establishment of the Machhkund hydroelectric project displaced 2938 different tribal households belonging to *Paroja, Gadaba and Kondh* communities who later on migrated to the lower part of the river and got settled in the hill terrains in their own arrangements. Most of the displaced suffered a lot due to the loss of their livelihood sources, kith and kin resources. Balimela Hydro power project the second joint enterprise of Government of Odisha and Andhra Pradesh on Sileru river established on 4.9.1062 has displaced around 2000 tribal families who later on also rehabilitated themselves largely on their own arrangements (Reddy,1992).

The impacts of these development projects are seen in the socio-economic life of the villagers in general and tribal people in particular. These projects have affected the bio-social and livelihood resources of the displaced. The leafy vegetables, fruits and roots, forest games, which were supporting the livelihood sustenance of the tribals, have been devastated. Collection of fuel, fodder and ethno medicines is also affected. The village ceremonies and the festivities were the arena to minimize the tensions. The holistic characters of the village were reflected in their customs and traditions through community based rituals and group sharing of liquor, communal dance, village fare, and festivals. Due to displacement members of lineage/clan dispersed in search of employment and livelihood. The resources available at destination could not accommodate them as per their cultural needs and exposed them to an alien culture. The double displacement of the *Kondh* and *Paroja* tribal people (once due to Machhkund hydro power project and again due to Balimela hydro power project) resulted in large scale eviction, loss of their lands, destruction of their places of worship and burial grounds, weakened their solidarity and made them vulnerable to the blandishment of the government (Stanley,1996).

Many of the newly created colonies are yet to became villages even after six decades and are lacking roads, electricity, regular school, anganwadi center, and required infrastructure facilities to supply basic life support systems on regular basis (Panigrahi,Ibid).

Health Infrastructure in Study Region

Kudumulugumma is one of the PHCs of the district, which covers 320 villages. The PHC has a Medical Officer and one pre-P.G Doctor. The PHC under its jurisdiction has one Additional PHC at Jodambo, one Subsidiary Health Center (SHC) at Janbai and three Mobile Health Units functioning under its operational area to deliver the health services in inaccessible villages. It covered a total population of 50,960 (2004). The average population covered under one health sub-center is 3640, which is above the norm adopted by the state (3000 population per one Health Sub-Centre) for tribal areas. Out of 14 Health Sub Centers of this PHC, 9 (64.28%) sub-centers had population strength beyond the population norm fixed by the state. The average number of villages and habitations covered per health sub-center consists of 22.85, are much higher to cover in hilly terrains. These villages are situated at a mean radial distance of 21.67 kms. It is impossible for a Female Health Worker to cover such a distance by foot inhilly terrines. In addition to the population criteria, the physical distance, number of villages/habitations covered, sex composition, road communication facilities, disease pattern etc of a region are the influencing factors for the delivery of outreach services. The natural barriers in the form of hills, forests and water reservoirs make the area inaccessible for easy movement. The low level of educational achievements and poor transport system within the region restricts the movement of the villagers (Tribal people). Even in case of serious ill health many times the villagers do not come to hospital. With the reformulation of new Gram Panchayats, new health sub-centers have not been established to match the changing demographic needs of the people. In case of Kudumulugumma PHC, the short fall of staff observed in the position of Multipurpose Health Workers for male was 54.54 percent (6 out of 11 were in place), and for female it was 21.42 percent (3 out of 14 were in place). Similarly, all the three posts sanctioned for Multipurpose Health Supervisor were found vacant; while among Female Health Supervisors 50 per cent (one out of two) of posts were found vacant. The shortfall in staff strength has highly influenced the delivery of health services, monitoring and supervision of health activities. In 2012 during the revisit by the authors to the study area found very little changes in the health infrastructures available in the region.

Additional P.H.C. Jodambo

The Additional PHC at Jodambo was established in the year 1970s and has the provision of one Doctor, one Pharmacist, one lady Multi-Purpose Health Worker, and one Medical Attendant to provide out-door health services. The operational area of this Public Health Institution (PHI) is divided into two Health Sub-Centers and is divided by big water reservoir of Balimela Dam Project and is linked by a Government motor launch, which covers 40 kms from Chitrakonda to Palaspodar a village of Jodambo Gram Panchayat and again to cover a walk of 8 kms through hill slopes so as to reach the PHI at Jodambo. The entire cut off area is not connected by power supply. Two female health workers working in the area were belonging to ST communities. Almost all the multipurpose health workers more or less stay at Kudumulugumma P.H.C headquarters, which is around 80 kms from the PHI. On an average they visit their operational area for 10 to 15 days per month. None of the health sub-center has sub-center building for accommodation. The PHI had no Doctor, whereas most of the time the Pharmacist was out of the headquarters. This was also observed by the research team and complained by the villagers during the stay at Jodambo. The local villagers told that the medical attendant many times manages the hospital and treat patients. One health sub-center on an average covers around 28 to 42 villages/ clusters/habitations, which are spread over an area of 18 to 22 kms. The population covered under this health sub-center ranges from 2770 to 3160. The Jodambo PHI area has a total number of 14 ICDS centers and 7 sub-centers of which only 11 centers have ICDS workers and 7 sub-centers have organisers.

Subsidiary Health Center (SHC), Janbai

The Subsidiary Health Center (SHC) at Janbai was started in the year 1974. Balimela Dam Project Reservoir separates the whole operational area of this health sector. It has been provisioned with one Doctor, one Pharmacist, one Female Multi-Purpose Health Worker, and one Medical Attendant. It provides only out-door health services to the local. The total operational area of the SHC at Janbai is divided into four Sub-Centers. The Male Multipurpose Health Workers posted in all the sub-centers were reported vacant. Of the total four Female Multipurpose Health Workers, there were only two working in the area of which one was a local tribal woman. Shortfall of staffs in all the technical and para-medico categories have reduced the delivery of health services. None of the sub-centers have own building for accommodation. The number of villages distributed over the sub-center ranges from 20 to 25 km, which are spread over a radius of 20 to 27 km. There were 550 to 780 households which covered 2300 to 3990 population covered under each sub center. The area had 11 ICDS centers and 9 ICDS sub-centers. During the interaction it was inferred that the Multipurpose Health Workers on an average stay for 10 to 15 days in their operational area and the rest of the period of the month they stay at Kudumulugumma. The SHC had one doctor, one Pharmacist who was also irregular in attending the hospital. The establishment of the new bridge linking to Janbai has brought some changes in the PHI at Janbai. Hardly any change is observed in the ICDS infrastructure and health services available as discussed with the PRI members of Jodambo and Janbai area.

Functioning of Mobile Health Units (MHU)

Mobile Health Unit is an approach started by Government of India to provide primary health services in the unreached pockets due to inaccessible operational area. The study has reviewed the progress of activities of the Mobile Health Units (MHUs) operating under Kudumulugumma PHC and Balimela Dam Project (BDP) hospital. The operational areas of these MHUs covered 4 GPs from Korkonda block, 2 GPs from Kalimela block and 12 GPs from Kudumulugumma block, consisting of 342 villages. It was observed from the records that treatment of female cases was less compared to male and children patient by all the MHUs. The average number of patients treated by a MHU per day was 36 to 68 persons. It was commonly complained that the supply of medicines to MHUs was not regular and many time short expiry medicines were also supplied. For example chloroquine, a basic medicine required in the area was not supplied on regular interval and as per the requirement. The villagers many times demand more injectables and syrups. Close coordination among health workers, MHU team and ICDS workers for the treatment of ANC and PNC. MHUs during their regular visit to the villages were rarely identifying special cases for treatment for TB and other diseases. It was observed that during the visit of MHUs to the villages during daytime, the villagers were found absent due to their engagement in agriculture and other activities (Observed by the researchers while accompanying MHUs in the field). Such situations many times do not justify the coverage of average treatment cases per day by MHUs.

Perception of Tribal People and Belief System on health

The *Kondhs* and the *Parojas* are the numerically dominant community in the study villages. They consider that the treatment of patients is specific to age, sex and nature of the ailment. Common diseases reported in the village were fever, respiratory tracts infection, skin diseases, dysentery, body injury, conjunctivitis, cataract, anemia, worm infection, etc. Belief system of these tribal communities is an organized body of ideas; attitudes and convictions centered on values and are considered as organic part of life processes. They believe that it is a community product of group experiences and are so deep rooted that many times the society does not question their validity and handed over to young generations by way of socialisation. The *Kondh* explains disease related beliefs as good and bad, right and wrong, links to natural and supernatural powers, which are both religious and magical by nature. All these beliefs guide their attitude and behavior. For example: they strongly believe that diseases like leprosy and TB are due to the curse of human being. The worldview of the *Kondhs and* the *Parojas* consists of nature and natural objectives, determines their life way processes and influences their behaviour pattern about life and death, health and sickness. They say: why some germs attack few people and not others? This provides them with an internal logic and acceptable explanations to believe on witchcrafts, evil spirits, evil eyes, anti social action and taboos related to living.

The folk world of these communities can also be classified on the basis of secular and non-secular belief pattern. The secular beliefs include physical and natural factors like effects of different seasons like hot, cold, rain, sunray, food pattern, addiction etc. while the non-secular beliefs can be classified as *karm (one's deeds),* sins, wreath of evil eyes, demons, evil spirits, religious events, etc. They consider health as a state of physical and mental fitness in which person can able to perform his/her natural responsibilities. The state of fitness of human health is interpreted as free of diseases. Both *Kondhs* and the Parojas pointed out various physical, dietary, natural factors as causes of disease. This may be multi-causal or mono-causal explanations. However, they believe that specific disease occurs due to specific reasons. However, the villagers spontaneously linked illness to traditional and supernatural factors. The socialization processes of the younger generations through oral transmission bears greater impact to believe on these factors. It is also important to know how the tribal belief becomes responsible for the spread of diseases. They believe that the disease needs a medium to spread from one place to another. They consider these mediums are natural like water, air and mosquito, as well as manmade like pollution of natural sources, animal contact, evil spirits, etc. Diseases, like TB, asthma and other organic deformities are hereditary in nature. Diseases like cholera, diarrhea, cough and cold, are transmitted through contamination of air and water. More or less the religious beliefs of *Kondh* and the Parojas influence their understanding and behavior pattern towards health and diseases. Very few of them are partly closer to the modern understanding that diseases are caused due to both natural and manmade factors. Thus, both the Kondhs and the Parojas have a holistic and integrated understanding on their life processes as a whole.

Physical Environment

In submerged villages shifting cultivation with forest economies were the major sources of livelihood for the Kondhs and the Parojas. The new settlements gave scope for generating new coping mechanisms and adoption processes to these changing environment. Perennial streams and tube-wells are the sources of water used for washing, cooking, drinking and other purposes. The small single room are used to prepare food, store grains, sleeping and keeping deities. Defecations by adult tribals are common in open field where as the children do it inside the village. This has enough contribution in contaminating water sources and resulting water borne diseases like dysentery, diarrhea and skin diseases. The animal sheds of both the tribes attached *to the* house breeds' mosquitoes, flies, and insects and makes poor sanitary situations which became very difficult for an outsider to get into the village. Animal dung, free movement of pigs and poultry largely pollutes while urine of animals and human being swamps. Creation of worms and other intestinal parasites of livestock many times attack their poor immune system of the children and the old. Distribution of houses in a compact space results ill ventilation and inadequate light inside the room. Spitting and urination by the children in front of their house pollutes the environmental sanitation of the village. A rapid visit in the study villages by the researchers after 10 years of the first study found little differences in the village physical environment when compared with the previous scenario.

Personal Hygiene

The tribal children below the age of seven years rarely clean the teeth as the adult members do. All the children and adult members use to take hot water bath during winter and rainy seasons. Because of their poor economic conditions the *Kondhs* normally have two pieces of clothes for each member of the family. The washing of all clothes (apart from the daily bath) is made during the occasion of pollution and purity due to birth and death ceremony. They use white powder of kitchen to clean their clothes and a few have started using soap. Smoking of locally made raw *pika* or cigarettes (*Dhungia*) are popular among both males and old females. Even a boy or girl of nine years old was also observed smoking. The tribal people consume various types of liquor made up of *raggi*, and *rice*, known as *pendum, landa*, and palm juice. Both men and women from their early age of nine to 10 start drinking liquor. The personal hygiene of these tribal groups is very much influenced by their traditional customs and practices. Above all the hygienic aspects of both the tribal communities are largely influenced by socio-cultural factors. The low level of education, poor awareness and lack of outward mobility makes their practices more traditional. Impact of market is seen in the possession of household articles which have influenced to some extent in adopting tooth brush, cleaning and bathing soaps, and detergent powder by few families who normally have better economic status in the society. Similarly, having more number of pairs of quality clothes were observed in few households shows the paying capacity and the attitude to purchase and invest more in this sector.

Health condition and health care services in study villages

Seasonal illness episodes of the *Kondhs* and *Parojas* were documented on the basis of their memory recall for a period of one year prior to the date of 1st survey. There were in all 809-illness episodes reported during the year. The common ailments reported were malaria, fever, body pain, headache, cough, joint pain, skin diseases and diarrhoea. Of the total diseases reported among the tribal people during the study, fever accounts for 57.62 percent of which malaria constitutes 61.81 percent, whereas, diarrhea (10,04%), skin (5.08%), APD (4.81%) have also been reported. The disease pattern among the *Kondhs* and *Parojas* shows that the females have been affected from 430 episodes (53.15%) than males who suffered from 379 episodes (46.84%). The major diseases affecting females' were 173 episodes of malaria (60.95%), 91 episodes of fever (52.36%), 22 episodes of joint pain (73.33%), whereas, males suffered from 51 episodes of body pain (51.11%), 21 episodes of cough (60.00%), 19 episodes of APD/Gastric (51.35%), and 22 episodes of skin diseases (52.38%).

The length of illness among the *Kondhs* and *Parojas* has been calculated till their first contact for treatment with any public health institution. In case of malaria and fever the average length of illness was relatively greater. Of the total reported cases, around 38.13 per cent of malaria patients (82) have suffered for 6 to 10 days, while 37.20 per cent (80) have suffered more than 10 days. Likewise, in case of normal fever, 31.88 percent (8) have suffered for more than 6 days, while 38.18 percent (97) have suffered for more than 10 days. In aggregate 28.92 percent (234) have suffered for 6 to 10 days, while 50.34 percent (408) have suffered for more than 10 days till they make use of health services from PHIs.

As regards the sources of treatment in total, 5.80 percent illness episodes (47) have not sought any treatment, while 431 (53.27%) treatment episodes have attended government hospital and 217 (26.82%) treatment episodes have attended private source. Around 114 (14.09%) episodes have attended both private and public health institutions for their treatment on priority basis. This clearly indicates the transition of the tribal society, which was once depending on ethno-medicines, who have started adopting allopathic treatments. There are few serious ailments, which could not be treated by private sources. This led them to depend on public PHIs after a long suferring. The villagers know that PHIs are the source to give specialised health services since it has trained health personnel. They viewed that the regular absence of government health personnel in their operational areas affects the villagers to get health services from PHIs. Seven quacks are operating from Janbai who moves from village to village with regular intervals and provide allopathic treatments. The quacks maintain a good rapport with the villagers. They prefer to give injectables to raise more income. Few Bengali quacks have been operating at Janbai to provide health services even for last 35 years. In Jodambo health sector, around 12.01 per cent have adopted private sources for treatment. The villagers feel quacks are more reliable and accessible at doorstep. In the second visit the team could talk with three quacks in the villages who were contacted in the first research study. The quacks expressed that they are satisfied in giving medicines to the people at their door steps where government health institutions have failed.

Traditional Birth Attendant (thus known as TBA or *Dhai*) in *Kondh* villages is popularly known as *'Dhokaris' who* play a very important role during pregnancy and childbirth. Due to the lack of facilities provided by PHIs for institutional deliveries in rural areas, TBAs have been playing an effective role. Due to their functional importance, government and non-government agencies have been providing training to TBAs *(Dhai)*. In-depth interviews were carried out with 14 TBAs distributed over all the health sectors. Of them, 9

(64.28%) were STs in which four TBAs in each are belonging to *Paroja* and *Kondha* tribe, 3 (21.42%) were SCs and the rest 2 (14.28%) were belonging to other caste groups. The age classification of these TBAs indicates that around 57.14 percent belonging to the age group of 41 to 60 years, while 35.71 percent were above 60 years of age. About 92.85 percent were reported as illiterate. All the *Kondh* and *Paroja* TBAs were active, while the *Kondh* TBAs were going beyond their village boundaries. The *Paroja* TBAs because of their old age were unable to go beyond the village boundaries to render their services. None of them have ever received any type of training from the government. While two of the *Kondh* TBAs have trained their young generations to act as TBA, the *Paroja TBAs* have complained about the non-participation of the younger generations for this purpose. The *Kondha* TBAs during last year on an average has attended 9 delivery cases, while a *Paroja* TBA has attended 5 number of delivery cases. The TBAs were normally paid in the form of kind, which is not a major source of income for them. They consider their skill as a service to their own people. Two number of TBAs were interviewed in second visit to the study area who replied that there is very little improvement in health services delivery. They are providing health services what they were doing 20 years back.

In cut-off area facilities for institutional delivery were not available. The Female Multi Purpose Health Workers were irregular and often not regularly found in their operational areas. The TBAs being local attend the deliveries. It was also observed that for better health service delivery the operational linkages have not been established between the female Multi Purpose Health Workers and TBAs in their day-to-day operations. As a result, the Health Workers were unable to make use of the TBAs while implementing their pre-and-post-natal immunization programmes. Due to this many health programmes have not reached the interior pockets of the area. The logic of the Health Workers for not involving the TBAs was that most of the TBAs were old enough to carry out the responsibilities in a demand driven and decentralized manner. The natural growth of new TBAs under the guidance of old TBAs was inadequate. The Health Workers feel that some of the TBAs still have operational viability, which can be made use for greater interest.

Traditional tribal healers or magico-religious specialists play a very important role in health related issues. They are popularly known as *Disari* who is also a specialist in ethnic medicine. They perform their role as a religious leader who forecasts the auspicious days and period to do festive occasions and also performs certain rituals. All *Disaris* do not play the role of traditional healer. The *Disaris* adopt the process of divination to invoke deities and spirits by chanting spells so as to ascertain the cause of affiliation. In almost all cases they prescribe certain food taboos and instruct to arrange for the prophylactic rite. Patients suffering from diseases caused due to physical and environmental factors have been treated directly with ethno-medicines. The study made in-depth interviews with 10 numbers of *Disaris* or traditional healers. The socio economic background of these *Disaris* reflects that around 90.00 percent of them belong to ST groups and were within the age group of 41 to 50 years. Around 40.00 percent of them were illiterate, while another 40.00 percent of them were just literate. Around 80.00 percent i.e. eight number of total TBAs provides health services within 5 to 10 number of villages, in a distance of 6 to 10 kms. Four healers (40.00%) have treated 11 to 15 patients each, while five (50.00 %) of them have treated more than 15 cases during last year. The study indicates that the ethno-practitioners are still playing important roles in the disease treatment regime of tribal societies. The transfer of skill on hereditary basis justifies the contribution of these agents to maintain good health in the village. They enjoy a substantial influence in and around the villages, which goes beyond ethnic boundaries. These traditional practitioners as a community of health service providers can be given training from time to time so as to infuse certain basic scientific knowledge pertaining to health and hygiene.

Conclusion

- Availability of health infrastructure in Malkangiri district is inadequate both in quantity and quality of inputs.
- Tribal health, disease, health care system and bio-cultural adaptation are to be seen as inter related and integrated one. The tribal people still recognise and are guided by both natural and super natural factors as the causes of diseases. They are more influenced by their belief patterns. The common diseases, which affect tribal people, were reported as malaria and fever followed by skin diseases and diarrhea are largely influenced by ecological factors. Therefore, in almost all cases the tribal people believe the religious heads, disharies, quacks, for initial treatments.
- The extension workers engaged in delivery of health services in Malkangiri district do not have a holistic understanding

of diseases suffered by the tribal people and their ecological resources which influence their life and living. As a result, tribal communities normally do not accept the prescriptions made by the Health Workers.

- It was observed that the operational linkages in whatever form were observed functioning between the female Multi Purpose Health Workers and local functional institutions like TBAs do not contribute much for better functioning of local health institutions and in improving outreach health service delivery system. Quacks are the first person to provide health services to the villagers even in remotest corners. Even they identify special TB cases and link them for sputum tests directly.
- In case of few serious ailments, which cannot be treated by private sources, the tribal patients are depending on Public Health Institutions (PHIs), but their poor economic conditions do not allow them to avail specialized treatments from outside. Absence of doctors at PHC and SHC very frequently even for long years restricts the delivery of treatments provided from PHIs.
- Out reach services provided by MHUs have reached many unreached villages during their short duration of visits to a village are unable to cover the chronic cases like TB and in providing follow ups to TB patients. There are consistent gaps in converg the health services with such special cases identified by the MHUs.

Major Suggestions

- The infrastructure development in the interior regions of tribal dominated Malkangiri district may be emphasized more in order to develop the access of the tribal people to health service institutions which will develop their quality of life.
- The plurality of medicines are found in tribal societies may be promoted by the State in tribal region.

References

Acharya S. 2011. State of health and health service delivery system in scheduled districts of Odisha. Journal of the Indian Anthropological Society. 47.

Alland AJR. 1970. *Adaptation in cultural evolution: an approach to medical anthropology.* New York: Columbia University Press.

Basu S. 1994. *Tribal Health.* National Institute of Health & Family Welfare, Manak Publication, New Delhi.

Behura NK. 2003. *Health Status, Health Care Facilities and Ethno Medicine in Odisha.* In Tribal Women and Reproductive Health (eds) by R.N Pati. APH Publishing Corporation, New Delhi.

Bodding PO. 1925. The Santhals and disease studies in Santhal medicine and connected folklore. *Memories of Asiatic Society of Bengal.* X:3.

Census of India. 2011. Available at http.\\www.censusindia.net\\00-06.html.

Charlotte SS. 1990. Macmillan dictionary of Anthropology. London: Macmillan Press,pp.187-188.

Chagnon NAY. 1992. The Fierce people. College Ed. Harcourt Brace Jovanovich College of Disease. *Archaeology and Ethnology.* 32:185-252.

Dalton ET 1872. *Descriptive ethnology of Bengal.* Government of Bengal.

Dash J, Pradhan SC. 2002. *The concept and treatment of disease among the Dongria Kondhs of Odisha*, in RN Pati, J Dash (eds). Tribal & Indigenous People of India Problems & Prospects, APH Publishing Corporation, New Delhi.

Debi S. 2007-08. *Health accounts of Odisha, sponsored by European Union (Unpublished)*, Report submitted to ICSSR Institute Dharwad.

Francine S, Serge G. 2005. *Anthropologies medicale, ancrages locaux, defies globaux (Medical anthropology, Local roots, global challenges)*, Quebec: Les presses de Universite Laval, Ma.

Green A. 1992. *An introduction to health planning in developing countries.* Oxford University Press, New York.

Government of Odisha. 2008. *District statistical handbook.* Malkangiri, Directorate of Economics and Statistics, Government of Odisha.

Health and Family Welfare Department. 2002. *Odisha state integrated health policy.*

Kroeger A. 1983. Anthropological and socio-medical health care research in developing countries. *Social Science Medicine.* 17.

Malden M. 2007. *Medical anthropology: regional perspectives and shares concerns.* Blackwell.

Odisha Vision. 2003. *2010-A Health Strategy*. Government of Odisha, 2003.

Statistical Abstract of Odisha. 2005. *Directorate of economics and statistics.* Bhubaneswar.

Mahapatra LK 1994. *Concept of health among the tribal population of India and its socio-cultural correlations*, in S.Basu (eds). Tribal Health in India,

Manak Publications, New Delhi

Majumdar DN. 1933. Disease, death and divination in certain primitive societies in India. *Man in India*. 13:115-159.

Mackintosh M. 2003. *Health care commercialization and the embedding of inequality, RUIG/Unrised Health Project Synthesis paper*.

McElroy A. 1996. *Medical Anthropology*, in DLevinson and MEmber, Encyclopedia of Cultural Anthropology. http://www.univie.ac.at/ethnomedicine/PDF/Medical%20Anthropologie.pdf.

Mohapatra RK and Ghosh Mallick SK.1995. Health situation of the Juang of Odisha.*South Asian Anthropologist*. 16:1.

Newill VA. 1975. The strength and weknesses of population studies in assessing the environmental health. *Journal of Health*. 26:133-146.

Padhi S and Mishra S. 2002. *Premature mortality health status and public health care facilities in Odisha: A study in accessibility and utilization*. Report of NKC Centre for Development Studies, Bhubaneswar.

Panigrahi N. 2004. *Reaching the unreached: access to health services for tribal communities of Malkangiri district*. Report submitted to DANTB, Odisha.

Patra NR. 2007. *Health Economics in India*. New Century Publications, New Delhi, India.

Pattnaik N, Rout SP, Ali A, Debi KB.1980. *Health and Nutrition: Hand Book on Pauri Bhuiny, An anthropological study of the Primitive Section of the Bhuiyan Tribe of Odisha, Adibasi Special*.XIX.

Ray Choudhuri J, Bhowmick A, Das P. 1976. Economics correlated of tribal fertility in Eastern India. *Bulletin of Cultural Research Institute*. 12.

Reddy IUB. 1992. *Displacement and Rehabilitation*. Delhi: Mittal Publications.

Sahu SK. 1986. Health culture of the Oraons in the context of different health institution. *Ethno Medicine*. VI.

Schultz TW. 1961. Investment in human capital.*American Economic Review*. 51:2.

Scotch NA. 1963. *Medical Anthropology*, in Bernard J.Siegel, Biennial Review of Anthropology,Stanford,California: Stanford University Press, pp.30-68.

Stanley W. 1996. Machkund, Upper Kolab and NALCO Projects in Koraput Districts, Orissa. *EPW*. 31: 1533-1538.

Thomas RB. 1973. *Human adaptation to a high andean energy flow system*. Occassional pares in Anthropology 7. University Park,Pennsylvania State University.

World Bank. 1990. *Orissa Health System Development Report*, Project

Appraisal Doccument Report No.17653-IN, India.

(The paper is based on the findings of the research project "Reaching the Unreached: Access to Health Services for the Tribal Communities of Malkangiri District, Orissa", carried out by Dr N Panigrahi the author which was sponsored by DANIDA Assisted Revised National Tuberculosis Control Programme, Bhubaneswar, 2004-05 and again restudied during 2012).

SECTION II

Chapter Five

HEALTH, ILLNESS AND SPIRITUAL HEALING: THE LEPCHA EXPERIENCE

SUMITABHA CHAKRABORTY

ABSTRACT

Life of an individual is concerned with 'health'. The idea of ill-health disturbs the rhythm of life and performance capabilities of the individual being. All human groups, no matter how small or technologically primitive, have always been devising ways and means for taking care of the health because health is a property and illness is a state. Health and illness have close linkages with the therapeutic and preventive practices, which have shown variations throughout the ages. The health-sickness process is a tangible veracity for all people all over the world. Spiritual healing is an integrative approach of the healers across the world might work on different premise and follow diverse practices however the main goal is to cure sickness and maintain good health. The Lepchas, an indigenous community of Darjeeling and Sikkim Himalayas and being an inhabitant to nature with their tangible knowledge utilizes the natural biotic resources in one hand and prefer to undertake therapy by means of belief system to identify illness causation and its cure. To them, knowledge is warranted by direct experience based upon cognitive spheres. It is entirely concerned with a range of intellectual products what they always try to maintain from generation to generation. The present article is an outcome of empirical research work conducted in various Lepcha villages in Darjeeling district and west and north districts of Sikkim in various phases from 2007-2010.

In this article an attempt has been made to highlight how effectively the Lepchas maintain such tradition and what they will do in critical health disorder.

Keywords: *Health, illness, tangible, spiritual healing*

INTRODUCTION

"Health is a state of complete physical, mental and social well-being and is not merely the absence of disease or infirmity" as propounded by World Health Organization (WHO, 1946). Life of an individual is always concerned with 'health'. The idea of ill-health disturbs the rhythm of life and the performances of the individual being. All human groups, no matter how small or technologically primitive, have always been devising ways and means for taking care of the health. Many definitions represent health and illness, which have conceptualized health as 'modes of relationship' – equilibrium and disequilibrium between man and his environment; involving human factors, ecological aspect and social structure (Lehriche, 1973). Health and illness have an integral association with the individual as well as society, where the health is a property and illness is a state. In one of his interpretation, Valabrega (1962) mentioned two notions of health and illness – first, the illness, behavior of the sick and medical practices are considered by endogenous (illness is caused by the magical theft of the individual soul) and exogenous (illness is caused by the real or symbolic intrusion of some objects into the patient's body) concept; secondly, illness may be caused by the action of another man or sorcerer or religious origin, produced by a god or a spirit.

Health and illness has close linkages with the therapeutic and preventive practices, which have shown variations throughout the ages. These therapeutic and preventive practices led by the human being is termed as 'ethno-medicine', which is referred to beliefs and practices relating to disease which are the products of indigenous cultural development (Hughes, 1968). In the sphere of ethno-medicine, man only depends on their surrounding 'biome' and developed an attachment with biotic and abiotic creature for coping up various health disorders and illness. The traditional way of nature cure with herbal medicine got tremendous popularity during the historical period. The first recorded treatise on the collection of 800 plant and plant products was mentioned in *Charak Samhita* (1000 – 800 B.C.) followed by *Sushruta Samhita* (800 – 700 B.C.). These are still identified as the baseline guidance for the practice of traditional herbal medicine for ever. In the path of development of ethno-medicine, there were two types of healing prevalent during the Vedic period – one was relied on magico – religious system while the other combined with medicinal herbs and medicines. In India, the concept of utilizing the natural and plant products to cure the ailments had appeared in the remote past, dating back to 4500-1600 B.C. during Rig Veda. On the other hand spiritual healing is an integrative approach has been accepted as a vital component of therapeutics. Spiritual healing is a cultural practices; hence the process of healing and the interpretation of illness reflect and reinforce the cultural definitions of the Lepcha health problem.

The Lepchas of Darjeeling Himalayas has tremendous significance and value in ethno-medicine because Darjeeling is the rich repository of many of such effective herbal plants and the Lepchas being the son of the soil acquire age old traditional system of power–healing from their forefathers and practice when they feel to be effective. The present article is based on the concept of health, illness and its curative measures of the people; how far the modern treatment can dilute the traditional system of application.

Area and the People

Nestled among the rolling mountains with the glistening Mt. Kanchenjunga towering over the azure sky, Darjeeling fondly called "Queen of the Hills" provides a perfect gateway for those seeking to be in harmony with nature. The name Darjeeling comes from the Tibetan words – *Dorje* (thunderbolt) and *Ling* (place or land), meaning the land of the thunderbolt. It is the northernmost district of the state of West Bengal in eastern India in the foothills of the Himalayas. The district is famous for its hill station and Darjeeling tea. The district has long history – most of area of the district formed a part of dominions of the Chogyal of Sikkim, who had been engaged in an unsuccessful warfare against the Gorkhas of Nepal. From 1780, the Gorkhas made several attempts to capture the entire region of Darjeeling. But all efforts were prevented by the British East India Company breaking out the Anglo-Gorkha was in 1814 and prevented over-running of the Gorkha from this area. Before 1861 and from 1870 to 1874, Darjeeling District was a "Non-Regulated Area" (where acts and regulations of the British Raj did not automatically apply in the district in line with rest of the country, unless specifically extended). From 1862 to 1870, it was considered a "Regulated Area". The phrase "Non-Regulated Area" was changed to "Scheduled District" in 1874 and again to "Backward Tracts" in 1919. The status was known as

"Partially Excluded Area" from 1935 until the independence of India. Darjeeling is famous for its hill stations and flavoured tea. Kalimpong, Kurseong, Mirik and Siliguri are the sub-divisional headquarters of the district. Today's Kalimpong subdivision was Damsang region of the Lepchas, which was earlier an independent country, ruled by Pano Gaeboo Achyok, the last Lepcha king from 1780 A.D. onwards. Being a son of Damsang area he had made this place famous as an important place of Lepcha tradition and culture. In Lepcha language Kalimpong is deduced from the name *Kalenpung*, which in Lepcha means – "Hillock of Assemblage".

The Study Area

The Lepcha dominated village named Pakang has been selected for this study. The village is situated in Gitdubling Gram Panchayat of Kalimpong Block II of Kalimpong subdivision, which is more than 55 kms., from Kalimpong town. According to Census data (2011) Gitdubling Gram Panchayat has second highest Scheduled Tribe population which is about 53.71 per cent and the Pakang busty has 99 per cent Lepcha population. The main occupation of the village is agriculture and the village lacks good roads, medical dispensaries etc. Though it is electrified and has one primary school.

The People

Once the ruling race, the Lepchas are the earliest settlers of Sikkim profoundly proclaimed as '*Rongkup*' (the son of the snowy peak) '*motanchi*' (term for intra-community identity). The history revealed that formerly the ruling dynasty of the Lepchas was extended from the Himalayas down to Titaliya, the plains of Bangladesh. To the east it was extended up to Gipmochi Mountain of present days Chinese Tibet and to the west it was up to Aroon river of Nepal (Tamsang, 1983). The Lepcha tradition depicted that in the beginning the first primo-genitors of the Lepchas, *Fodongthing* and *Nazaongnyo* were created by God from the pure, virgin snow of *Kingtsoomzaongboochoo's* (Khangchendzonga) pinnacle and sent them down to live, prosper and spread up all over the fairy land. Therefore, most of the Lepcha clan thus claims to have mythical connections with this mountain peak, which they worship as their guardian deity.

The derogatory word 'Lepcha' is derived from the Nepalese term *Lepchey*, which means scurrilous speakers. Originally, the term *Lepchey* was anglicized by the British people and coined the present term 'Lepcha', who proclaimed themselves as *Rongkup* or in short *Rong* that is 'snowy peak'. According to the tradition, there were ten divisions of ancient Lepcha families claiming their descent from the ten sons of *Fodongthing* and *Nazaongnyoo*. Those ten divisions of the ancient Lepcha families were called as '*Rong kup kati*', which means ten Lepchas. The Lepcha is also recognized as '*Rong Migyit*'. They have hereditary fixed clan or caste which called *agyit*, means a group of Lepcha people or family under the common ancestor.

The Lepchas are thought to have been living mostly through hunting and gathering from the forests. Since later phase of last century they took to settled cultivation and subsequently adopted the system of cash crop plantation, like cardamom, tea and ginger, in their terrace agricultural field, the Lepchas raise maize, paddy, wheat, barley and millet. The rice is the most important staple food Millet is commonly used for making local bear '*Chi*'. Fish is taken occasionally but meat – both fresh and dried are taken regularly. They do not have any inhibition in consuming beef, pork, rabbit, porcupine, monkey, deer etc. The Lepcha language as dubbed by many scholars as a 'mystery' language, because it is not related to any other language, prevalent in this region. Some have a belief that the language belongs to the Tibeto – Burman family, while others have found its root in the Austro-Asiatic family. Dr. Suniti Kumar Chatterjee had mentioned that the Lepcha language belongs to the Himalayan group of the Tibeto-Burman sub-family (Thakur, 1988).

Health, Illness and Disease: the Lepcha wisdom

The concept of health and illness among the Lepchas is fully guided by the belief in supernatural. According to the belief of the people, the cause of illness can be classified into two categories – (i) Disease caused by supernatural beings, their displeasure and actions, which are beyond their control; and (ii) diseases caused by the magical means. According to them, the system of cause, effect and cure is a circular and enclosed system of knowledge, which provides the manifestation of explanation and control in the face of disorders, chaos and inexplicable circumstances. It is their belief that if the cause of illness is a spirit, the effect is then spirit possession or other way if can be the cause of controlled spirit possession. The idea of health, illness and disease have own individual importance in Lepcha mind. The Lepcha feel that any kind of health disorder may not cause any disease all the time. Simple cough and cold, headache, bodyache is not experienced as an illness or disease to them. According to them, disease is of two categories – (a) Curable and (b) Non-curable. The people also have the opinion that due to carelessness some disease can be turned into a non-curable disease. According to their perception 'illness' has two aspects – i.e. (a) Psycho-analytical (based on the existence of spirits, ghosts, evil doers), (b) Medicinal (based on the existence of some noncurable fatal diseases like, tuberculosis, cancer, cholera, diarrhea etc.). The Psycho-analytical aspect of illness is cured only by means of propitiation of deities and appeasement of spirits, ghosts etc., while the 'medicinal' aspect is cured by the application of traditional herbal medicine first and if not cured then they apply modern allopathic medicine.

During the discussions, it is also pointed out that the faith in supernatural power, i.e. gods - *Rum* and demons – *Moong* ; is an age-old tradition. Both *Rum* (God) and *Moong* (demon) can be doing harm in the form of fatal injury, epidemics, mishaps, disease etc. and also can snatch out ones' life, if they really dissatisfied. At that time, the *Mun* and *Boongthing*, the folk-healer is to be consulted. The *muns* and *boongthings* are considered by the Lepcha to be the media for communication to the God (*rum*) and the devils or demons (*moongs*). It is believed by the people that the *boongthings* are supposed to be able to communicate with all the devils / demons (*Moongs*) except the 'Dom *moong*', who causes *Leprosy*. It is the opinion of the *mun* and *boongthing* that different types of illness are responsible by the deeds of different *moongs* (devil/demon) which can be treated with worship and devotion of respective *moongs* accompanied by animal sacrifice. The folk-healer (*mun & boomgthing*) stated that if those *rum* and *moong* (God and devil/demon) are ignored or any disrespect is shown to them by defiling or polluting by nature's call etc. may invite the suffering of the particular individual – the people may suffer from the serious sickness and sometimes even die. They mentioned one of such *moong* is 'Lungzee normally reside in the big stone present at the entrance of a *bustee* (hamlet). *Mun* and *boongthing* also agreed that if Rum(god) is angered it appears in malicious guise and then referred to as a demon, and may cause sickness and other misfortune. The sickness, disease may also cause by magical means, which is treated by exorcism. In this sphere the folk healer (*mun* and *boongthing*) took initiative steps. By counting of the rosary beads and throwing off the dice, the folk-healer divines what is actually troubling the patient and then suggested that sacrifice is actually necessary or not. In psycho-analytical aspect of illness, disease may caused by the evil spirit and according to them, all evil spirit reside in the upper part and as well as in the lower part of the earth. To get rid of those evil spirit, in almost all Lepcha houses of both in Yuksam and Dzongu, a kind of structure was found, what they termed *Namgo* (for the evil spirit of upper part of the earth) and *Sago* (for the evil spirit of lower part of the earth).

It is a common belief that this structure seemed to protect all kind of malevolent spirit.

It was informed that there are number of spirits, demons and deities in the Lepcha society, whose harmful action is responsible for disease and illness. Among all of them, few important, spirits, demons and deities are mentioned as follows:-

i. The demon *mung-nong-chuk* and its evil action.

ii. The deities *Rum-na-na-cho* become arrogant

iii. The spirit *Thing-na-na-cho* and its malevolent action.

iv. Jungle spirit *muzom-na-chuk-chumboo* and its harmful activities.

v. Household deities *Sakya-tofion-lee-Rum* and its harmful action.

vi. Principal household deities *Mukung-Rum* and its evil action.

vii. The deity *Veek-Run* and its evil action, believed to be present in the surrounding of a house, of a person.

viii. Nature spirit *yougebo* and its evil action.

ix. Nature spirit – Dzongo and its evil action.

x. The deity *Lungno* and their evil action.

xi. The spirit *Makryum, Sor,Dut-chaim* and their malevolent effect.

xii. The spirit *Muzom, sipundi, Anee* and their malevolent effect.

xiii. The demon (*mong*) – *Dut,* Tshen, *mamn, Cu, Gey-bo, Cyang-shergnyu, eetgnyn, Thyakdum,* pankar, tong-Thing.

It is narrated that due to the harmful effect of demon, deities and spirits the people become sick by heart disease (*alut-dak*), stomach disorder (*tubok-dak*), rheumatism (*aku-dak athung-dak*), vision problem, nose bleeding (*jukmar-vee*) etc. which can be cured by the magico-religious performances.

Cosmology In Relation To Health & Illness

During the study they also informed that they have strong faith in cosmology in relation to health, illness and disease. Both eclipses (Solar and Lunar), stages of waxing and waning of moon, falling of stars, sudden visibility of any constellation in the sky etc. are believed to have a direct effect on peoples' health, especially on the pregnant lady, new born baby and the children of lactating stage. Since pregnancy, both would be father and mother have to follow certain taboos, which are believed to be essential for safe delivery and as well as for the protection of any deformities of would be child. They also informed that any kind of disrespect of that taboos may cause epilepsy and blindness to the new born child. It is also in their faith that sacredness of the natural objects, like streams, lakes, rivers, trees, stones has direct or indirect relation with the illness and disease. They informed that whenever the sacred river, lakes and streams got polluted by any means of sinful activities, it become either dried up or displaced from its place of origin and this may cause epidemic in that area. They also have the opinion that the high density water in the sacred rivers and lakes would maintain the seasonal change, and indirectly would not affect the health of the people, on the other hand the low density of water would disturb the seasons and the people may fall ill or their health may be disturbed.

Beliefs and illness

The Lepchas, in one hand belief on ghost, demons and on the other hand they have the belief on Gods and goddesses. They also have the religious attitude towards various natural objects. All supernatural being, good and bad, though eternally living outside the world, have innumerable manifestations. These manifestations, or replicas, of the supernatural, chose various natural phenomena for semi permanent habitation, agreeable phenomena - lakes, or fruit trees or fruitful land – if the supernatural are generally benevolent, disagreeable places – useless trees, waterfalls, rocks or barren ground – if the supernatural are generally malevolent. Each type of supernatural has a preference particular kind of habitation, thus all the *dent moong* – fever devils – live in big isolated trees, *Sabdok moong* – skim disease devils – in outcrops of rock. According to them everything in the world possess a soul, for the soul is the animating principle of all life, without whose intermediary nothing could move or grow.

During the field work, there are few such devil's habitation were come across as per their information. One such spot was in between the area of Tingboong and Linzya just beside the road side gorge, where the two outcrops are believed as the homes of two malevolent spirits, i.e. *Sabdokmoong* and his wife *Loo moong*. This female devil causes a specific skin disease, and if a person / or a passerby urinate on that spot should suffer from a non-curable genital disease. Her stone will be anointed with holy water by a lama and with milk by a *Mun*.

It is believed to be informed that there is a lake 'Luksom partam', high up in Dzongu, from whence birth is meant to have originated. Sterile couples who wish for children should visit this lake, spend the night on its bank copulating, and then in the morning throw into the water a silver rupees and a *chimi* (altar light) to please the gods. It necessary this may be repeated annually for three years. The connection between water and birth runs all through the Mun mythology. It was informed that in divine world where the two gods *Tak-bo-thing* and *Narzong-nyou* live there is a stream called *Lungfung* which represents the birth of male children and a well called *Rungzel oong-lap* which represents the birth of female children. This well is guarded by a supernatural boy called *Sathi moong*, and on occasion a family which has many girls and no boys will get a Mun to make sacrifices to the boy and the two gods to make the two pieces of water change place.

Rituals curing of illness

The rituals are performed for the benefit of individuals, households and the habitation area at large. The people have the belief that performances of these rituals are essential for curing the illness. In these rituals, Mun, Boongthing and Lama play an overwhelming role as a witch, sorcerer or priest.

A. ***Cherim Ceremony:*** The *cherim* ceremony, held twice in a year; once at the beginning of rains, and again at the beginning of winter; to keep off epidemic diseases like malaria, typhoid etc. from the community. Altogether there are three separate rituals performed, two by *Mun*, and the third by Lamas. In such communal sacrifice at least one individual from each household has to be present, and each household contributes a little amount of grains. The first ceremony, *rum* consists of an off sing to the devils by giving a number of chief articles as a sacrifice to the demon. When the offerings have been made, the *mun*, sitting opposite to the people, intones a long chant to invoke the gods (*rum*) and then takes the eggs and holds them to his forehead while he shuts his eyes and concentrates; the line which he envisages inside the eggs foretells the future health of the community.

The second ceremony – '*Tsandong*' is also performed by Mun, consists of offerings to the Gods of Khangchendzonga and to the plains. The offerings consist of rice, butter, *chimi*, a rupee and eggs. The sacrifice is in two parts; first grain and strained *chi* are thrown out by the Mun and her assistant and later a goat is dedicated and then killed. In this ceremony prayers are also attributed to the God of mountains (*Sungmul*) from the protection from snow, hailstorm and blizzard. The people present in this ceremony are busy in cooking, eating, gossiping and watching the preparation.

The third ceremony is performed by the Lamas with the preparation of a very elaborate ceremonial object. The chief of these are the '*deu*', the 'nine – storied palace', consisting of elaborate regular polyhedral in different colour threads supported on bamboo splinters through a central bamboo. The foreground of the structure was occupied by an elaborate representation of the female demon *Mamoo Moong*, portrayed as a snake-haired female riding on a tiger, and surrounded by hundreds of lesser objects. The *Mamoo Moong* herself was summoned and gratified with the offerings of copper pots and clothes. It is a perception that if any animals have not devoured within three days, it is a sign that there will be serious sickness in the coming season. Before taking out the image a *Mun* sang a song alone for thanking the god for coming and begging them now to go back. On these occasions, *Mun* always sang more or les a sacred songs.

B. ***Shokbu – Rum Ceremony:*** This ceremony is followed by the Lepcha peole during the month of summer season to propitiate the *Yomgebo* god (rum) and nature spirit. It is a belief to the people that during onset of summer season people are affected by various seasonal diseases like diarrhea, dysentery, caugh & cold etc. which may cause by the ill effect of that *yomgebo* deity (rum) and the spirit residing in the nature. According to them, the sun god, *Yomgebo* is most powerful among the all. People should have to appease that sun god. The Lepcha people offered millet, maize, buckwheat flour to the *yomgebo* and the nature spirit. No animal is sacrificed in this ceremony. *Boongthing* plays an important role to propitiate the god and the spirit without taking any food. By seeing the yoke of the egg offered by every individual household, *Boongthing* can felt about the future health status of that particular household. Either the member of the household would really affected by any diseases or not during the coming season can be foretold by the *Boongthing*. At the time of initiation of this ceremony, *Boongthing* sits facing the east because the sun rises in the east side, he also decorated the place by making a platform made of bamboo poles, bamboo vessel for the offerings, wooden bowl for *maung chi* (country millet beer) etc. The whole propitiation is preferably done on the bank of a river or a stream. Because they have a faith on the sacred river Teesta.

C. ***Parnap festival:*** This ceremony is performed to appease a demon, known as *Zengo*, who is believed to be resided in Tolung gompha. This ceremony is performed every year turn wise by the every household. It is the perception of the people that the appeasement of the demon *Zengo* may protect their health from any dreadful diseases. It is also told that the Lepcha men, whenever completed the construction of his house, organized this ceremony in his newly built house as if to purify the house and no any demon can do any harm to the house. *Boongthing* or *Mun* are the responsible to propitiate the rituals in their traditional way. On the day of the ceremony one cock and one hen is sacrificed to the demon and on the next day the house-owner organize a feast where the relatives, kith and kin members and the neighbours are invited. On the other hand, during the span of one year every household within a *bustee* contribute the food grains (millet, maize, and buckwheat), money and *maung-chi* (millet-beer) as per their capacity and assimilated together. At the time of yearly festival, furring the month of June, one of the members of that *bustee* carried away those assimilated articles to the Tholung monastery and performed worship by a Lama. This *parnap* ceremony, according to them is performed for overall prosperity, happiness and well-being of the *bustee*. The people believed any kind of disregard and carelessness to that demon may cause harm to them and the people even died by the dreadful diseases.

D. ***Apang Moong / Sor moong:*** If get rid of genitor-urinary disease or violent death, a goat is tittered by a long rope which has three knots tied in its length, first of all, all the members of the afflicted household must touch the knots and then the Mun will call on all the devils to be contended with the blood of the sacrifice and not to take the patient, after which he throws the rope into the air. It the rope falls ends outwards (i.e. the end away from the goat falls towards the door), it means the devils will be satisfied and if it falls towards the house the prognosis is bad. After this the animal is killed and the *gazook* (the liver) and *sha-fot* (head) offered to the devil/demon and a pot filled with rice, a rupee and a ceremonial scarf (*Khada*), together with some of the invalid's ornaments and clothing and also a cup of *chi* with different grains in it. Then the *Mun* constructs a phallus out of wood, which is called in its guardian function *moong long tik*. This phallus is set up between two stones leaning slightly forward, somewhere in the forest, and anointed with the blood of the slain animal and *chi*. This will keep the devil/demon away from the area and household.

E. *Num-een moong*: The young children who become died by the infantile diarrhea is believed to be caused by a demon of a dead child named as *Num-eenmoong*. To drive away that demon (*moong*) the Lepcha people sacrificed a goat or a sheep. Even after the sacrifice of an animal if the person troubled by the *moong*, goes down to a narrow stream. The troubled person stands on the right of the stream and the *Mun* on the left of it. Then a 'gateway' is made over the stream of two bundles of elephant grass and brambles, while the *Mun* holds in each hand a bundle made out of wild raspberries, nettles and all other thorny and prickly plants. These bundles are dipped in water and peek over the sufferer several times. A bamboo filled with blood and *chi* are shut up at both ends, and a leaf filled with fried rice and meat and blood are peek over the patient and thrown through the gateway for the demon. The branches of thorny plants are thrown through the gateway and finally the gateway is filled up with thorny plants, so that it looks like a tree. The *Mun* does this at two other places, one is some way apart on the streams, and the other is either above or below the first one. After completing the *Mun* must return straight to his own house without meeting anybody. It was told that *Num-een moong* is the demon released by the death of young children under the age of about ten. This devil pursues living people and especially other children. Older people who die do not let loose a devil/demon. The *Num-een moong* persists for about three years after the child's death.

F. *Sipundi:* The Lepcha when attacked by food poison is believed to be caused due to the effect of an malevolent spirit called *sipundi*. It is also believed by the people that when the malevolent spirit *sipundi* made a tremendous effect on the Lepcha, they become died directly. Sometimes its effect gradually do harm to the people. At this time, the Lepcha are experienced with various physical ailments and their physique becomes reduced. Some of the people also got affected by jaundice and started decreasing their health. The Boongthing is called out and he is the person who can trace that what kind of supernatural power really affected the person. He also suggested the best way one Lepcha can do. Whenever the malevolent spirit *sipundi* affect the person, he/she will be cured by folk medicine of herbal medicine.

G. ***Amee:*** Another type of malevolent spirit usually believed to be reside in the fruits, vegetables and grains heaped outside the Lepcha house. This malevolent spirit may be the cause of limb pain whenever a Lepcha person got effected a limb pain it is believed that he or she once take out the other Lepcha's article without telling anything. They also believed that for the cure of the malevolent effect of *Amee* the affected person must have to go to the owner's house and confess his wrongdoings. It the owner' of the article simply rub the limb and effected person get relief.

H. ***Lung-Zee:*** One of the most special spirits is *Lung-zee*, interpreted as an equivalent sort of guardian spirit for a particular object of nature. These objects are such that they catch the eye straightaway may be a huge tree, a crag, a tarn, a cave, a cluster of trees, a special hillock and other natural objects. They are supposed to have some sort of a limit or boundary around the object in which they have come and taken up abode. The belief is that if the spirit is ignored, and the object defiled and polluted by answering the call of nature, or men and women have sexual connection anywhere in its vicinity, there is the possibility of the whole village suffering by any infections disease, or at least the culprit or culprits receiving punishment by a series of diseases and sometimes death may occur in the family. They also narrated that they generally do not perform any harm to the nature. They always abide by the rules pertaining to disturb or irritate the nature. For that matter they restrict themselves for cutting or chopping the wood of a tree, where lung-zee is apprehended to be resided. If they believe that a pond or a stream is the abode of a *lungzee*. They do not irritate if by throwing stones in ti. If it is believed that the *lung-zee* is present in a crag, they do not dare to collect honey combs, hornet grubs or flowering edible orchids from it. *Boongthing* and *Mun* perform the job to detect where the *lung-zee* originally resides and give the instruction accordingly.

Supernatural power and the illness

According to their opinion, the illness may occur due to the displeasure or dissatisfaction of the supernatural power beyond their control. This supernatural powers are sometimes benefited them and sometimes cursed them in the form of illness and diseases. This type of harmful supernatural power have its own jurisdiction which are trying to mention in the following tables (Tables 1-3).

Table 1: Malevolent power by the God (*Rum*)

Position	Local Name	Cause of Diseases
Village God	*Langrun*	Responsible for headache, fever, drowsiness
Household deity	*Tongthing*	Eye infection
Household deity	*Lee-run*	Cause the disease like diarrhea, dysentery, stomach, disorder etc.
Common deity	*Tsandong run*	Cause epidemic like malaria, jaundice
Common deity	*Lung-no run, Ajo Gyantho*	Responsible for severe stomach pain, diarrhea, dysentery.
Seasonal deity	Shukbu-run	Responsible for various seasonal disease like Cough & Cold, Phenomonia, diarrhea, dysentery etc.

Table 2: Malevolent power by the demon/devil/ghost (*moong*)

Position	Local Name	Cause of Diseases
Place of dense forest, rock and cave	*Duet-Tshen moong*	Responsible for rheumatism (*akn-dak / athmg dak*), headache, Bodyache, joint and limb pain, high fever
Places of flowing streams, rivers	*Manoo moong* (female ghost)	Responsible for whole body pain.
places of flowing streams, rivers	*Loo-moong* (female demon)	responsible for specific skin disease, wounds, fatal injury
Places inside the *bustee*	*Gey-bo-moong*	Responsible for severe headache, severe heat attack

Places of a village boundary	*Lyang shergynu* (female ghost)	Responsible for miscarriage, frequent vomiting, lose of appetite of the female folk.
Places of outcrops of a rock	*Sabdok moong*	Skin disease, sore etc. is caused due to the ill effect of the *moong*
Places of roadside area	*Arof moong*	Accident, suicide

Table 3: Malevolent power by the evil spirit

Position	Local name	Cause of diseases
Reside in the nature as a whole	*Dzengo*	Cause of different dreadful diseases like TB., Pneumonia lung disease.
Reside in the tree trunk	*Apang moong sor moong*	Cause of genitor-urinary disease. Cause for violent death.
Reside in the dead child's soul	*Num-een moong*	Cause of infantile diarrhea
Reside in the open barren field	*Sipundi*	Cause of food poison and jaundice
Reside in the fruits, vegetables and grains	*Amee*	Cause of limb pain, whole body pain
Reside in a huge tree, a crag, a taru, a cave, a cluster of trees, a hillock	*Lung-zee*	Cause of various infections disease. The whole village got affected.
Reside in the huge stone situated at the entry point of the *bustee*	*Sandong Long-chuk*	Cause of various common diseases like headache, bodyache, limb pain, nose bleeding (*jukmar-vee*), heart disease (*alut-dak*), stomach disorder (*tubok-dak*)
Reside in the open air just outside the house	*Maknyam*	Cause of vomiting, stomach pain, diarrhea
Reside in the dense forest	*Sor*	Cause of loose motion, piles, abnormal delivery etc.

From the list of few supernatural powers it can be assessed that the Lepcha world of vision is completely guided by beliefs. Even in nowadays, this tradition got importance. The Lepcha take the measure, to propitiate those supernatural evil power first by the *boongthing* and *Mun*, if it is not cured they opt, for the better option of Traditional herbal medicine by consulting the *pudim/boongthing*. If the health situation becomes aggravated, then they go to the Primary health centre and opt for modern medicine.

The role of *Pudim/Boongthing* and *Mun*

The Lepcha have their own ancient religion, named as *Boongthingism* and *Munism*. They believe in the existence of God called Run and to him the *boongthing* and *mun* offer their prayers and thanksgiving. *Pudim/Boongthing* and *Mun* perform all the rituals and religious ceremonies of the Lepchas. Many of the earlier writing mentioned that for the God fearing Lepchas, prayers supplication and worship is performed through *boongthing* and *mun*. It is not a superstition, not any flight of eloquence and not even lips homage to God. The living quality of *Boongthingism* and *Munism* is demonstrated by the loyalty it has commanded from its followers, the Lepchas. *Boongthing* and *Mun* is the mediator between God (*rums*), devil/demons (*moongs*) and the Lepchas. The *boongthing* ward-off the evil spirits by sacrificing the animals and other things. Both of them are invited to officiate during clan/community rituals or even for worshipping the family deities. Their assistance is also invariably sought for curing sickness of individuals. *Boongthing* are supposed to be able to communicate with the malevolent and benevolent demons/devils (*moongs*). The institution *mun* is hereditary in nature, but the institution *boongthing* can be learnt from the other *boongthing*. The Lepcha believed that apart from the service of warding off the malevolent spirits, *boongthing* are also sought for during the wedding to invoke the gods and goddesses. The *boongthings* are considered more popular among the Lepchas in general as their service is more frequently sought for particularly during illness. *Muns*' performance is restricted to different social functions. *Mun* plays a pivotal role in agricultural performance. *Muns* participation is compulsory in different ritual associated with agriculture. According to them the *Muns* are hierarchically classified with their status. Every classification has definite performance. *Pilden Muns* are the superior one who has the capacity to communicate with the dead person's soul. Some of the *muns*, known as *Mun Mook-Mun*, are thought to be the evil doers who cause hardship to the people. The *Mun-Jyum-Mun* category *mun* perform the activities as like the *Pilden mun*, except for that they cannot communicate with the dead person's soul, but they can cure the sick person by herbal medicine. The *mun*, having the specialized knowledge of using herbs is considered as *Tangli mun*.

Conclusion

In the prolong discussion of the foregoing pages it tries to delineate that irrespective of caste, class, creed; 'health' is an important feature to all human groups. The ill-health disturbs the rhythm of life and the performances of the individual being. On having a separate identity health and illness is always remain as both sides of a same coin. If health is a property, then illness is a state. The failure of health causes illness, whose cure is very necessary. Being an inhabitant of nature the Lepcha of the Damsang region and around Khangchendzonga Biosphere (KBR) including West and North district of Sikkim is not an exception of that. But according to their perception, every health disorder or health hazards are not contemplated as an 'illness'. Like other original son of the soil, the Lepcha also have dependency on age-old ethno-medicine. The health, illness, behaviour of the sick and medical practices among the Lepchas primarily follows the path of endogenous path of conception. Became according to their belief, everything in the world possess a 'soul', and illness is the reflection towards the disorder of that 'soul'.

While describing the illness and therapeutics, it has been found that the illness of the Lepcha is either caused by the dissatisfaction of various natural being which is considered to be an animate object, the arrogance and dissatisfaction of spirits, demons, and ghosts, believed to be residing in the nature; or by the displeasure of various deities related with nature. In accordance with the rules of prevention against the illness and diseases the Lepcha primarily follows the path of appeasement of various deities by worshipping them; or propitiating the malevolent spirits, demons, ghost by employing the service of the traditional spirit healer and priest, called as *mun* and *pudim/boongthing* following the path of power-healing. *Mun* acquire the knowledge from the older generation; it is their opinion that when a *Mun* is called to exorcise a specific devil that he has been divined, the *Mun* spends a night in his own home – *munthening* for summoning and communing with the possessing spirit. The question of causation is bound up with the conception of *tamtoom* – the necessary consequence of an earlier act; often this act was not committed by the sufferer, but by fairly remote ancestors. The *Mun* worships two supernatural, *Hit-rum* and *De-rum*, who are considered to be ancestral gods who look after all dead Lepchas. When a *Mun* has discovered as much as possible about the supernatural and immediate causes of the illness he indicates the necessary objects of sacrifice. These are almost always animals, but on occasion other objects are needed as well or instead. Sometimes these objects are valuables, which are just displayed to gratify the supernatural; sometimes other edibles – crops, chi, dried bird, dried fish, and ginger. According to the ceremony these are either abandoned to be eaten by wild animals, or consumed, as part of the ritual, by all present except the *Mun* himself.

References

Charles CH. 1968. *'Ethnomedicine'* in the *Encyclopedia of Social Sciences,* David L. Sills (eds.), Vol. 9-and 10, Pp. 88.

Department of Forest. Report of Khangchendzonga National Park and Biosphere Reserver (unpublished).

Fonning AR. 1987. *Lecpha, my vanishing tribe.* New Delhi, Sterling Publishing Co.

Gazetteer. 1931. *Gazetteer of Bengal and Sikkim.* A.E. Porter, Vol. V, part-I & II, Delhi: Usha Publication.

Gochman SD. 1982. Labels, systems and motives: some perspective for future research in D.S. Gochman and G.S. Parcel (eds.) Children Health, beliefs and health behavior (Spl. Issue). *Health Education Quarterly.* 9:167-174.

Gorer G. 2005. *The Lepcha of Sikkim.* New Delhi, Gyan Publishing House.

Government of India. 2001. *Population Atlas.* Census Report, Sikkim.

Khangchendzonga Conservation Committee. Brochure of Khangchendzonga and its people (unpublished).

Lehriche C, Danglas G. 1973. Health and illness: a social psychological analysis, London, Academic Press.

Maity D, Chauhan AS. 2001. *Kanchanjunga Biosphere Reserve.* In Floristic diversity and Conservation Strategies in India, Vol. V; (eds.) NP Singh and KP Singh. Kolkata, Botanical Survey of India.

Pattnaik B. 2005. Ecological bases of Indian traditions: search for an indigenous vision. *The Eastern Anthropologist.* 58.

Raina VK, Srivastava BS. 1981. *Tectonic evolution of Sikkim Himalayas.* Contemp Geosci,Resin Himalaya, vol. Dehradum.

Roy Burman JJ. 2003. *Tribal medicine: traditional practices and changes in India.* New Delhi, Mittal Publication.

Roychaudhury AK. 1988. *Man, malady and medicine: history of Indian medicine.* Calcutta, Das Gupta & Co. (P) Ltd.

Sharma R. 1983. *Images of Sikkim: the land, people and culture.* Sikkim, Department of Tourism, Gangtok, Ringsum Publication.

Sigerist HE. 1943. *Civilization and Disease.* University of Chicago. Press, Chicago.

Singh AK, Patil S. 2007. *Man in biosphere: Nilgiri Biosphere Reserve.* New Delhi, Gyan Publishing House.

Singh NP, Mudgal V, Khanna KK, Srivastava SC. 2001. *Medicinal plant in floristic diversity and conservation strategies in India*, vol. IV, Botanical Survey of India, Kolkata.

Tamsang KP. 1983. *The Unknown and Untold Reality about the Lepchas, Kalimpong, Lyangsong Tamsang.*

Thakur RN. 1988. *Himalayan Lepchas.* New Delhi; Archives Publisher and Distributors.

Valabrega JP. 1962. *La Relation Therapeutique, Malade et Medecin.* Cited in '*Social Tactors in relations to chronic Illness* by Graham Smith (1963).

Weiser S. 1984. *Tibetan Buddhist Medicine and Psychiatry.* New Delhi, Samuel Weiser Inc.

World Health Organization. 1946. Health and Illness, Bulletin, New York.

Chapter Six

SOCIAL DIMENSION OF HEALTH AND WELL BEING AMONG TRIBAL ELDERLY

Dipankar Chatterjee and Koustab Majumdar

Abstract

Every country in the World is experiencing increase in aged population both in numbers and proportion. With increasing numbers of aged population economic and social changes are essential to ensure progress in development. These changes are vital in achievement of the goals outlined in the 2030 Agenda for Sustainable Development. Understanding changes in the health of the elderly is a central policy issue. A healthier elderly population is able to work to later ages, spends less on medical care each year, and requires less informal care from family and friends. Efforts to promote population health are therefore central to many health reform proposals. Although the WHO definition of health, promulgated decades ago, includes social health as equal in importance to physical and psychological health, it has rarely been incorporated analytically in describing population health. The present research seeks to construct the community perception of elderly not simply as a chronological phase of life but with reference to social relationship that ensures the well-being of the elderly. In order to understand the issues in cross cultural perspective, the study is being carried out among the purposively selected six tribal communities of eastern part of India. This article addresses the conceptual underpinnings of various aspects of social wellbeing constructed in the context of tribal elderly. The findings from this inquiry may provide new insights capable of strengthening policies for the welfare of the elderly tribal people of the country.

***Keywords:** Social well-being, Tribal elderly, Eastern India*

Introduction

In 1948, the World Health Organization (WHO) defined health as ". . . a state of complete physical, mental and social well-being and not merely the absence of disease or infirmity" (Glenn and Weaver, 1979). Since then others have called for conceptualizations of health expanded to include positive health (Ryff and Singer, 1988) or successful aging (Rowe and Kahn, 1997), although these more inclusive definitions have rarely been applied to understanding the health of individuals or populations. This chapter addresses the conceptual underpinnings of various aspects of social wellbeing constructed in the context of tribal elderly of Eastern India. It presents commonly used measures of social well-being, rarely referred to as social health, and briefly reviews the relationship between these measures and other dimensions of health. It suggests ways that assessments of the health of individuals, groups, or populations could be expanded to include social health, and it discusses future directions for research on the demography of social well-being at older ages. Although the WHO definition of health, promulgated around half a century ago, includes social health as equal in importance to physical and psychological health, and some researchers have incorporated the social in their conceptual frameworks (Ryff and Singer, 1988; Rowe and Kahn, 1997;), it has rarely been incorporated analytically in describing population health. Addressing this lack is an important future direction for the social well-being of elderly, but it means that reviews of recent research have little to say on social well-being as a component of health and much more to say on social factors as causes of other dimensions of health. That lack shapes the discussion below on our understanding of the links between social well-being and health. When WHO added "social well-being" to its definition of health, what did it have in mind? No generally accepted definition of social wellbeing exists. Obviously, it should include adequate and well-functioning social relationships, adequate social support, little or no social strain, some social participation, social inclusion in one's society, strong and well-functioning social networks, and, perhaps, sexuality as one desires (Waite, 2005). Such parameters have profound influence in constructing elderly person in a community and social well-being as a component of health. The present research seeks to construct the community perception of elderly not simply as a chronological phase of life but with reference to social relationship that ensures the well-being of the elderly. In order to understand the issues in cross cultural perspective, the study is being carried out among the purposively selected six tribal communities of eastern part of India. The study finds that construction of elderly is a relative status marker, accomplished by passing through ritual transitions, and is not necessarily tied to extended chronological years across the studied tribal community. The study also entails that the cultural construction is more pertinent rather the chronological parameter of identifying elderly to assure material benefit through social security schemes overlooking the social embeddedness of well-being among the tribals. The findings from this inquiry may provide new insights capable of strengthening policies for the welfare of the elderly tribal people of the country.

Theoretical and Conceptual Approaches to Social Well-Being

The standard Medical Model of Health, sometimes called the biomedical model, had its origins in the 1910 Flexner Report (Flexner, 1910), which codified medical education through a focus on diseases, specifically their pathology, biochemistry, and physiology (Stevens, 1971; Starr, 1982; Beck, 2004; Annandale, 2014). In this model, health is the absence of disease, dysfunction, or injury. Engel's (1977) biopsychosocial model integrated traditional medicine with psychosocial factors, which stimulated the field of psychosomatic medicine. A focus on physical health and the avoidance of disease defined "successful aging" as conceptualized by Jack Rowe, a physician, and Robert Kahn, a psychologist. Successful aging was distinguished from normal aging, which might include health declines and chronic disease (Rowe and Kahn, 1997). Rowe (1990) defined "staying healthy" as not diseased, not disabled, with a hallmark of successful aging being a low risk of developing chronic disease. Later, Rowe and Kahn (1997) expanded the definition of success to include a low probability of disease and disease-related disability, high cognitive and physical functional capacity, and active engagement with life; one ages successfully if one achieves all three of these goals. No mention is made of good mental health. Subsequent research showed that very few people are able to maintain the high levels of functioning required to be classified as "successful" (Martin et al., 2015). Note that this definition of health includes one measure that may reflect social well-being: active engagement with life, defined as maintenance of personal relationships and engagement in paid or unpaid activities that produce goods or services of economic value (Rowe and Kahn, 1997). The related ideas of "positive health" and "successful aging" incorporate the presence or absence of disease, cognitive and functional capacity (Ryff and Singer, 1998), and active engagement with life (Rowe and Kahn, 1997, 1998). Ryff and Singer (1998) pointed to the importance of both mind and body in positive health and focused on the effect of each on the other, but they ignored the social. Rowe and Kahn (1997) privileged cognitive function and ignored psychological well-being. Recent work has moved little beyond this point. Lowsky et al. (2014) defined "healthy aging," using self-reported health, as getting no help with activities of daily living or instrumental activities of daily living, having no work limitations due to health, not having been diagnosed with any major chronic disease, and having a perfect score on the health-related quality-of-life scale. Recent research has focused on markers of physiological aging in young adults (Belsky et al., 2015), including physical functioning, cognitive function, and appearance. Social functioning is not included. And a sizable body of research has focused on the effect of social relationships on longevity (Yang et al., 2013, 2016), and the biological mechanisms through which these occur (Yang et al., 2013). These models are based on the assumption that social relationships affect health. But WHO includes social well-being as a component of health. Lindau et al. (2003) proposed an "interactive biopsychosocial model" in which three components, the psycho-cognitive, biophysical, and social health of each social partner, affect and are affected by each other within a social environment. Within the social environment, life changes influence individuals with varying frequency and intensity depending upon their location within the social structure (Tausig, 1982), and clearly, age is one important factor in determining that location. In fact, the transition through the life span, until older age, can be viewed as a series of role entrances and exits (Blau, 1981) with concomitant changes in social resources (such as social support), psychological states, and health status.

Community, Context and Methods

The research is based on the data generated from the fieldwork in phases across six tribal communities classified under two broad categories such as Particularly Vulnerable Tribal Groups (PVTG) [*Lodha*, *Asur*, and *Juang*] and Socially Dominant Tribal (SDT) [*Santal*, *Oraon*, *Bhuinya*] distributed in five district of three eastern Indian states namely Jharkhand, Odisha and West Bengal. The selection of the villages in different districts was based on the predominance of substantial amount of the targeted section of the tribal community. During the reconnoiter survey, five districts namely Ranchi and Gumla (Jharkhand), Kendujhar (Odisha) and Paschim Midnpore and Jhargram (West Bengal) were explored for final selection of villages inhabited by the targeted tribal communities. After preliminary investigation of different region of the three states, the studied villages were finally selected. The state-wise selected villages are given below in Table 1.

Table 1: State-wise selected villages

State	Ethnic Group	Villages
West Bengal	Santal	Nakuijuri, Rangamatiya, Tal Jamboni, Kendugari
	Lodha	Gobindapur, Lohamaliya, Korasol, Patasimul Muchibere
Jharkhand	Oraon	Rarha
	Asur	Sakhuapani, Polpolpat, Gorapat, Jobipat
Orissa	Bhuinya	Ichinda, Kainsari and Anjar
	Juang	Gonasika, Jantari and Baragarh

This research is an attempt to explore the social construction of old age and the state of wellbeing of the elderly of tribal community. The present research is a blend of cognitive anthropology and social constructionism since it adopts a mix of quantitative and qualitative techniques in data collection and analysis. Social constructionism is a term used by researchers and scholars to describe the construction of knowledge. The arrangement of this present research is based on 'Back' and 'Forth' approach (Vate, 2005), going between the data collected and analyzed from contemporary fieldwork and the review of related on hand literature, books, journals, government records etc. The primary data has been culled in phases incorporating six tribal communities from Jharkhand Odisha and West Bengal. A schedule comprising both open ended and closed ended questions were prepared to address the research objectives. A pilot testing of the schedule among the studied community was carried out for contextual validation of the schedule. The state and district of the study was purposely selected on the basis of the reconnoiter survey information. The informants were selected on the basis of simple random sampling stratifying the entire population on the basis of age and sex. The main data collection tools used to obtain quantitative data was a household survey schedule. The other specific tools used to interpret the objectives of the research includes participant observation, case study focused group discussions (FGDs) and recording narratives. Extensive field notes were taken which were subsequently coded and analyzed in a variety of ways.

Conceptualizing Tribal Elderly

When we talk about ageing and old age, there is very little room left for the voices of tribal elderly to tell their own reflexions on old age and experiences of ageing. A lack of scientific, public and media transmitted communication about old age and ageing of the actual, real persons, support numerous stereotypes, prejudices, and fatalistic, but also unrealistically affirmative perspectives of old age and needs of the older persons. There are also "apocalyptical" standpoints that treat old age as a social problem as well as media transmitted images that support a distorted conception of old age (and process of ageing) as "deviance from normalcy" (Hurd, 2011). Such, more or less explicit ageist approaches and contents suggest that "youth is good, desirable, and beautiful; old age is bad, repulsive, and ugly" (Hurd, 2011). In line with the discourse of humanist and social gerontology, that does not ignore the voices of older persons but, on the contrary, insists on the "interpretation and self-actualization" (Cruikshank, 2009), we would like to grasp thoroughly the real experience, feelings and reflexions of older persons – individual above and below 60 years of age. To achieve that, we posed a direct question: What is the old age for you? An analysis showed that there was no unanimous or dominant understanding of old age. Relationship towards old age depends to the largest extent on an entire life experience, including primarily personal biographic material, but also observation and critical evaluation of other people's lives and destinies. Following Zeman and Zeman (2015), we observed four basic types of old age interpretations from the position of research participants: fatalistic, affirmative, stoical and relativistic. Fatalistic standpoint supports the most widely spread narrative of old age as a loss and decline, dealing mainly with motives of illness and pain, weakness, loss of beauty and strength, accumulated fatigue, senility, dependency/loss of independency and definite end of life. In the context of this narrative an (older) person functions as a frail protagonist drawn by cruel lines of force and merciless physical and mental processes beyond her or his power. In that sense, for a respondent, old age is primarily connected to infirmity and loss: "Weakness. I often say old age is cruel, one looses beauty, looses teeth, looses hair, external appearance..." (*Asur*, Female, 64 years). Diametrically opposed to fatalistic is affirmative standpoint of ageing and old age. It is a standpoint that in old age see a new life opportunity, a new phase and a new quality of life can be seen. Advocates of this standpoint decide to look beyond limiting factors that are insisted on by fatalists, concentrating primarily on: freedom of existential worries they were occupied with while living active life, new qualities that are enriched their personalities and attitude towards external world – accumulated experience, wisdom, maturity, peace of mind/calmness and objectivity. Of course, here an emphasis has been made on the awareness of the need to find new interests (or renewing of some old ones), and, generally, old age is considered as a period of opening to new opportunities and finding new strength. This perspective is amazingly synthesized by reflection of another respondent, according to whom old age is "A collected wisdom of life, because this what I was telling you before, you draw some lessons from each of these years – if you want them" (*Oraon*, Female, 62 years). As antique stoicism required a life in accordance with nature and sense and inner peace as a result of accepting life circumstances, so do the examinees that share a perspective that we named stoical, see old age experienced and understood as a normal and unavoidable, natural phase of life, outcome of which is a peaceful and relatively relaxed attitude towards getting old. It seems that "necessity awareness" reconciles expectations with real situation and in so far relieve of needless frustration and excessive fear. Such an attitude is perfectly illustrated by Mr. Birsa's answer to our basic question: "What is the old age for you?". "It is a natural thing like day and night, drought and flood, hot and cold.... What else can it be?" (*Santal*, Male, 69 years). According to relativism that claims that nothing exists neither in absolute, nor in necessary terms, the examinees who take relativistic standpoint incline towards the statement that quality of somebody's old age depends to the largest extent on how a person will relate to this life period. This statement also implies a freedom of choice of the way of looking at actual life conditions and life in general: "My Grandfather, aged 71 years still working two hours daily in the agricultural field but I can't. It's a period of life. And how somebody experiences it, that's how it is for that person" (*Bhuinya*, Male, 32 years). It should be pointed out that, speaking about these four basic ways of understanding of old age, we deal with analytic constructions that arose through clarifying abundant empirical material collected from our examinees. Like ideal types of Max Weber, these forms of understanding old age (and life in general) appear sometimes in relatively pure state, but sometimes they come with more or less "admixture" of other standpoints... The only exception here being fatalistic view, that considerably complicates taking of more positive and more active attitude towards life by its passive-defensive character.

Out of the studied sample of elderly from the selected communities, both men and women were interviewed, the age range of the respondents varied from 60 to 73 years old. As to education, 99% cannot sign. But working with an aged population in the tribal area is to experience the wealth of diversified experiences and meanings. The daily contact with them is translated into an exchange of knowledge and the wealth of reports of a multiplicity of cases. We can see proud in them and they seldom think about old age as a negative moment in their life story. Old age arrived unperceived in subjects' life, was legitimated with the old age pension, which was uncommon among them. This perception becomes relevant because chronology specific elderly policy act as an agent that sensitizing unconsciously the fatalistic interpretation of old age among the tribals. Tribal people contemplates 'elderly' as the consequence of process of 'ageing' that should not be limited or restricted within a particular phase of life. Elderly is perceived not as merely a social-cultural attributes but physical and mental changes assimilated among the members that reflect the characteristics of an elder person. Hereby, the perception of elderly has been interpreted through two ways. One is the perception of elderly among youth and among the aged (sixty years and above).

Tribal Elderly and Social Well-Being

Everywhere the human cycle begins with dependency of the young on those who are older; and it ends, if late in life, with dependency of the old on those who are younger-and with both dependencies deeply rooted in kith and kin. With rare exceptions, and despite potentials for strife and tension, family relationships are more intimate, responsibilities more reciprocal, and personal ties more long-lasting than in any other association shared generally by human beings. To anthropologists, a tribal society is an uncentralized grouping of autonomous local communities linked by common cultural features and associations. These social entities are connected by kin-based organizations such as clan, or associations based on age grading or special activities such as ritual, which cross-cut kinship and territorial boundaries (Haviland, 2000). Households tend to be egalitarian, having relatively equal access to available material and social resources, although there can be significant differences based on gender and age. Tribal communities typically have an economic base in horticulture or animal herding, although foraging and hunting in rich environments sometimes supports this kind of socio-political organization. In such small scale, kin-focused societies, passage through the life span allows the accumulation of social debt and cultural knowledge that forms the basis of respect and support of older adults. In such cultural settings, the wide embrace of family frequently provides what Andrei Simic calls a life-term arena —a stable setting for the engagement of an entire life. The lack of economic specialization through a division of labor tends to enable people of all ages to link their changing abilities and knowledge to the varied tasks over the annual work cycle. There are two important effects from this that are common in tribal societies. First, work groups are often age heterogeneous, and second, these arrangements facilitate the learning of new work skills as one passes through the life cycle (Halperin, 1987).

The construct of a stage of elderhood or of later adulthood appears to exist in all tribal societies and is largely based on combining social and functional definitions of one's place in the life cycle. Often there is a distinction between elderhood as a marker of social maturity in relation to others in the community contrasted to boundaries of old age that can take some of the criteria of elderhood and combine them with how a person's physical being and behavior reflects the biological aging process. Elderhood on the one hand is a relative status marker, accomplished by passing through ritual transitions, and is not necessarily tied to extended chronological years. Persons who do not pass these ritual markers will not be considered elders no matter what their age. Older adulthood on the other hand links changes in the person's physical being (reduction of work capacity, beginning of menopause) with social changes (such as the birth of grandchildren) to create a culturally defined sense of oldness, which like elderhood, can have various gradations that can even extend beyond the point of death. The first notion of old age typically begins in tribal societies between the fourth and fifth decades of life, with a change in social/economic role being the most common beginning marker (Glascock and Feinman, 1981). Factors such as invalid status and senility are quite rare as primary indicators of a general designation of old, since tribal culture begins using such labels before such changes are likely. However, many tribal societies also recognize those truly ancient adults who show sharp declines in functional skills as a different category of old, which may lead to a dramatic loss of status and even neglect and actions that hasten a person's death (Glascock, 1997).

There is also a growing global interest in the promotion of wellbeing as an objective of public policy (Stiglitz, et al., 2009). A growing body of knowledge furthers our understanding of the subjective well-being of the general population and with this increase in understanding is a concomitant increase in interest in the subjective well-being of subcategories of the population such as the aged. Though well-being varies over the life span, it often does so in a manner that common sense would not predict. Findings show elderly persons to be generally more satisfied with their lives than other age groups (Herzog, et al., 1982), to worry less, except in regard to health (Campbell, 1981), and to evidence less negative affect (Zautra, 1983) and depression (Radloff, 1977). The stereotypes of older age as a period of decline in the quality of life do not hold up. In speaking of elderly persons, as with any large social category, we must interject a note of caution, for they are a heterogeneous group. As Blau insightfully points out, structural factors such as education, ethnicity, employment, and marital status mediate the effects of age upon physical and mental health and self-conception (Blau, 1981). In order to develop a more precise understanding of well-being among elderly persons, we need to focus upon particular aged populations and the psychosocial factors that influence their well-being.

Attributes of Wellbeing: Tribal Elderly Perspectives

The data from the FGDs generated different themes of wellbeing that can be categorized under three broad categories namely emotional, socio economic and health. The participants of each community were randomly divided into groups of four, irrespective of gender. All discussions and interviews took place at the community setting. The participants of each small group, facilitated by the researcher and a translator, discussed their needs freely, using both hindi and traditional language. The responses elicited during the small group discussions were followed up with individual interviews to explore certain issues that had emerged. Each small group discussion lasted an average of 30 minutes while the individual interviews lasted fifteen to twenty minutes each. The subjects responded to a variety of issues affecting their lives, namely health, finance, marriage, family support, housing etc.

Emotional

This category included themes of loneliness/isolation, sexuality/love/marriage, lifestyle/ behaviour and respect/dignity. These are discussed below.

Loneliness/isolation

A significant difference of opinion is observed between PVTG and SDT respondents in terms of degree of loneliness. Most of the participants of PVTG, who stayed with their children and grandchildren complained of being lonely most of the time. They explained that during the day their children were at work and when they came back from work they were either too tired to socialize with them or they went out for leisure. This dilemma is explained by the following quotation:

> 'I stay with my son who is married and have 8-year-old son. Both my son and daughter in law move out of the village every day to work as laborer in a construction site. Grandson now started to attend school. I am left in the house, for the entire day and await the arrival of my grandson from his school.' (*Lodha*, Female, 68 years)

> 'I am widow and have two married sons. Both sons work in the mine as labour and stay there with their family. I cannot even prepare meals for myself. I depend on meals from the residential school of the village, where I used to clean the room of the teacher' (*Asur*, Female, 62 years)

Those who are widowed miss the companionship they had with their late spouses, as when their partners were alive it was easy for them to engage in discussions of interest and of relevance to both. They mentioned that the spouses show love and they care for each other and provide good interaction, as one participant said:

> "I really miss my wife; we used to talk about a lot of issues and laugh. It is difficult to talk with children because they are rarely at home and in addition do not enjoy the topics that we old people like". (*Juang*, Male, 66 years)

During the FGD it was found that majority of the earning member of the PVTG communities work as a wage labourer away from the village while SDTs remain in the village to continue agricultural operation.

> 'During the cultivation season all adult members went to the field except aged female like me. It is difficult to spend whole day doing household work alone' (*Oraon*, Female, 65 years)

> 'My wife died 8 years ago. Earlier I used to visit the crop field every day but at this age it is difficult and spent the time alone in the house. Daughter in law stays in the house but you cannot talk to her all the time!'. (*Santal*, Male, 69 years)

The participants of the study complained of loneliness as well as social and emotional isolation, factors which are supported by the literature (Peplau and Perlman, 1982; Dugan and Kivett, 1994). Some studies reveal interplay of factors as causative factors of loneliness while Dugan and Kivett (1994) showed that changes in loneliness were related to transitional life events like changes in marital status, usually through loss of a spouse and health

Love/ Marriage

The widows felt that it was difficult for them to remarry because they lived with their children and grandchildren, with one mentioning:

> 'We are supposed to be good role models to our children and grandchildren. It becomes difficult to advise them if we do not act as good examples to them'. (*Santal*, Female, 61 years)

They said that marriage was entangling, as one of them explained:

> 'I was 35 years old when my husband died of an accident. Marrying again with a child is not allowed in the community. It means you as a woman moving into another home and if you have children they have to follow you to the new home and this could create a lot of problems. We cannot remarry'. (*Oraon*, Female, 63 years)

The widowers, however, expressed some desire to remarry, but complained of not finding the right partners as one said:

> 'When we try to remarry it is difficult to find the right woman, as most women want only to get married for the sake of money'. (*Bhuiyan*, Male, 62 years)

Those who were married said that life goes on as usual. All the groups, however, agreed that marriage provides better companionship as long as the spouses continue to love and care for each other.

> 'I am now spending more time with my husband than ever before. God Knows! How long we will be able to stay together?' (*Lodha*, Female, 62 years)

As also confirmed by this study, the loss of spouse was the single most important factor contributing to loneliness in later life (Berg et al., 1981; Kivett and Scott, 1979). Revenson (1986) observed greater loneliness among those elderly that never married, or became separated, divorced or widowed than married elderly persons also substantiated through the present findings.

Life Style/ Behaviour

A clear gendered differences is observed in that category where most of the female participant complained the abusive behavior of their husband and son. One of the respondent from *Asur* community expressed that the initiation of mining activities in the area plays an important role in changing lifestyles of the male members of the community

> 'We find it hard to get two square meals a day because my son spends most of his earnings for foreign liquor. It is easier to arrange foreign liquor than drinking water. Mining company transformed the lifestyle of new generation' (*Asur*, Female, 62 years)

In patriarchal societies like *Oraon* and *Bhuinya*, violence is used by men to control women, to suppress the latter's rebellion and resistance to male domination, and to enforce the differential status of men and women that have traditionally been translated into laws and customs, in order to serve collective interests of men. This unequal distribution of power between the sexes has resulted in a society that is dominated by men and that most women occupy subordinate positions of power, increasing their vulnerability to violence, especially within the family. One of the respondent stated that abusive behavior by men is a socially accepted behavior that cannot be changed,

> 'My husband used to abuse me every day in the evening in intoxicated condition, my son is repeating the same behavior with his wife. We are habituated with that behavior and it appears normal to us' (*Oraon*, Female, 62 years)

On the contrary, many men unlike women complaining of their spouses denying them their conjugal rights. Many explained that the presence of grandchildren was interference because in most cases, the elderly women shared their beds with their grandchildren. The elderly men therefore view their elderly wives as sexless. Elderly women are stereotyped as having lost their sexual appeal.

> 'Man remain man till he dies but women lost her appeal after forty years'. (*Santal*, Male, 60 years).

Respect and Dignity

Lack of attention and respect from the family and community is the reason most frequently given by participants in the interviews for the low wellbeing of older people. Most participants are of the view that older people need love, understanding and respect. They believe that a cordial supportive family environment brings happiness to older persons. The elderly people complained of the disrespectful behavior by the young generation, as one said:

> 'We never used to smoke and drink the way our children and grandchildren do. It was rare to see a youth to smoke and drink in the village, but nowadays things have changed. Children have the freedom to do what they want'. (*Oraon*, Male, 62 years).

Most of the participants blamed the intergenerational gap in culture and the urban influence for changing behavior of youth, thus resulting in the elderly losing their respect and dignity. Family relations are said to be the most important and salient social relationships in the life of older persons. One participant commented:

> 'I feel happy when I get attention and respect from children and grandchildren'. (*Santal*, Male, 65 years).
>
> 'Each child wants to live the way they want. If you try and intervene by suggesting that this is not the way we should live and treat each other, the children either ignore you or they tell you to mind your own business. Further, the problem is compounded by our dependency on the children both financially and materially. Our children do not respect us as it used to be in the olden days. Those olden days are gone for good". (*Juang*, Male, 70 years).

Respect by close kin is important for individual wellbeing across the lifespan but may be of particular importance in later life when occupational, economic, functional, and health challenges increase. Given links between cultural expectations of love, bonding, solidarity and family affiliation, the family, in particular, appears to be an important source of life satisfaction and wellbeing for aging adults.

Socio-Economic

Family Connectedness

Elderly tribal perceives the well-being as non-materialistic and obvious part of life satisfaction especially at the later phase of one's life. Being an elder member of the community or family they expect special priority by the family member and community members too. A bit mental frustration devours the elder person as they became incapable individual in family but still want to conduct the light works, taken care of the grand-children and go for grazing of the domestic animals. Even, actively taking part in the cultural and ritual programme (community level), teaching the cultural and moral values, telling moral stories to grand-children (family level). They indicated that this makes one's life happy and fulfilling. This is what some of the respondents had to say:

> 'I am happy enough. I have no problem except the pain that I often feel at my right leg. I have two sons and one daughter and each of them got married and capable of securing their livelihood. What else do I need? And, now I have two grandsons and one granddaughter. I am the responsible person for taking care of my grandchildren when all of them go for work outside the home. I share my old stories and other interesting moral stories to my grandchildren that make them astonished and absorbed. My sons love and respect me very much. (*Santal,* Female, 64 years).

The attributes such as secured livelihood, grandchildren, shared emotions, respect and love emerged as the principle aspects of family connectedness. The elder members are free to do anything that indicates the acceptance of elder member at the family instead of burden. The elder member is not forced within their choice as the majority of family members agreed that elderly is the last phase of life where, the elder members are allowed to have rest and enjoy their life according to their own choices.

> 'I am independent and I do not want to be associated in the financial matters of my family. I just want to have food in time, take rest and enjoy the community events, when occurred. And, I just want to go through like this in my remaining life." (*Lodha*, Male, 68 years).

However, it was found that some of the elderly individual of Asur community do work at the local schools as sweeper and earn money. Even the family members are allowed them to work and never force their old members to share the income for family expenditure.

> 'Yes! I do work in the school at evening specially to clean the surrounding areas. I get Rs. 350 monthly remunerations for this and I never share this to my family. I do spend it for my personal purpose especially buying cloths and *Bidi*. However, I spend the earnings for my granddaughter.' (*Asur* , Female, 62 years).

> 'I cannot do any work. I just take rest. My family members love me so much. They care me and consider my decision at the family level. (*Oraon*, Male, 63 years).

From respondents' perspectives, family connectedness could also be seen as having leisure time with family and giving a helping hand in taking care of others within the family. These bring about cohesion and unity that last.

Social Support

Most of the participants acknowledged the support they got from their children and immediate members of the family like brothers and sisters and sometimes from the neighbours. This support was mainly in the form of domestic chores, financial, material and transport, as one said:

> 'They do provide me with financial support. It is usually not enough but at least it is there. Sometimes it is difficult to get all you want at once because they have to manage their lives as well'. (*Oraon*, Male, 63 years).

The tribals are usually responsive in nature about the social status of the elder people. Community members recognize the elderly individual as valuable resource for the community especially in coping disaster and during communal worship. One of the youth narrate that,

> 'Elders are the most respected member in our village. Though they are physically weak and cannot participate in economic activities but their life experiences and knowledge especially on community rituals is much crucial for us. We do consult them whenever we are going to have any kind of decisions in critical situation because we think they have already encountered those situations earlier. (*Lodha*, Male, 43 years).

Some narrative shows that, in terms of resource and information control, only certain types of control, particularly administration, rituals and consultation, correlate with beneficent treatment of the elderly.

> 'During *Sarna* worship, we all elderly receive exceptional treatment like special seating arrangement, special food and dress. During name giving ceremony, eldest member of the family irrespective of gender have the right to name the child.' (*Santal*, Male, 65 years)

Some community members also help the elderly in the form of transport and visits in times of illness, as one said:

> 'When you have not been seen for a day or so some members of the community come to check on you and if you are very ill they do arrange transport to take you to the hospital'. (*Juang*, Female, 62 years).

Wilkin (1987) offers a useful definition of dependency as, "a state in which an individual is reliant upon others for assistance in meeting recognized needs". Clearly this is the prevailing situation in studied community where the elderly who participated in this study were dependent on their children or grandchildren. Even those who were married and staying alone were dependent on financial and material support from their children or grandchildren, because they no longer had a source of income of their own.

Spiritual Connectedness

Respondents described spiritual connectedness as having a strong relationship with supernatural forces and fully participating in religious activities. Some respondents indicated that they visit village temple or village deity almost every day that give them a feel of peace. They also conduct moral classes for the village youth citing examples of their ancestor. Some respondents had this to say:

> 'Spending time with God is my social connection. I am so happy that in spite of the fact that I cannot walk properly, I am very happy to be in *Sarna sthal*, which is a kilometer away from my house. The tranquility of the place make you feel that you are with your ancestor'. (*Santal*, Male, 61 years)
>
> 'I wish Karma festival to happen every day so that I can be with my friends, laugh, converse, encourage one another, and also gain more connections and privileges when coming to the place of rituals.' (*Oraon*, Male, 64 years)

The most important thing for respondents was to be fellowshipping with one another during community festivals and enjoying each other's company. In this, they found a sense of spiritual connectedness and a strong factor for their longevity. Sharing the Word of God with others as well as participating in religious activities served as the most important connection to the elderly.

Income/ Authority

The participants who receive pensions from government schemes seems to be happier than the other. It was also found that respondents' role as family head or their participation in decision making body of the community correlate strongly with the subjective wellbeing.

> 'Old age pension is necessary for the person like me to maintain the authority in the family otherwise nobody will value us as dependent' (*Juang*, Female, 64 years)

> 'My son considers me as a source of income because I am the beneficiary of widow pension' (*Bhuinya*, Female, 62 years)

It is emerged from the above narratives that pension not only give financial security but also the authority at the family level. One of the respondent explained the benefit of being old,

> 'Old age, when it come, is good for certain things. At old age you get the special status in the society. I am one of the member of village panchayat. It is a huge responsibility and everyone obey me because of my status.' (*Santal*, Male, 66 years).

Therefore, we can understand that old age is a complex process of changes in people's life path. Every context has its particularities which will change the life style of each and every one.

Health

Almost all older persons agreed that good health is their top priority, that enjoying physical mobility is necessary for their self-esteem, and that if they can maintain good health they are sure to be happy. This applies to older people of all ages, both sexes, all communities and place of residence. It can be concluded therefore that, in respect of health all older people in the study belong to the same homogeneous group.

Mobility

Most of the participants said that they were in good health despite having chronic respiratory problem, arthritis, hearing impairment and visual defects. The major difficulty, which was highlighted, was accessibility to health facilities. Transport was cited as one of the problems leading to difficulties in accessing health care facilities. Habitation of the PVTGs are mostly found in the hilly and forested areas that creates impediments for the elderly section to access health centre. Participants cited overcrowding at hospitals and standing in long queues is difficult for them, as one said:

> "We have to queue for a long time to see a doctor and sometimes medicine is not available". (*Asur*, Male, 64 years)

For many, decreased physical capacities in later life likely explain the decline in mobility, since activity limitations are found to have greater impact later in life. As an older woman stated:

> '... not everybody has the type of energy you need to go, to reach out to others, to do all these kinds of things. Some

> people are just, have so many interior problems, that they really can't.' (*Juang*, Female, 63 years)

All the studied location suffers from lack of public transport. People have to walk atleast five kilometer to reach the point to get public transport. Some respondents said that they were able to walk for over a hundred metres without serious problems, though slowly. One said:

> 'Though I do not go very far I am able to walk around the house and visit my neighbours. I do not walk very fast but at least I am able to walk on my own and do what I want in the house without overburdening my children'. (*Oraon*, Female, 63 years)

> 'My shoulder ached and my knees ached sometimes'. Even it is difficult to carry out regular domestic chores' (*Santal*, Female, 68 years)

It is apparent from the above narratives that the persons who felt old reported physical changes, mainly difficulty in walking and moving around impact their wellbeing.

Supporting aid

Another area of concern arises from the non-availability of assistive devises such as spectacles and hearing aids. Most of the elderly use walking aids which they manufacture from the branch of a tree that lasts hardly six months. Assistive devices were not obtainable anywhere in study area.

> 'I am depending on the walking stick for the last five years. After every six months I have to request my son to make a fresh one.' (*Bhuiyan*, Male, 63 years)

Those elderly persons who had spectacles said that the nearest place where they could obtain spectacles, although expensive, was from town which is about 30 kilometres away.

> 'I had an eye operation three years back organized by a voluntary agency through mobile eye checkup facility. They provide me spectacle but now it is not in a good condition.' (*Asur*, Male, 66 years)

They suggested the establishment of mobile services which could provide assistive aid. In a study by Ferreira and Charlton (1992), health was ranked first as a factor affecting the quality of life of the elderly people.

Functional Activities

All the participants mentioned that they did not experience any difficulties in activities of daily living such as bathing, eating, dressing, walking and use of the toilet. They noticed, however, that they were slow in some of these activities. Over half of the participants expressed having difficulties in doing one or two of their chores. Ploughing was cited as the most cumbersome for male and fetching water for female as the following quotations illustrated:

> 'I have lost the strength to plough the crop field'. (*Santal*, Male, 68 years)

> 'Earlier I used to fetch water from the spring which is located two kilometers downhill from my house. Now I find it difficult to carry a pot of water from the borewell located 100 metres away' (*Asur*, Female, 66 years)

The issue of reduced functional activities in old age is recognized by participants generally. Some of the participants seems redolent in expressing their activities of youth age that they cannot do at the later phase of life,

> I have lost my ability to swim in river or climb a tree, catch fish from the stream or hunt a wild pig....Ah! what a life that was? (*Lodha*, Male, 68 years).

The feeling of reduced functional activity not only make them unhappy but reiterating their past activities make them happy also.

Recreation

Recreation plays an important role in enhancing the quality of life of the tribal elderly. Majority of the respondents expressed that community festival and community centre is instrumental in reducing social disconnectedness. Every elderly usually visits the community centre to make them relax and meet the peers. As expressed by the respondents,

> '*Chabutra* (community meeting place) is a place where we meet every day to know about different information about the village or the region. It is the place where I find the people of my age group who understand each other'. (*Oraon*, Male, 68 years).

> 'I love to sing and dance. You cannot do it every day but during community festival we get that opportunity'. (*Juang*, Male, 64 years)

The participants expected to be involved in activities which would reduce their boredom. They realized later that the facilities, which were available at the village, were inadequate to provide the recreation, as one of them said:

> "Most of the time we come and sit around and do nothing. We need a place to be developed specifically for recreation so that we can learn to something to keep us active. We would like to participate in sewing and knitting". (*Santal*, Female, 62 years)
>
> 'Community pond earmarked for village women is an important place of recreation. We can enjoy our time without the interference of men'. (*Bhuiyan*, Female, 60 years).
>
> 'I await the day of weekly *haat* that held every Thursday in our village. People from different villages came and I got the opportunity to meet the outsider'. (*Asur*, Male, 63years).

The impression was that the tribal elderly rarely visits outside the village due to inaccessibility and find solace in the opportunity available within the community settings. Recreational activities are said to be important for the elderly people in helping them to 'enjoy' life and endure morbidity (Borgono 1989). It is well documented in the literature that healthy ageing could be influenced by a lot of factors such as interacting with others, participating in a lot of developmental tasks and feeling of worth that one is part of a developing society (Alvarez 1995; Ebersole and Hess 1990; Svanborg and Selker 1993). The elderly can influence and direct certain decision-making processes and hence be involved in the problem-solving process.

Conclusion

The findings of this study are similar to those of other studies (Berg et al., 1981; Borgono, 1989; Dugan and Kivett, 1994; Ferreira and Charlton, 1995; Hampson, 1995). The economic situation of these elderly is closely related to the changes taking place in the social conditions of society. Findings of this study supported the United Nations' description that social connectedness of the elderly is related to social involvement, social assistance, and social linkages, as well as enhancing the strength and health of the elderly (UN, 2013). Findings are also consistent with Thomas, et al. (2010), who explained social connectedness as a multifaceted and interconnected concept that has many different parts. The respondents of the current study described social connectedness as being responsible for relationships that give meaning to their lives. In their views, the quality of the relationship is important because the number of times one has the opportunity to meet with loved ones and spend quality time with them is to be considered. The pension which some of them receive is not adequate to meet most of their basic requirements but it does give sense of security among the elderly. Another very important issue is the interdependence of these categories. For instance, health is dependent on economic security, while care is dependent on the security of the household. Other issues that emerged from this study were loneliness, isolation, respect, dignity, health care, function, family and community support and recreation. It can, therefore, be inferred that, if the elderly is socially well connected, their quality of life will improve, and they can enjoy their old age. Active and healthy ageing could be promoted with greater participation of the elderly in income generating activities, greater participation within the community and better care giving within the family.

Acknowledgements

We gratefully thank Indian Council of Social Science Research (ICSSR), New Delhi for financial support under Major Research Project Scheme.

References

Alvarez TJ. 1995. The elderly are a potential resource. *World Health Forum*. 16: 361

Annandale E. 2014. *The Sociology of Health and Medicine: A Critical Introduction* (2nd ed.), Cambridge, UK: Polity Press.

Beck AH. 2004. The Flexner report and the standardization of American medical education. *Journal of the American Medical Association*. 291: 2139–2140.

Belsky DW, Caspi A, Houts R, Cohen HJ, CorcoranDL, Danese A, Harrington H, Israel S, Levine ME, Schaefer JD. 2015. Quantification of biological aging in young adults. *Proceedings of the National Academy of Sciences of the United States of America*. 112: 4104-4110.

Berg S, Mellstrom D, Persson G, Svanborg A. 1981. Loneliness in the Swedish aged. *Journal of Gerontology*. 36: 342-349.

Blau Z. 1981. *Aging in a Changing Society*. New York: Franklin Watts.

Borgono MJ. 1989. Old people should be seen as a distinct group with special social, cultural and health needs. *World Health Forum*. 10: 311.

Campbell A. 1981. *The Sense of Well-Being in America*. New York: McGraw-Hill.

Cruikshank, M. 2009. *Learning to be Old. Gender, Culture, and Aging.* Lanham, Boulder, New York, Toronto, Plymouth, UK: Rowman and Littlefield Publishers, Inc.

Dugan E, Kivett VR. 1994. The importance of Emotional and Social isolation to loneliness among very old rural adults. *Gerontologist.* 34: 340-346.

Ebersole P, Hess P. 1990. *Towards healthy aging.* St Louis: Mosby.

Engel GL. 1977. The need for a new medical model: A challenge for biomedicine. *Science.* 196: 129–136.

Ferreira M, Charlton K. 1995. Aging inequalities in South Africa. *World Health Forum,* 16: 268-270.

Flexner A. 1910. *Medical Education in the United States and Canada.* Washington, DC: Science and Health Publications.

Glascock A, Feinman S. 1981. *Social Asset or Social Burden: Treatment of the Aged in Non-Industrial Societies. In* C. Fry (ed.), Dimensions: Aging, Culture and Health. New York: Praeger.

Glascock A. 1997. *When Killing is Acceptable: The Moral Dilemma Surrounding Assisted Suicide in America and Other Societies. In* J. Sokolovsky (ed.), The Cultural Context of Aging: World-Wide Perspectives, 2d ed. Westport, Conn.: Bergin and Garvey.

Glenn ND, Weaver CN. 1979. A note on family situation and global happiness. *Social Forces.* 57: 960–967.

Hampson J. 1995. Threats to health and wellbeing in Africa. *World Health Forum.* 16: 359–360.

Haviland W. 2000. Anthropology, 9th ed. New York: Harcourt.

Herzog AR, W Rogers, J Woodworth. 1982. *Subjective Well-Being among Different Age Groups.* Ann Arbor, MI: Survey Research Center, Institute for Social Research, University of Michigan.

Hurd CL. 2011. *Facing Age. Women Growing Older in Anti-Aging Culture.* Lanham, Boulder, New York, Toronto, Plymouth, UK: Rowman and Littlefield Publishers, Inc.

Kivett VR, Scott JP. 1979. The rural by-passed elderly: Perspectives on status and needs (The Caswell Study). Raleigh, NC: Agricultural Research Service, Bulletin No. 260.

Lindau ST, Schumm P, Laumann EO, Levinson W, O'Muircheartaigh CA, Waite LJ. 2007. A national study of sexuality and health among older adults in the U.S. *New England Journal of Medicine.* 357: 762–774.

Lowsky DJ, Olshansky SJ, Bhattacharya J, Goldman DP. 2014. Heterogeneity in healthy aging. Journals of Gerontology, Series A: *Biological Sciences and Medical Sciences.* 69: 640–649.

Martin P, Kelly N, Kahana B, Kahana E, Willcox BJ, Willcox DC, Poon LW. 2015. Defining successful aging: A tangible or elusive concept? *Gerontologist*. 55: 14–25.

Peplau LA, Perlman D (eds.) 1982. *Loneliness, a sourcebook of current theory, research and therapy.* New York: Wiley.

Radloff L. 1977. The CES-D Scale: A Self-Report Depression Scale for Research in the General Population. *Applied Psychological Measurement*. I: 385-401.

Revenson TA. 1986.*Debunking the myth of loneliness in late life. In* Seidman E and Rappaport J (eds). Redefining social problems. New York: Plenum Press, pp 115–135

Rowe JW, Kahn RL. 1997. Successful aging. *Gerontologist*. 37: 433–440

Rowe JW, Kahn RL. 1998. Successful aging. *Aging (Milano)*. 10: 142–144.

Rowe JW. 1990. *Toward successful aging: Limitation of the morbidity associated with "normal" aging.In* W.R. Hazzard (Ed.), Principles of Geriatric Medicine and Gerontology (2nd ed.,). New York: McGraw-Hill, pp. 138–141

Ryff C, Singer B. 1998. The contours of positive health. *Psychological Inquiry*. 9:1-28.

Starr P. 1982. *The Social Transformation of American Medicine: The Rise of a Sovereign Profession and the Making of a Vast Industry*. New York: Basic Books.

Silverman, F. 1987. *The Elderly as Modern Pioneers*. Bloomington, Ind.: Indiana University Press.

Stevens R. 1971. *American Medicine and the Public Interest*. New Haven, CT: Yale University Press.

Stiglitz JE, Sen A, Fitoussi JP. 2009. *Report by the Commission on the Measurement of Economic Performance and Social Progress*. www.stiglitz-sen-fitoussi.fr.

Svanborg A, Selker L. 1993. Postponement of aging-related disability. *World Health Forum*. 14:150-157

Tausig M. 1982. Measuring Life Events. *Journal of Health and Social Behavior*. 23: 52-64.

Thomas S, Lewis S, Browning C. 2010. Social connectedness and musculoskeletal conditions: A review of the literature. Retrieved from http://arrow.monash.edu.au /hdl/1959.1/497884

United Nations. 2010. *Current status of the social situation, wellbeing, participation in development and rights of older persons worldwide*. United Nations Human Rights Office of the High Commissioner.

Vate V. 2005. *Maintaining Cohesion Through Rituals: Chukchi Herders and*

Hunters,a People of the Siberian Arctic. In Kazunobu Ikeya and Elliott Fratkin (eds.),Pastoralists and their Neighbors in Asia and Africa.Senri Ethnological Studies No. 69. Osaka: National Museum of Ethnology.

Waite LJ. 2005. *Marriage and family.In* D. Poston and M. Micklin (Eds.), Handbook of Population. Boston: Springer, pp. 87–108

Wilkin D. 1987. Conceptual problems in dependency research. *Social Science Medicine.* 24 :867-73.

Yang YC, McClintock MK, Kozloski M, Li T. 2013. Social isolation and adult mortality: The role of chronic inflammation and sex differences. *Journal of Health and Social Behavior.* 54: 183–203.

Yang YC, Schorpp K, Harris KM. 2014. Social support, social strain and inflammation: Evidence from a national longitudinal study of U.S. adults. *Social Science and Medicine.* 107: 124–135.

Zautra AJ. 1983. Social Resources and Quality of Life. *American Journal of Community Psychology.* 11: 275-290.

Zeman Z, MG Zeman. 2015. Young heart in old body: Experiences of ageing from older persons' perspectives. *Etnoloska Tribina.* 45:72-85.

ABSTRACT

Chapter Seven

POVERTY AND HEALTH: A STUDY AMONG THE ASUR COMMUNITY OF JHARKHAND

ABHIJIT GHOSAL AND MANOJ RAUL

The poor are more vulnerable to health hazards, economic down-turns, natural catastrophes, and even human-made violence than any other group. Shocks such as illness, injury, and loss of livelihood have dreadful impacts, and are significant causes of poverty. The present study was conducted among the vulnerable (PVTG) community of Asur of Bishunpur block in the Gumla district of Jharkhand. This study mainly focuses on the poverty and health system and how to inter-related to this both from the poorest people of the Asur community. This study observed that due to poorness, the studied populations could not go for better treatments because they have not the proper money and sources of income for this. This community is so poor that they cannot arrange foods for two times in a day properly. They do the works in mining, migrating labours, and daily labours for the purpose of two-time meals, and due to this work, they have suffered many diseases. They also enable crops only during the rainy season, but it is not sufficient for their food needs. Due to this, they are suffering nutritionally unhealthy and many health-related effects. They do not say and consider themselves miserable because of their vulnerability in socially, culturally, and psychologically. But yet, the government and NGOs are trying to develop their livelihoods and health-related practice, and other socio-economic development activities.

Keywords: *Poverty, Health, Asur, PVTG.*

INTRODUCTION

The health sector and related problems need special attention in the context of tribal communities. The tribal communities in general and primitive tribal groups, in particular, are highly disease-prone. The tribals in India have distinctive health problems depending on their habitat, rugged terrains, and ecological conditions. In our country, the health issues of the tribals have not been given timely priority, which has been further compounded by their poverty, illiteracy, ignorance about causes of diseases, hostile environment, blind beliefs, poor sanitation, lack of safe drinking water, lack of personal, hygiene and health education. Poverty and poor health throughout the world are inextricably linked with each other. The leading causes behind poor health for millions globally are rooted in political, social, and economic injustices. Behind poor health, debt is both a reason and an outcome. Poverty enhances the chances of poor health and, vice-versa, weak health traps communities in poverty. Infectious and neglected tropical diseases kill and weaken millions of the poorest and most vulnerable people each year. The study people of PVTG Asur community one of the very much most impoverished tribal communities of Jharkhand. But, they do not believe they are poor because they didn't give importance to money. Otherwise, they are not interested in education and literacy. Still recently, some of the Asur children are interested in education through the motivating of the nearest Jobhipat residential school and some NGOs work. The reduced income, low literacy, and daily food collection are the challenging issues of this communitys lives and life.

In a report entitled 'Community Involvement in health Development: Challenging Health Services' (1991) published by theWorld Health Organisation (WHO) argues that health will be best served if (1) People from a community – village, neighbourhood, or cultural or socio-economic grouping – take part in planning and implementing their health care, and (2) health systems are oriented towards preventive and primary rather than curative and specialty health care. In the context of health issue, it is argued that the social concept has "added potential for illuminating processes which link determining social structures-like income distribution, policies, local resources- to individual outcomes, and structures to the agency, or for clarifying our understanding of health inequalities and the role of place" (Cattell, 2001). Chambers (1995) brings forth lesser discussed dimensions of poverty and deprivation, such as vulnerability, isolation, and powerlessness, and proposed widening the definition to include these disadvantages as well. According to Anand and Sen (1997), poverty is now known as a multi-dimensional issue whose dimensions aggregate to holistic wellbeing. Anand and Sen stated that, "The need for a multi-dimensional view of poverty and deprivation guides the search for an adequate indicator of human poverty." The expansion of poverty definition to look beyond deprivation of food and income has been welcomed by researcher.

Objectives

1. To understand about community and poverty relation of Asur people.
2. To understand peoples perception of interrelation between poverty and health issues.
3. To identified diseases and how they were controlling.
4. To study about agency role of their health-related issues.

Methodology

The research has followed the scheduled method to collect family information and details. The study followed door-to-door interviews and also understood poverty and health-related issues for the arising question in our mind while talking both we and our informant to discuss relevant data collection. The overall data analyzed with demographically, narrative discourse, and case study based. And the area is selected based on purposively.

About the Community and Area

The research work has been conducted among the Asur community of Sakhuyapani village under the Gumla district of Jharkhand. The Asur is the PVTG tribal group in India. They are lived in the hill-forest area in Jharkhand. As per the 2011 census, the tribe has a population of around 23,000 in Latehar and Gumla districts. In the community, 50 percent of the population could barely speak in Asur language; they are not fluent in the language. According to C. Roy, Asur passed from Neolithic through the equivalent of copper, bronze, and iron ages but not necessarily in strict succession. In Jharkhand found Asur forts and cemeteries. Asura in Sanskrit literature were a pre-Aryan people with magical powers and practical knowledge of metals (Hutton, 1969).

The study area of Sakhuapani village (Forest-hill area) or other Asur villages is known as the Netarhat group of Jharkhand plateaus.

The Netarhat plateau forms the northwest corner of the Chotanagpur plateau. Physically the terrain has been harsh and, in the earlier days, not easy to access. But now, the road and paths wind about over the top of a lofty eminence, locally called as 'pat.' The Netarhat plateau hills are of a nearly uniform height of about 3,600 feet above the sea level and measuring about 485 square miles in the centre of which flows a small stream. The plateau is formed of lateritic rock. It is from these rocks; the Asur is used to extract iron ore for iron smelting. The region taken up for investigation stretches from Narma pat in the northeast to Rajadera in the southwest, mainly covered by hills and forests of Netarhat plateau (Gupta, 1976).

This study covered all families and members of the studied village. All 48 families were covered in this village. And the village population was divided into three broad age groups 0-17, 18-59, and 60 or above years for the purpose of understanding the health condition of child age, adult age and old age. In the age group, between 0-17 years, 63 (19.4%) are males, and 62 (39.1%) are females. While between the age group of 18-59 years, there are a total of 124 (38.8%) people, among which 52 (16.3%) are males, and 72 (22.5%) are females. Females are more than males in this age group. In the age group of 60 and above males are more 37 (11.6%) than females.

Economy, Poverty and Health

Each community, people want to grow their source of income regarding livelihoods according to time and situation. But, this is a big challenge for the Asur community people. Asur community people depend entirely on agriculture, forestry, mining labour, and migration labour to sustain their livelihood pattern.The majority of the family have their basic monthly income in between 3,000 to 5,000 rupees per month (Table 1), which clearly depicts the present economic condition of the community.

Table 1: Profile of village (based on occupation and income)

Variables			Frequency	Percentage
Occupation status	Agriculture		27	8.4
	labour	Mining	45	14.1
		Day labour	13	4.1
		Migration	31	9.7
	Forestry		76	23.8
	Business		3	0.9
	Private service		7	2.2
	Non-working people		118	36.9

Monthly income of total (48) family	10,001 & Above	2	4.2
	7,001-10,000	1	2.1
	5,001-7,000	4	8.3
	3,001-5,000	25	52.1
	Below 3000	16	33.3

A few years back, they depended upon occupations like iron smelting, hunting-gathering, and *Jhum* cultivation to sustain their livelihood. But, at present, they have transformed their food habits and lifestyle occupationally and accordingly. Due to change in their livelihood practices, they are face and suffer from many vital diseases, i.e., cough, viral fever, skin diseases, and blindness. which were unknown. It seems not possible to cure these diseases through their ethno-medicinal practice.

Moreover, block PHC is about 40 km from the village. They have not sufficient money for their proper treatment in the private health centres. On the other hand, there no good communication to reach the PHC and also a lack of doctors and other staff in the PHC. No proper curable medicines are available there. They buy some necessary medicines from outside shops. Since they have impoverished income and economy and thus, they cannot afford costly medicines fees and treatments in this situation. Asur people have more affinity in a give and take and barter exchange facilities between their communities and other nearby communities. They cannot buy their food needs, agriculture equipment, and their treatment due to a lack of money. Therefore, they prefer to go there traditional ethno-medicinal men such as *Ojha, Gunin, Baiydhji* for their treatment. If they get well, they cannot pay money to the ethno-medicinal man, but instead of that they prefer to pay them with rice, pulses, and sometimes they also give hunted animals from the forest to the house of that medicinal man as a cost of treatment.

Nilu Asur and other villagers have to say that-

"We eat what we get? Only God will help us."

Means, Asur community people also collect green leaves, vegetables, and honey except hunting-gathering. But, they mainly sustain their livelihoods on hunting and gathering. Beside this,, they can do agriculture practice only in the rainy season because irrigation facilities are not available. They cannot fulfill their needs and sustain livelihood depending on agriculture. They have the belief that God will arrange something in the forest for their food. Only God will save us.

Shantimoni Asur and her husband Prahlad Asur have to say that-

"They don't know about poverty at all but, the resources we are getting at present hare decreased now."

Money is not their primary needs. Only resource collection is the primary source for them. Therefore, what is poverty? It is tough to say for them. Except for this, they have to say that in earlier could get forest resources, land resources, natural resources, and environmental resources traditionally; they are not getting these things. The numbers of forest animals are decreased, and some are extinct (wild boar, wild buffalo, etc.). While at present, they hunt hens, deer's, rabbits, moose, snakes and ants etc. two or three days per month if maximum village members are present in their village. After cleaning the forest resources, they collect bauxite and irons from that land, and then by their traditional method, after melting; they make the blade, knife, hoes, and axes. But, at present, some companies like Hindalco and Birla have taken that land on lease and doing mining works here. Due to these interferences by the private company, the Asur people are helpless to leave the lands. In natural resources, they are dependent upon spring water. They have divided this spring into many parts for their defecation, bathing, washing, and drinking and agriculture purpose. But, they face many problems regarding water in the summer season. They cannot fulfill their water needs in this season properly.

They think of climates as their environmental resources. During agricultural practices and works in the field, they consider rain as an ecological resource. They calculate the differences between natural resources and ecological resources during this season. So, they have not heard and awarded from their ancestors that natural resources will deplete so high.

Poverty, Health and Food Habit

The kind of food one consumes is directly associated with his health. If a proper diet is not available, it can be lead to malfunctioning of the body and mind. They have not any adequate idea about poverty, but yet due to the unavailability of resources, they are transforming occupation, food habits as well as livelihood practices. These changes in their lifestyle are affecting their health status. Earlier, they used to hunt and gather practices and used to eat the hunted animals after baking in the open fire and also the collected forest products after boiling. But, at the present time, they are cooking foods as modern types like adding spices, oils, salt, mixed some spices etc. Due to this practice; they are suffering from various diseases like acidity, gas, indigestion and so on. Moreover, the people who were working in Hindalco and Birla Companies face skin problems and eye problems like red eyes and eye pain due to heavy iron dust. Some of them have gone blind during works. Asur people have to say that sometimes due to heavy tasks, they get to suffer from headaches, cough, fever, eye pains, and burning. The most important case is that due to the lack of food they take a meal twice only -in the morning and at night. They eat boiled corn, rice, pulse, potato, and gourd vegetables (Papaya, *Nenuya*, and other vegetables). Middle-aged people do not take meals in the morning due to shortage and availability of foods, and they drink traditional *Mahua* wine instead of a morning meal. Maximum people of the village drink *Mahua* wine during appetite and get rid of body pains. Due to the heavy food intake, many of them die aged between 35-50 years old. The major problem which was quite apparent among the children was malnutrition. Though they are getting carbohydrate content from rice but in protein consumption, it is relatively undernourished since they are not taking milk in proper quantity, fish, and other protein items in their regular diet. Besides this, the main cause was their poverty, hence not being able to get proper food; the parents too are careless and ignorant. The children were more malnourished, having a large abdomen, which shows the ideal condition of malnourishment.

Table 2 depicts that pregnant women and 0-5 years of children take meals thrice in a day, i.e., in the morning, noon, and at night. And the rest of the people take meals twice a day in the morning and at night. 6-17 years aged people eat boiled corn, rice, and vegetables. However,people between 15-17 years group themselves intake *Mahua* wine occasionally. The most prominent case is that 18 – 60 and above-aged people, both males and females, take a meal twice in the morning and at night. They drink *Mahua* wine at noon. According to their wish and appetite, the workers and old aged people intake Mahua wines at any time in a day. They intake *Mahua* wine for relaxation and calm down their appetites.

Table 2: Intake of food (age wise)

Age group	Morning	Noon	Night
Pregnant women	Boiled corn, rice, pulses, and vegetables.	Rice, pulses, vegetables.	Boiled corn, rice, pulses, and vegetables.
0-5 years child	Mothers milk, cow milks, boiled corn	Mothers milk, cow milks, boiled corn	Mothers milk, cow milks, boiled corn
6-17 years people	Boiled corn, rice, pulses, and vegetables	Occasionally *Mahua* intake	Boiled corn, rice, pulses, and vegetables
18-59 years people	Boiled corn, rice, pulses, and vegetables, *Mahua*	*Mahua*	Boiled corn, rice, pulses, and vegetables, *Mahua*
60 & above	Boiled corn, rice, pulses, and vegetables, *Mahua*	*Mahua*	Boiled corn, rice, pulses, and vegetables, *Mahua*

Morbidity profile, Common Diseases and Nature of Treatment

It is necessary to take a balanced foods and good work to keep the body healthy. Due to work pressure, modernization and the industrialization process, our health status is degrading day by day. The information gathered from the studied village, PHC, *Anganwadi* centre regarding morbidity profile, was presented in Table 3. It can be seen that intestinal disorder, arthropod-born diseases (malaria, unknown fever), nutritional deficiencies, diseases of blood-forming organs (anemia), respiratory disorders, diseases of the digestive system, skin diseases are relatively common. This is understandable because of morbidity pattern reflects the existing health care practices, environmental sanitation, food habits, and lifestyle of the studied population.

Mostly traditional and modern medicine was found prominently among those patients. One of the most commonly seen diseases among them is diarrhea. The frequency of affected people is more because of ill sources of drinking water. People of all ages are affected by this disease. A number of tuberculosis patients were found from the studied village. Most of the affected persons were belong to the more impoverished family. Skin diseases were recorded from the studied community. People had skin diseases that could occurs due to harmful and contaminated water, working in mines, wearing dirty clothes, and being communicable. They took the help of both modern and traditional medicine for this purpose. The frequency of malaria and dengue cases was reported from the area. The main reason for affecting is the lack of mosquito net use though they know that the cause of malaria, but due to hot, they did not use it. The frequency is more during the summer and rainy seasons. Another reason is deforestation, which provokes most of the vector-borne diseases in forests and adjacent areas. Other significant conditions are anemia, ulcer, jaundice, etc. During hunting, they get fractures and feel pain, mainly foot, and hand as well as body aches by their mistakes. Moreover, due to the miniry work of Hindalco/Birla Companies every day, mining dust covers areas and peoples feel eye pain, and also some people become blinded. The outbreak of the impact of jaundice is also seen in that area due to a hot climate, improper facility of water, and more intakes of *Mahua*. Some people have to say that *Mahua* wine is their medicine and relaxes them from aches. According to them some problems like joint pains and body pains are not felt.

For the treatment, they seek help from the traditional healer (*baidh*), allopathic, ayurvedic service providers, both private and government. If the treatment given by the local healer is not effective, then they go to consult a doctor or vice-versa. To get an idea of the treatment preferences of the studied population, the family members were asked to rank the method of treatment. Treatment preferences are indicated in Table 4.

Table 3: Health status of different aged people in studied village

Variables	Age group		
	0-17	18-59	60 and above
Cough, cold and viral fever	22(6.9)	14(4.4)	39(12.2)
Fever (Dengue/Malaria)	3(0.9)	9(2.8)	-
Jaundice	1(0.3)	5(1.6)	-
T.B.	-	18(5.6)	23(7.2)
Fracture	8(2.5)	3(0.9)	2(0.6)
Chicken Pox	-	4(1.3)	-
Anemia	17(5.3)	20(6.3)	-
Pneumonia	1(0.3)	-	-
Blind	-	11(3.4)	9(2.8)
Skin disease	2(0.6)	31(9.7)	14(4.4)
Diarrhea	-	17(5.3)	25(7.8)

Table 4: Mode of treatment

Mode of Treatment	1st Preference	2nd Preference
Traditional Medicine man	72	29
Allopathic Medicine	18	47

They accept two types of treatment methods. The first is the traditional method, and they go to conventional medicinal men who practice ethno-medicine to treat people. The other is the allopathic treatment method in which they go to the nearest block PHC centre or hospital. In the first instance, they prefer to go with the traditional way, and if it doesn't cure them properly only, they visit in nearest allopathic centre for treatment. So, these people believe and going in allopathic treatments for a better cure.

Case Studies on disease and nature of treatment (traditional and modern system of medicine)

Case I:

Sidiu Asur was affected by '*pilia*' (jaundice). He thought that the said disease could attack anyone due to natural causes. But he was not sure of the specific reason behind the case. He visited the traditional healer for remedy. The patient and the healer were confident about the disease through the yellow colour of urine, eyes, and body. Taking of high proteinous and fat food was restricted. A single dose of liquid herbal medicine was given to him. He had to follow the restriction for two months. He had paid Rs.20/- to the healer for the medication. He was cured within two months.

Case II:

Sadhuram Asur, a 47 years old man, was suffering from stomach problems. First of all, he consulted with the *ojha* and was told by him that some spirits intrusion occured inside his body. By doing several procedures and spending Rs.50/- and a hen behind this, he was not cured. Then he visited the traditional medicine man of the village and some herbal medicines are also prescribed by him for remedial purposes. He had to collect herbs from the forest, but the healer prepared it. The medications were taken two times a day, and also, there were some restrictions on taking non-vegetarian food. He has to paid Rs.30/- or 1 kg of rice each time he visited to the medicine man. But, he was not fully cured. Then he decided to visit an allopathic doctor in the town but could not manage any money for the said purpose.

Case III:

Jingi Asur, a 37 years old lady, was suffering from female diseases for a few years. As a first step, she visited an allopathic doctor in the town after taking medicines; she was not cured. And she spend Rs.350/- for this purpose. As a second step, she visited a traditional medicine man and, a typical herbal medicine was given to her, which had to be taken twice a day with some food restrictions. After three weeks, she was cured, and she did not have any such problems.

Role of Government and NGOs

Bishiunpur block PHC of government authority cell is playing an essential role in the well being of poor Asur community people. This PHC support motivated them to Allopathic treatment. This PHC also motivated pregnant women to come within its campus for delivery. A Bikash Bharti NGO situated in Bishunpur block was 35 km from the studied Asur village. This NGO has started an awareness program and treatment like free health check-ups, food distribution, and also trained in hand-made materials making process for their resources based livelihood practices. Also, the Anganwadi of this village plays a vital role in the life of pregnant women and child health.

In the present study, it was found that those women having a good socio-economic background goes for the ante-natal check-ups during their pregnancy period. Sometimes they also take help of the government service providers. As for the Tetanus Toxoid (TT) injections are concerned, very few of them have received doses of TT. They are provided with iron and folic acid (IFA) tablets from the *Anganwadi* centres. But the scenario is totally different in case of poor and illiterate people. They are just unaware of these facts, but very few of the cases were found where they have taken injections and iron and folic acid from the *Anganwadi* centres. From 1 year to 5 years meals of the baby is also offered by the Anganwadi. They teach them how to read and write. Primary education is provided by the members of Anganbadi to the child till the age of 5 years. They also provide nutritious food to the child. Mid-Day Meal (MDM) is also being provided. A sum of Rs.1,500/-is provided by the government for the safe delivery of the baby. Nutrition is also provided along with required medicines to the mother.

Conclusion

According to the study, it has been revealed that these studied people are not only poor in their works and income but also very poor in understanding of psychological and social as well, which is the leading cause for their backwardness and poverty. The study has shown that the concept of poverty and health is intertwined with several factors among them. Besides physical constraints, the people face their traditional ideologies that many times act as determining factors in health and health-seeking behavior of the people prevalence of malnutrition and consequent of health hazard. This matter and issue force them to think about their health and sustainable livelihood. Therefore, they are facing various new diseases and problems. Thus, their beliefs are getting potent towards allopathic doctors than the traditional ethno-medicinal man.

Suggestions

1. The nutrition status of pregnant women directly influences their reproductive performance and the birth weight of their children. This factor is crucial to informant chances of survival and its subsequent growth and development.
2. The health care system to the needs of this area Awareness programs are mainly crucial in this area, which changes their socio-economic and mental health care system.
3. They should be focused on their traditional daily food system.
4. The government should provide a drinking water facility and source in the village.
5. The mining companies must care for the health of workers and the people.
6. They should be focus on how to increase their education go for new employments rather than the present one.

References

Cattell V. 2011. *Poverty, community and health: co-operation and the good society*. Springer.

Gupta SP, 1976. The Asur, Ethno-Biological Profile. Bihar Tribal Welfare Research Institute, Ranchi.

Hutton JH. 1961. *Caste in India-its nature, function and origins. Oxford University Press, London.*

World Health Organization. 1991. *Community Involvement in health Development: Challenging Health Services.* WHO Technical Report Series 809.

Chapter Eight

FACTORS AFFECTING TRIBAL HEALTH: A REFLECTION FROM JHARKHAND

SUDHANSHU SHEKHAR MAHATO

ABSTRACT

For all nations either developing or developed, health remains a concern of priority in their agenda. Health is one of the most significant aspects of an individual life which needs to be nourished and maintained. The progress and prosperity of the person concerned, the family to which he belongs and community and society at large depends upon the sound health of its members. This sound health can be ensured to a large extent when properly planned from individual level to that of the Government in power. Usually, nutritious food and diseases have direct impact on health but across time and space, things are changing rapidly and a number of other factors too affect health indirectly resulting into atrocious consequences. In the present paper an effort has been made to explore the decisive factors causing health problems among tribal people of Jharkhand. The study is based on observation of the researcher during his field visit to various tribal settlement areas of Jharkhand in connection with various research projects undertaken from time to time. The tribal people under consideration here include Santhal, Oraon, Munda, Birhor, Bedia and Ho. The secondary data is brought into use to support and justify the statement concluded. The study reveals that it is not merely the nutritious food and diseases that affects their health but there are other factors like alcoholism and drug addiction, belief system, indigenous health practices, occupation pattern and poor economy, deforestation, education and lack of awareness, migration, mining and involuntary displacement etc. The policy planners and implementing agency therefore need to give due consideration to all the factors to secure achievement in health for all and specially among tribal.

Keywords: *Tribal Health, Jharkhand, Indigenous Pharmacopeia, Health Care.*

INTRODUCTION

In the development agenda of contemporary world, health occupies a significant place. The synonym of health is '*Swasthya*' in Sanskrit, meaning establishment in one's natural state. The health is determined by numerous factors and a single yardstick is not sufficient enough to measure it in totality. Traditionally, health refers to absence of disease and the disease is absence of biological norm (Brahmesananda, 2004). Therefore, in order to encompass all those issues that regulates and signifies the health status of an individual, the World Health Organization (WHO) has propounded a broader definition of Health. According to WHO, health is defined as a state of complete physical, mental and social well-being and not merely absence of diseases or infirmity. In fact, this well-being character is not permanent but works as a process that seeks continuous adjustment to the changing environment. The tribal who has been residing close to the nature since his early days of settlement, prefer to continue over there not because of pollution free environment but for supply of resources which support their living. However, the people's greed of over exploiting the nature for reaping maximum benefit, the concept of sustainability is simply kept aside. Consequently, it makes direct impact on the health of living being. The health issue of an individual begins much before the birth of an individual and this is why a lot of precaution is taken during pregnancy. However, after birth, child health comes under the direct influence of a number of factors that ranges from social and physical environment, cultural factors, cleanliness, diseases, water and food taken and so on. This continues to be a lifelong process. The ability of an individual to perform an activity successfully depends much upon the physical, mental and free from diseases. A good health stimulates in positive thinking for achieving the goal one determines in his life. But the ageing in tribal which happens to be the last phase of life cycle of an individual is associated with deterioration in health that changes attitude, psychology and their role as member of the family and the community (Mahato, 2006). In the present era of industrialization, urbanization and globalization, the health of rural people in general and tribal people in particular in a state like Jharkhand is also affected by some other factors in which they have no control.

Area Profile and the Tribal Situation

The land of Jharkhand bears a special characteristic of having variety of natural resources on its earth's surface as well as underneath. Some of the most important resources available underneath comprises of iron ore, copper ore, manganese ore, nickel ore, uranium ore, bauxite ore, mica, graphite, coal, dolomite, quartz, feldspar etc. There is a huge reserve of these minerals. On the land surface, there is vast expansion of deciduous forest that favours the growth of variety of trees and bushes making its climate soothing for both man and animals and providing its product in different forms for people's utilization. A number of indigenous people have inhabited this particular region since remote past. The state of Jharkhand was curved out from erstwhile Bihar on 15 November, 2000. It has a total geographical area of 75,545.36 Sq. Km. and a total population of 3.296 crore (Census, 2011). Ranchi happens to be the capital city of Jharkhand while Dumka remains as the sub-capital. The state is proud to have Dhanbad as the coal capital of India while Jamshedpur and Bokaro stands as prosperous industrial cities. From administrative point of view, it has been divided into five division viz. South Chotanagpur Division with Ranchi, Khunti, Simdega, Gumla and Lohardaga district, North Chotanagpur Division with Hazaribagh, Ramgarh, Chatra, Koderma, Giridih , Bokaro and Dhanbad district, Kolhan Division with East Singhbhum, West Singhbhum and Saraikela-Kharswan Districts, Palamu Division with Palamu, Garwa and Latehar district and Santhal Pargana Division with Sahebganj, Pakur, Jamtara, Deoghar, Dumka and Godda district.

There are 32 ethnic groups each bearing a distinctive socio-cultural character of their own, have been identified as Scheduled Tribe under the constitution of India. Moreover, there are other indigenous groups of people who were recognized as tribes till 1931 census but were not included in the list of schedule tribe framed after independence. As cited by Ekka and Asif (2000), "in the 1931 census there were listed as many as 49 tribes and semi-tribes which could be called indigenous people of Jharkhand (Lacey 1933:285-288). But the Indian constitution put them under three different lists-the Scheduled Tribes, The Scheduled Castes and Other Backward Communities, albeit providing them constitutional guarantees for justice. This constitutional break up, however, did not safeguard the indigenous identity of these groups like the Pan, the Ghasi, the Kurmi , the Bhuinya , the Turi and the Khetauri to mention a few. These were not added to the scheduled tribes list of the constitution nor are recognized today as indigenous people of the country by the government". Those people still believe and practice their traditional tribal culture and if included, it will completely change the tribal demographic structure in the region. The most prominent schedule tribe communities are Santhal, Oraon, Munda, Ho, Kharia, Bedia, Asur, Chero, Lohra, Mahli, Karmali etc. Santhal happens to be the most populous tribe constituting 34 percent of the total Schedule Tribe population in the state followed by Oraon and Munda. According to 2011 Census, Khunti (73.26%) has the highest concentration of tribals followed by Simdega (70.78%), Gumla (68.94%), West Singhbhum (67.37%) and Lohardaga (56.89%). The Schedule Tribes in Jharkhand, all together represents 26.2 percent of the total population of the state. Based on their economic activities undertaken, they are classified as hunter-gatherer, shifting cultivators, simple artisan and settled agriculturist. Eight of the total scheduled tribe groups namely Asur, Birhor, Birjia, Korwa, Savar, Paharia, Malpaharia and Sauria Paharia were identified as Primitive Tribal Groups for their distinctive feature like declining or almost stagnant population, low level of literacy, pre-agricultural level of technology and economical backwardness. These characteristics obviously imply poor health status and currently they are termed as Particularly Vulnerable Tribal Groups (PVTGs). They are, therefore, dealt with special privileges to bring them at par with the main stream of the society. Thus, it is very difficult to get a crystal clear picture of the health status of all the tribal groups in the region.

Materials and Methods

The present study is an outcome of the analysis of primary and secondary data that was collected on different occasion in connection with researcher's association with various project works. The study of Bedia community was a part of M. Phil. dissertation whereas Birhor were intentionally selected out of researcher's personnel interest for having opportunity to make observation on longitudinal basis. Some of the projects are worth mentioning that brought the researcher in close contact with various tribal groups and observe them from a close distance. The socio-economic survey of project affected persons under Farakka NTPC Project for the railway track that runs from Farakka (W.B.) to Lalmatia (Jharkhand) was very important in this regard. Here majority of the people were from Santhal community.

Similarly the socio-economic survey of the families to be affected by Koel Karo Hydroelectric Project conducted on behalf of Bihar Tribal Welfare Research Institute, the Development Induced Displacement and Rehabilitation in Jharkhand (South Bihar) 1951-1995 by Indian Social Institute, New Delhi and Swa–shakti Project supported by Ministry of Welfare and World Bank, brought the researcher in close contact with various indigenous people of Jharkhand. Focused Group Discussion and collection of secondary data from government offices served for the authenticity of the sources. The magnitude of tribal people's suffering and misery is clearly reflected in the status of their health.

Factors Affecting Tribal Health

The issue of tribal health in Jharkhand is a major concern for the government and policy makers. Though, by birth they are healthy but subsequently, they undergo changes from time to time under the influence of various factors. Some of the most prominent factors that regulate tribal health in the state of Jharkhand may be categorized as follows:

Food, Water and Sanitation

Food is an essential intake with ingredients like protein, vitamin, carbohydrates, starch, minerals and fibers for the proper growth of the body. The deficiency of any one of them is marked with certain symptoms which the individual might or might not be aware of. The tribal supplemented these requirements from their surrounding as seasonal collection even without knowing their nutritious value. Some are collected in the form of root, shoot, vegetables, fruits, flowers etc. from the natural ecology where as others are grown as agricultural products or as horticulture product. Seasonal hunting sometimes provides meat but otherwise they domesticate few animals both for consumption and economic gain. But with mass deforestation, poaching, climate change and population explosion, there is huge scarcity of these natural resources and the tribal people who depends much on the natural products of forest and surroundings areas are finding it quite difficult to manage them. This has direct impact on the growth of their body and physical well-being. The food insecurity is the sole cause for increase in morbidity and mortality. Even the implementation of forest act and enactment of forest policy by the government has largely affected their natural rights of having access to minor forest products. The deprivation has affected them not only physically but also emotionally.

Water considered to be the elixir of life was earlier available in plenty from natural springs, riverbed, *Dadi,* ponds and well both for consumption as well as cultivation. But now it is quite difficult to have access to pure drinking water specially in the remote isolated villages. The impure and contaminated water directly helps in growing water borne and associated diseases that attack the least health conscious tribal people. The utensils are usually washed either in front or backward of the houses and the water gets collected into the ditch meant for it. This stagnant water becomes the breeding ground for mosquitoes. In the absence of the habit of using mosquito net, they become vulnerable to malaria and typhoid. Even the unhygienic condition which arises due to lack of health consciousness becomes sources of origin of a number of other diseases. The tribal people's continuous attachment with mud in the field, in the agricultural land and in the surroundings areas, the clothes easily becomes dirty but their poor economic condition does not permit them to get it cleaned regularly. From hygienic point of view, the Santhal houses are relatively better when compared with other tribal groups. This is due to the Santhal women personal initiative which they cultivate in themselves as a part of socialization process during their upbringing. But when the external condition like mining in the area takes place, it is beyond their capacity to protect themselves from such hazards.

Common Disease

The disease not only brings down their health but also forbids them from sincerely performing the daily activities since the work performed is often tedious. A large part of their economy is spent in its treatment. Some of the most common diseases found in the tribal areas of Jharkhand are malaria, jaundice, typhoid, dysentery, diarrhea, stomachache, vomiting, and headache, arthritis etc. The stagnant water of ravine in the forest fringe area becomes the breeding ground for mosquitoes. The absence of mosquito net and repellent while sleeping makes the mosquito bite easier. Further, the habit of consuming stale food often favours the growth of certain diseases as the food many a times gets contaminated. The unavailability of pure drinking water is another major problem that becomes acute during rainy season. Incidence of waterborne diseases such as malaria, schistosomiasis, dengue, encephalitis, filariasis, hookworm, guinea worm, cholera and gastro-enteritis due to construction of large scale hydroelectric dams and other water impoundment schemes, have been reported from the area of Maithon Dam in Godda, the Mayurakshi Dam in Dumka and Auranga Dam in Palamu districts are only a few to mention (Ekka and Asif, 2000).

Alcoholism and Drug Addiction

Consumption of country liquor locally called *Handia* and *Mohua phuli/chulan/chulai*, is an inherited cultural habit which most of the tribal people cherish for the rest of their life. They do not mind in transmitting such habits to the younger generation. The locally brewed distilled liquor specially Mohua, is a very hard drink and often becomes injurious to health. But the tribal people in rural areas hardly realize its consequence as it is practiced by almost each and every member irrespective of age or sex. During sowing and harvesting period there is a culture of rendering service for service to the neighbours, community men or to friends even in the neighboring village as there happens to be shortage of labour. In return, the host is expected to entertain the service provider with non-vegetarian food and hard drinks. Here quality of food and drinks is not a priority but quantity matters. Obviously, it includes mostly pigs and poultry along with country liquor. The same process is repeated when there is return of service. There is no hard and fast rule but a short of mutual understanding that strengthens the bond of relationship in between the two families. More over according to them, it is a means of relaxing the tiredness and get ready for agricultural activity with enthusiasm on the subsequent day. But in long run, the process is injurious to health, which they hardly realize. Besides in all festive occasion and life cycle rituals, the relatives and guests are served with hard drinks as symbol of customary practice. A good number of them in due course of time get addicted and in the absence of regular income, they even mortgage their property including the immovable one. This, at the end ruins not only the individual concerned but the entire family.

Belief System

The tribal people cherish firm faith in totemic objects. They also belief in ghost, witchcraft and sorcery. Any kind of disease or unwell being among the members of the family is believed to be due to dissatisfaction of their ancestors, Gods, Spirits and consequence of black magic. Thus they rely heavily on the *Ojha/Guni/Sakha* who are considered to be the expert in giving treatment through their *mantra* power. Sometimes, sacrifice are made to appease gods and ancestors but most of the times the disease gets enough time for attaining maturity, resulting into fatal incidence. There are a number of cases where witch beating including killing becomes the headline in the daily newspaper. They belief that diseases caused by spirits must be treated by spiritual power to get rid of it. The application of modern treatment becomes useless until and unless their deity is satisfied. So, they prefer to stick to traditional mode of treatment.

Indigenous Health Practice

The ecology of Jharkhand is very rich in variety of flora and fauna which serves as the major source of indigenous medicine. Since the dawn of their settlement, there have been certain medicine men those are expertise in recognizing the medicinal value of the wild plants and applied them very efficiently for the treatment of almost all kind of diseases. Sharma (2008) is of the opinion that, "According to an estimate about 80% of the world's rural population relies on herbal traditional medicine for their health care". Realizing this fact perhaps, WHO while declaring its goal of health for all by 2000 AD, drew the attention of its member state to the strategic role that could be played by traditional system of medicine, especially in the context of primary health care needs of the rural and tribal communities of the world (Sharma, 2008: 2). This is also true in case Jharkhand. Singh (2008) remarks that "Jharkhand is a land of forest, where many tribes dwell such as the Santhals, the Kurmis, the Hos, The Mundas, the Oraons, the Hill Kharias, the Birhors, the Asurs and many others. The tribal people who are the inhabitant of this land very competently practice indigenous medical system for their health care". But the problem that arises in such health practice is that the medicine men do not have any scientific mechanism to diagnose the disease specially when it is matter of internal problem. They solely depends on patient's complain and symptoms. So there is possibility of inaccurate treatment and even delay in identifying exactly the real cause. Sometimes the people take the problem casually and look for treatment only when it becomes serious. As such the suffering of the people enhances manifold. Further due to dwindling of forest, many plants of medicinal value are getting extinct and thus the treatment becomes difficult. However, under certain circumstances, allopathic treatment is preferable for immediate relief but tribal people neither realize it nor does their pocket allow them.

Occupation Pattern and Poor Economy

In the era of science and technology, it is the money power that can manage everything to make one's life comfortable and lead a better life. But unfortunately the income from traditional occupation has gone down and it is not sufficient enough to fulfill the desire expectation to cope up with the rapidly advancing civilization. The settled agriculturist does not have enough production because of untimely monsoon. Besides in the areas of their settlement, the irrigation facilities are either least or totally absent to support them in undertaking agricultural activities. The population has increased but productions have decreased. The situation has compelled many of the tribal to leave their traditional homeland in search of alternative income for their survival. The artisan groups are not in a position to compete with factory products and accordingly, their income is not adequate enough to support them. The traditional *Jajmany* system which supported them is getting vanished. The shifting cultivator does not find enough ground to alternate their practice and the pressure from forest department and forest policy does not gives freedom to clear the forest area for the purpose of cultivation as practiced earlier. The condition of hunter-gatherer is further worst. Although, constitution has given reservation in government jobs but low level of education does not favours everyone to get a job. The economic status except a few per cent of families is constantly deteriorating bringing direct impact on their health. The stress and strain confronted by tribal people leaves adverse effect on their health as well as psychology too.

Deforestation

Vidyarthy (1963) through his study on Maler not only have tried to establish the relationship among nature, man and spirit but at the same time exposes the interdependency and mutually complimentary supports to each other component for their sustainable development. The culture of Indigenous people originated in the lap of nature and subsequently developed and flourished in it. The people to a large extend depends on forest for their growth, prosperity and development. Even food and drink is obtained through hunting and gathering. Their economy revolves around forest and their pharmacopeia depends on it. But unfortunately, the population pressure, Industrialization and urbanization process have motivated the greedy wood merchants for illegal deforestation that have direct impact on the health and life of those people who depends on it largely and prefer to choose it as their abode. The deforestation and poaching is so terrible that even the big wild animals are bound to leave their natural habitation and trouble the people in the country side.

Education and Lack of Awareness

Education is one of the most influential factors for bringing transformation in the life of an individual. This is also true for the people belonging to schedule tribe category. The social, economic, political as well as even religious status of schedule tribe to a large extent is determined by their educational status. The rate of literacy among schedule tribe population in the state is 57.10 percent as against 59 percent of schedule tribe communities in India. The male and female literacy rate among schedule tribes in Jharkhand is 68.20 and 46.20 percent respectively. But the irony of the fact is that the enrollment is highest in the elementary level only. The percentage is relatively very low in secondary and higher secondary level and the figure continue to deteriorate further at the tertiary level. As a result of low rate of literacy and level of education, the awareness among tribal population especially in the field of health care is comparatively very poor. Mahato (2008) remarks that lack of education and exposure to outside world especially urban centers, keeps them away from the concept of quality life and accordingly there is no desire for the same. The people in the rural areas hardly adopt preventive measures to get rid of sickness. Awareness building therefore is the need of the hour in Jharkhand that can serve a long way in ensuring better health amongst the schedule tribe population.

Migration

The push and pull factor of rural and urban areas respectively are the sole cause of tribal migration in the contemporary period. A sudden shift from pollution free natural environment to cities mostly suffering from air pollution is a big challenge for the tribal to make adjustment specially when their pocket is too short to make their life comfortable. The only option left with them is to find a habitation in the slums area which is again undoubtedly dangerous. A good number of them get involved in illegal activities. Thus the expectation with which they migrated is kept aside and ultimately becoming the prey of sufferings. In a bureau report published in daily newspaper, Sharma (2020) stated that 45.3 percent of tribal in rural areas live below poverty line and citing the report of the expert committee on tribal health claims that 55 percent of India's tribal population lives outside the tribal majority block. In a state like Jharkhand, proliferations of Naxal movement have challenged the peaceful existence of innocent rural people including tribal communities. Migration under such circumstances often demands adjustment in new environment. This, in long run causes devastating impact on their health where children and women are the worst sufferer when compared with adult male.

Mining

Industrialization is the steering wheel of developing economy and the possibility of industrialization to a large extent depends on mineral reserves and mining activities. Jharkhand being the land of mineral wealth, the mining activities are at rampant. However, the absences of appropriate policy measures have caused a great deal of suffering not only to the miners but the people living around the mining areas which mostly comprises of the tribal. Many a times the suffering proves to be fatal. A report in Hindustan times (Mar 3, 2009) reveals that "in places like Jagannathpur, Noamundi, Gua in Jharkhand and Jamda and Badbil in Orissa where 30 percent of iron ore reserve lies, the tribal were in good health before the reckless mining activity begun but now most of them die before stepping into old age due to constant exposure to Iron ore dust. Silica is the common chemical compound found in iron ore and other minerals mined extensively in Jharkhand's West Singhbhum area. A small quantity of silica dust inhaled overtimes can lead to silicosis, a form of cancer. The dust gets lodged in the lungs and continuously irritates them, reducing lungs capacity as silica does not dissolve over times (Murty, 2009). The suffering of tribal people is worst in the uranium mining areas of Jadugoda due to radio activity. On completion of a research in five villages near the mines owned by Uranium Corporation of India Limited, Pallavi (2015) found, "cases of congenital deformity, sterility, spontaneous abortion and cancers were alarmingly high among the villagers mostly from the Ho, Santhal, Munda and Mahali tribes". Jharkhand is one of the four states in India where coal mining takes place at a very large scale through open cast and underground mining to support production of steel and thermal power electricity. It is the only state in the country where three coal companies are simultaneously excavating coals from its mineral rich soil. Coal mining is spread over a number of districts. Most popularly recognized coal producing districts are, Dhanbad, Giridih, Hazaribagh, Ramgarh, Bokaro, Chatra, Palamu and Ranchi. These districts are also the habitational areas to number of schedule tribes and indigenous people. Sangeetha (2018) identifies, "air pollutants and dust mixed with silica are the two major factors that affect the health of coal mine workers. Some of the diseases caused by coal mine are chronic pulmonary obstructive diseases (COPD), coal workers pneumoconiosis (CWP), asthma and massive Fibrosis. Prolonged exposure to coal mine dust cause variety of diseases like tuberculosis, chronic bronchitis, heart diseases, lung cancer, pneumonia, liver disease, kidney damage and reproductive disorder". It is not only the workers but even the non- worker residing in the region or exposed to such pollution are likely to get infected. Almost all kind of mining has some kind of occupational hazards. Therefore the magnitude of mining impact on the health of tribal people is very alarming that needs to be brought under control immediately for better life.

Involuntary Displacement

Land acquisition in Jharkhand for various project have remained a matter of priority for the government in the name of development. The availability of enormous natural resources stimulates the industrialization process in the region for which land has been acquired since colonial period in India. Such development initiatives either displace people or deprive them from their livelihood resources. In a state like Jharkhand, most of the land belongs to indigenous people of which Schedule Tribe (26.26%) and Tribe like Kudmi (23.2%) (Non-government Tribe according to the report of the Committee on Jharkhand Matters) are major component and therefore, obviously, they becomes the looser of land which was their main source of livelihood. Although compensation was paid but it was not sufficient enough to sustain the future generation. Further innocent tribal people were not in a position to circulate the money as an investment and regenerate out of it. So within a few years, the people became empty handed and were left with no option but to work as labour or to migrate to some other places. Such pathetic situation is bound to cause stress and strain that ultimately brings down the health status. Ekka and Asif (2000) conclude that in addition to the adverse environmental and socio- cultural ramifications, involuntary resettlement has a direct consequence on the health of the resettlers. It can result in the spread of infectious diseases and nutritional stress and thereby increase morbidity and mortality. The magnitude of the problem can very well be estimated from the quantum of land acquired by the government, as shown in Table-1.

Government Initiative

The government of India launched a number of health programme from time to time to curb out health hazards. Family Planning in 1952, National Malaria Control Programme in 1953, Integrated Child Development Service in 1975, Immunization Programme in 1978, Pulse Polio Immunization in 1995, National Vector Borne Diseases Control Programme in 2003-04, National Viral Hepatitis Control Programme and Ayushman Bharat Yojna in 2018 are only a few worth mentioning in the series. A broad classification of the programme includes Reproductive, Maternal, Neonatal, Child and Adolescent Programme, National Nutritional Programme, Communicable Diseases, Non communicable Diseases and Health System Strengthening Programme. However, lack of information, isolated habitational area and the shy nature of tribal people forbid them from availing benefit of the above programme in true sense. Further it is also evident from above facts that the root cause of their ill health is not the variety of diseases that proliferates in the absence of preventive measures but certain undesired circumstances engulf them in such a manner that it is difficult to escape. Although efforts are made to ensure health facilities even at Panchayet level but the sheer uncongenial circumstances compels the tribal to find an alternative at local level. The public hospitals and health centers in suburban areas are always in short supply of medicine, medical appliances, beds and auxiliary manpower. In case of emergency, priority is given to patients who possess good contact and high connection (Haldar, 2006). Therefore, the simple and poor tribal give up their trust and looks for some alternatives.

Table 1: Total land acquired for development scheme in Jharkhand (acres)

Category of Project	Private Land	%	Common Land	%	Forest Land	%	Total Land	%
Water Resources	364646.00	71.7	94808.00	18.7	48498.00	09.6	507952.00	34.0
Industries	98525.59	56.1	63768.68	36.3	13435.91	07.6	175730.18	11.7
Thermal Power	2598.45	43.1	2534.38	42.1	894.04	14.8	6026.87	00.4
Mines	184169.00	35.7	156341.19	30.4	174614.40	33.9	515124.59	34.4
Defense Establish-ment	22543.61	20.1	11134.93	09.9	78610.57	70.0	112289.11	07.5
Misc. Scheme	152000.65	85.0	8941.21	05.0	17882.43	10.0	178824.29	12.0
Sub Total	824483.30	55.1	337528.39	22.6	333935.35	22.3	1495947.04	100.0
Missing Scheme	27550.00	55.1	11300.00	22.6	11150.00	22.3	50000.00	
Grand Total	852033.30		348828.39		345085.35		1545947.04	

Source: Ekka and Asif, 2000.

Conclusion

The health of tribal has been witnessing a deterioration trend and in the recent years, it is perhaps more alarming. There are a number of factors that contribute to the persistence of the problem. The economic status of tribal people has gone down the subsistence level. Accordingly, they are unable to combat the health hazard that seems fatal irrespective of age and sex. The socio-economic and cultural habit forbids them to get rid of the problem whereas in case mining areas, it is beyond their capacity to control it. The Government needs to intervene sympathetically to protect them from the life threatening circumstances which have emerged due to unprotected activities in the name of development. Awareness building and enhancement in the rate as well as level of education can help to a large extent in minimizing and controlling the health problem confronted by them. The tribal are integral part of Indian population and in a growing democracy like India, they deserve to grow with natural justice.

References

Brahmeshananda S. 2004. *Health medicine and religion.* Chennai. Sri Ramakrishna Math Printing Press.

Ekka A, Asif M. 2000. *Development Induced Displacement and Rehabilitation in Jharkhand, 1951-1995: A Database on its Extent and Nature,* New Delhi: Indian Social Institute.

Haldar S. 2006. *Management of health and health related problems of the tribal aged,* in AK Haldar and AK Jana (eds.) Tribal Ageing,Sparks from Bidisha, Vol.VI, Kharagpur: The Institute of Social Research & Applied Anthropology.

Mahato SS. 2006. *Impact of mass media on aged Bedia,* in AK Haldar and K Jana (eds.) Tribal Ageing, Sparks from Bidisha, Vol.VI, Kharagpur: The Institute of Social Research and Applied Anthropology.

Murty BV. 2009. *Kids face health hazards near iron ore mines in Jharkhand.* Hindustan Times, March 03, 2009.

Pallavi A. 2015. *Uranium mine waste imperils villages in Jadugoda.* Down to Earth.

Sangeetha R. 2018. Health implications of exposure to coal mine dust in workers-a review. International Journal of Research in Pharmaceutical Science.

SharmaVS. 2008. *Strengthening the Scope of Practice of Ethno-medicinal Plant Cultivation among the Tribal Communities Using Self Help Group Strategy in Jharkhand,* in A. K. Haldar, P. K. Singh and P. C. Coomar (eds.) Tribal Ethno medicine- Problem and Prospect, Sparks from Bidisha, Vol. VII, Kharagpur: The Institute of Social Research & Applied Anthropology.

Sharma YS. 2020. *Reverse Migration of People due to Lockdown may Destroy India's Tribal Communities,* Economic Times, April 07, 2020.

Singh PK. 2008. *The indigenous medical system and the new patent regime,* in A. K. Haldar, PK Singh and PC Coomar (eds.) Tribal Ethno medicine-Problem and Prospect, Sparks from Bidisha, Vol. VII, Kharagpur: The Institute of Social Research and Applied Anthropology.

Vidyarthy LP. 1963. *The Maler: a study in nature-man-spirit complex of a hill Tribe.* Calcutta. Bookland Private Limited.

Chapter Nine

LIVING WITH CHRONIC PAIN: MALADIES OF SANTAL AND LODHA ELDERLY OF PURULIA AND JHARGRAM, WEST BENGAL

JAYDEEP SENGUPTA, SUDIPTA DEY AND PRASENJIT MAHATO

ABSTRACT

Background: Chronic pain (CP) has received poor attention in medicine all over the world, particularly in India, where it is widespread. A couple of Indian literature that confirm wide prevalence of CP is just a tip of an iceberg. Myriads of other complexities, ranging from functional disability to erratic referrals depression and behavioural changes that are associated with CP are under reported and unaddressed. Moreover, since chronic pain aggravates with age, people who are elderly, belonging to tribal communities, financially poor, socially marginalised, and located in geographically 'hard-to-reach areas' suffer most. Their sufferings are not adequately represented in academics as well as in policy interventions. Purpose: This article pays particular attention to maladies of elderly belonging to tribal communities of Santal and Lodha of West Bengal and suffering from various forms of CP. Methodology: Based on first-hand information collected during fieldworks through surveys and in-depth interviews from 2018 to 2020 the article gives an overview of the CP condition of tribal vis-à-vis the national situation. Findings: Overall, there is an information-deficiton CP. Moreover,poor public healthcare delivery system, unavailability of appropriate facilities, reluctance of physicians to address CP, and low awareness level of people aggravates the situation of chronic pain.Conclusion: The article strongly suggests for tribal-specific information, CP addressal mechanism from primary healthcare level, public health campaigns to raise awareness, and structural changes to prioritise CP as an essential healthcare intervention.

Keywords: *Chronic pain, elderly, Santal, Lodha*

Introduction

Chronic pain (CP)isa ubiquitous experience in modern times.With nearly 10 percent of world population experiencing CP in one form or the other, it is undeniably a public health crisis of the present time (Jackson, et al., 2014). A more serious concern is the unequal distribution of the CP burden in low and middle-income countries. The high unment need of CP burden in these countries reflect poor healthcare services.

In India CP is widely prevalent among adults. In a nation-wide study conducted by Saxena, et al. (2018), 19.3% of the adult population was found to suffer from CP. They also found prevalence of CP was higher in females than males. Similarly, Dureja et al. (2014) found prevalence of CP to be 13% in eight Indian cities. 37% to 63% of them suffer from chronic moderate to severe pain with mean pain intensity to be as high as 6.93. Pain in knees, legs and joints was more than other body parts. Study conducted among elderly population of Tamil Nadu showed 47.6% of the elderly suffer from chronic pain especially in knee joints and lower backache (Kirubakaran and Dongre,2019). Somade et al. (2011) assessed chronic pain among adults of age 30 to 60 years in the village of Kasegaon, Maharashtra and found 21 out of 27 residents suffered from pain with score of 2-3 assessed as per McGill (PPI) and Visual Analogue Scale. The SAGE-India (Wave 1) report also showed large number of elderly to be suffering from CP, although the report did not give further insights (Arokiasamy et al., 2013). Ahdi et al. (2016) in acommunity-based cross-sectional study, conducted among 250 women in the age group of 30-65 years residing near a tertiary medical institution in Puducherry, found low back pain as the most common complication among women (42%). Majority of these women (60.9%) experienced moderate disability. The survey was done using Numerical Pain Scale, a modified Oswestry Low Back Pain Disability Questionnaire and WHO-BREFscale to assess the QOL. What attracts serious attention from the reports is the fact that CP intensity has a direct correlation with age progression. In other words, sensation of pain intensifies as one continues to age. Global studies estimate 25 to 50percent of the community-dwelling elderly suffer from CP (Fayaz et al., 2016; Hanks-Bell, et al., 2004). Moreover, AGS Panel on Persistent Pain in Older Persons (2002) suggests that pain doubles after 60 years and thereafter escalates in every ten years. Although, such assertion awaits further validation but it is true that chronic pain adversely affects healthy ageing. Another inference from the global literature is ageing and pain have acomplex interplay (Docking et al., 2011; Thomas, 2010). Literature suggest CP leads to anxiety, depression, sleep disturbances and other psychosomatic disorders (Morete et al., 2018; Daskalaki et al., 2017; Denard et al., 2010). Johnson and McElhaney (2009) point out that those aged above 80 years have nearly three times (21%) more chances of post-herpetic neuralgia than the younger cohort aged 50-54 years (8%).

The International Association for the Study of Pain revised its earlier definition of CP as *An aversive sensory and emotional experience typically caused by, or resembling that caused by, actual or potential tissue injury* (IASP, 2019).It implies CP has a deep bearing not only on physical functioning, but also on psychological and social well-being. IASP further defines that CP is a subjective experience as individuals learn to cope and respond through their life experiences. Thus according to the new definition, CP management entails multidisciplinary approach. However, in the Indian context there are several challenges in providing multidisciplinary care to the patients, especially if the patient is elderly belonging from the marginalized section of the community. Some of the lacunae found in the healthcare system are:

a. Lack of population-specific knowledge about the prevalence of CP, especially of the tribal people
b. Lack of resources to address chronic pain
c. Barriers in communicating pain
d. Difficulties in pain assessment

Information Deficit about Prevalence of Chronic Pain among Tribal Population

As said earlier there is a lack of population-specific information about prevalence of chronic pain, especially of the tribal population. Even the national level reports like the SAGE-India (Wave-1) gives an aggregate figure with no indication of the situation of tribal people. Nevertheless, it is widely known the changing epidemiology of chronic illness among the tribal population. Studies affirming rising trend of diabetes and hypertension are rising in numbers (Sathiyanarayananet al., 2019; Singh et al., 2019; Kshatriya, 2015; Jain et al., 2015).In comparison, there are lesser studies and paucity of information on chronic pain. A study by Basu, Mondal and Roy (2018) find 73.3% of tribal elderly of West Bengal suffer from low back and joint pain. Apart from this, there are no major studies to highlight burden of chronic pain among them. It shows poor academic attention to this problem that otherwise has a severe consequence. On the other hand, unpublished dissertations and field reports prepared by students of the Department of Anthropology, SKBU, from 2016 onwards have confirmed prevalence of chronic diseases mainly backpain, arthritis, rheumatoid joint pain, among elderly belonging to Santal and Lodha communities. A rough estimate shows that 67 to 73 percent of elderly suffer from low back pain, and pain in joints of arm and legs.

A very recently concluded study conducted in the district of Jhargramon 78 Lodha people and 83 Santal (N=161), all above 60 years of age, in two select villages show 71.4% suffer from back pain followed by joint pain (36.6%) and pain in either of the arms (approximately 10 to 11%) (Sengupta and Dey, 2020). Around 62.1% felt the pain to badly affect their lives on daily basis. Many reported that turning around in the bed is difficult that in turn resulted in sleep disturbances. Another study set in the block Purulia-II of the district Purulia has come up with a similar finding (Mahato and Sengupta, 2020). The study showed 56% of the elderly women belonging to the Kudmi Mahato community (categorized as Other Backward Class-B in the state of West Bengal) suffer from chronic pain as against 44% of the males. Knee and lower back pain was most common. During the study the respondents reported to bear the heavy burden of CP for 4-5 years. It infers that CP initiated quite early; for some it started even before they reached the age of 60 years. In both the studies mentioned there were fewer cases of cancer-related pain.

A severe consequence of CP is loss of functionality. While tribal communities mostly engage in labour-intensive jobs like agricultural activities, mining, and manual labour, CP prevents them to continue their work. Many are left out from government-aided livelihood opportunities like MGNREGA. The field visits also confirm the dismal situation of the elderly. However, contrary to the common notion that loss of job leads to anxiety and depression, the tribal communities were found to have a social norm to cope with the loss. All the respondents considered CP as a natural sign of ageing. Without showing much anxiety they compensated the loss of functionality by taking up household chores—a traditional model of changing social role. While men engaged in minor household jobs like gardening, watering the dusty roads that ran over their village, rearing cattle, collecting forest woods, and so on, women spent time with their grandchildren.

Lack of resources to address chronic pain

In India pain clinics are rare. It seems the health policy-makers are yet to realise the epidemics of chronic pain. Poor attention to chronic pain in the country owes much to the poor healthcare policies, both at national as well as regional level. The newly revised National Health Policy (NHP) of 2017 and the National Program for the Health Care of the Elderly (NPHCE) propose pain management but the roadmap seems sketchy. While NHP conceptualises 'Wellness Centres' at the primary healthcare level to deliver comprehensive preventive, promotive, curative and rehabilitative services, NPHC recommends physiotherapy unit for geriatric patients at CHC, district hospital and Regional Geriatric Centres. Both these policy documents leave readers to only speculate that the package of services would include pain management for geriatric patients. The NPHCE's commitment to provide physiotherapy and rehabilitative services at the CHC means many elderly living alone in remote locations or in bed-bound condition would be unable to access the institutional service. Moreover, complete absence of chronic pain management in the list of non-communicable diseases, prepared by the Ministry of Health and Family Welfare, Government of India for the capacity development of Multi-purpose front line health workers, confirms this doubt all the more. The list only includes diabetes, hypertension and cancer. The later subsumes pain, leaving out large number of patients suffering from nociceptive pain, like arthritis. Even in case of cancer-related pain, it is widely known in India the problems of availing and accessing opioids due to administrative hurdles. This made India to be identified as one of the countries with least use of opioids for pain relief since 1985 (Vallat et al., 2017). It was only in 2014 when the Narcotic Drugs and Psychotropic Substances (NDPS) Act was amended as a result of which opioid can now be easily obtained for palliative care. Under the Act six drugs, namely morphine, fentanyl, methadone, oxycodone, codeine and hydrocodone are included as "essential narcotic drugs". Even then few concerns still remain. One is the recent inclusion of Tramadol in the list. The drug is a low cost, easily available and weak-opioid but is notoriously know for making patients easily inclined to take over-dose and be addicted. The other concerns arepoor awareness among physicians and different misconceptions among patients about opioids (Jacob and Mathew, 2017). Moreover, in the context of tribal medicine the proposed models of 'Wellness clinics', 'AYUSH system of healthcare' or 'essential narcotic drugs' are not vetted. Even at the global level, pain management has largely remained unaddressed. A Delphi study conducted to ascertain gap areas in pain management and include them in the WHO documents shows that chronic pain has been exclusively understood in relation to cancer, whereas non-malignant chronic pain has remained unaddressed (Kumar, 2007). Clinical practitioners in different branches of pain management recommend for guidelines that is age-specific: children, adults and older adults; patient-specific: co-morbid conditions, terminally ill etc. and need-based: substance-abuse, emergencies, home-based etc. These recommendations may be helpful to effectively address pain issues of different population.

Most tribal communities in India are known to stay in geographically inaccessible areas, shy away from interacting with members outside their communities, and rely on traditional healthcare resources. As a matter of fact, tribal health is still understood in the context of magico-religion (Raushan and Acharya, 2019). Faith healing and folk medicines play major roles in determining treatment-seeking behaviour of the tribal people. However, presently the trend is changing as many are getting drawn to bio-medicine. Raushan and Acharya (2019) in their analytical study of treatment-seeking behaviour of Indian tribes using Indian Human Development Survey-2 of 2011-12 dataset show 82 percent seek some form of treatment for chronic ailments while 18 percent do not. Among those who seek treatment, majority visits private clinics and physicians (54.0%) in their first consultation followed by government facilities (30.8%) and others (3.1%). The later includes folk healers, shamans and home remedies. However, during the second consultation, visit to government facilities drastically reduces (25.3%) whereas over- the-counter purchase and visit to local healers increasesmanifolds. This data indicate a couple of possibilities. One, private facilities and over-the-counters are easily accessible to tribal people than government facilities, second, the trust on institutional care dwindles, and third institutional care set-ups lack culture-appropriate long-term care plans. This is somewhat confirmed during our first-hand data collection and observation in Purulia and Jhargram on health-seeking behaviour of Santals and Lodhas for CP management. Majority of the elderlyreported visiting allopathic physicians (95%), few visited

Ayurveda practitioners (3%) and rest to homeopath. Proximity of the facility centres from their villages and compassionate caregiving are said to be the major driving forces. Thus, pain clinics at village level, opioid supply, compassionate caregiving and patient-physician trust that are very important in the context of chronic pain management seems to be grossly missing in these tribal villages and rural India at large.

Barriers in communicating pain and difficulties in pain assessment

Addressing chronic pain is a challenge to clinicians because it involves host of non-clinical factors to take into consideration. Gender, ethnic background, culture and communications are some of the issues that matter in reporting pain (Glajchen, 2000). In fact, pain being a subjective experience causes a major difficulty to the physicians to assess it on any standardised scales. It mostly depends how patients describes their sensation and experiences. Nevertheless, there is a continuous effort among the clinicians to sophisticate pain assessment scales for different population: infant, children, adolescent, adults, elderly, cognitively and verbally challenged. Some of the widely available pain scales are Wong — Baker Faces Pain Rating Scale, Visual analogue scale, McGill Pain Questionnaire (MPQ), Descriptor Differential scale (DDS), Faces Pain Scale-Revised, Numerical 11-point box scale (BS-11), Numeric Rating Scale (NRS-11), Dolorimeter Pain Index (DPI), Brief Pain Inventory (BPI), Walid — Robinson Pain Index (WRI) — computed asintensity on admission (0-10) × length (in months). Among them VAS, MPQ and BPI are more popular because of their application in wide range of settings, easy-to-use, and cover population of different age groups. However, as Kumar and Tripathi (2014) opinenone of the scales are perfect because after all pain is a subjective experience. Moreover, there is not enough information how effective are each of the scales inaccurately assessing pain when patient makes transition from one care setting to other, for instance from home to hospital to critical care unit. In India, 49.7 percent physicians believe pain assessment is a challenging task (Bhatnagar et al., 2018).This may be largely attributed to the culture of patients reporting pain very late and language barrier.

On the other hand, our research team came across different expressions of pain in the local language of tribal and folk communities of Santals and Lodhas. Some of these dialects are presented in table no.1, below:

Table 1: Expressions of Chronic Pain in local dialects

Expression of Chronic pain	English translation
"এক জায়গায় বশে থাকলে কমড়টা ধকধক করে" *(Dakhin Soren, Male, 60+ years)*	Hip throbs and feels heavy
কোমড়ে ও পিছে ও বুকে ধকধক করে। *Srinath Mandi, M*	Hip, back and chest throbs fast
হাঁটু রোজই কনকন করে। *(Panmoni Soren, F, 59 yrs.)*	Sharp pain in the knees
কোমড়ে হাল্কা চীনচীণে ব্যাথা হয়। *(Laxmansoren, M, 60 yrs.)*	Pricking sensation in the hips
কোমড় প্রচন্ড কনকন করে ও হাঁটু চিবুয়। *(Bani Tudu, 62 yrs.)*	The hip and finger tips feels a burning sensation
কোমড় প্রচন্ড কনকন করে ও হাঁটু চিবুয়। *(Ram Tudu, M, 60+yrs.)*	Intense and sharp pain in the hip. Grinding pain in the knees
পায়ের পাতা জ্বলন ধরে। কমড়টা কামড়ে ধরে। *(Ramchandra Soren, M, 65 yrs)*	Dorsal portion of the fee burns. Biting ache in the hip
কোমড়ে খিঁচ করে(শিড়াটান) হাঁটতে পারিনা। *(Mona Murmu, F, 55+yrs. & Chandmoni Soren, F, 70+ yrs.)*	Gripping pain in the hip. Cannot walk properly
মাঝে মাঝে কোমড়ে কনকনে ব্যাথা হয়। *(Kalachandtudu, M, 55+ yrs.)*	Sometimes there is aching in the hip
মাথা কনকন করে। *(Meghnad Soren, M, 55+ yrs.)*	The head aches
কাঁধ, হাত, কনুঁই কনকন ও জ্বালা করে।	The shoulder, arm and elbow aches and burns
বাঁ হাঁটুচাকতি কন কন করে। (Brihaspati Mallik, M, 45 yrs.)	The kneecap (patella) of the left leg numbs
শীতকালে কোমড়ে খিল ধরে। Baijoyonti Mallik, F, 45+ yrs.	In winter the hip bone joints gets stuck (illium rotates posteriorly)
মেঘলাদিনে হাঁটু কনকন করে। (Gouri, F, 55 yrs.)	During cloudy weather (rainy season) a sharp pain in the knee is felt
জৈষ্ঠ মাসের শেষে কোমড়ে ও পিঠে ধকধক ব্যাথা করে। (Sunil Mullick, M, 45 years)	Late summer (when monsoon onsets) heavy pain in the back and hip is felt
কোমড়ে ও ঘাড়ে খিঁচ ধরে। (Mohur Nayek, M, 45 yrs.)	The Shoulder and the hip feels a gripping pain

From the above table few inferences can be drawn. Firstly, there is an indigenous way to express chronic pain. Terms like, *চিবুয়* (Grinding),

চীনচীণে (Pricking) কনকন (sharp pain), খিঁচ (muscle twitch), খিল (bone joints lock), ঝনঝন (numbness) and so on corresponds to the standard expressions of pain; either the sensation or cause of pain. However, in some cases terms are non-classificatory like ধকধক that implicates both heavy and throbbing pain. Second, the patients could communicate the frequency and location of the pain in their own language. For example কোমড় (hip), lower back, হাঁটু (knee), হাঁটুচাকতি (kneecap), ঘাড় (neck), পা পাতা (feet) and মাথা (head) etc. Terms like মাঝেমাঝে (sometimes) and রোজই (everyday/continuous) indicate the frequency of pain. Third, there are seasonal variations indicated like winter শীতকাল (winter), মেঘলা (cloudy/rainy season), জৈষ্ঠ (late May to Early June/onset of monsoon) when CP aggravates. Finally, an in-depth analysis of the expression can lead the physicians classify pain as nociceptive, neuropathic or idiopathic. Overall, it can be inferred that familiarity with the local dialects can facilitate physicians diagnose and assess pain. Apart from the tribal people, the KudmiMahato a dominant caste in Purulia has a unique way to classify chronic pain. The classification of mild, moderate and severe pain is presented in the figure below:

Table 2: Classification of pain in Kudmali language of the Mahatos of Purulia

Dukhachhe	Mild pain
Kutchhe	
Bedna	
Bajchhe	
Konkonachhe	Moderate pain
Vokvokachhe	
Jhonjhonkorche	
Tortorkorchee	Severe pain
Tenelichhe	

These expressions enlisted in Table 2 have major role in making pain assessment tools effective, if physicians pay attention to them. Even if the standard tools are not available or the physician is unable to use them, these expressions can serve as proxy indices. Thus the local languages need to be documented and standardized.

Conclusion

Chronic pain has suffered negligence in the medical discourse, globally. Mao (2012) points out several hindering factors to translational pain research: firstly animal models that are used to study pain fail to reproduce multiple dimensions of pain including cognitive and affective changes. Moreover, animal behaviour experience does not assess subjective pain experience of human beings; second, preclinical data provide little information for development of new analgesic. He explained that few drugs that worked successfully in animals either lack clinical efficacy in humans or cause significant side effects; third, lack of understanding of pharmacokinetic, pharmacodynamics and pharmacogenomic profiles and their interactions make study of pain in human beings fuzzy; fourth clinical trials precludes subjective experiences of pain and fail to capture the multidisciplinary consequences of co-morbid chronic pain; and finally, assessment tools does not consider influence of genetic and psycho-social influence of pain. Moreover, aaccording to Schatman (2007) physicians and healthcare professionals for long showed reluctance to address pain, possibly because ethical issues that complicated painaddressal further.

Apart from these limitations in pain research, in India there are host of other drawbacks to implement pain management. Most important among them are reluctance of policy-makers to prioritise pain management as essential healthcare services, non-accreditation of pain medicine as a specialisation by Medical Council of India, inadequate infrastructure to offer multidisciplinary care to patients suffering from CP and lack of expertise to assess, counsel and manage CP. These limitations have adversely affected all sections of society, especially elderly belonging to tribal communities, who are geographically isolated and socio-economically poor. While lack of pain clinics, specialist physicians and drugs particularly in rural areas have resulted in huge unmet need for addressing CP, reluctance to report chronic pain has also affected effective pain management. The latter is largely attributed to lack of awareness and sensitisation to prioritise chronic pain. There is also paucity of in-depth information how people live and age with chronic pain, how they cope with it and what are its implications to mental health, caregiving, and social participation are unknown. Based on these above-mentioned limitations, the authors strongly suggest for:

1. Disaggregated data on prevalence of CP with particular reference to tribal people
2. Multidisciplinary pain addressal and management at the door-step of aged and ailing patients, particularly those who

are bed-bound

3. Awareness at all levels through sensitisation and health campaigns: ranging from patients (to report pain early) to health policy-makers (to prioritise pain research)
4. Devise and adopt culturally-appropriate, robust pain assessment procedure

According to Brennan et al. (2007) *heavy burden of chronic pain not only reflects poor medical service, but also a violation abrogation of fundamental human right. Moreover, living with CP* interferes with health ageing and quality of life. Unless these issues are resolved tribal elderly in India will continue to live with multiple maladies, physically and mentally.

References

AGS Panel on persistent pain in older persons. 2002. The management of persistent pain in older persons. Journal of the American Geriatrics Society. 50: S205–S224.

Ahdhi GS, Subramanian R, Saya GK, Yamuna TV. 2016. Prevalence of low back pain and its relation to quality of life and disability among women in rural area of Puducherry, India. Indian Journal of Pain. 30:111.

Arokiasamy P, Parasuraman S, Sekher TV, Lhungdim H. 2013. Study on global ageing and adult health (SAGE) Wave 1, India National Report. International Institute for Population Sciences. Geneva: World Health Organization.

Basu G, Mondal P, Roy SK. 2018. Health of elderly tribes: a community based clinico-epidemiological study in West Bengal, India. International Journal of Community Medicine and Public Health. 5: 970.

Bhatnagar S, Patel A, Raja SN. 2018. Aspiring pain practitioners in India: assessing challenges and building opportunities. Indian Journal of Palliative Care. 24: 93.

Brennan F, Carr DB, Cousins M. 2007. Pain management: a fundamental human right. Anesthesia and Analgesia. 105: 205-221.

Denard PJ, Holton KF, Miller J, Fink HA, Kado DM, Marshall LM, Osteoporotic Fractures in Men (MrOS) Study Group. 2010. Back pain, neurogenic symptoms, and physical function in relation to spondylolisthesis among elderly men. The Spine Journal. 10: 865-873.

Docking R, Fleming J, Brayne C. 2011. Epidemiology of back pain in older adults: prevalence and risk factors for back pain onset. Rheumatology, 50: 1645e53

Chapter Ten

AN ANALYSIS OF COVARIATES OF POST-PARTUM AMENORRHOEA AMONG THE MISHING TRIBE OF ASSAM

MAITREYEE SHARMA

ABSTRACT

Our in-built biology always finds a way to increase the survival chance of it through certain mechanisms. One of such a mechanism is Post-Partum Amenorrhoea (PPA) which is a temporary period of sterility that follows immediately after every child birth. In a society with natural fertility, this is the only period that tends to act as a space between two successive births. Though PPA is biological, earlier findings suggest that it is regulated by various socio-cultural and demographic factors, both implicitly and explicitly. In this paper, an investigation is done to observe the extent to which various socio-demographic explanatory variables may have an influence and association using Log-Rank test and Cox's Proportional-Hazards Model. A sample of 400 mothers with atleast one living child belonging to the Mishing tribeof Assamwas selected for the purpose. These women so considered never used any kind of contraceptives till now. The median duration of PPA was observed to be 7.8 months. Ten (10) explanatory variables were considered for statistical analysis, of which only four (04) variables, namely, duration of breastfeeding, birth order, family type and the survival status of the preceeding child were found to show significant association and correlation with PPA.

Keywords: *Postpartum amenorrhoea, socio-demographic variables, cross-sectional studies, survival experience, statistical association.*

Introduction

A mother, after every childbirth, has to go through a period in which she is temporarily sterile. This period is the post-partum amenorrhoea (PPA) and it varies from one woman to another and also after every childbirth of the same woman. This period of temporary sterility tends to reduce the effective reproductive span of a woman, thus, acts as a natural contraceptive mechanism. Longer the PPA period, longer is the spacing between two successive births. This is a kind of in-built survival mechanism of women. Interestingly, though PPA period is a physiological factor that affects fertility but it is found to be associated with many demographic and socio-cultural factors (Singh et al., 2012) such as duration of breastfeeding, parity, age at entry into marriage, child and maternal nutritional status (Delgado et al., 1982; Aguirre and Jones, 2005). Various researches of PPA have shown that the duration of PPA is strongly and positively associated with the duration of breastfeeding (Heinig, 1994; Aryal, 2006; Dwivedi, 2012; Singh et al., 2012). It is extremely interesting that in any cultural community, the duration of breastfeeding is regulated by the norms and taboos as prescribed by the society. The duration of PPA is longer in most of the traditional hunter-gatherer populations where mothers breastfeed their infants for three years and more (Konner, 2005) as well as giving longer and frequent bouts (Wood, 1994).

Materials and Methods

This anthropological empirical study was conducted among the Mishing tribe, located in the Dhemaji district of Assam, Northeast India. This study was approved by the research council of GauhatiUniversity. The evermarried women having atleast one live birth were selected for the purpose. A pre-tested semi-structured interview schedule was prepared to harness the required information. The sample consists of 400 eligible women. The duration of PPA is considered as the response variable and the resumption of menstruation after childbirth is regarded as the end of amenorrhoea period. The mothers who had reported termination of PPA before the survey date were also included in the study and considered as uncensored cases, however, the mothers who were still in amenorrhoea upto the end of the survey were considered as censored cases. The mothers who had more than one live birth, the PPA duration of the last birth was asked to minimize the data recall error.

Various demographic covariates include duration of breast

feeding, birth order, age at marriage of the mother, sex of the child, type of family, educational and occupational status of the couples and survival status of the preceeding child were considered. The covariates considered are interdependent and therefore, had to quantify these to adjust the effects of other covariates (Singh et al., 2012).

The Log-Rank test (Chi-square) was adopted to compare the survival experience of the groups as categorized in the tables and Cox's Proportional Hazards model was utilized to know if the duration of PPA is associated with any of the selected demographic variables. The Cox's Proportional Hazards Model was applied to investigate the effects of the explanatory variables on the time of resumption of menstruation after child birth.

The Cox's Proportional Hazards model: $\lambda(t;z)= \lambda_0(t) \exp(z\beta)$,

Where, $\lambda(t;z)$ refers to the time a specific event takes to happen (here, it is resumption of menses); $\lambda_0(t)$ is the baseline hazard function when all covariates are set to zero and β is a vector of regression coefficients (Cox, 1972). Therefore, the ratio: $\lambda(t;z)/ \lambda_0(t)= \exp(z\beta)$ represents the 'relative risk'(rr) of resumption of menstruation in the present study. When the value for the relative risk for a group is greater than one and lesser than unity for the reference group indicate that the risk of resumption of menstruation is higher and lower for this group respectively when compared with the baseline group (Singh *et al.*, 2012).

Results

Table 1 indicates the median durations of PPA according to some demographic characteristics of the couples. It is quite obvious that the median durations of PPA of the women increased with the increasing duration of breastfeeding. The overall median duration of PPA in the study is found to be 7.8 months. Log rank univariate analysis suggests a significant positive correlation between the duration of breastfeeding and PPA (39.49, $p<0.01$). Similarly, a significant and positive association was revealed between birth order and PPA (21.22, $p<0.01$). It is evident from the study that the duration of PPA increased from the lower to the higher birth order. A negative association was found between the duration of PPA and the age at marriage of the women (26.45, $p<0.01$). The sex of the child does not seem to influence the duration of PPA. However, it is interesting that the survival status of the preceeding child (surviving or death) shows a strong influence on the duration of PPA (8.16, $p<0.01$). Comparatively, longer duration of PPA is found in women who have experienced the death of the previous child than the women who have not. The women in the joint family show comparatively higher median duration of PPA (8.6 months) than who are in the nuclear family (6.0 months). By the Log rank test, the type of family also has an association with PPA. The pattern of variation in the median durations of PPA according to the educational status of the husband and the wife shows a negative linear trend and a strong correlation. The women engaged in cultivation shows the highest median duration of PPA (8.8 months) and the women engaged in service shows the lowest duration of PPA (5.8 months).

Table 1: Univariate analysis of duration of post-partum amenorrhea with some demographic variables

Duration of breastfeeding (years)	Median of PPA (months)	Log-rank test ($\chi 2$)
<1	5.8	39.49, p<0.01
1-2	7.6	
3-4	8.8	
Birth order		
1	5.6	21.22, p<0.01
2-3	6.1	
4-5	6.5	
6+	7.6	
Age at marriage of the woman (years)		
<18	8.1	26.45, p<0.01
18-23	7.2	
23-28	6.8	
Sex of the child		
Male	6.8	2.81, p>0.01
Female	7.3	
Survival status of the preceeding child		
Surviving	6.1	8.76, p<0.01
Death	7.8	
Type of Family		
Joint	8.6	6.63, p<0.05
Nuclear	6.0	
Educational Status of Husband		
Illiterate	7.6	13.22, p<0.01
Primary Standard	7.1	
Middle Standard	6.5	
Secondary Standard and above	5.2	
Educational Status of Wife		

Illiterate	7.8	14.67, p<0.01
Primary Standard	6.7	
Middle Standard	6.4	
Secondary Standard and above	5.0	
Occupational Status of Husband		
Cultivation	7.8	14.84, p<0.01
Petty Business	6.6	
Skilled work	6.8	
Service	5.3	
Occupational Status of Wife		
Cultivation	8.8	15.32, p<0.01
Petty Business	6.7	
Skilled work	6.2	
Service	5.8	
Overall	7.8	

Table 2: Cox's Proportional Hazards Analysis of PPA

VARIABLES	COEFFICIENT (β)	WALD TEST (p value)	Relative Risk (eβ)	95% CI for Relative Risk
Duration of breastfeeding (years)	-0.017	12.577, p<0.01	0.976	0.965-0.996
Birth order	-0.022	6.018, p<0.05	0.887	0.776-0.903
Age at marriage of the woman (years)	0.009	1.501, p>0.05	0.999	0.997-1.101
Sex of the child	0.005	1.435, p>0.05	0.987	0.886-1.012
Survival status of the preceeding child	-0.308	8.044, p<0.01	0.868	0.565-0.999
Type of Family	-0.217	7.341, p<0.05	0.739	0.735-0.876
Educational Status of Husband	0.005	0.381, p>0.05	0.1008	0.995-1.111
Educational Status of Wife	-0.037	0.861 p>0.05	0.733	0.866-1.003
Occupational Status of Husband	0.004	0.446, p>0.05	0.1008	0.995-1.001
Occupational Status of Wife	0.004	0.446, p>0.05	0.1008	0.995-1.102

In order to estimate the partial effects of the explanatory

variables on the relative risk of the resumption of menstruation after child birth, Cox's multivariate proportional hazard model was applied (Table 2). It is observed from the study that after controlling the other covariates, the relative risk of termination of the duration of PPA decreases with the increasing duration of breastfeeding (RR=0.976, $p<0.01$). In addition to that, the risk for resumption of menstruation decreases by 1.6 percent with every one month increase in the duration of breastfeeding. Birth order is found to be another significant variate; the relative risk of the termination of PPA decreases with the higher birth order than that of the lower birth order ($e\beta=0.887$, 6.018, $p<0.05$). The survival status of the preceeding child during infancy had a significant association on the relative risk of returning into menstruation after childbirth. The risk of termination of PPA is 0.66 times higher for those who have not experienced a death of the previous child (RR=0.668, 8.044, $p<0.01$) than those who had experienced a previous infant death. The type of family is found to have a significant effect (7.341, $p<0.05$) on the risk of returning into menstruation. The women in the joint family shows a lower risk of resumption than those who are in the nuclear family. Of the other predictor variables, the occupational status of the husband and the wife, their educational status and the age at marriage of the women are found to be insignificant predictors of the relative risk of termination of PPA.

Discussion

The duration of PPA of a particular woman is though biological but affected by many demographic variables within a certain socio-cultural matrix. In the present population, the PPA period is considered to be a natural biological phenomenon by the couples. The aged females responded that the temporary absence of menstruation for a few months helps in better child-rearing process by the mother as well as for healing of the mother's womb. In the present study, the overall median PPA is found to be 7.8 months but found to be associated with many demographic predictor variables. The duration of breastfeeding is found to be significantly associated with the lower risk of PPA period. This result corroborates with the results of Yadava and Jain (1998), Pinto (2005), and Singh et al., (2012). The process of breastfeeding is found to be universal in this particular population. It is also apparent from the study that the youngest child, irrespective of the gender, is breastfed for longer period than the previous children. As a result, the birth order is also one of the covariates that tend to be associated with the duration of PPA. The birth order of the child is operating indirectly through the duration of breastfeeding on the duration of PPA. The study reveals a strong and significant association between the duration of PPA and the survival status of (alive or death) the previous infant or child. The mothers who had experienced a child death preceeding the child in question have shown a higher duration of PPA than the mothers who have not experienced such an incident. Here, it may be reasoned that the succeeding child (the child in question) after the dead child tends to get relatively more attention and emotional attachment of the mother in the form of longer breastfeeding and frequent bouts. The women in the joint family show higher median duration of PPA than those women who are in the nuclear family since their marriage. The possible reason for this may be that in the joint family, there are other female relatives who share the household chores and thus, the mother can attend to the demands of the new born whenever required. However, in the nuclear family, the mother, in addition to childrearing, she has to engage in all the other household chores and responsibilities. Here, again, the duration and frequency of breastfeeding play its role implicitly which is manifested through the type of family. The effects of the sex of the child (in question) and age at marriage of the mother, educational and occupational status of the couples are not found to be significant predictors. This is in consistent with the study made by Singh et al., (2012).

References

Aguirre GP, Jones RE. 2005. Breastfeeding and post-partum amenorrhea in rural Guatemala. *Pollaciony Saluden Masoamerica*. 3: 1-18.

Aryal TR. 2006. Retrospective reporting of the duration of post-partum amenorrhea: asurvival analysis. *Kathmandu University Medical Journal*, 4: 211-7.

Cox DR.1972. Regression models and life tables. *Journal of the Royal Statistical Society*. 34:187-220.

Delgado H, MartorellR, BrinemanE, Klein RE.1982. Nutritional, lactational and birth interval components in rural Guatemala.*American Journal of Clinical Nutrition*. 31: 1468-1476.

Dwivedi LK, Dixit P. 2012. Relationship between breastfeeding and postpartum amenorrhea among Indian women: an epidemiological appraisal.*African Journal of Basic and Applied Sciences*. 4: 30-37.

Heinig MJ, Nommsen-Rivers LA, Peerson JM, Dewey KG. 1994. Factors related to duration of postpartum amenorrhoea among USA women with prolonged lactation. *Journal of Biosocial Science*. 26: 517-527.

Konner MJ, Worthman C. 1980. Nursing frequency, gonadal function, and birth spacing among Kung hunter-gatherers. *Science.* 207: 788–791.

Pinto G. 2006. Breastfeeding and postpartum amenorrhea among Bolivian women: asurvival analysis. madison, WI: University of Wisconsin-Madison: 55 (Center for Demography and Ecology working paper no. 2005-01).

Singh NS, Singh NS, Narendra RK. 2012. Postpartum amenorrhoea among Manipuri women: asurvival analysis. *Journal of Health, Population and Nutrition.* 30: 93-98.

Wood JW. 1994. *Dynamics of Human Reproduction: Biology, Biometry, Demography.* Aldine de Gruyter, New York.

Yadava KNS, Jain SK. 1998. Post-partum amenorrhea in rural eastern Uttar Pradesh, India. *Journal of Biosocial Science.* 30: 227-243.

SECTION III

Chapter Eleven

ZINC DEFICIENCY AND HUMAN HEALTH

ANTARA BOSE AND JAYDIP SEN

ABSTRACT

Zinc is among a trace element which plays an essential role in maintaining the proper health and development of the body. Zinc plays a significant role in cell development, growth, cell differentiation, and also helps in the replication process. It is an essential component that plays a structural role in various types of proteins, functional role to several enzymes as well as helps in normal growth, wound healing and plays a critical role in brain and neurobehavioral development. Zinc deficiency is a major public health issue that results in disbalances in the body's immune system, causing irritation, depression, anger, alopecia, and diseases such as diarrhea. India is a multi-ethnic country that provides insufficient information about the zinc status among the Indian population where the tribal are also included. The insufficiency is mainly due to fewer studies and lack of reliable parameters. The present chapter highlights the importance, recommended dietary allowances, effect, the targeted group including the tribal health about zinc, and its deficiency in India. The chapter also discusses the biomarkers used, the supplementations, and interventions approach to lower the rate of zinc deficiency.

Keywords: *Biomarkers, Deficiency, Health, Tribal, Supplementations*

Introduction

Nutrients in the form of both micro and macro form are an essential component for the overall growth and development of the body. Nutrients promote normal body growth, maintenance, and repair mechanism. Nutrients comprise carbohydrates, proteins, fats which are the major form of nutrients, the other forms which include vitamins and minerals, which are crucial but are required in very less amount. Minerals though required in small amounts is necessary for healthy well-being. The body requires moderate to very less quantity of major minerals and trace minerals for the smooth performance in maintaining the overall strength of the body. Trace elements are present are less than 0.1% by weight or 100 parts per million (ppm) which is further classified into essential and toxic depending on their function (Dorjee and Sen, 2016). The harmful trace elements constitute the lead, mercury, and arsenic which when accumulates in the body cause ill-effects and toxicants the overall development of the body whereas the essential elements which consist of zinc, copper, iron, cobalt, fluorine, iodine, selenium, manganese and chromium are important for proper metabolic functions. Micronutrient deficiencies are most widespread among people of all ages (WHO, 2006; Murray et al., 2012) including the tribal population where zinc deficiencies count the most. Middle to low-income countries is mostly affected by micronutrient deficiencies due to which these countries face the rise in mortality and morbidity (WHO, 2006; Victoria et al., 2008). Studies conducted during decades consider zinc deficiency as a widespread phenomenon leading to the global burden of diseases.

Zinc is an essential form of trace elements that plays a major role in cell differentiation maintains the maturation level and also helps in the replication process (Prasad, 2013; Dorjee and Sen, 2016). Zinc is the trace elements which occupies almost all organ and tissues which solely includes the brain, kidney, liver, hair whereas cerebellum contains zinc in higher amount then the cerebrum (Prasad 2013). Zinc is an essential component as it has a catalytic, structural, and regulatory function (Cousins, 1996; Bhowmick et al., 2010), where deficiency causes loss of activities. Zinc as it is not conserved inside the body so the dietary intake quantity of zinc depends upon its adequacy. Zinc is naturally present in few foods whereas are absent in others. Zinc is an essential element to maintain the steady-state of the body (Rink and Gabreil, 2000) as it also acts as catalysis for more than three hundred enzymes (IMPM, 2001; Dorjee and Das, 2013). The inadequate intake of zinc through diet thus contributes to zinc deficiency. Zinc in any form whether deficiency or in excess accumulation inside the body causes different infections and diseases which further lowers the survival rate. Non-specific symptoms are very prevalent with zinc deficiencies which often coincides with other health issues. Figure 1 highlights some of the effects caused by both deficiencies as well as in the excess amount of zinc accumulation. Undernutrition results in 3.1 million child deaths annually which further are caused due to stunting, wasting, minimum breastfeeding, micronutrient deficiencies which includes mainly vitamin A and zinc deficiency (Black et al., 2013).

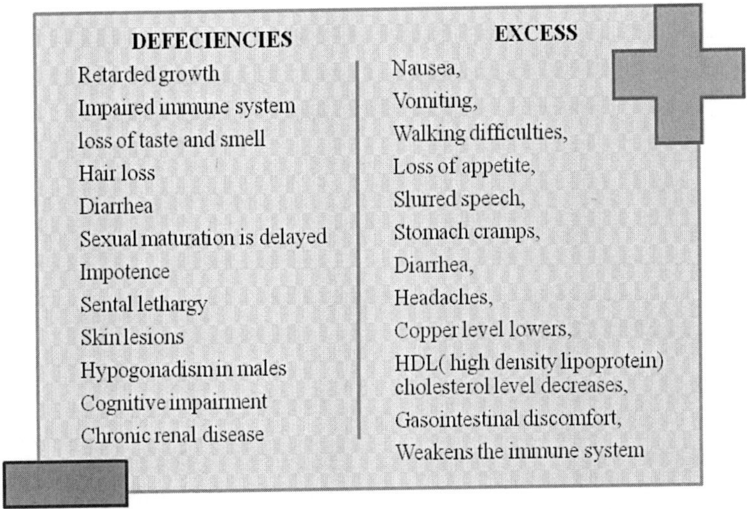

Figure 1. Zinc effects in the form of both excess and deficiency

The datasheet from the recent Comprehensive National Nutrition Survey (CNNS, 2016-2018) showed that adolescent females (28%) were less affected by zinc deficiency than males (35%). State-wise prevalence showed huge differences as Nagaland showed lowest prevalence of zinc deficiency among pre-school, school children, and also among adolescents whereas prevalence was higher in Himachal Pradesh (41% and 38%) among children belonging from 1 to 9 years of age where Gujrat showed 55% of adolescents to be zinc deficit. The Northeastern and eastern states showed prevalence of zinc deficiency to be highest in Jharkhand (28.4%), Assam (27.1%) and Manipur (26.6%) among pre-school children. The prevalence was higher in Manipur (35.3%) followed by Meghalaya (23.3%) and Jharkhand (21.9%) among children belonging to 5-9 years. The adolescents are the transitional group where micronutrients are essential for rapid growth and development. The states which showed high prevalence of zinc deficiency among this group were Manipur (52.8%) from the Northeastern states followed by Jharkhand (49.8%) in the east and then Meghalaya (49.3%) again from the Northeastern region.

Recommended Dietary Allowances (RDA)

The dietary intake of zinc depends on the Recommended Dietary Allowances (RDA) which determines the average intake of zinc in the form of a daily basis which further meets the nutritional requirements depending upon the age and sex of the individual. The recommendation of zinc intake is determined by Dietary References Intakes (DRIs) which is developed by the Food and Nutrition Board (FNB) are summarized in Table 1.

Table 1: Recommended dietary allowances for Zinc(mg/day)

Age	Male	Female	Pregnant women	Lactating women
0-6 months	2	2	-	-
7-12 months	3	3	-	-
1-3 years	3	3	-	-
4-8 years	5	5	-	-
9-13 years	8	8	-	-
14-18 years	11	9	12	13
19 years and above	11	8	11	12

The Adequate Intake (AI) level of zinc determines the adequacy to maintain the RDA level, the tolerable upper intake level determines the maximum daily intake level of zinc. The Indian Council of Medical Research (ICMR) (Nair and Augustine, 2018) recommended 5-9 mg intake of zinc for children belonging to 1 to 12 years, 11-12 mg for 13-17 years of age, and 10-12 mg for males and females. The RDA for both pregnant and lactating women is 12 mg of zinc per day. The details RDA values by ICMR (2010) are provided in Table 2 which has been further revised the year 2019.

Table 2: Recommended dietary allowances for Zinc (Indian population)

Groups		Age	Zinc (mg/day)
Children		1-3 years	5
		4-6 years	7
		7-9 years	8
Adolescents		10-12 years	9
		13-15 years	11
		16-17 years	12
Adult Women	Non- pregnant/ non-lactating Women	-	10
	Pregnant Women	-	12
	Lactating women	-	12
Adult Men		-	12

Source: Recommended Dietary Allowances (RDA) for zinc in India (ICMR 2010, 2019)

Zinc Deficiencies and its effect

Zinc deficiencies can be in any form: severe, moderate to mild conditions. The severe form is very rare as compared to the mild and moderate forms of zinc deficiency. Cereals protein-containing phytate serves as a major factor for zinc deficiencies (Prasad, 2013). Zinc deficiency in severe form causes acrodermatitis enteropathica, which is a rare autosomal recessive lethal disease (Gammoh and Rink, 2017), bullous pustular dermatitis. Eyes are also affected causing several diseases such as corneal opacities, conjunctivitis, and photophobia. An inadequate amount of zinc causes fluctuation in emotions, retardation in growth, loss of weight, cerebellar ataxia, and many more (Dorjee and Das, 2013). The males are affected by hypogonadism. Disorders related to the nervous system and sensory organs are also very common. The severe form of zinc deficiencies needs utmost care where when untreated can cause death risk (Prasad, 2013; Yasuda and Tsutsui, 2016). Zinc deficiencies in the form of moderate and mild are common among children as the rate of infections increases (Aggarwal, 2005). Maternal zinc deficiency adversely affects the health of the fetus thus increases the chance of complications during pregnancy. Zinc deficiency dysfunctions the immune system where chances of being affected by different pathogens increases (Gammoh and Rink, 2017). Zinc malfunction is directly the cause of malnutrition and various diseases such as diabetes and several types of cancer (oesophageal and breast). Deficiency in zinc also causes various infectious diseases as malaria, diarrhea, human immune virus, pneumonia (Maret, 2013). Mild effects of zinc are diverse and detectable through various metabolic processes which can be further corrected by the usage of zinc supplementation (IMPM, 2001). Mild zinc deficiency during the old age disbalances the adaptive immune responses which includes the production of immunoglobulins reduces B-cell functioning and increases the effect of proinflammatory cytokines (Mossink, 2020). Zinc deficiency decreases the neutrophil functional activities, the number of lymphocytes also decreases (Mossink, 2020), production of antibodies also lowers (Gammoh and Rink, 2017), the activity of phagocytosis also decreases (Haase and Rink, 2009; Wessels et al., 2017; Mossink, 2020). The T helper cells cytokine secretion is disturbed which decreases the production of interferonγ (INFγ) (Gammoh and Rink, 2017) whereas thymic atropy increases thus chances of infection also increases (Maggini et al., 2018). The recent data from CNNS shows that zinc deficiency is prevalent among preschool children (19%), school children (17%), and 32 percent among the adolescents group. The effect of zinc deficiency more in rural areas than urban areas where pre-school children (20%, 16%), school children (18%, 14%) as well as the adolescents group showed such similarities.

Zinc and its importance

Zinc though required in small amounts serves as a second messenger to immune cells further helping in the signalling process (Prasad, 2013). Litchten et al., (2001) has reported that human genome codes proteins which contain zinc accounts to more than 10 percent. Zinc intake in sufficient amount depends on the age, sex, and the diet consumed. The bioavailability of zinc depends on the diet patterns where ligands (phytate), lignin chelate decreases zinc contents in food whereas whole grains, cereals, red meats, seafood contain zinc in higher amounts. The foods from animal sources contain zinc in a higher amount than plant-based foods, thus people consuming more plant-based foods are more prone to zinc deficiency. The quality of dietary intake due to poverty, poor hygiene, and also food taboos contribute to an increase in infections further lowering the zinc concentration where both the environmental as well as hereditary factors play a major role (Sandstrom et al., 2000). The ZIP-Zrt/Irt-like proteins transport zinc inside the cytosol and the ZnT-Zinc transporter consists of 10 transporters which transport zinc out of the cytosol thus provides stimulus to both deficiency and excess contain zinc inside the body further maintaining the stability of the body (Wellenreuther et al., 2009; Kimura and Kambe, 2016; Gammoh and Rink, 2017). Zinc deficiency causes damage to the host cell which further causes inflammation of cells, as zinc acts as a regulator of proinflammatory response (Gammoh and Rink, 2017). Zinc due to its catalytic activity is called the Lewis acid and acts as an electron acceptor. It helps in the activation of T-lymphocytes and decreases the chances of infection through sepsis and acts as an antibacterial immune response which suppresses the viral activity of pneumonia (Lechein et al., 2020). It is associated with the metabolic activity of bone by increasing the level of vitamin D and the synthesizing of DNA also increases (Dorjee and Sen, 2016). It also acts as a neurotoxin further helping in the proper functioning of the central nervous system (Bitanihirwe and Cunningham, 2009).

Zinc Inadequacy and the Targeted Group

Zinc deficiency causes various health problems which if untreated takes a severe form and becomes fatal. It is distributed throughout the body which is the reason for being difficult to measure thus its deficiency gives rise to clinically risk factors. Zinc deficiencies effects several targeted age groups having risk factors which commonly includes people with alcohol consumption will low zinc due to decrease in intestinal absorption with an increase in zinc concentration in urine (Prasad, 2002), infants who are more than six months of age but fully depends on breastmilk (IMPM, 2001; Hambidge and Krebs, 2007), children and adults with sickle cell anemia where zinc is in lower concentration within the plasma concentration due to poor nutritional status (Zemel et al., 2002). Pregnant women requires an excessive amount of zinc (Berhe et al., 2019) than non-pregnant females as the fetal grows the zinc requirement also increases thus causes zinc deficiency, as well as lactating women, also requires maximum zinc as the growing infants depend on the breastmilk which should further contain the required amount of zinc for the first six months as the infant solely depends on exclusively breastfeeding practices. Zinc is important during pregnancy as its deficiency can give birth to babies with low birth weight as well as the fetus would have retarded growth rate during the gestational periods. Zinc deficiency shows high prevalence among vegetarians who fully depends on the plant-based diet which contains phytic acid (myo-inositol hexaphosphate) where the bioavailability of zinc is very low. Individuals with malabsorption syndromes like Crohn's disease, short bowel syndrome, and ulcerative colitis are more prone to zinc loss through urine (IMPM, 2001). Zinc absorption decreases due to chronic diseases related to renal and liver (Prasad, 2003). Gastrointestinal infections, diabetes, and chronic diarrhea also contribute to zinc loss from the body (Prasad, 2004).

Zinc and Tribal Health

Zinc deficiency contributes to about 30 percent in South Asian countries (Wessells and Brown, 2012). The prevalence of zinc deficiencies varies depending on various factors which include the socio-economic, demographic factors. The consumption of diet pattern, climate, and educational level directly have positive to negative effects on health. The tribal population is considered as the vulnerable group and the most underprivileged group (Mishra, 2005) where malnutrition in terms of under nutrition and micronutrient deficiencies exists. The tribal population consists of 8.6 percent of India's population according to the 2011 census from were 89.97 percent lives in the rural areas and 10.03 percent resides in the urban areas. The rural areas are mainly the forest areas where basic necessary condition of living amenities are absent such as clean and safe drinking water, proper sanitation, proper nutrition, safe and hygienic birth practices leading to the rise in degraded environmental conditions. One major factor associated with zinc deficiency may be the cultural practices that differentiate them based on language, norms, different political and social institutions which may restrict them to the consumption of animal-based foods or supplementation offered by the government through various programmes and interventions. The prevalence of zinc deficiency is directly related to diseases where maternal zinc deficiency weakens the immunological system of the growing infants whose effect persists throughout the whole lifespan. The scarcity of data for zinc on the tribal population has made it very difficult for determining the health consequences. Recently a study by Smith et al. (2019) shows that southern and the Northeastern states which are dominated by rice consuming diets show a high prevalence of zinc inadequacy (38%) when compared to the states of northern, eastern, central, and the western region (17%). Local eating habits region-wise shows diversification in zinc deficiency. The level of carbon dioxide susceptible to the food crops on which the Indian population solely depends causes deficiency in zinc concentration as the CO_2 (carbon-dioxide) level increases by 550 ppm, thus hampering the normal intake levels (Smith et al., 2019). The tribal communities mostly belong to the poor households where the majority consume plant-based foods that contain low zinc and anti-nutritional compounds, thus leading to a rise in zinc deficiency. The tribal people live in a perilous atmospheric condition where limited resources are available for food thus gives rise to deficiency with abysmal living conditions. Tribal people show a high prevalence of nutritional deficiency, chronic energy deficiency as well as micronutrient deficiencies which seriously contributes to mortality and morbidity. A study by Mittal and Srivastava (2006) shows that the intake amount of proteins and calories are very less among the tribal group. The serum zinc levels among the adult tribal of Jharkhand were <70µg/dl which showed the prevalence of zinc deficiency (Kapil et al., 2003). Agte et al., (2005) showed that zinc intake among the tribal is lower than the non-tribal groups. Zinc deficiency contributes to rising in intestinal infections and diarrhea further causes malabsorption (Osei and Hamer, 2008).

Biomarkers and Zinc detection

Zinc deficiencies at all ages have resulted in the introduction of zinc supplementation as well as fortified foods containing zinc. The prevalence of zinc deficiency is commonly estimated through plasma or serum zinc concentration (Lowe et al., 2009). Table 3 classifies the serum zinc concentration level to a diagnosis of zinc deficiency among children and adolescents. Plasma or serum zinc concentration is less reliable in case of the increased burden of infections as well as during inflammation where falsified high estimates can show the prevalence of zinc deficiency. Serum zinc concentration indicates the dietary amount of zinc intaked. It also responds to the intake of zinc supplementation as well as available for almost all age. Clinical management with metabolic syndromes serves as a sensitive form of biomarkers (Reed et al., 2014; Freitas et al., 2017). Studies suggest that 24-hour urine excretion containing zinc serves as a recently adopted biomarker though supportive evidence is much less regarding valediction and effectiveness (Wieringa et al., 2015; Lowe, 2016). Studies also suggest that erythrocyte zinc can be used as a biomarker for the study of zinc in terms of cellular form (Freitas et al., 2017). Very recently the Polyacrylamide Gel Electrophoresis (PAGE) is being used to detect the amount of phytic acid in foods that would help in extraction and separation of the acid, thus decreasing the negative impact of absorption of zinc, further by preventing zinc deficiency. Zinc status has been recently analyzed in relation to the blood gene expression with the analysis of zinc transporters (ZIP4 and ZNT1) which showed that children with plasma zinc deficiency consist of high ZnT1 mRNA expression whereas have low ZIP4 mRNA expressions which show the regulation of homeostasis of minerals which further influences the nutritional status (Reis et al., 2020).

Table 3: Serum zinc concentration among children and adolescents to assess zinc deficiency

Age–Childrenand Adolescents	Fasting-Status (Morning)	Non-fasting Status (Morning)
<10 years	<65μg/dl	<65μg/dl
≥10 years		
Females (non-pregnant)	<70μg/dl	<70μg/dl
Males	<66μg/dl	<70μg/dl

Source: International Zinc Nutrition Consultative Group (2012)

Supplementation and Interventions to tackle Zinc deficiency

The plant-based food consumption provides an inadequate source of zinc thus demands zinc supplements (Brieger and Rink, 2010). To reduce the rate of mortality and morbidity due to deficiencies of zinc, biofortification of crops would serve as a nutritional intervention through agronomic pathways and classical breeding through genetic processes (Bouis et al., 2011; Saltzman et al., 2013). Exclusively breastfeeding infants suffer from zinc deficiency as breast milk contains inadequate zinc which further causes various infections which further can be overcome by providing oral zinc supplementation (Huang and Tepaamorndech, 2013). Zinc supplements are available in various forms which include sulfate, acetate, and gluconate which various in percentage. Zinc supplementation helps to improve weight and also acts as an inflammatory biomarker for the insulin resistance effect (Khorsandi et al., 2019). Zinc supplementation increases the lymphocyte's response to mitogens (Prasad 2000; Wintergerst et al., 2007), use in treatment for skin, leg, and arteriole ulcers (Wilkinson and Hawke, 2000). Zinc deficiency during pregnancy leads to low birth weight of the baby. Zinc supplementation to sickle cell anemia patients improves the ammonia level of plasma and secondary sexual characteristics. It helps to increase its amount in the blood composition consisting of the plasma, erythrocytes, and neutrophils, whereas also corrects the hypersensitive activity of the patient (Prasad, 2013). Zinc serves as an "anti-copper drug" for Wilson's disease where metallothionein when induced has a high affinity to bind with copper which prevents the transfer of serosal of copper to blood thus producing a negative effect, hence effective in the treatment of the disease (Prasad, 2013). Therapeutic use of zinc in daily dose also decreases the signs of age-related macular degeneration hence also reduces the mortality rate. Zinc supplementation according to bioavailability consists of different compositions which include zinc gluconate, picolinate, and citrate (Santos et al., 2020). A recent study by Kewcharoenwong et al. (2020) among rural children of Laotian shows that T-cell concentrations of cytokines show an effect on zinc supplementation. Zinc supplementation reduces the rate of diarrhea and pneumonia among children residing in the low-income countries, thus decreasing the rate of mortality and morbidity among them (Brown et al., 2009; Kewcharoenwong et al., 2020). Zinc supplementation serves as a preventive measure against diarrhea and pneumonia among children.

Very little strategies have been developed to improve the condition of zinc deficiencies, where supplementations are recommended directly which proves effective against the deficiency. As this does not secure for long term effect, interventions are necessary to lower the rate of zinc deficiency by long term impact on the overall health. To increase the dietary zinc amount direct approaches should be implemented towards the health of the tribal groups in terms of reducing the inhibitors and increasing the absorption which would cause an increase in the zinc quantity level. An alternative method introduced to tackle the problem of zinc deficiency is fortification were the staple foods with zinc is made available that further improves the serum zinc concentration. (Shah et al., 2016). Though fortification is difficult to apply, fortified meals can be made available to the targeted groups mainly encompassing the children group in the form of zinc sprinkles (Osei and Hamer, 2008). Oral zinc also helps in the treatment of diarrhea (Lazzerini and Wanzira, 2016). Biofortification of food crops (Petry et al., 2016) with a high amount of zinc are also some recent interventions put forward by the government to combat the zinc deficiency status among the population. Dietary diversity with an adequate amount of zinc-rich diets serves effectively towards zinc deficiency. Zinc deficiency is a major concerning public issue which should be thoroughly monitored and interventions concerning a permanent reduction in the deficiency must be envisaged upon the targeted population. Zinc in additional form is available as micronutrient powders and blended fortified foods.

Conclusion

Essential multiple functions of the life cycle are affected by zinc deficiency as zinc is an essential trace element that plays a vital role in growth and development. Dietary inadequacy, malabsorption, and an increase in utilization process further challenge the zinc status among the tribal populations. Zinc supplementation should be made available to the tribal population at a minimal amount or free of cost. Zinc deficiency should be monitored and treated in form of supplementations and various interventions should be implemented at the community level which would help to reduce the burden of mortality, morbidity, and prevalence of infectious diseases thus contributing to strengthening the neuro-behavioral development and hence proper functioning of the immune system leading to normal growth and development. Strategies in determining the causes of zinc deficiency and planning accordingly would contribute to proper health consequences and reduce the rate of being infected by the asymptotic feature of zinc deficiency.

Acknowledgment

The authors acknowledge the help of the Department of Anthropology, University of North Bengal.

References

Aggarwal AK. 2005. Zinc Deficiency: Public Health Perspective. *Indian Journal of Community Medicine.* 30: 73-74.

Agte VV, Chiplonkar SA, Tarwadi KV. 2005. Factors influencing zinc status of apparently healthy infants. *Journal of the American College of Nutrition.* 24: 334-341.

Berhe K, Gebrearegay F, Gebremariam H. 2019. Prevalence and associated factors of zinc deficiency among pregnant women and children in Ethiopia: a systematic review and meta-analysis. *BMC Public Health.* 19: 1663.

Bhowmik D, Chiranjib KP, Kumar S. 2010. A potential medicinal importance of zinc in human health and chronic disease. *International Journal of Pharmaceutical and Biomedical Science.* 1: 5-11.

Bitanihirwe BK, Cunningham MG. 2009. Zinc: The brain's dark horse. *Synapse.* 63: 1029-1049.

Black RE, Victora CG, Walker SP, Bhutta ZA, Christian P, de Onis M, Ezzati M, Grantham-McGregor S, Katz J, Martorell R, Uauy R, MCNSG. 2013. Maternal and child undernutrition and overweight in low-income and middle-income countries. *Lancet.* 382: 427–451.

Bouis HE, Hotz C, McClafferty B, Meenakshi JV, Pfeiffer WH. 2011. Biofortification: a new tool to reduce micronutrient malnutrition. *Food and Nutrition Bulletin.* 32:S31-40.

Brieger A, Rink L. 2010. Zinc and Immune Functions. *Nutrition & Medicine.* 25: 156-160.

Brown KH, Peerson JM, Baker SK, Hess SY. 2009. Preventive zinc supplementation among infants, preschoolers, and older prepubertal children. *Food and Nutrition Bulletin*. 30: S12–40.

Comprehensive National Nutrition Survey (CNNS). 2019. *National Report*. Ministry of Health and Family Welfare (MoHFW), Government of India, UNICEF and Population Council. New Delhi.

Cousins RJ. 1998. A role of zinc in the regulation of gene expression. *Proceedings of the Nutrition Society*. 57: 307-311.

Dorjee B, Das S. 2013. Zinc Deficiency among Indian Children. *Southeast Asian Anthropologies*. 13: 103-109.

Dorjee B, Sen J. 2016. Trace Elements, Nutritional Anthropology and Zinc. *Southeast Asian Anthropologies*, 16: 167-177.

Freitas EP, Cunha AT, Aquino SL, Pedrosa LF, Lima SC, Lima JG, Almeida MG, Sena-Evangelista, KC. 2017. Zinc Status Biomarkers and Cardiometabolic Risk Factors in Metabolic Syndrome: A Case Control Study. *Nutrition*. 9: 175.

Gammoh NZ, Rink L. 2017. Zinc in infection and inflammation. *Nutrition*. 9: 624.

Haase H, Rink L. 2009. Functional significance of zinc-related signaling pathways in immune cells. *Annual Review of Nutrition*. 29: 133-152.

Hambidge KM, Krebs NF. 2007. Zinc deficiency: a special challenge. *Journal of Nutrition*. 137(4): 1101-1105.

Huang L, Tepaamorndech S. 2013. The SLC30 family of zinc transporters. *Molecular Aspects of Medicine*. 34: 612-619.

ICMR, 2010. Nutrition Requirements and Recommended Dietary Allowances for Indians. A Report of the Expert Group of the Indian Council of Medical Research. ICMR: New Delhi.

Institute of Medicine (US) Panel on Micronutrients (IMPM). 2001.*Dietary Reference Intakes for Vitamin A, Vitamin K, Arsenic, Boron, Chromium, Copper, Iodine, Iron, Manganese, Molybdenum, Nickel, Silicon, Vanadium, and Zinc. Washington (DC): National Academies Press (US):12, Zinc*. Available from: https://www.ncbi.nlm.nih.gov/books/NBK222317/

International Zinc Nutrition Consultative Group (IZiNCG). 2012. Assessing population zinc status with serum zinc concentration: Technical Brief. 2(2): USA.

Kapil U, Singh P, Pathak P. 2003. Serum zinc levels amongst tribal population in a district of Jharkhand State, India: a pilot study. *Eastern Journal of Medicine*. 8: 33-34.

Kewcharoenwong C, Schuster GU, Wessells KR, Hinnouho GM, Barffour MA, Kounnavong S, Brown KH, Hess SY, Samer W, Tussakhon I, Peerson JM, Lertmemongkolchai G, Stephensen CB. 2020. Daily Preventive Zinc Supplementation Decreases Lymphocyte and Eosinophil Concentrations in Rural Laotian Children from Communities with a High Prevalence of Zinc Deficiency: Results of a Randomized Controlled Trial. *Journal of Nutrition*. 150: 204–221.

Khorsandi H, Nikpayam O, Yousefi R, Parandoosh M, Hosseinzadeh N, Saidpour A, Ghorbani A. 2019. Zinc supplementation improves body weight management, infammatory biomarkers and insulin resistance in individuals with obesity: a randomized, placebo-controlled, double-blind trial. *Diabetes & Metabolic Syndrome*. 11: 101.

Kimura T, Kambe T. 2016. The Functions of Mettallothionein and ZIP and ZnT Transporters: An Overview and Prespective. *International Journal of Molecular Sciences*. 17:336.

Lanzzerini M, Wanzira H. 2016. Oral zinc for treating diarrhoea in children. *Cochrane Database of Systematic Reviews*.12: CD005436.

Lechien JR, Chiesa-Estomba CM, De Siati DR, Horoi M, Le Bon SD, Rodriguez A, Dequanter D, Blecic S, El Afia F, Distinguin L, Chekkoury-Idrissi Y, Hans S, Delgado IL, Calvo-Henriquez C, Lavigne P, Falanga C, Barillari, MR, Cammaroto G, Khalife, M, Leich P, Souchay C, Rossi C, Journe F, Hsieh J, Edjlali M, Carlier R, Ris L, Lovato A, Filippis CD, Coppee F, Fakhry N, Ayad T, Saussez S. 2020. Olfactory and gustatory dysfunctions as a clinical presentation of mild-to-moderate forms of the coronavirus disease (COVID-19): a multicenter European study. *European Archives of Oto-Rhino-Laryngology. 277:* 2251–2261.

Lichten LA, Ryu MS, Guo L, Embury J, Cousins JR .2001. MTF-1-Mediated Repression of the Zinc Transporter Zip10 Is Alleviated by Zinc Restriction. *PLoS One*. 6: e21526.

Lowe NM, Fekete K, Decsi T. 2009. Methods of assessment of zinc status in humans: A systematic review. *The American Journal of Clinical Nutrition*. 89: 2040S–2051S.

Lowe NM. 2016. Assessing zinc in humans. *Current Opinion in Clinical Nutrition & Metabolic Care*. 19: 321–327.

Maggini S, Pierre A, Calder PC. 2018. Immune function and micronutrient requirments change over the life course. *The Journal of Nutrition*. 10:1531.

Maret W. 2013. Zinc and Human Disease. In *Interrelations between Essential Metal Ions and Human Diseases*. Sigel A, Sigel H, Sigel RK (eds.) Springer: Dordrecht, The Netherlands. pp. 389-414.

Mishra, N. R. 2005. Dynamics of caste-based deprivation in child under-nutrition in India." Report Presented at the National Seminar on *Development of Scheduled Castes in India: An Appraisal of Implementation of Programmes*. at MPISSR, Ujjain, Madha Pradesh, January 17-19.

Mittal PC, Srivastava S. 2006. Diet, nutritional status and food related traditions of Oraon tribes of New Mal (West Bengal), India. *Intr Elec J*

Rur Rem Health Res Edu Prac Pol. 6: 385.

Mossink JP. 2020. Zinc as nutritional intervention and prevention measure for COVID-19 disease. *BMJ Nutrition, Prevention & Health.* 3: e000095.

Murray CJL, Vos T, Lozano R, Naghavi M, Flaxman AD, Michaud C, Ezzati M, Shibuya K, Salomon JA, Abdalla S, et al.2012. Disability-adjusted life years (DALYs) for 291 diseases and injuries in 21 regions, 1990-2010: A systematic analysis for the Global Burden of Disease Study 2010. *Lancet.* 380(9859): 2197-2223.

Nair KPM, Augustine LF. 2018. Country-specific nutrient requirements & recommended dietary allowances for Indians: Current status & future direction. *Indian Journal of Medical Research.* 148(5): 522-530.

Osei AK, Hamer DH. 2008. Zinc Nutrition and Tribal Health in India In *Health and Nutritional Problems of Indigenous population: Tribes and Tribals.* Kaushik Bose editor. Kamla-Raj Enterprises. 2: 111-119

Petry N, Olofin I, Boy E, Angel MD, Rohner F. 2016. The Effect of Low Dose Iron and Zinc Intake on Child Micronutrient Status and Development during the First 1000 Days of Life: A Systematic Review and Meta-Analysis. *The Journal of Nutrition.* 8: 773.

Prasad AS. 2000. Effects of zinc deficiency on Th1 and Th2 cytokine shifts. *The Journal of Nutrition.* 182: S62-568.

Prasad AS. 2002. Zinc deficiency in patients with sickle cell disease. *The American Journal of Clinical Nutrition.* 75: 181-182.

Prasad AS. 2003. Zinc deficiency. *British Medical Journal.* 326: 409-10.

Prasad AS. 2004. Zinc deficiency: its characterization and treatment. *Metal Ions in Biological Systems.* 41: 103-137.

Prasad AS. 2013. Discovery of Human Zinc Deficiency: its Impact on Human Health and Disease. *American Society of Nutrition and advance Nutrition.* 4: 176-190.

Reed S, Qin X, Ran-Ressler R, Brenna JT, Glahn RP, Take E. 2014. Dietary zinc deficiency affects blood linoleic acid: Dihomo-γ-linolenic acid (LA:DGLA) ratio; a sensitive physiological marker of zinc status in vivo (Gallus gallus). *The Journal of Nutrition.* 6: 1164–1180.

Reis BZ, dos SantosVieira DA, da Costa Maynard D, da Silva DG, Mendes-Netto RS, Cozzolino SMF. 2020. Zinc nutritional status influences ZnT1 and ZIP4 gene expression in children with a high risk of zinc deficiency. *Journal of Trace Elements in Medicine and Biology.* 61: 126537.

Rink L, Gabreil P. 2000. Zinc and the immune system. *Proceedings of the Nutrition Society.* 59: 541-552.

Saltzman A, Birol E, Bouis HE, Boy E, De MFF, Islam Y, Pfeiffer WH. 2013. Biofortification: progress toward a more nursing future. *Global Food Security.* 2: 9-17.

Sandstrom B, Bugel S, McGaw BA, Price J, Reid MD. 2000. A high oat-bran intake does not impair zinc absorption in humans when added to a low-fiber animal protein-based diet. *Journal of Nutrition*. 130: 594-599.

Santos HO, Teixeira FJ, Schoenfeld BJ. 2020. Dietary vs pharmacological doses of zinc: a clinical review. 39: 1345-1353

Shah D, Sachdev HS, Gera T, De-Regil LM, Pen˜aRosas JP. 2016. Fortification of staple foods with zinc for improving zinc status and other health outcomes in the general population. *Cochrane Database of Systematic Reviews*. 6: CD010697.

Smith MR, DeFries R, Chhatre A, Ghosh-Jerath S, Myers SS. 2019. Inadequate Zinc Intake in India: Past, Present, and Future. *Food and Nutrition Bulletin*. 40: 26-40.

Victoria CG, Adair L, Fall C, Hallal PC, Martorell R, Richter L, Sachdev HS, Study MCU. 2008. Maternal and child undernutrition: consequences for adult health and human capital. *TheLancet*. 371: 340-357.

Wellenreuther G, Cianci M, Tucoulou R, Meyer-Klaucke W, Haase H. 2009. The ligand environment of zinc stored in vessels. *Biochemical and Biophysical Research Communications*. 380: 198-203.

Wessells KR, Brown KH. 2012. Estimating the global prevalence of zinc deficiency: results based on zinc availability in national food supplies and the prevalence of stunting. *PLoS One*. 7: e50568.

Wessels I, Maywald M, Rink L. 2017. Zinc as a gatekeeper of immune function. *The Journal of Nutrition*. 9: 1286.

Wieringa FT, Dijkhuizen MA, Fiorentino M, Laillou A, Berger J. 2015. Determination of zinc status in humans: Which indicator should we use? *The Journal of Nutrition*. 7: 3252–3263.

Wilkinson EA, Hawke CI. 2000. Oral zinc for arterial and venous leg ulcers. *Cochrane Database of Systematic Reviews*. 2: CD001273.

Wintergerst ES, Maggini S, Horing DH. 2007. Contribution of selected vitamins and trace elements to immune function. *Annals of Nutrition and Metabolism*. 51: 301-23.

World Health Organization. (WHO). 2006. Guidelines for Food Fortification; World Health Organization: Geneva, Switzerland. Available from: https://www.who.int/nutrition/publications/guide_food_fortification_micronutrients.pdf (accessed on 20 August 2020).

Yasuda H, Tsutsui T. 2016. Infants and elderlies are susceptible to zinc deficiency. *Scientific Reports*. 6: 21850.

Zemel BS, Kawach DA, Fung EB, Ohene-Frempong K, Stallings VA. 2002. Effect of zinc supplementation on growth and body composition in children with sickle cell disease. *The American Journal of Clinical Nutrition*. 75: 300-307.

Chapter Twelve

NUTRITIONAL ANEMIA AMONG THE TRIBAL POPULATION OF NORTH BENGAL

BIDYUT KRISHNA GOSWAMI

ABSTRACT

Background and Objective: Despite tremendous improvement in standard of life, easily preventable nutritional anemia is the most common cause of anemia among the Tribal populations of Northern districts of West Bengal, popularly known as North Bengal. The present study was undertaken to assess the magnitude of nutritional anemia in tribals of North Bengal with review of available literature in this regard. Materials and Methods: A descriptive study is done on the tribal individuals during a period of 3 year study (April 2015 to March 2018) with CBC (complete Blood Count) hemoglobin variants, Serum iron, ferritin, total iron binding capacity, Vitamin B12, and folic acid were measured along with other relevant investigations wherever needed. For review of articles, a search using Google and Pubmed was made and reviewed chronologically. Results: 320 (59.2%) of the cases (n=540) screened were found to be anemic and 250 (78.1%) of anemic cases were nutritional with Iron deficiency being the most common (41.5%) of cases. Abnormal hemoglobin variants were responsible in about 15% of anemic patients, and of these patients, nearly half (50%) had associated nutritional deficiency, masquerading the picture. Contrary to the conventional concept, in combined iron and folate deficiency, about 70% showed microcytic hypochromic RBCs in peripheral blood film where 30 % were with dimorphic picture, Conclusion: Among the tribals of northern region of West Bengal, Iron and folic acid deficiency is the most important cause. Study of RBC morphology alone can not establish the diagnosis of causes. Moreover, abnormal hemoglobin variants, one important cause of anemia among various tribes of this zone, may be complicated with nutritional deficiencies making situation more difficult for diagnosis. A systematic approach involving clinical, hematological, and biochemical parameters is prudent for the accurate diagnosis and thereby effective treatment of anemia, highlighting the need for a screening for the causes of anemia in this population, prior to introduction of any medications or blood transfusion.

Keywords: *Anemia, Tribal Population, North Bengal, Hemoglobin, Nutrition*

Introduction

Among major public health problems in India, anemia, that is reduction in hemoglobin, is considered one most important issue, especially in the rural India, inhabitants of poor socio-economic classes including Tribal population. More than 1.6 billion people, almost a quarter of the world's population, are anemic (Mcleam et al., 2009). As compared to other developing countries, the prevalence of anemia among all age groups is higher in India (DeMaeyer and Adiels-Tegman, 1985; Kalaivani et al., 2009). Iron deficiency anemia accounts for about half the world's anemia burden (World Health Organization., 2001). In a study at Toronto, Forty seven percent of Asian Indians are reported to have Vitamin B12 deficiency (Gupta et al., 2004). Folate deficiency, another important cause of anemia of nutritional deficiency, has traditionally been linked to poverty, which (by Indian standards) afflicts around 33 percent of the population of India (Nath et al., 1998). India is a home of almost more than half of the world's tribal population. Over 84 million people belonging to 698 communities are identified as members of scheduled tribes (Ministry of Tribal Affairs., 2014), including 75 primitive tribal communities (Sharma et al., 2015). India has more than 250 different tribal groups and many more sub groups. Out of them, Bhil, Gond, Ho, Khond, Mina, Munda, Woga, Oraon and Santhal are the major or large groups, constitute more than 25 percent of the total tribal population. Of these groups, the Bhils, Gonds and Santhals predominate. The small tribal communities comprising less than 100 people include the Andamanese, Onge, Shampen and Toda, whereas the Bhil, Santal, Oraon, Munda, Mina, Khond and Saora had more than one million people each. According to latest data, tribal population is considered one of the most vulnerable sectors of the population of a country in terms of social development constitutes 8.19 percent of Indian population. Being resident of remote and Isolated places, with rigid customs, high illiteracy and separation from modern amenities, they are more prone to many health hazards. Though published literatures of isolated IDA or vit-B12 or Folate deficiency are available, but no comprehensive data of the prevalence of nutritional deficiencies among tribals are available, except a small study from Dhanuka et al., (2019) under guidance of present author, especially in northern districts of West Bengal, where tribal populations constitute an important percentage. The present study may be considered one extension of its primary work, involving more population in relation to anemia and its correlation with status of iron, vit-B12, and folic acid level in tribal population of northern districts of West Bengal.

Materials and Methods

From April 2015 to March 2018, in three years, a total of 540 tribal volunteers were studied exclusively from northern districts of West Bengal attending the Thalassemia control Unit (TCU) of North Bengal Medical College (NBMCH) for screening and from the camps arranged by TCU, for pallor or weakness, were selected for this study. Prior to study, informed consent was taken from all the individuals, participated. Exclusion criteria were diagnosed patients of hematologic malignancies or any chronic illness, patients receiving hematinics or any other marrow stimulating agents, patients who received blood transfusion recently, and pregnant ladies. In a pre-structured format, Clinical history was taken and complete clinical examination was done for each individual, followed by collection of Blood samples were studied using 5-Part automated cell counter (Sysmax 800*i*, Japan) along with study of direct peripheral blood smear for cell morphology and reticulocyte count. Those who were found to be anemic, based on their hemoglobin levels were graded as mild, moderate, or severely anemic using the WHO criteria for anemia (WHO, 2011). Similar to previous study, apart from CBC, serum ferritin, vitamin B12, and folic acid were measured by automated immunofluorescence assay method using TOSOH AIA System Analyzers,Japan, in all patients and assay of Serum iron and total iron–binding capacity were done for all anemic patients. Simultaneously, the presence of abnormal hemoglobin variants was assessed by cationexchange high–performance liquid chromatography (ce-HPLC) principle, using Variant 2 (Bio–Rad, USA) automated HPLC. Quality control for the tests was assessed by the internal quality control program of the institution's laboratory. Similar to previous study,Standard statistical techniques (Chi-square test and *t*-test) were used for calculation, using Microsoft™ Excel.

Results

Out of total 540 tribal persons, 320 (59.2%) were found to be anemic, and majority of them belonged to 2nd to 3rd decade of their life. Non-anemic persons were predominated by male 147/220 (66.8%) with a male–to–female ratio of 2.01:1.00, But in the anemic population, female were the predominant (195 out of 320, 60.93%),with male-to-female ratio 1: 1.56 One hundred and thirty one patients had 'feeling of weakness' and was the most common presenting complaint among the 320 anemic patient (41%). Most of the cases of the study population were non-vegetarians, of all anemic patients, 8 were vegetarians (2.5%). Of all anemic patients, 92(28.7%) did not have any pallor on clinical examination(Table1). As per the WHO criteria of grading of anemia nearly 15 percent had severe anemia while nearly 60 percent of them were mildly anemic (Table 2). All patients who were found to be severely anemic showed clinical pallor. Hemoglobin level among the females was low comparatively and the number of females suffering from moderate and severe anemia was higher as compared to that of the males (Table 3.) However, one aspect is to be kept under consideration that these case were collected from TCU, NBMC, one tertiary referral center of this zone, not necessarily reflecting the exact demographic pattern.

Table 1: Demographic details and clinical features of anemia cases (*n*=320)

Demographic and clinical features		Observation (%)
Age (years)		
	Mean age	36.77
	Most common age group	18-37 (47.31%)
Sex		
	Male	125 (37.5)
	Female	195 (62.5)
	Male: female ratio	1:1.56
Diet		
	Non-vegetarian	312 (100 (97.5%)
Symptoms		
	Body ache	55 (17.2%)
	Dizziness	48 (15%)
	Fever	18 (5.6%)
	Weakness	131 (41%)
	Loss of appetite	42 (13%)
	Asymptomatic	112 (35)
Signs		
	Pallor	228 (71.3%)

Most cases are female and weakness is the most common symptom

Table 2: Clinical status (pallor) vs grade of anemia

Status of pallor	Grade of anemia		
	Mild	Moderate	Severe
Without pallor	85	15	Nil
Pallor	90	89	41

Most cases had mild degree of pallor

Though there are several nutritional factors in causation of anemia, we tested for the most important factors, i.e. Serum Iron, TIBC, ferritin, serum vitB12 and folic acid. Out of 320 anemic population, 250 (78.12%) had at least one nutritional factor deficiency, and the remaining patients i.e. 70 (22%) had no evidence of nutritional deficiency. Iron deficiency (IDA) ranked the top (41.25%), seen in 132 anemic patients (Tables 3 and 4).Pure Folate deficiency was observed in 43 (13.43%). As a whole Vit-B12 deficiency was reported very low, only 3 (0.93%) in all 320 cases, and remaining cases(72) were found to be with concomitant Iron and FA deficiency, 3 cases of combined deficiency showed VitB12 deficiency as well.

Majority (78%) of IDA (103 out of 132) presented with microcytic hypochromic red blood cells (RBCs) with presence of leptocytes, pencil cells and cigar cells in PBFs (Figure 2) depicted by decrease in MCV, MCH & MCHC. In combined iron and folate deficiency, 47 of 72 (65.28%) showed predominantly microcytic hypochromic morphology and 25 of 72 (34.72%) were with dimorphic picture with presence of both microcytic hypchromic RBCs and Macrocytic RBCs (Figure 4) with moderate to marked anisocytosis as indicated by raised RDW in cell counter. Only 13 of 43 (30.23%) of pure folic acid-deficient population showed macrocytic RBCs, as indicated my presence of Macrocytes, macroovalocytes with PMNs showing shift to the right and occasional presence of Macropolycytes in PBF and raised MCV.

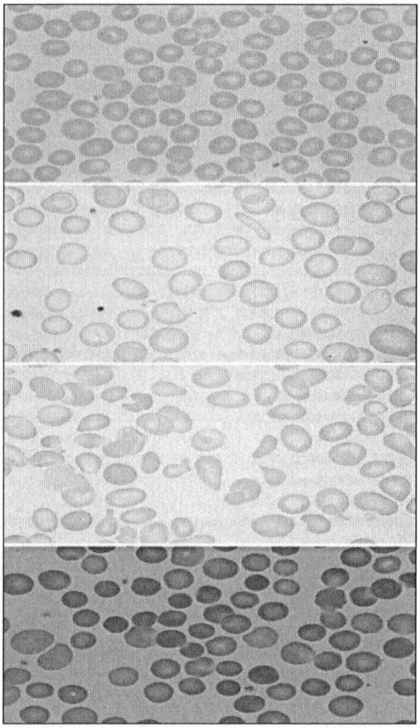

Figure 1: Normal

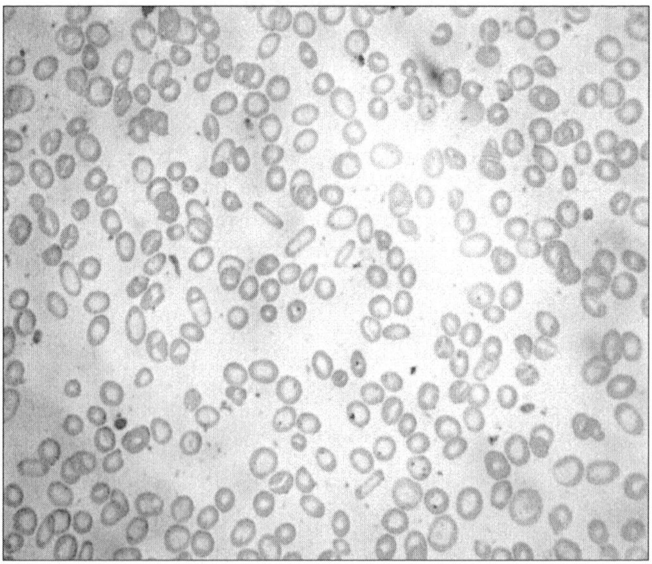

Figure 2: Microcytic and hypochromic in IDA

Table 3: Severity, grade, and type of anemia among males and females

Parameter	Females (%)	Males (%)
Severity of anemia (Hb level)		
Minimum Hb (g/dl)	4.87	5.35
Maximum Hb (g/dl)	11.65	12.90
Average Hb (g/dl)	9.60	11.16
Grade of anemia (number of cases)*		
Mild anemia	99 (49.50)	94 (78.33)
Moderate anemia	70 (35)	09 (07.50)
Severe anemia	31 (15.5)	17 (14.16)
Type of anemia (number of cases)*		
Iron deficiency	94 (53.4)	37 (50.00)
Folic acid deficiency	17 (9.65)	26 (35.13)
ID+FAD+ Vitamin B12 deficiency	3 (1.70)	0 (0.0)
Iron + folate deficiency	62 (35.2)	11(14.86)

Degree of anemia is more severe in female, though statistically not significant. Iron deficiency is the most common type of anemia in both sexes.

*Chi-square statistic: 3.3106. P: 0.191033. The result is not significant at $p<0.05$. Hb: Hemoglobin, ID=Iron deficiency, FAD= Folic acid deficiency

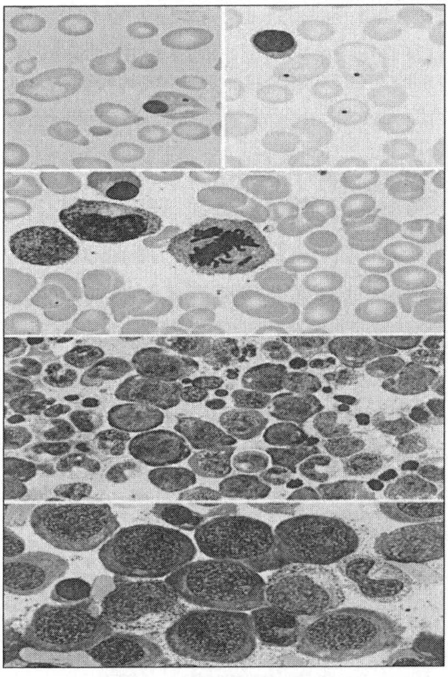

Figure 3: Macrocytic

Table 4: Distribution of red blood cell morphology in different deficiencies

Deficient factor	M/H (%)	N/N (%)	Macrocytic(%)	Dimorphic (%)	Total
Iron	103 (78.03)	22 (16.66)	0	7 (5.30)	132
Folic acid	15 (34.88)	15 (34.88)	13 (30.23)	0	43
Vitamin B12	-	-	2 (66.6)	1 (33.3)	3
Iron and folic acid	47 (65.28)	0	0	25 (34.72)	72
Total	165	37	15	33	250

(M/H= Microcytic and Hypochromic, N/N= Normochromic and Normocytic)

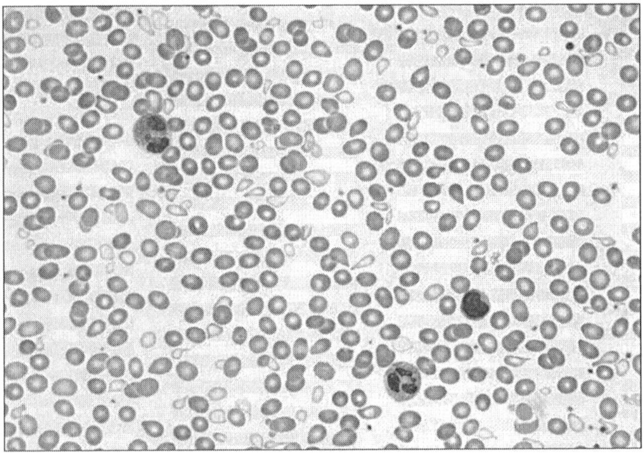

Figure 4: Dimrphic (IDA+FAD)

In this total study, 48 cases had abnormal hemoglobin, 34 were beta-thalassemia carriers (9 with iron deficiency, 3 with both Iron deficiency & folic acid deficiency and 2 with only FA deficiency) 3 had Hb-E trait (2 with either of Iron or FA deficiency), all these cases presented with moderate to markedly microcytic hypchromic RBCs with moderate to marked anisopoilocytosis, along with presence of target cells and occasional fragmented RBCs. Eleven(11) cases were found to be sickle cell carriers (5 with concomitant Iron deficiency, 1 with Vit B12, FA and iron deficiency and 2 with pure FA deficiency. None of them showed in PBF, Sickle test was also negative in all of them. A statistically significant difference was observed between RBC indices of iron and folic acid deficiency in respect of Mean Corpuscular Volume (MCV) and Mean Corpuscular Hemoglobin

(MCH) but not in Mean Corpuscular Hemoglobin Concentration (MCHC) and Red cell Distribution Width (RDW)

DISCUSSION

Due to various factors such as geographical and cultural isolation, low levels of literacy, primitive occupations, and extreme levels of poverty, most of the Indian tribals remain at the lowest stratum of the society (Bala Thiruselvakumar, 2009). The state of West Bengal is home to 38 scheduled tribes (ST) constituting 5.5 percent of the total population of the state (numbering 80,176,197) which includes Oraon, Minj, Lakra, Kujur, Tigga, Ekka, Kaka and Toppo, among the broad group Santhals, which represent more than half of the total ST population of the state (51.8%). The other population groups in ST are Munda, Bhumij, Kora, Lodha, Mahali, Bhutia, Bedia, and Savar. More than half of the total ST population of the state are concentrated in four districts, namely Medinipur, Jalpaiguri, Purulia, and Barddhaman (Ministry of Tribal Affairs, 2014)

The present study included 540 individuals, of which 320 (59.25%) were found to be anemic, which is similar to a study on prevalence of anemia in tribal women in Udupi taluk, Karnataka, which showed 55.9% to be anemic (Kamath et al., 2013). The burden of anemia is overwhelmingly higher among indigenous groups compared to the general population and represents a moderate (20-39.9%) to severe (≥40%) public health problem. as indicated by the results of a study done at Royal North Shore Hospital, New South Wales, Sydney, Australia, in which 50 studies published from 13 countries including India using PubMed/MEDLINE and Embase were analyzed (Khambalia et al., 2011). Abnormal hemoglobin variants are very common among different population groups in northern districts of West Bengal (Goswami et al., 2014). A study for coexistence of hemoglobinopathies and iron deficiency in tribal population of East India shows that 39.92 percent and 76.4 percent of tribal populations are anemic in Assam and West Bengal, respectively (Chatterjee et al., 2011). However picture regarding reporting of concomitant nutritional anemia in a case of abnormal hemoglobin variant are not clear. Dhanuka *et al.*, (2019) in their study reported the co-incidence of Hb-variants and nutrional deficiency, but case numbers are very few. In this extended study, though numbers are increased relatively but still less to be statistically significant. What is evident that good number of cases of BTT, Hb-S Hemoglobinopathies, even Hb-E Hemoglobinopathies are found with co-existent nutritional deficiencies, masquerading the total morphological analysis of anemia from PBF alone.

So far gender status is concerned, it was seen In the present study that, out of the 320 anemic patients, 213 (66.5%) were females, reflecting gender discrimination from birth, inequitable distribution of health resources, and early and frequent reproductive cycles, apart from overall poverty, the health status of women in India. This high rates of anemia among Indian women, make them vulnerable socially and biologically, both within society and the household (Bentley and Griffiths, 2003). Not only was the occurrence of anemia, the severity of anemia also found to be higher in females as compared to that of males.

A study on malnutrition and anemia in tribal population of Purnia district, Bihar, by showed that only 21.9 percent of tribal children had normal hemoglobin level. Thirty six percent of Munda and 16.11 percent of Oraon children had moderate anemia. Overall, 78.1 percent of children were found to be anemic (Rao and Vijay, 2006). The most common presenting symptom in this study was weakness, noted in 14 (29.16%) out of 48 cases. This is similar to a recent study done in a tertiary care center (Prakash et al., 2015). However, 14 cases with anemia were asymptomatic. It had been argued that patients would adapt to low hemoglobin levels if anemia developed slowly. This has led to the concept of asymptomatic anemia. In truth, asymptomatic reflects the fact that impairments in physical condition, quality of life,and cognitive function may be unrecognized by both patients and their doctors (Gasche et al., 2004). In our extended study, iron deficiency was found in 132 (41.25%) anemic cases, folic acid deficiency in 43 (13.43%), and combined iron and folic acid deficiency in 72 (22.5%). These results regarding the prevalence of these deficiencies among the tribal population of Northern regions of West Bengal is found to be close to the previous study . In this extended study, very few cases (only 3 cases) of Vitamin B12 deficiency were found, may be because all the cases studied were non-vegetarians and as per published literature, dietary Vitamin B12 deficiency is not prevalent in Asia, except in vegetarians (Stabler and Allen, 2004).

In the present study, abnormal hemoglobin variants were found in 48 out of 320 (15%) cases. A study on spectrum of hemoglobin variants in northern region of West Bengal showed a high prevalence of hemoglobinopathies in this region, especially among the ethnic races. Though Hb-E hemoglobinopathy is the most frequently observed Hb-variants among prevalent races in this zone, but among the Scheduled Tribes as listed here, Beta Thalassemia and Hb-S hemoglobinopathies are observed more than Hb-E Hemoglobinopathies (Goswami et al., 2014). In the present study, iron-deficiency was the commonest nutritional deficiency with BTT, and Hb-S hemoglobinopathies followed by folate deficiency. According to a study on coexistence of hemoglobinopathies and iron deficiency in the development of anemia in the tribal population in East India, HbE was the most common hemoglobinopathy among the studied groups of the Northeast. The prevalence of beta–thalassemia (1.6%) was almost nil in the tribal groups (Chatterjee et al., 2016).

In this study, cases having iron deficiency showed microcytic hypochromic RBC morphology in 103 out of 132 cases(78 %). A study on iron deficiency anemia, peripheral smear showed microcytosis and hypochromia in all cases with severe anemia, 61.5% and 22.5% of those with moderate and mild anemia, respectively (Vishwanath et al., 2001). One of the most important and distinguished observations in the present study was the morphological type of nutritional anemia as result of combined iron and folic acid deficiency. Contrary to the belief, in combined deficiency of Iron and Folic acid the peripheral blood picture was microcytic hypochromic in 65.28 percent and dimorphic in the rest. This observation is similar with some difference to our initial one (Dhanuka et al., 2019), may be related to increase in the number of cases. No other published literature with this type of observation in this part of the country has been found in the mean time.

So far the clinical presentation, pallor was the commonest one. Out of 320 cases of anemia, 107 (33.3%) of them did not have any clinical pallor. Ninety-Six (90%) out of these 107 cases had mild anemia and 11 had moderate anemia. As tribes are hard working, palmar crease does not reflect the pallor properly and palpebral conjunctival pallor may be a more accurate indicator of the presence or absence of anemia than pallor of the palms or nail beds.

Conclusion

Among the tribal population of Northern districts of West Bengal, popularly known as North Bengal, Anemia due to nutritional deficiency, especially of iron and folic acid either in single or in combination, is very common, more in females with more severity compared to male. Among the nutrients, Vit - B12 deficiency is not common in this population. Although microcytic hypochromic RBC morphology is an important observation in iron deficiency anemia, alone it lacks the specificity for the diagnosis of causes, as the same morphology is quite commonly observed in a huge percentage of patients with both Iron deficiency and Folate deficiency. Furthermore, occurance of abnormal hemoglobin, specially Beta-Thalassemia and Hb-E hemoglobinopathies, is not negligible in these population groups and co-existance of nutriotional deficiency pose a great problem in diagnosis from morphological assessment alone. Hence a thorough clinical examination, hematological parameters including study of direct PBF and biochemical correlation, specially of assay of iron status, V-B12 and folate assay along with study of Hemoglobin variants are required for the accurate diagnosis and effective treatment of anemia, and thereby necessitating the need for a detail screening for the causes of anemia in this population population, preferably prior to introduction of any medications or blood transfusion.

Informed consent

Informed consent was obtained from all individual participants included in the study.

Declaration of patient consent

The authors certify that they have obtained all appropriate patient consent forms. In the form, the patients have given their consent for their images and other clinical information to be reported in the journal. The patients understand that their names and initials will not be published and due efforts will be made to conceal their identity, but anonymity cannot be guaranteed, preferably prior to introduction of any medications or blood transfusion.

Financial support and sponsorship

Nil

Conflicts of interest

There are no conflicts of interest.

AcknowledgementS

We are highly indebted to the appropriate authority, and all staff of TCU, North Bengal Medical College, Sushrutanagar, Darjeeling, all colleagues, Department of Pathology, North Bengal Medical College, Sushrutanagar Darjeeling for their kind cooperation and Dr. Soham Basu, Final Year PGT (Pathology),NBMC for assisting.

References

Bala SM, Thiruselvakumar D. 2009. Overcoming problems in the practice of public health among tribals of India. *Indian Journal of Community Medicine.* 34: 283-287.

Bentley ME, Griffiths PL. 2003. The burden of anemia among women in India. *European Journal of Clinical Nutrition.* 57: 52-60.

Chatterjee S, Dhar S, Sengupta B, Sengupta S, Mazumder L, Chakrabarti S. 2011a. Studies of tribes and tribals. *Studies of Tribes and Tribals.* 9: 111-121.

Chatterjee S, Dhar S, Sengupta B, Sengupta S, Mazumder L,Chakrabarti S. 2011b. Coexistence of haemoglobinopathies and iron deficiency in the development of anemias in the tribal population Eastern India. *Studies of Tribes and Tribals.* 9: 111-121.

DeMaeyer E, Adiels-Tegman M. 1985. The prevalence of anaemia in the world. *World Health Statistics Quarterly.* 38: 302-316.

Dhanuka A, Goswami BK, Goswami SB, Chakrabarti S. 2019. Profile of nutritional anemia and its correlation with serum iron, Vit B12 and folic acid levels among the tribal population of northern districts of West Bengal, India. *Archives of Medicine and Health Sciences.* 7: 201-205.

Gasche C, Lomer MC, Cavill I, Weiss G. 2004. Iron, anaemia, and inflammatory bowel diseases. *Gut.* 53: 1190-1197.

Goswami BK, Pramanik R, Chakrabarty S, Pal PP, Banerjee S, Bandhopadhayay A. 2014. Spectrum of hemoglobin variants in the population of Northern region of West Bengal: An ethnogenetic proposition. *Journal of Family Medicine and Primary Care.* 3: 219-223.

Gupta AK, Damji A, Uppaluri A. 2004. Vitamin B12 deficiency. Prevalence among South Asians at a Toronto clinic. *Canadian Family Physician.* 50: 743-747.

Kalaivani K. 2009. Prevalence and consequences of anaemia in pregnancy. *Indian Journal of Medical Research.* 130: 627-633.

Kamath R, Majeed JA, Chandrasekaran V, Pattanshetty SM. 2013. Prevalence of anemia among tribal women of reproductive age in Udupi Taluk, Karnataka. *Journal of Family Medicine and Primary Care.* 2: 345-348.

Khambalia AZ, Aimone AM, Zlotkin SH. 2011. Burden of anemia among indigenous populations. *Nutrition Reviews.* 69: 693-719.

McLean E, Cogswell M, Egli I Wojdylad, de Benoist B. 2009. Worldwide prevalence of anaemia, WHO vitamin and mineral nutrition information system, 1993-2005. *Public Health Nutrition.* 12: 444-454.

Ministry of Tribal Affairs. 2014. *Tribal profile at a glance 2014.* Available https://tribal.nic.in/ST/Tribal%20Profile.pdf

Nath I, Reddy KS, Dinshaw KA, Bhisey AN, Krishnaswami K, Bhan MK, Ganguly NK, Kaur s, Panda SK, Jameels S, Srinivasan K, Thankappan KA, Valiathan MS. 1998. Country profile: India. *Lancet*. 351: 1265-1275.

Prakash KG, Devendrappa KR, Madhukumar MH, Priyashree R, Avinash BH. 2015. Cinical profile of anemia in elderly: a cross sectional study from a tertiary care centre. *Scholars Journal of Applied Medical Sciences*. 3: 1266-1270.

Rao TV, Vijay T. 2006. Malnutrition and anemia in tribal pediatric population of Purnia district (Bihar). *Indian Pediatrics*. 43: 181-182.

Sharma RK, Thakor HG, Saha KB, Sonal GS, Dhaniwal AC, Singh N, 2015. Malaria situation in India with special reference to tribal areas. *Indian Journal of Medical Research*. 141: 537-545

Stabler SP, Allen RH. 2004. Vitamin B12 deficiency as a worldwide problem. *Annual Review of Nutrition*. 24: 299-326.

Viswanath D, Hegde R, Murthy V, Nagashree S, Shah R. 2001. Red cell distribution width in the diagnosis of iron deficiency anemia. *Indian Journal of Pediatrics*. 68: 1117-1119.

World Health Organization. 2011. *Haemoglobin Concentrations for the Diagnosis of Anaemia and Assessment of Severity*. Vitamin and Mineral Nutrition Information System. Geneva: World Health Organization.

World Health Organization/UNICEF/UNU. 2001.*Iron Deficiency Anaemia: Assessment, Prevention, and Control. A Guide for Programme Managers*. Geneva, Switzerland: World Health Organization.

Chapter Thirteen

ASSESSMENT OF NUTRITIONAL STATUS USING ANTHROPOMETRIC VARIABLES AMONG THE LOTHA NAGAS OF NAGALAND, INDIA

JENNY JAMI AND D K LIMBU

ABSTRACT

Background: An adequate diet with proper nutrients in the right amounts as required by the body is considered to make an individual healthy while a poor diet characterized by inadequate or excess nutrients in relation to need can adversely affect the normal functioning of the body. Nutritional status is an important health and wellness indicator of a population. In developing countries like India which are often faced with the dual burden of malnutrition, the relevance of nutritional status on public health at both the local and national levels is indispensable. In this regard, nutritional status assessments are important, particularly among the marginalized sections of the population. This paper highlights the nutritional status of the Lotha Naga, a tribal community of Nagaland, Northeast India. Methods: A cross-sectional study was conducted among 708 Lotha Naga individuals (354 males and 354 females) aged between 20 and 70 years from Wokha Town of Nagaland, using a two-way cluster sampling method. Height, weight and waist circumference were recorded using standard procedures. The World Health Organization (WHO) classification of BMI based on the Asian cut-off points (WHO, 2000b, 2004, 2011c) was taken and for waist circumference cut-offs, WHO recommended International Diabetes Federation (IDF) cut-offs for South Asians was used (WHO, 2011c). The data was analysed for percentage distribution, independent t-test and chi-square test using SPSS (version 18.0). Results: The percentage of underweight, normal weight, overweight and/obese individuals were 6.07%, 52.26%, 18.22% and 23.14% respectively. The percentage of central obesity in respect of waist circumference was 35.73% which is significantly higher in women (54.52%) than observed in man (16.95%). Conclusion: There is an emerging trend of overnutrition even among tribal communities, thereby calling for increased research and awareness initiatives on these aspects, especially among those communities transitioning to an urban setting.

Keywords: *Nutritional Status, Body Mass Index, Waist Circumference, Central Obesity*

Introduction

Concepts of nutrition, health and well-being are universal and many researches are increasingly being focused on such issues. In the World Food Summit (Food and Agriculture Organization, 1996), it was recognized that more than 800 million people throughout the world, particularly in developing countries do not have enough food to meet their basic nutritional needs and hence, a resolution to reduce the number of undernourished people to half the level by the year 2015 was made. Similar goals with a renewed resolution to reduce extreme poverty and hunger by the year 2015 were declared as part of the Millennium Development Goals during the United Nations Millennium Summit (United Nations, 2000). Despite such commitments followed by several interventions and efforts by governmental agencies and international bodies, undernutrition still remains persistently high and continues to be the most important risk factor for the burden of disease in most developing countries (Müller and Krawinkel, 2005; FAO et al., 2014). High undernutrition levels in these countries are further aggravated by high prevalence of bacterial and parasitic diseases where malnutrition increases a person's susceptibility to infection and likewise, infectious diseases also contributes to malnutrition resulting in the vicious cycle of malnutrition and infectious diseases which ultimately leads to lesser productivity and higher mortality rates (Müller and Krawinkel, 2005; Katona and Katona-Apte, 2008). This scenario is especially more pronounced in a developing country like India which has one of the highest number of undernourished people in the world (190 million), representing 15.2 % of its entire population (FAO et al., 2014).

In addition to undernutrition, prevalence of overweight and obesity has also increasingly been reported not only in developed nations but also in developing countries, particularly in urban areas (Popkin 1998, 2002; WHO, 2000a, 2000b; Prentice, 2005; Schmid et al., 2006; Kelly et al., 2008; Cusick and Kuch, 2012). As a result of such changes in the global nutrition dynamics (Popkin, 2006), overnutrition, which was generally considered a problem only in high-income countries, has also emerged as a serious health concern even in the poorer countries in recent years. In particular, the rising epidemic of obesity presents a major public health burden due to its association with a host of morbidities such as cardiovascular diseases, type 2 diabetes, hypertension, dyslipidaemia, ischaemic stroke, sleep apnea, degenerative joint disease, gallstones, fertility problems and some forms of cancer (Gill et al., 2002; WHO, 2000b; 2002). Most of these non-communicable diseases (NCDs) are the leading causes of death worldwide with nearly 80 percent of NCD deaths occurring in low and middle income countries (WHO, 2011a). Several studies have now recognised obesity as one of the initiating factor for many of these chronic diseases including heart diseases, hypertension and cancers such as colon cancer, prostate cancer and breast cancer (Shaper 1996; Kopelman 2000; Poirier and Eckel 2002; Pérez et al., 2007; Yang et al., 2011; Kearns et al., 2014; Shukla et al., 2014), thus, highlighting the severity of the risk associated with the condition.

In a developing country like India where both ends of the spectrum of malnutrition are equally present, the relevance of nutritional status on public health at both the local and national levels is indispensable. In this regard, nutritional status assessments are important, particularly among the marginalized sections of the population. This paper highlights the nutritional status among the Lotha Nagas, a tribal community of Nagaland. The objective is to assess the nutritional status of the adult Lotha Nagas using anthropometric variables.

Materials and Methods

A cross-sectional study was conducted among the Lotha Naga adults of Wokha Town, Nagaland during the period between May 2014 and January 2016. For the present study, a two-way cluster sampling method was implemented where five wards were selected. No statistical random sampling of individuals was possible due to the unavailability of the required sampling frame of the population. However, the population was stratified based on gender and attempt was made to include all consenting adults (20 – 70 years) who were willing to participate in the study following house to house visit. A total of 708 individuals (354 men and 354 women) from 470 households participated in the present study.

Wokha is a town and a municipality in the state of Nagaland, India. It is the headquarters of Wokha district and is located about 75 km north of the state capital Kohima. Wokha literally means head count or census in Lotha language. It is predominantly inhabited by the Lotha Nagas. Lothas belong to the Mongoloid racial stock and speak the Lotha language (*kyong yi*) classified under the Tibeto-Burman language family. Traditionally, they have an egalitarian society without any social stratification. Social structure of the community is mainly based on phratry, clan and village affiliation. The tribe is divided into three phratries, namely, *Tonphyaksu-rui, Ezomontsu-rui and Miphongshan-rui* (Kikon 2002). Clan exogamy is strictly maintained in most cases i.e., any Lotha cannot marry within his/her own clan, though marriage between members of different kinders of the same clan is permitted in some villages of the Southern Lothas. Monogamy is the common form of marriage. Christianity is the predominant religion comprising of about 95 percent of the population, out of which 85 percent are Baptist (Edzung, 2014). Agriculture is the mainstay of the people, with 60.54 percent of the total working population of the Wokha district are engaged in cultivation or employed as agricultural labourers (Census of India, 2011b). The Lothas are agriculturist and thus, most aspects of their life including their rituals, ceremonies and festivals are related to agriculture. In urban areas, majority of the population (86.27%) are listed as non-agricultural workers such as teachers, office employees, clergy man, business, political and social work. Kikon (2002) had opined, "The Lothas are undergoing a transitional phase and their culture is also in a process of flux and change. In response to such change they are adapting to a new way of life, discharging their old way of life".

Anthropometric measurements

For the present study, anthropometric measurements such as height, weight, and waist circumference were included. Standard techniques of taking the measurements, as suggested by Weiner and Lourie (1981) under the aegis of Human Adaptability Section of the International Biological Programme (HAIBP), National Health and Nutrition Examination Survey (NHANES) anthropometry procedures manual (Centers for Disease Control and Prevention,

2012) and World Health Organization guidelines (WHO, 2011b) were employed.

Nutritional status

Nutritional status is assessed through anthropometric measurements and indices include body mass index (BMI) and waist circumference (WC).

BMI has been calculated using the formula

$$BMI = \frac{Weight(Kg.)}{Height(m^2)}$$

The criteria used for the classification of the nutritional status have been described in Table 1. For screening purposes based on BMI, the World Health Organization (WHO) classification of BMI based on the Asian cut-off points (WHO, 2000b, 2004, 2011c) was taken and for waist circumference cut-offs, WHO recommended International Diabetes Federation (IDF) cut-offs for South Asians was used(WHO, 2011c). The latter values have also been recommended as level 2 cut-offs points for WC in Asian Indians (Misra et al., 2006).

Table 1: Criteria for classification of nutritional status

Anthropometric variables	Nutritional Status	Cut-off points	
Body Mass Index (kg/m^2)	Underweight Normal Overweight Obese	< 18.5 18.5 – 22.9 23 – 24.9 ≥25	
Waist Circumference (cm)		Men	Women
	Normal Obese	< 90 ≥ 90	< 80 ≥ 80

Statistical analysis

Data analyses were carried out with SPSS 18.0 software for Windows. Percentage distribution, independent t-test and chi-square test were the common statistical tests used in the present study. The level of significance was set at $p < 0.05$.

Results and Discussion

Anthropometric variables

Table 2 presents the descriptive statistics of age, selected anthropometric traits and body mass index of both men and women. The values of skewness and 'excess' kurtosis were also given for all the measurements and indices to understand the distribution of the data. The values of skewness for all measurements and indices were within acceptable limits of skewness i.e., within an absolute skew value <2 or an absolute kurtosis (proper) <7 (Kim, 2013) and hence, the data are assumed to be normally distributed. An independent-samples t-test was conducted to compare the gender differences in the selected anthropometric traits and BMI. The mean weight for men and women were found to be 60.49 kg and 54.25 kg respectively. Similarly, the mean height of men and women were 163.95 cm and 153.56 cm respectively. The mean values of waist circumference of men and women were 79.70 cm and 81.40 cm respectively. It is evident that the Lotha men have significantly higher mean values of height, and weight than their women counterpart. It is also apparent that women showed higher mean values of waist circumference and body mass index than men. Statistically significant differences between men and women were observed for all these variables.

Table 2: Descriptive statistics of age, weight, height, waist circumference and BMI in both men and women

Variables	**Men (n = 354)**				**Women (n = 354)**				***t*- values**
	Mean	***SD***	***Sk***	***Kr***	**Mean**	***SD***	***Sk***	***Kr***	
Age (years)	37.12	15.03	0.58	-0.85	38.16	12.67	0.47	-0.64	
Weight (kg)	60.49	8.97	0.71	0.18	54.25	9.01	0.75	0.79	9.18***
Height (cm)	163.96	5.23	0.11	0.07	153.56	5.13	-0.16	0.94	26.69***
WC (cm)	79.90	9.40	0.50	-0.39	81.40	10.45	0.31	-0.28	2.00*
BMI (kg/m^2)	22.49	3.04	0.73	0.26	22.98	3.45	0.75	0.94	2.09*
Sk: Skewness, *Kr*: Kurtosis, $^*p< 0.05$, $^{***}p< 0.0005$									

Table 3: Nutritional status according to BMI

Nutritional Status	**Men (N = 354)**		**Women (N = 354)**		**Total (N = 708)**	
	No.	**%**	**No.**	**%**	**No.**	**%**
Underweight (<18.5 kg/m^2)	19	5.37	24	6.78	43	6.07
Normal (18.5 – 22.9 kg/m^2)	202	57.06	168	47.46	370	52.26
Overweight (23 – 24.9 kg/m^2)	60	16.95	69	19.49	129	18.22
Obesity (≥ 25 kg/m^2)	73	20.62	93	26.27	165	23.45
	χ^2= 6.75, df = 3, p = 0.08					

Nutritional status based on BMI

The nutritional status of the participants according to BMI categories is shown in Table 3. When both the sexes were combined, the percentage of underweight individuals (6.07%) was found lowest followed by the overweight (18.22%) and thereafter the obese category (23.45%).The normal category individuals formed the majority i.e., the highest percentage (52.26%). A similar trend is observed in both the men and women when observed separately. The percentages of the underweight category among men (5.37%) found lower than the women (6.78%). The percentages of overweight men and women were 16.95% and 19.49% respectively. The occurrence of obese men was 20.62% and women were 26.27%. Although a majority of people had normal or healthy BMI (52.26%) and is slightly tilted in favour of the males (57.06%), however, this percentage is far lacking from an ideal scenario of an entirely healthy population.

By and large, theprevalence of overweight and/ or obesity were observed slightly higher among the women than in men. However, the association between gender and nutritional status was found statistically not significant ($\chi2 = 6.75$, $p = 0.08$).

Nutritional status based on WC

Table 4 shows the distribution of central obesity (CO) for men and women according to their waist circumference. It was observed that majority of the individuals had normal waist circumference (64.27%), although the percentage of obese category was also found considerably high (35.73%) in the present population. The percentage of CO was found threefold times higher among the female (54.52%) than their male counterpart (16.95%). A statistically significant association between the waist circumference and gender ($\chi2(1) = 1.09$, $p< 0.0005$) was observed. The association was moderately strong, $\phi = 0.39$.

Table 4: Central obesity by waist circumference in men and women

Categories	Men ($N = 354$)		Women ($N=354$)		Total ($N = 708$)	
	No.	%	No.	%	No.	%
Normal	294	83.05	161	45.48	455	64.27
Obese	60	16.95	193	54.52	253	35.73
	$\chi^2= 1.09$, $df = 1$, $p < 0.0005$					

The present study was conducted among the Lotha Nagas, a tribal population of Nagaland to assess the nutritional status and thereby understand the nutritional dynamics in tribal communities undergoing a transition towards urbanization. Present findings reveals that while the prevalence of under nutrition among the urban residing Lotha Nagas was low, on the contrary, the overall prevalence of overweight and/obese was found high. Women showed higher tendency of being overweight or obese than then their men counterpart, however, this association between gender and nutritional status was not found statistically significant. The prevalence of central obesity based on waist circumference was also found significantly high among the female than the male.

These results are crucial because it present the emerging trend of overnutrition even among tribal communities who were otherwise known to have a higher prevalence of undernutrition (Das and Bose, 2012; Kapoor and Dhall, 2016). In fact, a growing trend towards obesity is now being observed from many tribal communities. This shift is indeed a matter of concern as obesity or overweight is a global epidemic that is linked with a host of co-morbidities with most of these diseases being the leading causes of deaths worldwide. As a result of the increased rate of morbidity and mortality associated with the condition, there is not only much economic burden but also considerable emotional and psychological pressure on the individual and the family members as well as the society in general, an aspect which is often neglected in many studies (Turner and Kelly, 2000). Such problems may be further compounded as more tribal communities make a rapid transition from rural to urban settings, as has been witnessed within the past decade. Even in the present context, Nagaland state has registered a decadal growth of 66 percent in the urban sector which is much higher than the national average rate of 31 percent (Census of India, 2011). Despite all these ramifications, there is comparatively less awareness on this crucial issue among the communities of Northeast India as can be evident by the lack of substantial literature on nutritional status, especially of adults. For instance, works on adult nutrition among the Nagas are limited to reports of national surveys viz., the National Family Health Surveys and District Level Household Surveys (excluding Phase-3) surveys; and fragmented studies among the Ao Nagas of Nagaland (Temsutola 2010), the Tangkhul Nagas of Manipur (Mungreiphy et al., 2010, 2011, 2012) and the Rengma Nagas of Assam (Rengma et al., 2015). Although the National Surveys play an indispensable role in the nutritional status assessment of the population, however, there are cited limitations associated with such large scale surveys (Kelley et al., 2003), that particularly also hold true in the context of heterogeneous tribal communities like the Nagas that have several listed tribes within and across the boundaries of their recognised native state, each with their own set of unique cultural practices and traditional way of life. Hence, even though it is not fully understood how we can tackle this problem, it is imperative to spread awareness about overweight or obesity and the various chronic health risks associated with the condition. This need to educate the masses on the consequences of risk factors and economic costs associated with overweight and obesity, the importance of monitoring our fat distribution and BMI as well as the importance of prevention early in life were also voiced by other researchers of the region such as Singh and Dkhar (2013).

The relevance of nutritional status on public health at both the local and national level is indispensable; however, apart from the national surveys, very limited studies had been conducted in Northeast India till date. Besides the few populations of Meghalaya, Assam and Manipur that had been studied, very less work has been done in populations of the other Northeastern states. This sincere dearth of nutritional studies in the region has in fact been highlighted in most of the works that have been done in the region (Khongsdier, 1995; Maken and Varte, 2012; Longkumer, 2013a, 2013b; Singh and Devi, 2013). Thus, it can be observed that nutritional studies in Northeast India is still at a formative stage and hence, it should be given due importance as a crucial subject of research interest. While it is seen that some works have been initiated, much is still left to be explored both in terms of the communities to be studied as well as the research questions to be developed.

Conclusion

To conclude, it can be succinctly stated from the overall findings and discussions of the present study that there is a serious emerging trend of overnutrition among the Lotha Nagas which is a consequence of changes in various interrelated factors such as socio-demographic conditions, dietary habits and physical activity. These changes, in turn, are a manifestation of the continuing stage of transition from traditional to modern that Nagas are still embroiled in and trying to adapt to. In either case, the expression, as required by the body or in relation to need holds significant meaning especially in the modern context of increasing urbanization, changing lifestyle, dietary habits and occupational work patterns. A bio-cultural approach towards a better understanding of the physical and cultural dimensions within which all these factors operate is fundamental for formulating health policies applicable for the people.

References

Centers for Disease Control and Prevention. 2012. *National Health and Nutrition Examination Survey (NHANES) anthropometry procedures manual; 2011*. Hyattsville, MD: NHANES.

Census of India. 2011. *Rural Urban Distribution of Population - India, Census of India 2011 (PCA Final Data)*. New Delhi, India: Office of the Registrar General and Census Commissioner.

Cusick S E. Kuch A E.2012.Determinants of undernutrition and overnutrition among adolescents in developing countries. *Adolescent Medicine: State of the Art Reviews*. 23: 440.

Das S. Bose K. 2012. Nutritional deprivation among Indian tribals: A cause for concern. *Anthropological Notebooks*. 18: 5-16.

Ezung M. 2014.*Traditional religion of the Lotha Nagas and the impact of Christianity*. Ph.D.dissertation, Nagaland University.

Food and Agriculture Organization of the United Nations.1996. *Rome Declaration on World Food Security*. Rome, Italy: FAO.

Food and Agriculture Organization of the United Nations. 2014. *The state of food insecurity in the world 2014: Strengthening the enabling environment for food security and nutrition*. Rome, Italy: FAO.

Gill T, Hughes R, Tunidau-Schultz J, Nishida C, Galea G, Cavalli-Sforza T. 2002.*Obesity in the Pacific: Too big to ignore*. Noumea, New Caledonia: World Health Organization Regional Office for the Western Pacific, Secretariat of the Pacific Community.

Kapoor A K, Dhall M. 2016. Poverty, malnutrition and biological dynamics among tribes of India. *Health Science Journal*. 10:1.

Katona P, Katona-Apte J. 2008. The interaction between nutrition and infection. *Clinical Infectious Diseases*. 46: 1582-1588.

Kearns K, Dee A, Fitzgerald A P, Doherty E, Perry I J. 2014. Chronic disease burden associated with overweight and obesity in Ireland: the effects of a small BMI reduction at population level. *BMC Public Health*. 14: 143.

Kelley K, Clark B, Brown V, Sitzia J. 2003. Good practice in the conduct and reporting of survey research. *International Journal for Quality in Health Care*.15: 261-266.

Kelly T, Yang W, Chen C S, Reynolds K, He J. 2008. Global burden of obesity in 2005 and projections to 2030. *International Journal of Obesity*. 32: 1431.

Khongsdier R.1995. *A study on nutrition and health status in relation to some bio-social factors among the War Khasi of Meghalaya*. Ph.D.dissertation, North-Eastern Hill University.

Kikon M.2002.*Culture Change among the Lotha Nagas: A case study of Wokha and Akuk village in Nagaland.* Ph.D.dissertation, North-Eastern Hill University.

Kim H Y. 2013. Statistical notes for clinical researchers: assessing normal distribution (2) using skewness and kurtosis. *Restorative Dentistry andEndodontics*. 38: 52-54.

Kopelman P G. 2000. Obesity as a medical problem. Nature. 404: 635-643.

Longkumer T. 2013a. *Physical growth and nutritional status among Ao Naga children of Nagaland, Northeast* India. Journal of Anthropology, 2013, http://dx.doi.org/10.1155/2013/291239, accessed September 6, 2017.

Longkumer T. 2013b. *A study of somatotypes and nutritional status among the Ao children of Mokokchung District, Nagaland*. Ph.D. dissertation, North-Eastern Hill University.

Maken T, Varte L. 2012. Nutritional status of children as indicated by z-scores of the Hmars: a tribe of NE India. *Antrocom Online Journal of Anthropology*. 8: 213-227.

Misra A, Vikram N K, Gupta R, Pandey R M, Wasir J S, Gupta V P. 2006. Waist circumference cut-off points and action levels for Asian Indians for identification of abdominal obesity. *International Journal of Obesity*. 30: 106-111.

Müller O, Krawinkel M. 2005. Malnutrition and health in developing countries. *Canadian Medical Association Journal*. 173: 279-286.

Mungreiphy N K, Kapoor S. 2010. Socioeconomic changes as covariates of overweight and obesity among Tangkhul Naga tribal women of Manipur, North-East India. *Journal of Biosocial Science*. 42: 289-305.

Mungreiphy N K, Kapoor S, Sinha R. 2011. Association between BMI, blood pressure, and age: study among Tangkhul Naga tribal males of Northeast India. *Journal of Anthropology*, http://dx.doi.org/10.1155/2011/748147, accessed March 12, 2018.

Mungreiphy N K, Kapoor S, Sinha R. 2012. Relationship between nutritional status, respiratory performance and age: study among Tangkhul Naga females of Northeast India.*Acta Universitatis Szeqediensis*. 56: 31-36.

Pérez A P, Munoz J Y, Cortés V B, de Pablos Velasco P. 2007. Obesity and cardiovascular disease. *Public Health Nutrition*. 10: 1156-1163.

Poirier P, Eckel R H. 2002. Obesity and cardiovascular disease. *Current Atherosclerosis Reports*. 4: 448-453.

Popkin BM. 1998. The nutrition transition and its health implications in lower-income countries.*Public Health Nutrition*. 1: 5-22.

Popkin BM. 2002. An overview on the nutrition transition and its health implications: the Bellagio Meeting. *Public Health Nutrition*, 5: 93-103.

Popkin B M.2006. Global nutrition dynamics: the world is shifting rapidly toward a diet linked with noncommunicable diseases. *The American Journal of Clinical Nutrition*. 84: 289-298.

Prentice A M. 2005.The emerging epidemic of obesity in developing countries. *International Journal of Epidemiology*. 35: 93-99.

Rengma M S, Sen J, Mondal N. 2015.Socio-Economic, Demographic and Lifestyle Determinants of Overweight and Obesity mong Adults of Northeast India.*Ethiopian Journal of Health Science*. 25: 199-208.

Schmid MA. Egeland GM. Salomeyesudas B. Satheesh PV. Kuhnlein HV. 2006. Traditional food consumption and nutritional status of Dalit mothers in rural Andhra Pradesh, South India.*European Journal of Clinical Nutrition*. 60: 1277-1283.

Shaper AG.1996. *Obesity and Cardiovascular* Disease, *In* DJChadwick and G Cardew(eds.),Ciba Foundation Symposium 201-The Origins and Consequences of Obesity.pp.90-107, https://doi.org/10.1002/9780470514962.ch6, accessed December 8, 2017.

Shukla A, Kumar K, Singh A. 2014. Association between obesity and selected morbidities: a study of BRICS countries. *PloSone*. 9: e94433.

Singh M S, Devi R K. 2013. Nutritional status among the urban Meitei children and adolescents of Manipur, Northeast India. *Journal of Anthropology*, http://dx.doi.org/10.1155/2013/983845, accessed February 17, 2018.

Singh MS, Dkhar JW. 2013.Growing Obese in Manipur: Relationship between Age and Obesity among the Meitei Males of Manipur, India. *The Anthropologist*.16: 753-756.

Temsutola T. 2010. *Body Composition and Nutritional Status among the Ao adults*.Ph.D.dissertation, North-Eastern Hill University.

Turner J, Kelly B. (2000). Emotional dimensions of chronic disease. *Western Journal of Medicine*. 172: 124.

United Nations. 2000. *Resolution adopted by the General Assembly*.United Nations Millennium Declaration. New York, NY: UN.

Weiner J S, Lourie J A. 1981. *Practical human biology*. London, England: Academic Press.

World Health Organization.2000a. *Obesity: Preventing and managing the Global Epidemic – Report of a WHO Consultation*. WHO Technical Report Series. No. 894. Geneva, Switzerland: WHO.

World Health Organization.2000b. *The Asia-Pacific perspective: redefining obesity and its treatment*. Geneva, Switzerland: WHO.

World Health Organization. 2002. *The world health report 2002: reducing risks, promoting healthy life*.Geneva, Switzerland: WHO.

World Health Organization.2004. *Appropriate body-mass index for Asian populations and its implications for policy and intervention strategies*. Lancet. 363: 157-163.

World Health Organization.2011a. *Global status report on noncommunicable diseases 2010*. Geneva, Switzerland: WHO .

World Health Organization. 2011b. *Physical status: the use and interpretation of anthropometry.* WHO technical report series. 854: 2009-2016.

World Health Organization. 2011c. *Waist circumference and waist-hip ratio: Report of a WHO expert consultation*. Geneva, Switzerland: WHO.

Yang C Y, Peng C Y, Liu Y C, Chen W Z, Chiou W K. 2011. Surface anthropometric indices in obesity-related metabolic diseases and cancers. *Chang Gung Medical Journal*. 34: 1-22.

Chapter Fourteen

NUTRITIONAL STATUS OF TRIBAL WOMEN IN VISAKHAPATNAM DISTRICT, ANDHRA PRADESH

M. SIVA DURGA PRASAD NAYAK AND SUNITA SREEGIRI

ABSTRACT

Background: India is a diversified country with a blend of people living in urban, rural& tribal areas. According to NFHS-3, 46.6 percent of tribal women had Body Mass Index (BMI) below 18.5, indicating chronic energy deficiency. Based on this background this study was conducted in the tribal population of ITDA paderu division in Visakhapatnam district to assess the nutritional status of tribal women. Methods: It is a cross-sectional study conducted in ITDA Paderu division of Visakhapatnam district among 225 randomly selected reproductive age group tribal women. Multistage simple random sampling technique was applied to select villages. A prior consent was taken from selected women& a pre-tested semi structured schedule was used to collect the information. Anthropometric measurements such as height& weight were measured& Body mass index was calculated. Pallor was observed by examining the conjunctiva. MS-Excel 2007, SPSS trail version-21 softwares were used for statistical analysis. Results: *In the study population mean height of study population was 147.95±6.33 cm and mean weight was 45.01± 6.372 kgs. Prevalence of thinness among the study women was 18.2 percent. Among them 15.1% had moderate thinness and 3.1 percent had mild thinness. Pallor was observed among 61 percent of study women. Women from families with continuous earnings & debt free condition had BMI above 18.5. Conclusions: One fifth of the study population were at risk of further nutritional deficiency. Continuous earnings of families throughout year and debt free condition influence the nutritional status of women.*

Keywords: Body Mass Index, Chronic Energy Deficiency, Nutritional Status, Prime Tribe Group, Tribal Women

Introduction

The world is now bearing dual burden of both over nutrition and under nutrition. This can be called as nutritional transition phase, which means that over weight and obesity predominate as diet related health problems in industrialized countries, where as under nutrition still exists among large segments of world's population especially vulnerable sections such as tribal communities. India is a diversified country with a blend of people living in urban, rural and tribal are as. National Family Health Survey –3 (2005-06) brought out data on health and nutritional indicators and provides a clear picture of the status of tribal women. According to NFHS-3, 46.6 percent of tribal women had Body Mass Index (BMI) below 18.5, indicating chronic energy deficiency (Ministry of Women and Child Development, 2011).

Several research studies on tribal population of India revealed that prevalence of chronic energy deficiency was high among tribal population. Women being vulnerable section, the impact on their health is much higher. Health and nutritional status of tribal population clearly indicates that, the goal of Health for all cannot be fully achieved unless due attention is paid to the vulnerable sections of the society i.e., tribals and especially tribal women. Based on this background this study was conducted in the tribal population of ITDA Paderu division in Visakhapatnam district to assess the nutritional status of tribal women.

Methodology

A cross-sectional study was conducted in ITDA Paderu division of Visakhapatnam district among the reproductive age group tribal women. The study was conducted during the period from April 2014 to October 2014. Sample size was calculated as 225 based on the prevalence of malnutrition as 64 percent as reported by previous studies (Kupputhai and Mallika., 1993). Multistage simple random sampling technique was applied to select villages. In the first stage, 3

Community Health and Nutritional Centres were selected randomly among the six CHNCs in ITDA paderu division. In the second stage, 3 PHCs were selected from each selected CHNC. In the third stage, one village was selected from each PHC. A house to house survey was conducted to interview 25 women in reproductive age group in each village. In case of less populated villages/ small hamlets where 25 women could not be covered, the subsequent hamlet / village was included for the study. Written Permission was obtained from ITDA Additional District Medical and Health Officer (DM&HO) for conducting the study and taking help from the PHC staff. Help of Local Multi-purpose Health worker Female (MPHW-F) and Accredited Social Health Activist (ASHA) was taken for identification, initial contact and for translation of conversation where ever required. Tribal women in reproductive age group (15-49 years) available at home at the time of study and those who were willing to participate were included in the study. Pregnant and lactating women, and those women with chronic infectious diseases were excluded from study. A prior consent was taken from selected women and a pre-tested semi structured schedule was used to collect the information. Economic classification was done based on guidelines of Planning Commission of India. Planning commission defined poverty line as expenditure class-wise distribution of persons less than Rs.560/- per person per month in urban are a and below Rs.368/-in rural are a at 2004-2005 prices (Lal and Pankaj., 2011). As there is no separate definition for tribal area, definition of rural are a had been applied to tribal area. Continuous earning capacity of the family through out the year was enquired. If the family had opportunities for 5 days work per week through out the year, without any break in any season, summer, rainy or winter seasons, then the family considered as it had continuous earning capacity through out year.

Anthropometric measurements such as height and weight were measured and Body mass index was calculated. According to the WHO classification of BMI, study subjects were categorized as Under weight (<18.50 kg/m^2), Normal (18.50-24.99 kg/m^2) and Overweight (≥ 25.00 kg/m^2). Based on the additional cut-off points, women in the normal range were again classified in to two categories such as class1 (18.50-22.99 kg/m^2) and class 2 (23.00-24.99 kg/m^2) and women in pre-obese category were also classified as pre-obese class 1 (25.00-27.49 kg/m^2) and pre-obese class 2 (27.50-29.99 kg/m^2). Pallor was observed by examining the conjunctiva of study women in day light. MS Excel 2007, SPSS trailversion-21 softwares were used for statistical analysis. Chi-square test was used to test the significance of results.

Observations and Results

Table 1 shows that 75.17 percent of the women were in the age of 15–30 years and 24.9 percent in 31 to 49 years age group. About 60 percent were illiterates. 28 percent were unemployed/ remained at home where as 72 percent were working women. Majority of the women (64%)belong to nuclear family. Most of the women (96.4%) were married. Around three fourth of women (75.2%) had<2 living children and 24.8% had>2 children. Only two religions were predominantly followed among the study population. 78.7% belong to Hindu religion. Remaining 21.3 percent belong to Christianity. Women in the study belong to three PTG tribes (Khonds, Gadabas and Porijas) and six non-PTG tribes. PTGs constituted around 40 percent and Non-PTGs were 60 percent. Out of the 225 women, 41.3 percent of women were below poverty line. Majority of them (71.6%) did not have continuous earnings throughout the year. Around one third of women (35.6%) had debts.

Table 1: Socio demographic profile of tribal women

Variables	Number (%) n=225
Age group	
15-30	169 (75.1)
31-49	56 (24.9)
Education	
Illiterate	135(60)
Literates	90 (40)
Occupation	
Unemployed/Housewives	63(28)
Working women	162(72)
Type of Family	
Nuclear family	144(64)
Joint family	81(36)
Marital status	
Married	217(96.4)
Unmarried	8(3.6)

Number of children	
<2 children	169(75.2)
>2 children	56 (24.8)
Religion	
Hinduism	177(78.7)
Christianity	48(21.3)
Economic status	
Above Poverty Line	132 (58.7)
Below Poverty Line	93 (41.3)
Continuous earnings through out year	
Present	64 (28.4)
Not Present	161 (71.6)
Debts	
Yes	80 (35.6)
No	145 (64.4)

In the study population height ranged from 130–167 cm, majority of women (182 out of 225) had height between 140 cm to 156cm. Mean height of study population was 147.95±6.33 cm. Weight of the study women ranged from 35.7 - 66.9 kgs. Half (50.2%) of the women weighed between 40 kgs to 50 kgs weight. Mean weight was 45.01 kgs with a standard deviation of 6.372 kgs. BMI was calculated for all the study subjects. Figure 1 shows that, prevalence of thinness among the study women was 18.2%. Among them 15.1% had moderate thinness, and 3.1 percent had mild thinness. 65.3 percent women were in normal class 1, 13.3 percent were in normal class 2. Very less number (0.9%, 2.3%) were categorized as preobese class 1 and class 2 categories. Among the study women about 61 percent of study women had pallor and 39 percent had no pallor as depicted in Figure 2.

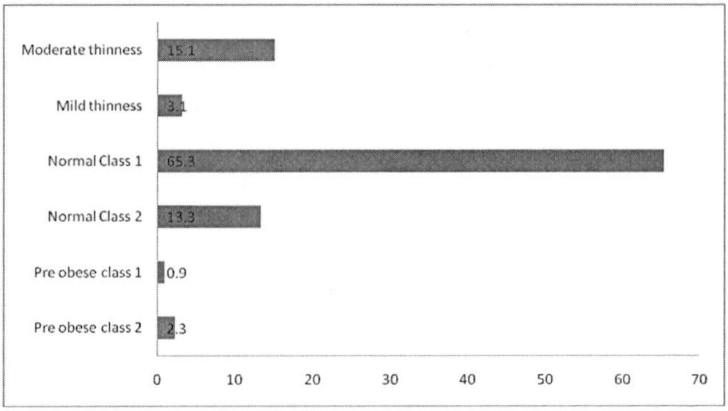

Figure 1: Distribution of study population according to nutritional status

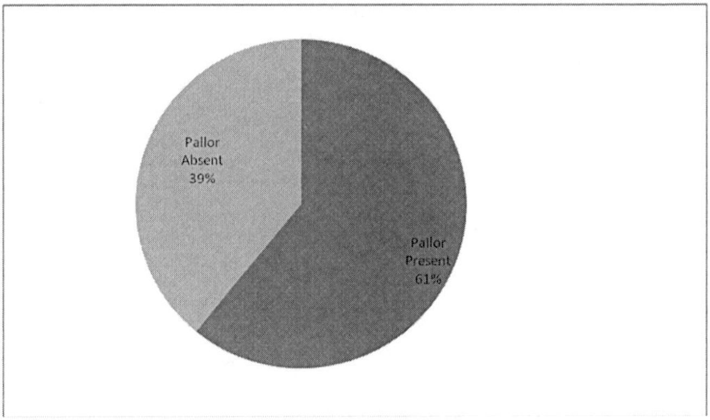

Figure 2: Distribution of study population according to pallor

Table 2 shows younger women in the age group of 15–30 years were having BMI less than 18.5 as compared to those in 31–40 years age group. These differences were statistically significant. A significant association was also observed between continuous earnings & debt free condition of the family and the BMI of the women. Women from such families had BMI above 18.5. Similarly women from prime tribe group had significantly better BMI as compared to the non-prime tribe groups.

Discussion

The anthropometric measurements of the tribal women in this study reveal that there is deficit in both weight and height as compared to the standards. The Indian Council of Medical Research (ICMR) has set a standard of 151cms as average height for Indian women and 55 kg as average body weight for Indian reference women. However the mean height among the study population was found to be 147.95cm and the mean weight was 45.01 kg which shows the tribal women are shorter by 2 percent and have a deficit of 18.16 percent in their weight as compared to the average Indian women.

Table 2: Socio-demographic variables vs. BMI

Socio-demographic Variable		BMI <18.5 Number (%)	BMI >18.5 Number (%)	X^2(p value)
Agegroups	15-30years	39 (23)	130 (77)	10.73 (0.001)
	31-49years	2 (3.5)	54 (96.5)	
Occupation	Unemployed and Housewives	10 (15.8)	53 (84.2)	0.32 (0.56)
	Working women	31 (19.1)	131 (80.9)	
Religion	Hinduism	12 (25)	36 (75)	1.88 (0.17)
	Christianity	29 (16.3)	148 (83.7)	
Caste	Prime Tribe Groups	8 (8.6)	84 (91.4)	9.47 (0.002)
	Non-Prime Tribe Groups	33 (24.8)	100 (75.2)	
Type of family	Nuclear family	31 (21.5)	113 (78.5)	2.99 (0.08)
	Joint family	10 (12.3)	71 (87.7)	
Number of children	<2 children	33 (19.5)	136 (80.5)	0.77(0.37)
	>2 children	8 (14.2)	48 (85.8)	
Continuous earnings for families through out year	Continuous earnings present	18 (28.1)	46 (71.9)	5.88 (0.01)
	Continuous earnings Not present	68 (42.2)	93 (57.8)	
Debts condition	Debts present	21 (26.25)	59 (73.75)	5.36 (0.02)
	Debts not present	58 (13.8)	87 (86.2)	
Economic statusof Families	Above poverty line	23 (17.4)	109 (82.6)	0.13 (0.71)
	Below poverty line	18 (19.3)	75 (80.7)	

This finding is consistent with that of other studies such as Ghosh and Malik, (2007) and Kupputhaiet and Mallika, (1993). In contrast to these findings various studies conducted in Andhra Pradesh

(Varadarajan and Prasad, 2009) as well as in different settings have reported the mean height to be higher ranging from 152cm to 160cm (Banik, 2011). This difference may be due to the ethnic variation as there was a representation of tribals from different regions in some studies as per the anthropometric measurements, it was found that majority were in normal category, very less percentage were found to be in pre-obese category, showing low risk towards lifestyle disorders. Around 18.2 percent of tribal women were having BMI less than 18.5 reflecting underweight status of these women. Various studies also have reported underweight among women ranging from10–27 percent (Varadarajan and Prasad, 2009).

Around one fifth of the women were in moderate to mild categories which suggests that any further nutritional deficiency may lead to severe deficiency. Contrasting findings have been reported by various studies conducted in different parts of the world. Very high prevalence of thinness was reported in some Indian studies Ghosh and Malik, 2007; Varadarajan and Prasad, 2009; Banik, 2011; Jaiswal, 2013). In countries like Brazil and Australia it was as low as 2 percent to 7 percent (Burns and Thomson, 2008) Even though tribals worldwide have similarities in several aspects, there may be difference in the dietary intake,(the quantity and quality of diet) and genetic variation of the indigenous groups may influence their BMI status. It is also observed that studies in the past (Taneja and Saxena, 1998; Ghosh and Malik, 2007)have shown a higher the prevalence of underweight compared to the recent findings including the present study, suggesting an improvement in the nutritional status in the past decade.

A significant difference in the BMI status is found between women of different age groups. In the present study, it is observed younger women are having better nutritional status as compared to older women in the age group of 31-49 years. Studies (Rao, 2012) have shown that among tribal families around 70 percent of the monthly income is spent on food. Continuous earnings through out the year and debt free condition of the family provides the women as well as the family the opportunity of having nutritious food thus having better BMI. The same is reflected in our study as continuous earnings through out they ear and debt free condition of the family have been found to behaving significant influence on BMI.

The prevalence of anaemia in the current study population was 60.9 percent. This finding was higher than the national average prevalence of anaemia in reproductive age group women according to NFHS-3 i.e 55 percent (National Nutrition Monitoring Bureau, 2006). Sree Lakshmi et al., reported a high prevalence of anaemia in tribal women in their studies than the current study result, whereas Kamath and Majeed, (2013) reported a low prevalence of anaemia in tribal women when compared to the present study.

Conclusions

The anthropometric parameters of tribal women are lower than the ICMR standards. Although majority were normal showing low risk lifestyle diseases still one fifth were at risk of further nutritional deficiency. Education of women, continuous earnings of families through out year and debt free condition influence the nutritional status of women.

Acknowledgements

We are thankful to Additional DM and HO, ITDA Paderu division, Medical officers and field staff and of PHCs for their full cooperation in conducting the study. We are thankful to the study participants and village heads for their full cooperation to conduct the study.

References

Banik SD. 2011. Nutritional status adiposity and a body composition of Oraon and Sarak females in Ranchi District, India-a comparision. *Ecology of Food and Nutrition*. 50: 43-62.

Burns J, Thomson N. 2008. Review of nutrition and growth among Indigenous peoples. Australian Indigenous Health. InfoNet.

Ghosh S and Malik SL. 2007. Sex differences in body size and shape among Santhals of West Bengal. *Anthropologist*. 9: 143-149.

Jaiswal A. 2013. Health and nutritional status of aprimitive tribe of Madhya Pradesh. *Global Journal of Human Social Science*. 13: 1.

Kamath R, Majeed JA, Chandrasekaran V, Pattanshetty SM. 2013. *Journal of Family Medicine and Primary Care*. 2: 345–348.

Kupputhai U, Mallika N. 1993. Nutritional status of adult women Belonging to Khond, Gadaba and Porjatribes of Andhra Pradesh. *The Indian Journal of Nutrition and Dietetics*. 30: 173-179.

Lal S, Pankaj A. 2011. *Text book of community medicine: preventive and social medicine*. 4th Edition. CBS publishers. pp. 1-18.

Ministry of Women and Child development. 2011. *Scheduled tribe women and children: issues and challenges for development*. New Delhi; Ministry of Women and Child development. Available from: http://www.pib.nic.

in/newsite/erelease.aspx?relid=72382

National Nutrition Monitoring Bureau. 2006. *Diet and Nutritional Status of Rural Population and Prevalence of Hypertension among adults in Rural Areas*, NNMB Technical Report No. 24, NNMB, NIN, Hyderabad.

Taneja PV, Saxena M. 1998. Nutritional anthropometry of Bhil women in Jhabua district of Madhya Pradesh. *The Indian Journal of Nutrition and Dietetics*. 35: 98-102.

Varadarajan A, Prasad S. 2009.Regional variations in nutritional status among tribals of Andhra Pradesh. *Studies of Tribes and Tribals*. 7: 137-141.

Chapter Fifteen

DIETARY HABITS OF TRIBAL WOMEN IN VISAKHAPATNAM DISTRICT, ANDHRA PRADESH

M Siva Durga Prasad Nayak and Sunita Sreegiri

Abstract

Introduction: India is a diversified country with a blend of people living in urban, rural and tribal areas. The dietary habits of tribals are distinct from rest of the people. Various research studies on tribal population revealed that their diets are nutritionally deficient. Methodology: It is a population based cross-sectional survey conducted in ITDA Paderu division of Visakhapatnam district among 225 tribal women in the age group of 15-49 years during the period from April to October 2014. Data was collected using two formats 1) food frequency questionnaire (FFQ) 2) 24-hour dietary recall questionnaire. MS Excel 2007, SPSS and Dietsoft softwares were used for statistical analysis. Results: Rice is the most common staple food and ambali is the most common breakfast. Top five foods providing energy to the women were rice, ambali, vegetables, tea with milk and dal. The Mean Calorie intake of energy by tribal women was 1931 Kcal per day. Average consumption of carbohydrates per each day was 367.14 gm and it accounts for 76.6 percent of total energy consumption. Protein intake was 49.83 gm and it was equal to 10.5 percent of total energy and fat consumption was 27.67 gm and it accounts for 12.9 percent of total energy. Conclusions: One third of women were consuming less than 80 percent RDA of energy i.e, 1784 Kcal per day and two fifths of women were consuming protein less than 80 percent RDA i.e., 44 grams per day. It indicates the need of nutritional education to avoid taboos and improve health.

Keywords: *Andhra Pradesh, Dietary Habits, Food Frequency Questionnaire, Nutritional Status, Tribal Women.*

INTRODUCTION

India is a diversified country with a blend of people living in urban, rural and tribal areas. Anthropologically tribe is a system of social organisation which includes several local groups – villages, districts on lineage and normally includes a common culture, a common name, political system, simple economy, religion and belief, primitive law and education system (Indian Tribal Belt, 2014). They primarily live in various ecological and geo-climatic conditions ranging from plains, forests, hills and inaccessible areas. The traditional and cultural distinction of each tribal community has made them distinguishable from each other and also from people living in plain areas (India Tourism E-Catalougue, 2019).Their dietary habits too are distinct from rest of the community.

Various research studies on tribal population of India in the past two decades have revealed that their diets are nutritionally deficient (Varadarajan and Prasad, 2009; Ministry of Women and Child Development. 2011). These nutritionally deficient diets lead to chronic energy deficiency and related diseases, low capacity for work, increased susceptibility to various ill health conditions and thereby to deterioration in the health status of the individuals. Women being vulnerable section, the impact on their health are much higher. Based on this background this study was conducted in the tribal population of Integrated Tribal Development Agency (ITDA) Paderu division in Visakhapatnam district to study the dietary habits of tribal women and .assess their nutrient intake.

SUBJECTS AND METHODS

It is a population based cross-sectional survey conducted in ITDA Paderu division of Visakhapatnam district among tribal women in the age group of 15-49 years during the period from April to October 2014. Sample size was calculated with Epi-info software for population survey. Population of ITDA Paderu division according to Census 2011 was 604047. At 5 percent confidence limits and 30 percent expected frequency of deficient nutrient intake the sample size was calculated as 225. Simple random technique was used to select 9 PHCs out of total of 37 PHCs in ITDA Paderu division.

From each selected PHC, one village was selected for covering a sample of 225. A house to house survey was conducted to interview 25 women in reproductive age group from each randomly selected village. In case of less populated villages/small hamlets where 25 women could not be covered, the subsequent hamlet/village were included for the study.

Written permission was obtained from ITDA Additional District Medical and Health Officer (DM and HO) for conducting the study and taking help from the PHC staff. Help of Local Auxiliary Nurse Midwife (ANM) and Accredited Social Health Activist (ASHA) was taken for identification, initial contact and for translation of conversation where ever required. Tribal women in reproductive age group (15-49 years) available at home at the time of study and those who were willing to participate were included in the study. Pregnant and lactating women and those women with chronic diseases were excluded from study.

Data was collected using two formats. 1) Information regarding dietary habits was obtained using food frequency questionnaire (FFQ). As the dietary habits of tribal people are not fixed every day, frequency of consumption of various types of foods by the tribal women in the previous week was obtained using FFQ considering one week as one dietary cycle. Food consumed by the study participants were classified as different groups, such as cereals, millets, oils, pulses, vegetables, green leafy vegetables, milk and milk products, flesh food, eggs, fruits and nuts, homemade preserved foods, packed foods, alcohol. Homemade foods made up of fruits or meat such as pickles and dried meat were considered as preserved foods and ready to eat food items such as biscuits, packed snacks etc. purchased from the market were considered as packed foods. 2) Information on complete diet history of the study participants was obtained using a modified 24-hour dietary recall questionnaire for the previous day, developed by Public Health Foundation of India. Details of all the food items consumed at various intervals during the day were noted. The amount of food intake of each item was calculated with the help of standard measuring units- 5ml, 15ml spoons, 50gms, 100gms, 150gms, 200gms, 250gms bowls. The measuring units were shown to the study participants and were asked to tell about dietary intake in terms of these vessels. The nutritive values of all consumed foods were added to calculate the total intake of energy and macro nutrients by the study participants using dietsoft software. As per Indian

Council of Medical Research (ICMR) guidelines recommended daily allowance (RDA) for energy intake for an Indian reference women is 2230 Kcal. Consumption of energy above 80 percent of RDA (>-2SD)was considered as normal, and consumption below 80 percent of RDA (<-2SD) was considered as deficient intake. MS Excel 2007, SPSS and Dietsoft software's were used for statistical analysis.

Results

Women in the study belong to three Prime Tribe Group (PTG) tribes (Khonds, Gadabas and Porijas) and six non-PTG tribes. Table 1 shows that 11.1 percent of the study participants were in the age group of 15 to 20 years, 64 percent were in the age of 21–30 years and 19.6 percent in 31–40 years age. About 60 percent were illiterates. Around 12.9 percent were educated up to graduation or above. Twenty eight percent women were unemployed/remained at home where as 72 percent were working. Out of the 225 women, 41.3 percent of women were below poverty line. Majority (78.7%) belong to Hindu religion remaining 21.3 percent belong to Christianity.

Table 1: Socio demographic and economic profile of tribal women

Age groups	Number (%) (n=225)
15-20 years	25 (11.1)
21-30 years	144 (64)
31-40 years	44 (19.6)
41-49 years	12 (5.3)
Education	
Illiterate	135 (60)
Up to High school	47 (20.9)
Intermediate/Post High school diploma	14 (6.2)
Graduate and above	29 (12.9)
Occupation	
Unemployed/Housewives	63 (28)
Working women	162 (72)
Economic status	
Above Poverty Line	132 (58.7)
Below Poverty Line	93 (41.3)
Religion	
Hinduism	177 (78.7)
Christianity	48 (21.3)

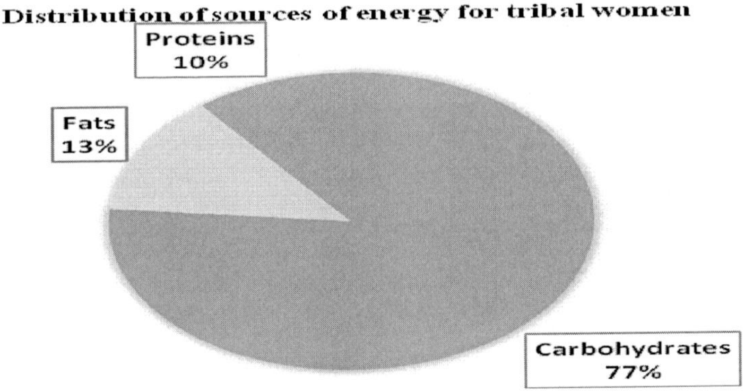

Figure 1: Distribution of sources of energy for study women

Table 2: Frequency of consumption of various foods in oneweek duration

Type of food	Not Consumed (%)	Once (%)	Twice (%)	Thrice (%)	>Thrice (%)
Rice	0(0)	0(0)	0(0)	0(0)	100(100)
Ragi	0(0)	0(0)	0(0)	0(0)	100(100)
Red Gram	7(3.1)	34(15.1)	80(35.6)	66(29.3)	38(16.9)
Black Gram	171(76)	27(12)	16(7.1)	5(2.2)	6(2.7)
Vegetables	2(1.0)	10(4.4)	25(11.1)	84(37.3)	104(46.2)
Green Leafy Vegetables	9(4)	18(8)	49(21.8)	98(43.6)	51(22.6)
Flesh	29(12.9)	145(64.4)	41(18.2)	10(4.5)	0(0)
Egg	48(21.3)	93(41.3)	49(21.8)	29(12.9)	6(2.7)
Milk	101(44.9)	22(9.8)	36(16)	21(9.3)	45(20)
Fruits	27(12)	30(13.3)	50(22.2)	54(24)	64(28.5)
Preserved Foods	142(63.1)	35(15.6)	9(4)	16(7.1)	23(10.2)
Packed foods	84(37.3)	54(24)	45(20)	25(11.1)	17(7.6)
Oils (palm oil)	0(0)	0(0)	0(0)	0(0)	144(63.9)
Oils (other oils)	0(0)	0(0)	0(0)	0(0)	81(36.1)

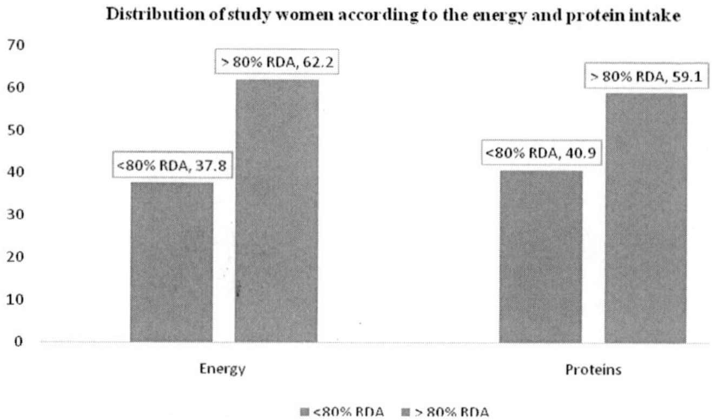

Figure 2: Distribution of study women according to the energy and protein intake

Table 3: Dietary intake of tribal women based on 24 hour Recall method

Items	Measuring units	Total number of servings	Energy in kilo calories
Rice	250 gm	454	192950
Ambali	500 ml	264	116335
Vegetables	100 gm	204	34680
Green Leafy Vegetables	150 gm	58	5800
Dal	50 gm	165	16500
Chicken	150 gm	38	9120
Eggs	1 egg	17	1530
Curd	100 gm	29	3190
Fruits	100 gm	66	5940
Breakfast	3 Idlies	53	7950
Tea without milk	120 ml	136	5440
Tea with Milk	120 ml	66	21120
Snacks	3 Biscuits	57	11400
Pickles	30 gm	11	1320
Pea Nuts	100 gm	10	900
Lemon Juice	200 ml	5	300

Table 2 and Table 3 depict the frequency of food intake, dietary practices of tribal women in ITDA Paderu division based on food frequency questionnaire and 24 hour Recall method. Rice is the most common staple food and ambali is the most common breakfast. Top five foods providing energy to the women were rice, ambali, vegetables, tea with milk and dal. Table 2 shows that majority of the women consumed rice (99.1%) and ragi (75.6%) every day. Consumption of wheat was almost negligible. Red gram is the commonly consumed dal among tribal women. Almost all the women (96.9%) were consuming redgram. Regarding the frequency, 46.2 percent women were consuming redgram atleast three days in a week. Comparatively consumption of blackgram was less. About two thirds of the women (76%) had not consumed black gram in the previous week. Only 24 percent of women were consuming blackgram. Vegetables were consumed at least three times in a week by 83.5 percent of women and green leafy vegetables by 66.2 percent of women. Consumption of saturated oils such a palm oil was observed among 63.9 percent as compared to other oils (36.1%).

Around two thirds (64.4%) of the women were consuming flesh food once in aweek and two fifths (41.3%) were consuming eggs once in a week. Only 20 percent of the women were consuming more than thrice in a week. One third of the women (44.9%) not consumed milk. About half of the women (52.5%) were consuming fruits atleast three times in a week. Around (63.1%) of the study population never consumed preserved foods and one tenth (11%) were consuming packed foods thrice in a week.

Regarding the practices of sharing the meal together, Majority (89%) of tribal women were eating food along with other family members whereas 11 percent of women were eating food after other family members had finished. Alcohol consumption was observed in 13.3 percent of tribal women.

Regarding the nutrient intake it is observed that the mean calorie intake of energy by tribal women was 1931 Kcal per day. Figure 1 shows that, in the present study, average consumption of Carbohydrates per each day was 367.14 gm and it accounts for 76.6 percent of total energy consumption. Protein intake was 49.83 gm and it was equal to 10.5 percent of total energy and fat consumption was 27.67 gm and it accounts for 12.9 percent of total energy.

Recommended daily allowance of energy for moderate working women is 2230 Kcal and 80 percent of RDA is 1784 Kcal. Figure 2 shows that, 37.8 percent of women were consuming less than 80 percent RDA of energy i.e., 1784 Kcal per day. Recommended daily intake for Indian reference women of 55kg weight is 55 grams per day and 80 percent RDA is 44 grams per day. Figure 2 shows that, 40.9 percent of women were consuming protein lessthan 80 percent RDA i.e., 44 grams per day.

Discussion

In this study, it was observed that rice and ragi were the major cereals consumed by tribal women. Both rice as well as ragi is cultivated by these tribals in their fields and that might be the reason for such consumption. This finding is consistent with the results of other studies conducted among tribal people (Mittal and Srivastava, 2006; Pradhan and Kamlesh, 2011; Tribal Welfare Department 2012; Jaiswal. 2013) Red gram and blackgram were the preferred pulses. Black gram intake was comparatively less, only 32 percent of women were consuming Blackgram. Almost all the women (96.9%) were consuming Redgram inthe form of *dal* and *pappucharu*. However the frequency of consumption of pulses was only once or twice in a week. This finding is in concurrence with the results of some other studies (Kumar et al., 2000; Murugkar and Pal, 2004; Mittal and Srivastava, 2006; Jaiswal, 2013). The consumption of pulses is very low in both the seasons as reported by ITDA in 1993 (Tribal Welfare Department 2012). Consumption of saturated oils such as palm oil was more among the women as compared to other refined oils may be because palmoline oil is marketed at a cheaper price in comparison to refined alternatives.

Some of the practices such as consumption of leafy and other vegetables was found to be good. Majority of the women (85.6%) were consuming vegetables including green leafy (66.7%) at least three times in a week. Regarding fruits, locally available seasonal fruits such as jack fruit and mangoes were consumed more as they were accessible to these tribal women. It was observed that, about half of the women (52.4%) were consuming fruits at least three times in a week. Similar results are reported by Ray et al., (2000) Murugkar and Pal (2004), Qamra et al. (2006), in their studies.

Flesh foods such as red meat, poultry and eggs were less frequently consumed as compared to the vegetables. The frequency was once weeks usually after the sandy days as the local shandies were the common purchasing points for these foods. Red meat was consumed by 64.4 percent of the women in a week where as 41.3 percent of women were consuming eggs once in a week. Consumption of fish/seafood was not common. In one of the villages called Gammeli, consumption of fish was a taboo as the villagers feel that the local diety protects these fishes.

Milking of cow is a taboo among tribal population and consumption of milk is comparatively less by these tribal women as compared with other food groups. In the present study it is observed that 44.9 percent of the women had never consumed milk. Similar findings have been reported by other research studies (Murugkar and Pal, 2004; Mittal and Srivastava, 2006; Kusuma and Babu, 2011; Jaiswal. 2013).

Tribals have a traditional practice of preserving foods such as meat and fruits for consumption at later days especially for rainy season when hunting and forest activities are not feasible. However in the recent times the traditional way of consuming such preserved foods is not so commonly seen among these tribal women. In our study, 58.2 percent of the women never consumed homemade preserved foods.

Alcohol consumption is common in tribal communities among both men and women. The alcohol consumed by them is usually locally prepared liquor called Toddy – 'Jeeluga Kallu'. Among the study population less number of women (13.3%) was consuming alcohol regularly which may be due to changing cultural patterns and influence of education. Rest of the women were consuming only during festival days. Kusuma and Babu (2011),also reported women have reported to consume only on festive occasions.

In our study the mean intake of calories by tribal women was found to be 1930 Kcal which is 86.5 percent of the recommended allowance with a mean deficiency of 13 percent. These findings are in concurrence with Kupputhai and Mallika (1993), who reported a 20 percent deficiency. Various studies on all age groups of tribal population including women revealed that the calorie deficiency ranged between 38 to 50 (Yadav and Singh, 1999; Mittal and Srivastava, 2006). Mean intake of carbohydrates in tribal women was 367gm per day which provides1468 Kcal of energy. This was equal to 76 percent of total energy consumption which is as per the recommendation.

In our study mean consumption of protein by tribal women was 49.8 gm. per day. The daily requirement of protein is 1 gm. per Kg body weight. It is recommended that the calorie contribution from protein should be atleast 10 percent of total energy. If the total energy intake is 1930 Kcal then a minimum of 193 kcal should be contributed by proteins. As one gm. of protein provides 4 Kcal of energy, for 193 Kcal 48.25 gm protein consumption per day would meet the requirement. In our study it was observed that mean protein intake was 49.8 gm per day which indicates that the protein intake satisfactory. An adequate intake of protein is also reported by Murugkar and Pal (2004), and Laxmaiah et al. (2007). However Kupputhai and Mallika (1993) reported that there was 30-40 percent deficiency in protein intake.

In our study fat consumption by tribal women was 27.6 gm, the main source being oil and flesh food, which provides 248 Kcal. This was equal to 12.9 percent of total energy intake. As per recommendation Fats should contributeto10-30 percent of total energy intake. In our study although the fat consumption is adequate it is in the lower end of the range. More over the fat consumed was more in the form of saturated oil compared to refined oil which may adversely affect the health of these women. However in contrast to this findings of Laxmaiah et al., (2007) who reported a 47 percent of total fat deficit intake by tribal women in Khammam district.

Conclusions

Dietary habits among tribal women were deficient of pulses and un-saturated oils. Presence of food taboos limiting their consumption of milk. One third of women were consuming less than 80% RDA of energy i.e., 1784 Kcal per day and two fifths of women were consuming protein less than 80 percent RDA i.e., 44 grams per day. It indicates the need of nutritional education to avoid taboos and improve health.

Recommendations

Education focussing on food taboos and misconceptions on various food groups among the women and families should be taken up by the Health Workers/ASHAs.

Acknowledgements

We are thankful to Additional DM&HO ITDA Paderu division, Medical officers and field staff and of PHCs for their full cooperation in conducting the study. We are thankful to the study participants and village heads for their full cooperation to conduct the study.

References

India Tourism E-catalougue. Tribal Life in India. 2019. Available from: http://www.indiatourismecatalog.com/india_tribal_rural/tribal_rural_india.html

Indian Tribal Belt. 2014. [cited2014 April 16] Available from: http://en.wikipedia.org/wiki/Indian_tribal_belt.

Jaiswal A. 2013. Health and nutritional status of primitive tribe of Madhya Pradesh. *Global Journal of Human Social Science*. 13: 1.

Kupputhai U, Mallika N. 1993. Nutritional status of adult women belonging to Khond, Gadaba and Porjatribes of Andhra Pradesh. *The Indian Journal of Nutrition and Dietetics*. 30: 173-179.

KusumaYS, Babu BV. 2011. An ethnographic note on Khondh, a primitive tribe and Valmiki, an acculturating tribe from Andhra Pradesh, India. *Antrocom Online Journal of Anthropology*. 7: 2.

Laxmaiah A,Rao MK, Kumar KR, Arlappa N, VenkaiahK, Brahmam GNV. 2007. Diet and nutritional status of tribal population in ITDA project areas of Khammam district, Andhra Pradesh. *Journal of Human Ecology*. 21: 79-86.

Ministry of Women and Child Development. 2011. Scheduled tribe women and children: issues and challenges for development. New Delhi; Ministry of Women and Child development. 2011. Available from:http://www.pib.nic.in/newsite/erelease.aspx?relid=72382

Mittal PC, SrivastavaS. 2006. Diet,nutritional status and food related traditions of Oraontribes of NewMal (West Bengal), India. *Rural and Remote Health*. 6: 385.

Murugkar DA, Pal PP. 2004. In take of nutrients and food sources of nutrients among Khasi tribal women of India. *Nutrition*. 20: 268-273.

Pradhan S, Kamlesh S. 2011. Nutritional status of Bhiltribal children in Madhya Pradesh, India: a cross sectional study. *Studies of Tribes and Tribals*. 9: 37-40.

Qamra SR, Roy J, Mishra DK. 2006. *Food consumption pattern and associated habits of the Bhil tribe of Dhar district of Madhya Pradesh*. Proceedings on National Symposium on Tribal Health. pp. 211-219.

Ray SK, Biswas AB, Kumar S. 2000. A study of dietary pattern, household food security andutritional profile of under-five chidren of a community of West Bengal. *Journal of Indian Medical Association*. 98: 3.

Tribal Welfare Department. 2012a. The dietary habits and nutrition status of the Chenchus. Available from: http;//aptribes.gov.in

Tribal Welfare Department. 2012b. Dietary survey among tribals of Visakhaptanam district. Available from: http;//aptribes.gov.in

Varadarajan A, Prasad S. 2009. Regional variations in nutritional status among tribals of Andhra Pradesh. *Studies of Tribes and Tribals*. 7: 137-141.

Yadav RJ, Singh P. 1999. Nutritional status and dietary in take in tribal children of Bihar. *Indian Pediatrics*. 36: 37-42.

Chapter Sixteen

RELATIONSHIP BETWEEN MATERNAL NUTRITIONAL STATUS AND PHYSICAL GROWTH MEASURES OF TRIBAL CHILDREN (<5 YEARS) OF ARUNACHAL PRADESH, NORTHEAST INDIA

NITAMONI BHARALI, NITISH MONDAL AND KH. NARENDRA SINGH

ABSTRACT

Introduction: The prevalence of undernutrition in children continues to be a major public health problem in developing countries. The maternal nutritional status found associated with reproductive outcomes and physical growth of children. Objectives: The objectives of the present investigation are to determine the relationship between maternal nutritional status and physical growth measures of tribal children (<5 years). Subjects and Methods: A community-based cross-sectional investigation was undertaken among 520 Nyishi tribal mother and children pairs of Arunachal Pradesh, Northeast India. Anthropometric measurements of weight and height were obtained using standard procedures and Body Mass Index (BMI=weight/height^2, kg/m^2) was calculated. The L, M and S growth references were used to calculate the age-sex specific Z-score of weight-for-age (WAZ), height-for-age (HAZ) and BMI-for-age (BMIAZ) (WHO, 2007). Maternal nutritional status was assessed utilizing recommended BMI classification of Asia pacific population (WHO, 2000). The statistical analysis of descriptive statistics, Pearson correlation and regression were done using the SPSS (version, 16.0). Results: The mean maternal anthropometric measures of height, weight and BMI was observed to be 154.82±5.94 cm, 50.55±5.96 kg and 21.08±2.18 kg/m^2. The age-sex combined mean of the physical growth measures of WAZ, HAZ and BMIAZ *were −0.57±1.43, −1.33 ±1.68 and 0.05±1.84, respectively. Pearson correlation coefficient analysis showed that maternal BMI was significantly (p<0.01) correlated with WAZ (r=0.314), HAZ (r=0.246) and BMIAZ (r=0.108). The linear regression analysis showed the significant (p<0.01) associations between maternal BMI and children WAZ, HAZ and BMIZ. Conclusion: Present investigation indicates the significant association and effect of mothers' nutritional status and anthropometric measures with children's physical growth variables. Thus, appropriate interventions by improving the maternal nutritional status are important and could have the significant role to improve the physical growth/undernutrition in pre-school children.*

Keywords: *Anthropometry, Physical Growth, Public health, Undernutrition.*

INTRODUCTION

Undernutrition continues to be a serious public health problem in many developing countries. Women, infants and children are considered to be most nutritionally vulnerable segments in population. Women health plays a major role in the physical growth and nutritional status of children, and the prevalence of under nutrition weakens the ability to survive childbirth, makes them with fewer reserves to recover from chronic illness, low birth weight of the infant, undernourished and physical growth retardation among children (Ojha and Malla, 2007; Mitra et al., 2012; Black et al., 2013; Vir and Malik, 2015; Pawar and Kumar, 2017; Mondal et al., 2018; Dey et al., 2019). The prevalence of under nutrition is associated with 2.2 million children deaths and 21 percent of disability-adjusted life years lost and more than 178 million children are stunted (low height-for-age) in developing countries. It is estimated that 45%-60% of child mortality (aged <5 years) is caused due to under nutrition and children's under nutrition which strongly correlated with mothers' poor nutritional status (Pelletier and Frongillo, 2003). Anthropometry is widely used non-invasive and easy-to-use techniques to assess the physical growth, body composition and nutritional status in children and adults (WHO, 1995, Hall et al., 2007). The Body Mass Index (BMI) is a surrogate anthropometric measure to determine the body composition and nutritional in population (WHO, 1995; Hall et al., 2007). The WHO has proposed the Z-score measure and classification (i.e., −2SD, undernutrition) to assess the physical growth and malnutrition (e.g., under and/or overnutrition). The conventional anthropometric measures of height-for-age (HAZ), weight-for-age (WAZ), weight-for-height (WHZ) and BMI-for-age (BMIAZ) were most widely utilized to assess the physical growth pattern and under nutrition status in pre-school children (WHO, 1995, 2007; Hall et al., 2007). Several studies have reported that maternal nutritional and/ or body composition (e.g., height, weight or BMI) is related with reproductive outcomes and survival of infants and children (Black et al., 2008; Sen et al., 2010; Bisai, 2012; Black et al., 2013; Aguayo et al., 2016; Tigga and Sen, 2016; Tayade et al., 2018; Dey et al., 2019). Prevalence of undernutrition is a serious public health concern and poor nutrition attainments (e.g., height/BMI or anaemia) among women begins during infancy and continues throughout their lifetime and it could affect the physical growth pattern, health condition, mortality, morbidities and nutritional status of their children (Subramanian et al., 2009; Bisai, 2012; Addo et al., 2013; Bhutta et al., 2013; Felisbino-Mende et al., 2014; Girma and Genebo, 2015; Tigga and Sen, 2016; Tayade et al., 2018; Dey et al., 2019).

Maternal nutritional status (e.g., BMI) is more important than any other factors on birth-weight attainments in children (Ojha and Malla, 2007; Mitra et al., 2012; Mumbare et al., 2012; Aguayo et al., 2016; Pawar and Kumar, 2017; Mondal et al., 2018; Dey et al., 2019). The women are belonging to the reproductive ages are subject to have several stresses affecting health and well-being so these things could affect the physical growth attainment in children in India (Subramanian et al., 2009; Sen et al., 2009; Sen et al., 2010; Gholamalizadeh el al., 2014; Adams et al., 2018; Hasan et al., 2018; Mondal et al., 2018). Recent studies have shown that maternal nutritional status influences several adverse outcomes (e.g., morbidity and mortality) in the offspring that also included nutritional outcomes in later life (Subramanian et al., 2009; Addo et al., 2013; Felisbino-Mendes et al., 2014; Girma and Genebo, 2015; Negash et al., 2015; Tigga and Sen, 2016; Tayade et al., 2018). Studies have shown maternal body composition or nutritional status (e.g., BMI) influence on physical growth patterns of children (G´ea-Horta et al., 2016; Rachmi et al., 2016; Tigga and Sen, 2016; Khan and Mohanty, 2018). Several studies have reported that the maternal body composition/nutritional status has shown associated with child growth pattern and undernutrition (Bisai, 2012; Tigga and Sen, 2016; Tayade et al., 2018; Dey et al., 2019). However, there is the paucity of studies on the association of maternal nutritional status and physical growth pattern among vulnerable segments in India. The assessment of the nutritional status of these groups hence becomes a priority because maternal nutritional status is closely associated with physical growth and nutritional status of children. Therefore, the present investigation was undertaken to determine the relationship between maternal nutritional status and growth pattern among Nyishi tribal women and children of Arunachal Pradesh, Northeast India.

Material and Methods

The present community based cross-sectional investigation conducted among 520 mothers (aged 15-44 years) and their 520 Nyishi tribal children (<5 years) of Kimin and Kakoi Blocks (Latitude 26^{0}55'N to 28^{0}40'N and Longitude 92^{0}40'E to 94^{0}21'E) of Papum Pare district, Arunachal Pradesh, India. The district has the total area covering of 2875 square kilometre. According to the National Census (2001), the total population of Arunachal Pradesh was 1,097,968 populations out of which the district consist 1,76,385 (males: 90,447 females: 85,938) individuals having a population density of 51 inhabitants per square kilometre and literacy rate 82.14 percent (males: 77.27%; females: 60.35%). The scheduled tribe population constitutes 56.60 percent of the Papum Pare district, which found to be 9.80 percent of total scheduled tribe population of the state. Ethnically, the Nyishi tribal populations are belonging to the Sino-Tibetan family and showing a close ethnic affinity with the quasi-Tibetan origin populations. The community block consists of predominant ethnic communities like Nyishi, Hill Miri and Adi ethnic populations. Initially, subjects are identified in the present investigation were belonging to the major dominant ethnic groups of this region includes Nyishi ethnic group. The literacy rate of this Nyishi population is 46.20 percent (male-55.70%; female-36.8%). The subjects belonging to the children (aged 0-5 years) and their mother (aged 15-44 years) were identified by utilizing the stratified random sampling method. Age of the subjects was collected using their birth certificates and relevant official records issued by the local government officials.

Collection of socio-economic and demographic data

Demographic data including age, sex, family income, sanitation, dependent children and parental education and occupation were collected using a structured schedule by household visits and interviewing the parents. A modified scale of Kuppuswamy's (Mishra and Singh, 2003; Kumar et al., 2007) was used to assess the socio-economic status (SES) of the research participants. The scale determines the SES based on a score calculated from education, occupation and family income. It was found that all selected children belonged to a lower to middle SES group. The research participants were free from any physical deformities, diseases and previous histories related to medical and surgical episodes were excluded to avoid the subject selection biases. A verbal consent was obtained from the parent's before the collection of socio-economic and anthropometric data. The investigation permission was obtained from local village level authorities and the Department of Anthropology, Assam University (Diphu Campus) before the data collection. The participation of the mothers and their children were voluntary in nature and the present investigation was undertaken in accordance with the ethical guidelines for human experiments as laid down in the Helsinki Declaration (Touitou et al., 2004).

Anthropometric measurements obtained

Anthropometric measurements were collected from the women (i.e., mothers) and their children using the standard procedures (Hall et al., 2007). The anthropometric measures of weight and height were recorded on both women and children by using Weighing scale, Anthropometer Rod and Infantometer (in case 0-2 year child). The differences in anthropometric measurements were also determined by testing the coefficient of reliability [$R=\{1-(TEM)^2/SD^2\}$, the SD= standard deviation of all measurements] using the technical error measurement {$TEM=\sqrt{(\Sigma D^2/2N)}$, D=difference between the measurements, N= number of individuals measured} following the method of Ulijaszek and Kerr (1999). A high values of R (>0.985) were obtained for height and weight using TEM analysis and values were found to be within the cut-off values (0.95) (Ulijaszek and Kerr, 1999). The anthropometric measurements were obtained with ample care to avoid the systematic errors in landmarks used and check the accuracy of the anthropometric instruments during the collection of the data. However, repeated/multiple measurements were also performed to check the possible reliability of the anthropometric measurements.

Assessment of Child Nutritional Status

The physical growth pattern assessment in the present investigation was done using three conventional anthropometric indices of height-for-age, weight-for-age and BMI-for-age (WHO, 1995; 2007). The interpretation of the three anthropometric indices involves the Z-score calculation using the international reference population to determine the physical growth assessment as recommended by the World Health Organization (WHO, 2007). The age-sex specific Z-score values were calculated using the LMS-method. This method is based on three important curves known as L (lambda), M (mu), and S (sigma) curves. The M-curve is the median or a 50th percentile curve, the S-curve is a measure of the coefficient of variation, and the L-curve is the power of the Box-Cox transformation, which measures the changing skewness of the distribution with age. The age-specific Z-score was calculated using the following equation: $Z = \{(X/M)^{*}L-1\}/(L^{*}S)$, where: X = height/weight/BMI, L, M and S are the age-specific values of the appropriate table corresponding reference populations. Therefore, the Z-score values of the anthropometric indices of height-for-age (HAZ), weight-for-age (WAZ) and BMI-for-age (BMIAZ) were calculated to assess the physical growth status of children. The standard sample size estimation was calculated by (Lwanga and Lemeshow, 1991). In this method, the anticipated population proportion of 50%, absolute precision of 5% and confidence interval of 95% are taken into consideration. The minimum sample size estimated for the present study was 384 individuals. The estimated sample size was also checked and recalculated using the online sample size estimation package of Raosoft sample size calculator (2004).

Assessments of Maternal Nutritional Status

The nutritional status of Nyishi women was assessed using Body mass index [BMI (kg/meter^2) =Weight (kg)/ Height^2 (meter^2)]. The BMI is being considered being a suitable indicator to estimate the intensity of undernutrition or chronic energy deficiency (CED) and overnutrition (e.g., overweight and obesity) status of individuals or populations. Nutritional status has been assessed using the accepted BMI guidelines as suggested by the WHO (WHO, 1995, 2000). The standard cut-off points were used to assess the nutritional status of the Nyishi women (WHO, 1995, 2000). Where, BMI <18.50 kg/m^2, BMI 23.00 -24.99 kg/m^2 and ≥ 25.00 kg/m^2 are considered being undernutrition, overweight and obesity, respectively.

Statistical Analysis

The data were analyzed using Statistical Package for Social Sciences (SPSS, Inc., Chicago, IL; version 17.0).The anthropometric data was presented in terms of descriptive statistics (mean and standard deviation). The Pearson correlation coefficient analysis was done to assess the relationship between maternal anthropometric variable and physical growth variables of children. Linear regression analysis was performed to assess the association between the maternal variable and anthropometric measures of children. One way analysis of variance (ANOVA) using the Scheffe procedure was done to assess mean differences in physical growth variables of children with different levels of maternal nutritional status. A p-value of less than <0.05 and <0.01 were considered being statistically significant.

Results

Descriptive statistics (mean ± SD) of mother and child anthropometric growth variables of mothers and their children were depicted in Table 1. The descriptive statistics (mean ±SD) of age, height, weight, and BMI were 32.56±8.84 years, 154.82±5.94 cm, 50.55±5.95 kg, and 21.08±2.18 kg/m^2 among women, respectively. The overall descriptive statistics of physical growth measures were −0.57±1.43, −1.33±1.68, and 0.052±1.84 of WAZ, HAZ and BMIAZ among pre-school children (Table 1).The results of the Pearson Correlation coefficient analysis between the maternal BMI with physical growth variables (e.g., WAZ, HAZ and BMIAZ) were shown in Table 2. The Pearson correlation coefficient values were observed to be statistically significant ($p<0.01$) in WAZ ($r=0.314$), HAZ ($r=0.246$) and BMIAZ ($r=0.108$). The results of the linear regression analysis of maternal BMI (independent variables) with child's physical growth measures as dependent variables (e.g., WAZ, HAZ and BMIZ) among preschool children is depicted in Table 3. The results reveal that BMI was an important predictor variable of WAZ, HAZ and BMIZ in children. The maternal BMI as an independent variable explained for 9.70%, 5.90% and 1.00% of variations in these three dependent variables of WAZ, HAZ and BMIAZ, respectively. The linear regression analysis showed statistically significant association between maternal BMI with HAZ, WAZ and BMI among pre-school children($p<0.01$).

Descriptive statistics (mean ± standard deviation) of child anthropometric variables according to maternal nutritional status categories among Nyishi pre-school children is depicted in Table 4. The overall prevalence of mother undernutrition, risk group, normal was found to be 10.96 percent, 25.96 percent and 46.35 percent among the tribal women, and their child mean and standard deviation of anthropometric variables are WAZ, HAZ and BMIAZ are −0.79±1.82, −1.83±1.46 and −0.31±1.65, −1.31±1.06, −1.65±1.76 and −0.36±1.60 and −0.34±1.31, −1.25±1.72 and 0.34±1.98, respectively. The overall prevalence of overweight (≥BMI 23.00 kg/m^2) and obesity (≥BMI 25.00 kg/m^2) among mother was found to be 10.19 percent and 6.54 percent, and their children with anthropometric variables WAZ, HAZ and BMIAZ are 0.21±1.52, −0.88±1.21 and −0.12±1.92 and −0.07±.39, −0.55±1.64 and 0.50±1.40, respectively. The results showed that as the mother BMI was increasing with the Z-score is also increasing in children. Using ANOVA, the mean differences in physical growth variables with different maternal nutritional categories were observed to be significant in WAZ (F=17.90; p<0.01), HAZ (F=5.55; p<0.01) and BMIAZ (F=4.47; p<0.01) (Table 4).

Table 1: Descriptive statistics of mother and physical growth variables among children

Variable	Mean±SD	N
Mother		
Age	32.56 ±8.84	520
Height	154.82±5.94	520
Weight	50.55±5.95	520
BMI	21.08±2.18	520
Children		
WAZ	-0.57±1.43	520
HAZ	-1.33±1.68	520
BMIAZ	0.052±1.84	520

Table 2: Pearson correlation analysis between Maternal BMI with Z-Score of physical growth variables in children

Maternal Anthropometric Characteristic	Child Z-score	R	p-value
BMI	WAZ	0.314	0.000
BMI	HAZ	0.246	0.000
BMI	BMIAZ	0.108	0.000

Table 3: Linear regression analysis of maternal BMI (Independent Variable) with physical growth variables in children

Dependent variables	Independent variables	B	SEB	T	Sig.	Adj.R^2
WAZ	Constant	-4.922	0.582	-8.463	0.000	0.097
	BMI	0.207	0.027	7.527	0.000	
HAZ	Constant	-5.335	0.696	-7.660	0.000	0.059
	BMI	0.190	0.033	5.777	0.000	
BMIAZ	Constant	-1.867	0.781	-2.390	0.017	0.010
	BMI	0.091	0.037	2.470	0.014	

Table 4: Maternal nutritional status and descriptive statistics of physical growth variables of children

Maternal Nutritional Status	N=520	WAZ	HAZ	BMIAZ
BMI<18.50 kg/m^2	57 (10.96)	−0.79±1.82	−1.83±1.46	−0.31±1.65
BMI 18.50-20.00 kg/m^2	135 (25.96)	−1.31±1.06	−1.65±1.76	−0.36±1.60
BMI 20.01-22.99 kg/m^2	241 (46.35)	−0.34±1.31	−1.25±1.72	0.34±1.98
BMI 23.00-24.99 kg/m^2	53 (10.19)	0.21±1.52	−0.88±1.21	−0.12±1.92
BMI >=25.00 kg/m^2	34 (6.54)	−0.07±0.39	−0.55±1.64	0.50±1.40
F-value		17.90*	5.55*	4.47*

Values are in parenthesis indicates percentages, p<0.01

Discussion

India is amid of socio-economic, demographic, nutritional and epidemiological transition and undernutrition continues to affect large vulnerable segments (e.g., children and women) of the population. The present cross-sectional investigation has shown the direct association between maternal anthropometric variables, nutritional status (e.g., BMI) and physical growth pattern of children (e.g., WAZ, HAZ and BMAZ) among Nyishi tribal population of Arunachal Pradesh, India. The results of the correlation coefficient analysis showed that positive correlation/associations between the maternal BMI and physical growth variables of WAZ, HAZ and BMIAZ among pre-school children (p<0.01) (Table 2). Several investigation have reported a positive association with the maternal anthropometric variables/body composition (e.g., height, weight or BMI) with physical growth variables in children (Subramanian et al., 2009; Bisai, 2012; Mitra et al., 2012; Addo et al., 2013; Felisbino-Mende et al., 2014; Girma and Genebo, 2015; Tigga and Sen, 2016; Tayade et al., 2018; Dey et al., 2019). The results of the linear regression model analysis revealed that maternal BMI was the most predictive variable of anthropometric growth parameters (e.g., HAZ, WAZ, and BMIAZ) and this explained the significant variations in these three dependent anthropometric variables in pre-school children (Table 3). Results showed that correlations between maternal and children anthropometric variables were observed to be significant and the maternal BMI explained for 9.70% (in WAZ), 5.90% (in HAZ) and 1.00% (in BMIAZ) of variations in the Z-score among children (Table 3). Therefore, these findings showed a strong genetic component between maternal and anthropometric physical growth variables among pre-school children. Santos et al. (2009) have reported the significant correlation ($p<0.01$) between children's BMI Z-score and their mothers' BMI, both among boys (Spearman rho = 0.26) and girls (Spearman rho = 0.30). The results of the present investigation showed that the maternal undernutrition (BMI<18.50 kg/m^2) had significant effect onthe children to became more susceptible to physical growth variables (HAZ, WAZ and BMIAZ) and the increase in maternal BMI increases the child Z-score values of the children, but the obese mother (BMI>=25.00 kg/m^2) had lower Z-score value in WAZ of children (−0.07±.39) (Table 4). Further, the mean differences in physical growth variables of WAZ, HAZ and BMIAZ in different maternal nutritional status levels were observed to be significant (p<0.05) (Table 4). Therefore, the maternal anthropometric variables and nutritional status has significant effect on children physical growth variables among Nyishi tribal pre-school children (<5 years). Several researchers have reported an increase in maternal body composition or adiposity (i.e., BMI) and/or nutritional status was significantly associated with a lower prevalence of under nutrition in pre-school children (<5 years) (Subramaniun et al., 2009, Mitra et al., 2012; Addo et al., 2013; Felisbino-Mende et al., 2014; Tigga and Sen, 2016; Tayade et al., 2018; Dey et al., 2019).

Several research studies have confirmed direct association between maternal body composition and nutritional with physical growth attainments or nutritional status among pre-school children (Rahman et al. 1993; Ajslev et al., 2014; Negash et al. 2015; Tigga and Sen, 2016). Rahman et al. (1993) reported that that a child's physical growth variables (i.e., WAZ) was associated with maternal BMI in Bangladesh ($p<0.001$). Islam et al. (1994) showed that mothers who were underweight were 2.50 times more likely to have underweight children in Bangladesh. Kulasekaran (2012) reported that women with poor nutritional status (e.g., BMI) had registered the higher risk of severe stunting (HAZ) and severe underweight (WAZ) (27.10% and 23.30%, respectively) among children. The present investigation also showed similar incidence of maternal undernutrition (BMI<18.50 kg/m^2) with lower physical growth attainments in children (Table 4). Similar study by Negash et al. (2015) have reported that HAZ was associated with maternal height (p<0.05). Recent investigation has reported that maternal BMI (r= 0.16; p< 0.05) was correlated with WHZ of children, whereas the maternal height (r =0.20; p< 0.05) was correlated with HAZ of children (Fleten et al., 2012). The positive association between maternal BMI or nutritional status with BMI of children (Ajslev et al., 2014; Tigga and Sen, 2016). The present investigation also showed the highly significant correlation (r) between mothers BMI and child Z-score (WAZ=0.314, HAZ=0.246 and BMIAZ=0.108). Khan and Mohanty (2018) have reported that the coefficient of maternal BMI in spatial error model was largest found for underweight (β=0.38, 95% CI: 0.29-0.48) followed by stunting (β=0.23, 95% CI: 0.14-0.33) and wasting (β=0.11, 95% CI: 0.01-0.22). Mitra et al. (2012) have reported that maternal BMI was the significant predictor of neonatal birth weight on multiple regression analysis (ß=0.340, p = 0.01). Therefore, present investigation has confirmed that the anthropometric measurements were useful in identifying mothers with higher anthropometric measures (e.g., BMI) with greater Z-score in physical growth measures among Nyishi pre-school children. It is important to note that the relationship between mother and child undernutrition is mostly affected by biological consequences of maternal malnutrition during lactation in infant and children (Tigga and Sen, 2016). Researchers have reported that necessary efforts must be given to improving the maternal nutritional status, dietary quality (e.g., fats, energy and nutrients) during weaning period and improving infants diet have a significant effect to attain appropriate physical growth and nutritional status in children (Deleuze et al., 2005; WHO, 2013; Adair, 2014; Owais et al., 2017). Moreover, prevalence of undernutrition in children will manifested as long-term effect on the physical growth attainments or reducing growth potentials, health and survivals, cognitive developments, lower attained schooling, decreased economic potential, reproductive performance, and onset of chronic illness in adulthood (Shrimpton et al., 2001; Pelletier and Frongillo, 2003; Black et al., 2013; WHO, 2013). It is attributed to the overall maternal health condition has adverse impact on pre- and postnatal growth and nutritional outcome of pre-school children, thus the implementation of appropriate intervention programme, nutrition sensitive approaches and overall dietary quality are needed to improve maternal nutritional and child health status could have a significant role in the overall improvement of physical growth pattern attainment (e.g., Z-score) and nutritional status.

Conclusion

The results showed the existence of low maternal BMI and/or undernutrition was seems to be one of the major concern of poor physical growth attainments or Z-score values in HAZ, WAZ and BMIAZ among Nyishi tribal children. This will trigger the vicious cycle of undernutrition in the population and phenomenon could be remedied by improving maternal nutritional status. A comprehensive nutritional intervention programme and strategies are needs to developed and operationalized for the overall improvement of nutritional status and physical growth attainments among Nyishi mother and children. Furthermore, it is essential to evaluate the efficacy of ongoing nutritional intervention programme to improve the health and nutritional status in population. Moreover, the maternal nutritional status found to be an important health determinant of a child's physical growth and nutritional status and should be considered to improve the health condition to address the appropriate intervention programmes in population.

Acknowledgements

The authors duly acknowledge the help and co-operation of the community members of the study area, parents of all the subjects, local community leaders and village headman during the fieldwork. The help and co-operation of the Department of Anthropology, Assam University (Diphu Campus) is also acknowledged.

References

Adair LS. 2014. Long-term consequences of nutrition and growth in early childhood and possible preventive interventions. *Nestlé Nutrition Institute Workshop Series*. 78: 111-120.

Adams KP, Lybbert TJ, Vosti SA, Ayifah E, Arimond M, Adu-Afarwuah S, Dewey KG. 2018. Unintended effects of a targeted maternal and child nutrition intervention on household expenditures, labor income, and the nutritional status of non-targeted siblings in Ghana. *World Development*. 107: 138-150.

Addo OY, Stein AD, Fall CH. 2013. Maternal height and child growth patterns. *The Journal of Pediatrics*. 163: 549-554.

Aguayo VM, Nair R, Badgaiyan N, Krishna V. 2016. Determinants of stunting and poor linear growth in children under 2 years of age in India: an in-depth analysis of Maharashtra's comprehensive nutrition survey. *Maternal & Child Nutrition*. 12: 121-140.

Ajslev TA, Angquist L, Silventoinen K, Baker JL, Sorensen TIA. 2014. Trends in parent-child correlations of childhood body mass index during the development of the obesity epidemic. *PLoS ONE*. 9: 109932.

Bhutta ZA, Das JK, Rizvi A, Gaffey MF, Walker N, Horton S. 2013. Evidence-based interventions for improvement of maternal and child nutrition: what can be done and at what cost? *The Lancet*. 382: 452–477.

Black RE, Victora CG, Walker SP, Bhutta ZA, Christian P, de Onis M, Ezzati M, Grantham-McGregor S, Katz J, Martorell R, Uauy R. 2013. Maternal and Child Nutrition Study Group. Maternal and child undernutrition and overweight in low-income and middle-income countries. *The*

Lancet. 382: 427-451.

Deleuze NBG, Fayomi B, Delisle H. 2005. Child malnutrition and maternal overweight in same households in poor urban areas of Benin. *Sante*. 15: 263-270.

Dey S, Mondal N, Dasgupta P. 2019. Head circumference and birth length as predictor of low birth weight among Bengali Hindu Population of Kolkata, West Bengal, India. *Journal of Clinical and Diagnostic Research*. 13: LC01-LC05

Felisbino-Mendes MSE. Villamor, G. Velasquez-Melendez, Nugent RA. 2014. Association of maternal and child nutritional status in brazil: a population based cross-sectional study. *PLoS ONE*. 9: 87486.

G´ea-Horta T, Silva Rd., Fiaccone RL, Barreto ML, Vel´asquez-Mel´endez G. 2016. Factors associated with nutritional outcomes in the mother-child dyad: a population-based crosssectional study. *Public Health Nutrition*. 19: 2725– 2733.

Gholamalizadeh M, Entezari MH, Paknahad Z, Hassanzadeh A, Doaei S. 2014.The study of association between mother weight efficacy life-style with feeding practices, food groups intake and body mass index in children aged 3-6 Years. *International Journal of Preventive Medicine*. 5: 21-28.

Hall JG, Allanson JE, Gripp KW, Slavotinek AM. 2007. *Handbook of Physical Measurements*. Oxford, UK: Oxford University Press.

Hasan M, Islam MM, Mubarak E, Haque MA, Choudhury N, Ahmed T. 2018. Mother's dietary diversity and association with stunting among children <2 years old in a low socio-economic environment: A case-control study in an urban care setting in Dhaka, Bangladesh. *Maternal & Child Nutrition*. 14: e12665.

Islam MA, Rahman MM, Mahalanabis D. 1994. Maternal and socioeconomic factors and the risk of severe malnutrition in a child: a case-control study. *European Journal of Clinical Nutrition*. 4: 416–424.

Khan J, Mohanty SK. 2018. Spatial heterogeneity and correlates of child malnutrition in districts of India. *BMC Public Health*. 17: 1027.

Kulasekaran RA. 2012. Influence of mothers' chronic energy deficiency on the nutritional status of preschool children in Empowered Action Group states in India. *International Journal of Nutrition, Pharmacology and Neurological Disorders*. 2:198–209.

Kumar N, Shekhar C, Kumar P, Kundu AS. 2007. Kuppuswamy's socio-economic status scale-updating for 2007. *Indian Journal of Pediatrics*. 74: 1131-1132.

Mishra D, Singh HP. 2003. Kuppuswamy's socio-economic status scale--a revision. *Indian Journal of Pediatrics*. 70: 273-274.

Mitra S, Misra S, Nayak PK, Sahoo JP. 2012. Effect of maternal anthropometry and metabolic parameters on fetal growth. *Indian Journal of Endocrinology and Metabolism*. 16: 754-758.

Mondal N, Dey S, Sen J. 2018. Association of Maternal Age, Pregnancy Order and Seasonal Variations in Low Birth Weight (LBW) in West Bengal. *India. Journal of Life Science*. 10: 1-9.

Negash. N, Whiting SJ, Henry CJ, Belachew T, Hailemariam TG. 2015. Association between maternal and child nutritional status in Hula, rural Southern Ethiopia: a cross sectional study. *PLoS ONE*. 10: 0142301.

Ojha N, Malla D. 2006. Low birth weight at term: relationship with maternal anthropometry. *J Nepal Med Association*. 46: 166: 52-56.

Owais A, Schwartz B, Kleinbaum DG, Suchdev PS, Faruque ASG, Das SK, Rahman S, Stein AD. 2017. A nutrition education program in rural bangladesh was associated with improved feeding practices but not with child growth. *Journal of Nutrition*. 147: 948-954.

Pawar A, Kumar D. 2017. Maternal factors associated with low birth weight: A case control study in rural Kerala. *International Journal of Community Medicine and Public Health*. 4: 3793-3795.

Pelletier DL, Frongillo EA. 2003. Changes in child survival are strongly associated with changes in malnutrition in developing countries. *Journal of Nutrition*. 13: 107-19.

Rachmi CN, Agho KE, Li M, Baur LA, Zhang Y. 2016. Stunting, underweight and overweight in children aged 2.0– 4.9 years in Indonesia: prevalence trends and associated risk factors. *PLoS ONE*. 11: e0154756.

Rahman M, Roy SK, Ali M, Mitra AK, Alam AN, Akbar MS. 1993. Maternal nutritional status as a determinant of child health. *Journal of Tropical Pediatrics*. 39:86–88.

Santos JL, Kain J, Dominguez-V´asquez P. 2009. Maternal anthropometry and feeding behavior toward preschool children: association with childhood body mass index in an observational study of Chilean families. *International Journal of Nutrition and Physical Activity*. 6: 93.

Sen J, Roy A, Mondal N. 2010. Association of maternal nutritional status, body composition and socio-economic variables with low birth weight in India. *Journal of Tropical Pediatrics*. 56: 254-259.

Shrimpton R, Victora CG, de Onis M, Lima RC, Blössner M, Clugston G. 2001.Worldwide timing of growth faltering: implications for nutritional interventions. *Pediatrics*. 107: e75.

Subramanian SV, Ackerson LK, Davey Smith G, John NA. 2009. Association of maternal height with child mortality, anthropometric failure, and anemia in India. *Journal of American Medical Association*. 301: 1691-1701.

Tayade S, Singh R, Kore J, Gangane N. 2018. Maternal anthropometric measurements, pre-pregnancy body mass index, and fetal growth parameters - A rural experience. *Obstetrics & Gynecology*. 1: 51-64.

Tigga PL, Sen J. 2016. Maternal Body mass index is strongly associated with children Z-scores for height and BMI. *Journal of Anthropology*. 6538235: 6538235.

Touitou Y, Portaluppi F, Smolensky MH, Rensing L. 2004. Ethical principles and standards for the conduct of human and animal biological rhythm research. *Chronobiology International*. 21: 161–170.

Ulijaszek SJ, Kerr DA. 1999. Anthropometric measurement error and the assessment of the nutritional status. *British Journal of Nutrition*. 82: 165-177.

Vir SC, Malik R. 2015. Nutrition situation of women in India: Current status, implications on child undernutrition and challenges ahead. *Statistics Applications*. 13: 71-84.

World Health Organization. 2013. *Essential Nutrition Actions: Improving Maternal, Newborn, Infant and Young Child Health and Nutrition*, World Health Organization, Geneva, Switzerland, 2013.

World Health Organization. 1995. *Physical status: The use and interpretation of Anthropometry*. Report of a WHO expert committee. World Health Organization Geneva.

World Health Organization. 2000. *The Asia Pacific Perspective. Redefining Obesity and its Treatment*. International Diabetes Institute. Health Communications Australia Pty Ltd.

Chapter Seventeen

EVALUATION OF NUTRITIONAL STATUS AMONG PRIMARY SCHOOL GOING CHILDREN FROM A SUB-URBAN AREA OF WEST BENGAL, INDIA

GOPAL CHANDRA MANDAL AND JAYANTY MITRA

ABSTRACT

Background: Good nutrition is the foundation to proper growth and development in every human, in the absence of which individuals are subjected to multiple health complications. Chronic malnutrition experienced during early life inhibits growth, retards mental development; reduces motivation and energy levels, causing a reduction of educational attainments. Primary school age is a dynamic period of physical growth and mental development of the child. Objective: The objective of the present study was to evaluate the nutritional status by both prevalence of thinness (low BMI for age) and obesity among the primary school children. Materials and methods: The present cross-sectional study was undertaken among the 452 students aged 5-10 years from 4 primary schools (Netaji Vidyatan, Eksara Primary School, Nobomukul Primary School and Majherhat Khirodmohini Primary School) situated in the sub urban area of Howrah District, West Bengal, India. The height and weight were measured using standard techniques. The derived variable, BMI (kg/m^2) was calculated following standard equation (WHO, 1995). Thinness and overweight were evaluated by using Cole et al. cut offs (2000 and 2007). Results: No significant sex differences were noticed in case of height, weight and weight. The overall prevalence of undernutrition was 62.4% (Boys, 63.0% and Girls, 61.8%), although the difference was not statistically significant. The *prevalence of overweight and obese was 4.4%. Conclusion: Although, some of the primary school children showed overnutrition but the occurrence of undernutrition as a whole measured by thinness was very high and that could affect the growth and development of these children.*

Keywords: *Primary school children, BMI, thinness, sub urban, West Bengal.*

Introduction

In any community health programme, screening for health problems in children is an important aspect. Because, children spend most of their time at school which is not only an ideal place for learning and playing, but also for screening of health problems. A school health programme helps in early detection of health issues and thereby early evaluation and treatment (Kumar et al., 2018). Malnutrition is one of the largest public health problems in developing country like India. India constitutes one third of the total malnourished children in the world (WHO, 1998). According to National family health survey-4, 35.7 % of children under 5 years of age are underweight, 38.4 % are stunted and 21.0 % are wasted in 2015-2016 (NFSH-4, 2017). Malnutrition leads to delay in physical growth and motor development, lower intelligent quotient, behavioural problems and poor social skills and an increase in the risk of morbidity and mortality (UNICEF, 2013). Chronic malnutrition experienced during early life inhibits growth, retards mental development; re-duce motivation and energy level, causing a reduction of educational attainments. Understanding the nature of the causal relationship between health and education is important to determine the exact relation between them (Ghosh et al., 2013).

Good nutrition is the foundation to proper growth and development in every human, the absence of which individuals are subjected to multiple health complications. Malnutrition still remains a significant problem all over the world, especially among children (Do et al., 2015). But mid-day meal is provided only in the government schools but not in private schools. There is dearth of studies focusing on the nutritional status of children in private schools and also those trying to assess the relationship between malnutrition and scholastic performance (Rashmi et al., 2015). In a developing country like India, there are many health problems in school children who are the wealth and future of our country, and they require special attention to meet their needs.

Primary school age is a dynamic period of physical growth and mental development of the child. Research indicates that nutritional deficiencies and poor health in primary school age children are among the causes of low school enrolment, high absenteeism, early dropout and poor classroom performance (WHO, 1997). Regular monitoring of growth of primary school children and health education session for the mothers is going to be effective in prevention of malnutrition among the children (Yankanchi et al., 2018). Malnutrition in young children puts them at a higher risk of experiencing health problems such as stunted growth, mental retardation, and increased susceptibility to infectious diseases (IIPS-NFHS-3). However, in our country there is a nutrition programme, Mid-Day Meal running in Primary Schools since the long time. But still the results are not satisfactory. There are various measures of assessing undernutrition like, stunting, underweight, wasting, thinness and so on. Here, we restricted ourselves only on the thinness (low BMI for age) as proposed by Cole et al., (2007).

Considering the above, the objective of the present study was to evaluate the nutritional status by both, prevalence of thinness (low BMI for age) and obesity among the primary school children.

Materials and Methods

Study Area

The present cross-sectional study was undertaken in 4 primary schools (Netaji Vidyatan, Eksara Primary School, Nobomukul Primary School and Majherhat Khirodmohini Primary School) situated in the sub urban area of Howrah District, West Bengal, India.

Participants

A total of 452 children aged 5-10 years old enrolled in these schools were studied. Among them mostly were from Hindu and some of them were from Muslim community who were excluded from the present study. Most of the families to which the children belonged were either of middle or low socio-economic status. The distribution of the studied population is given in table no 1. Permission for conducting the study was also obtained from each school authority. Informed consent was obtained from each participant as well.

Table 1. Distribution of participants according to age and sex

Age in years	Boys	Girls	Total
5	15	27	42
6	48	30	78
7	54	52	106
8	46	66	112
9	42	45	87
10	12	15	27
Total	217	235	452

Anthropometric Measurements

For the present study the anthropometric measurements like height and weight were measured using standard techniques (Lohmann et al., 1988) by the second author (JM). The derived variable, BMI (kg/m^2) was calculated following standard equation (WHO, 1995). The technical error of measurements (TEM) was calculated for height and weight and they were found to be within reference values as given by Ulijaszek and Kerr (1999). Thus, TEM were not incorporated in any analyses. Besides the anthropometric measurements some non anthropometric parameters were also taken. These were age, sex, ethnicity, parity etc.

Evaluation of Undernutrition

Evaluation of nutritional status as measured by thinness (Low BMI for age) was done following age and sex specific internationally accepted standard cut offs as proposed by Cole and others (2007). All the undernourished adolescents were categorized as Grade I, II, and III for severity of thinness. The overweight and obese levels were evaluated by using Cole et al., cut offs of Cole et al. (2000).

Table 2. The BMI (kg/m^2) Cut-off Points for Thinness Grades III, II and I for 5-10 years old children as proposed by Cole et al. (2007)

Age groups (years)	Boys			Girls		
	Grade III	**Grade II**	**Grade I**	**Grade III**	**Grade II**	**Grade I**
5	12.66	13.31	14.21	12.5	13.09	13.94
6	12.50	13.15	14.07	12.32	12.93	13.82
7	12.42	13.08	14.04	12.26	12.91	13.86
8	12.42	13.11	14.15	12.31	13.0	14.02
9	12.50	13.24	14.35	12.44	13.18	14.28
10	12.66	13.45	14.64	12.64	13.43	14.61

Statistical Analysis

After taking measurements and collecting information, analyses were done using SPSS-PC package for social sciences (Version 16.0). To test the significant sex difference of anthropometric variables, t-test was done. χ^2 - was (2 X 2) done to test sex differences of thinness between them.

Results

Table 3. Mean (SD) and sex differences of height, weight and BMI of the participants

Variables	Sex	Age in years						Total
		5	6	7	8	9	10	
Height (cm)	Boys	105.4	108.1	116.3	117.5	124.7	126.0	116.7
	Girls	103.4	107.2	113.9	118.6	123.3	127.0	116.1
	t	1.2	0.5	1.5	-0.8	1.0	-0.3	0.6
Weight (Kg)	Boys	14.8	16.3	18.7	19.9	23.3	23.2	19.6
	Girls	14.8	15.1	18.1	19.8	22.0	23.7	19.1
	t	0.03	2.8**	0.8	0.1	1.3	-0.3	1.0
BMI (kg/m²)	Boys	13.3	13.9	13.8	14.3	14.9	14.5	14.2
	Girls	13.8	13.2	13.9	14.0	14.3	14.6	14.0
	t	-1.0	1.8	-0.3	0.7	1.1	-0.1	1.2

** = $p < 0.01$

The Table 3 represents the mean and sex differences of height (cm), weight (kg) and BMI (kg/m^2) along with standard deviation of the studied children. Age combined values of all three variables showed no sizable differences between two sexes. Hence, there were no significant sex differences. Considering the age specific values only weight in case of children of age group 6 years represented the significant sex difference ($p < 0.01$). The gradual increase of the values following the increase of age among these children was also noticed.

Table 4. Prevalence of thinness by age and sex among the studied primary school children

Age (years)	Boys					Girls				
	Grade III	Grade II	Grade I	Overall	Normal	Grade III	Grade II	Grade I	Overall	Normal
5	4 (1.8)	3 (1.4)	2 (0.9)	9 (4.1)	6 (2.8)	4 (1.7)	6 (2.6)	6 (2.6)	16 (6.8)	11 (4.7)
6	15 (6.9)	10 (4.6)	6 (2.8)	31 (14.3)	17 (7.8)	7 (3.0)	6 (2.6)	7 (3.0)	20 (8.5)	10 (4.3)
7	9 (4.1)	18 (8.3)	8 (3.7)	35 (16.1)	19 (8.8)	7 (3.0)	9 (3.8)	18 (7.7)	34 (14.5)	18 (7.7)
8	6 (2.8)	9 (4.1)	11 (5.1)	26 (12.0)	20 (9.2)	12 (5.1)	16 (6.8)	14 (6.0)	42 (17.9)	24 (10.2)
9	7 (3.2)	8 (3.7)	11 (5.1)	26 (12.0)	16 (7.4)	10 (4.3)	6 (2.6)	11 (4.7)	27 (11.5)	18 (7.7)
10	2 (0.9)	2 (0.9)	3 (1.4)	7 (3.2)	5 (2.3)	2 (0.9)	3 (1.3)	4 (1.7)	9 (3.8)	6 (2.8)
Total	43 (19.8)	50 (23.0)	41 (17.2)	134 (61.8)	83 (38.2)	42 (17.9)	46 (19.6)	60 (25.5)	148 (63.0)	87 (37.0)
	217 (100.0)					235 (100.0)				
Grand Total	Thinness - 282 (62.4) : Normal - 170 (37.6)									

Percentages are given in the parentheses

Table 4 shows the prevalence of thinness by age and sex among the studied primary school children. It is evident that the overall (age and sex combined) prevalence of undernutrition as measured low BMI for age was 62.4%. Sex specific age combined rate denotes that, this was slightly higher among girls (63.0%) than the boys (61.8%), although, the difference was not statistically significant. Interestingly, prevalence of thinness in Grade III and Grade II among the boys (19.3% and 23.0% respectively) was comparatively higher than the girls (17.9% and 19.6% respectively). It indicates the severity of thinness was much more among boys than the girls. In case of Grade I, the rate was higher (25.5%) among girls than the boys (17.2%). The prevalence of thinness was higher in case of lower age group children among both boys and girls and it gradually decreases with the increase of age.

Table 5. Prevalence of overweigh and obese among the studied children

Sex	Overweight	Obese	Total
Boys	8	1	9 (2.0)
Girls	10	1	11 (2.4)
Total	18 (4.0)	2 (0.4)	20 (4.4)

Percentages are given in the parentheses

The prevalence of overweight and obese was expressed through Table 5. It is noticed that, age and sex combined overall rate was 4.4%. Out of which, 4.0 % children was overweight and only 0.4% was obese. Here also we found more or less similar prevalence of over-nutrition in both the sexes.

Discussion

In present study the mean Height among the boys was 116.7 cm and the same among the girls was 116.1 cm. Mean heights among the boys and girls of children of Nandigram, East Midnapur (Bose et al., 2006) were more-or less similar (in case of boys it was 117.2 cm and in case of girls it was 115.98 cm). In case of weight, the mean among the boys was 19.6 kg and among the girls it was 19.1 kg. The mean weight of the children of Nandigram was 19.02 kg among the boys and 18.69 kg among the girls. The mean height and weight showed no significance sex difference in the present study. A study in Santal Children of Ghatsila and Bolpur (Chackraborty et al., 2008) was also showed no significance sex difference of these two anthropometric variables. The derived variable i.e. BMI (kg/m^2), of the children of the present study (14.2 among boys and 14.0 among girls) was similar (14.0 and 14.1 among boys and girls respectively) among the 5-12 years aged primary school children from Phanshidewa block of Darjeeling District, West Bengal (Mondal and Sen, 2010).

Wickramasinghe and others (2004) pointed out that under-nutrition remains an important public problem in many Asian countries although the economic development in the region is noticed. Despite the availability of surplus food grains in India and in South Asia, the region is still facing high levels of hunger (Gupta, 2004). Among the school children aged 5–10 years from Purba Midnapore District, West Bengal, the prevalence of thinness was 62.2% (Chakraborty and Bose, 2009) which was almost similar with that of the present one (62.4%). In a study done by Mondal and others (2015) among the primary school children of various districts of West Bengal mentioned that, the prevalence of thinness among boys was 65.4% and among girls it was 65.3%. Medhi and others (2006) reported much better situation of nutritional condition among the 6–14 years school children of Dibrugarh district, Assam, India where the overall rate of thinness was 53.2%. The children aged 5-12 years of Darjeeling District, W.B. showed slightly higher (69.4%) prevalence (Mondal and Sen, 2010). Much higher prevalence (79.4%) of thinness was observed among the school going children aged 6-12 years from Aligarh District, Uttar Pradesh, India (Sultan, 2014). Moderate occurrence of thinness (36.96%) was noticed among the primary school children of Pauri Garwal District, Uttarakhand, India (Limbu and Arya, 2018). Fazili et al, (2012) reported a prevalence of thinness was 29% among the school children from Kashmir region, India. The higher (75.95%) prevalence of thinness was also found among the migrated Santal primary school children from Arambagh, West Bengal (Mandal and Bose, 2014). The lowest prevalence of thinness (10.1%) was reported among sub-urban school children from Chennai, India (Kumar et al., 2018). A noteworthy point was that all the studies reported that both sexes had more-or-less similar rates of thinness. However, there was a significant sex differences in thinness between the sexes among the rural school going children from Phansidewa, Darjeeling, West Bengal (Debnath et al., 2018), where 31.0% boys and 24.4% girls were thin. The overall prevalence of thinness among these children was much lower (27.7%) in comparison to the present study.

However, besides high prevalence of undernutrition, 4.4 % children of the present study also belonged to either overweight (4.0%) or obese (0.4) %). Here also no significant sex specific prevalence was noticed. Similar result was reported from Chennai, India (Kumar et al., 2018) where 8.6% children showed either overweight or obese.

In a study by Kamath et al. (2012) also found that 5.03% children were found to be undernourished, 2.3% were overweight and 1% were obese.

Will this be termed as "double burden"? WHO (2006) also pointed out about the "double burden" threats in many countries. It is noticeable that undernutrition and obesity coexistence within the same country, community and even within the same household. Lack of inadequate nutrition may causes this double burden to the pre-natal, infant and young child due to exposure of energy-dense, high-fat, poor micronutrient and poor physical activity (Rema, 2011). In the present study, we also noticed although the prevalence of undernutrition as measured by thinness was very high, simultaneously overnutrition was also evident.

Conclusion

From the above discussion, it can be concluded that, although, some of the primary school children showed over-nutrition but the occurrence of undernutrition as a whole measured by thinness was very high and that could affect the growth and development of these children who are vulnerable for infection and nutritional states. We also agree with Rahaman and others' (2019) opinion that, nutritional seminar should be conducted to increase of nutritional knowledge in school level by nutritionist. The result of the present study will be helpful for the Government authorities to understand the real situation of the states of nutrition which ultimately encourages to the policy makers to formulate the plans and programmes for betterment of the children as well as for the society.

Conflict of Interest

None

Acknowledgements

All subjects who participated in the study are gratefully acknowledged. Special thanks are due to the parents and the School authorities for their kind cooperation and help.

References

Bose K, Bhunia D, Paul G, Mukhopadhyay A. Chakraborty R. 2006. Age and sex variations in undernutrition of rural Bengalee primary school children of East Midnapore district, West Bengal, India. In Ecology, Culture, Nutrition, Health and Disease. *Human Ecology*. 14: 71-75.

Chakraborty U, Dutta Chowdhury S, Dutta G, Ghosh T. 2008. A comparative study of physical growth and nutritional status in Santal children of Ghatshila and Bolpur. In Health and Nutritional problems of Indigenous populations. *Tribes and Tribals.* 2: 79-86.

Chakraborty R, Bose K. 2009. Very high prevalence of thinness using new international body mass index cut off points among 5-10 year old school children of Nandigram, West Bengal, India. *Journal of Research in Medical Sciences.* 14: 129–133.

Debnath S, Mondal N, Sen J. 2018. Socio-economic and demographic correlates of stunting and thinness among rural school-going children (aged 5-12 years) of North Bengal, Eastern India. *Journal of Life Sciences.* 10: 29-46.

Do M, Monteiro C, Akré J, Clugston G. 2015. *Global Database on Child Growth and Malnutrition The worldwide magnitude of protein energy malnutrition: an overview from the WHO Global Database on Child Growth.* Bull World Health Organ.

Fazili A, Mir AA, Pandit IM, Bhat IA, Rohul J, Shamila H. 2012. Nutritional status of school age children (5-14 years) in a rural health block of North India (Kashmir) using WHO Z-score system. *The Online Journal of Health and Allied Sciences.* 11:11–3.

Ghosh S, Rakshit S, Bhattacharya M. 2013. Academic perfor-mance and nutritional status – A case Study on college stu-dents in North Tripura. *IOSR Journal of Research and Method in Education.* 1: 57-68.

Gupta SP. 2004. *India Vision 2020, Report of the Committee on India Vision 2020*, Planning Commission, Government of India, New Delhi, pp. 30-35.

World Health Orgamization (WHO). 1998. *Health across life span (Internet).* Available from http://www.who.int/whr/1998/en/whr98_ch3.pdf?ua=1 (accessed June 10, 2017).

International Institute for Population Sciences (IIPS). 2007. *International Institute for Population Sciences and Macro International, National Family Health Survey (NFHS III) 2005-2006.* Mumbai. 2007.

Kamath R, Kumar M, Pattanshetty S, Kamath A. 2012. Nutritional status assessment of school children in Mangalore city using the multicenter growth reference study WHO 2007 Z-scores. *International Journal of Nutrition, Pharmacology, Neurological Diseases.* 2: 233-6.

Kumar S, Pasupathy S, Chinnasami B, Ramraj B. 2018. Prevalence of health problems in sub urban schools in Chennai, India. *International Journal of Contemporary Pediatrics.* 5: 101-105.

Lohman TG, Roche AF, Martorell R. 1988. *Anthropometric Standardization Reference Manual.* Chicago: Human Kinetics Books.

Limbu R, Arya M. 2018. Nutritional status of primary school children in Pauri Garhwal District of Uttarakhand. *Journal of Krishi Vigyan*. 7: 111-114.

Mandal GC, Bose K. 2014. Thinness among migrated Santal primary school children from Arambagh, West Bengal, India. *International Journal of Food Safety, Nutrition and Public Health*. 5: 46-53.

Medhi GK, Barua A, Mahanta J. 2006. Growth and nutritional status of school age children (6–14 years) of tea garden worker of Assam. *Journal of Human Ecology*. 19: 83-85.

Mondal N, Sen J. 2010.hinness is a major underlying problem among Indian children. Journal of *Tropical Pediatrics* 2010; (http://tropij.oxfordjournals.org/content/early/2010/03/07/tropij .fmqo14., accessed on 27.03.2019)

Mondal T, Mondal S, Biswas M. 2015. An assessment of nutritional status of children of Government aided primary school of West Bengal. *International Journal of Elementary Education*. 4: 41-45.

International Institute for Population Sciences. 2017. *National Family Health Survey 4, India Fact Sheet 2015-16*. Mumbai. Available from http://rchiips.org/nfhs/pdf/NFHS4/India.pdf (accessed June 10, 2019).

Rahaman SK, Das S, Dash SK, Giri B, Ali KM. 2019. Nutritional status of primary school children in different parts of India: A Review. *International Journal of Current Research and Review*. 11:1-4.

Rashmi MR, Shweta BM, Fathima FN, Agrawal T, Shah M, Sequeira R. 2015. Prevalence of malnutrition and relationship with scholastic performance among primary and secondary school children in two select private schools in Bangalore Rural District (India). *Indian Journal of Community Medicine*. 40: 97-102.

Rema N, Vasanthaman G. 2011. Prevalence of nutritional and lifestyle disorders among school going children in urban and rural areas of Coimbatore in Tamil Nadu, India. *Indian Journal of Science and Technology*. 4: 131-140.

Sultan S. 2014. Prevalence of stunting and thinness among school-age children of working and non-working mothers in rural areas of Aligarh District. *Indian Journal of Basic and Applied Medical Research*. 3: 51-57.

Ulijaszek SJ, Kerr DA. 1999. Anthropometric measurement error and the assessment of nutritional status. *British Journal of Nutrition*. 82: 165-177.

UNICEF. 2013. *Improving child nutrition: The achievable imperative for global progress*. In: Division of Communication UNICEF; pp. 1–132.

Wickramasinghe VP, Lamabadusuriya SP, Atapattu N, Sathyadas G, Uruparanantha S, Karunarathne P. 2004. Nutritional status of school children in an urban area of Sri Lanka. *Ceylon Medical Journal.* 49: 114-118.

Yankanchi SG, Ganganahalli P, Udgiri R, Patil SS. 2018. Assessment of nutritional status of primary school children in urban field practice area, Vijayapura. *International Journal Of Community Medicine And Public Health.* 5: 779-783.

World Health Organization. 1995. *Physical status: the use and interpretation of anthropometry.* Technical report No. 854. Geneva.

World Health Organization. 1997. *Expert Committee on Comprehensive School Health Education and Promotion Health Through Schools,* Report of a Geneva, WHO Technical Series, No. 870.

World Health Organization. 1998. *Health situation in the South East Asia Region1994-1997.* WHO regional office for South East Asia, New Delhi.

World Health Organization. 2006. Child growth standards based on length/height, weight and age, *Acta Paediatrica*, 450: 76–85.

SECTION IV

Chapter Eighteen

ASSOCIATION OF PHYSICAL ACTIVITY LEVEL WITH CENTRAL OBESITY AND CARDIO-METABOLIC RISK FACTORS AMONG THE WANCHOS OF ARUNACHAL PRADESH AND ASSAM

JOHN BASUMATARY AND GULRUKH BEGUM

ABSTRACT

Objectives: The objective of this study is to assess how different physical activity level of the adult hill and the plain Wancho impact on cardio-metabolic risk defined by central obesity. Materials and Methods: A total of 400 adult Wancho (292 hills: 162 males; 130 females and 108 plains: 59 males, 49 females) ranging from 20 to 60 years of age were measured for height, weight, waist circumference, BMR, skinfold measurements and blood pressure. Central obesity parameters waist circumference, conicity index and waist-height ratio were used to ascertain the prevalence of cardio-metabolic risk factors among the adult Wanchos. WHO Step-wise instrument version 3.2, 2004 was used for determining the physical activity level of the adult Wancho. Results: Adult plain Wancho are more vigorously active than hill Wancho in most number of days in a week. The adult hill Wancho are showing higher prevalence of central obesity across all three parameters than the adult plain Wancho. All three central obesity parameters showed that females are more at risk than males both in hills and plains. The prevalence of hypertension is found to be higher among the males, who are more vigorously active than females in both hills and plains in most days of a week. All three central obesity parameters are positively associated with physical activity both in hills (at a significant level) and plains.Central obesity defined by waist circumference and waist-height ratio were found to be the strongest in association with variables among the hill and the plain Wanchos respectively. Conclusion: Among the hill Wancho cardio-metabolic risk is considerably much higher than plain Wancho. The hills Wancho are living in a much difficult terrain doing moderate to vigorous physical activity every day. This is found to be positively associated with central obesity defined cardio-metabolic risk. They are relatively more at risk than the plain Wancho, who despite sharing the same ethnicity and culture are geographically and ecologically living in a less challenging environment.

Keywords: *Physical Activity, Central Obesity, Cardio-metabolic Risk, Hill Wancho, Plain Wancho*

INTRODUCTION

According to the World Health Organization (2009), physical activity is defined as any bodily movement produced by skeletal muscles that require energy expenditure. Physical inactivity has been identified as the fourth leading risk factor for global mortality causing an estimated 3.2 million deaths globally. Regular physical activity has long been considered necessary for the achievement and the maintenance of an optimal health status.

The World Health Organization (2003) also emphasizes on different dimensions of physical activity and stretches on the fact that regular moderate physical activity such as walking, cycling or participating in sports has significant benefits for health. Epidemiologic research has demonstrated protective effects of varying strength between physical activity and risk for several chronic diseases including coronary heart disease, hypertension, non-insulin-dependent diabetes mellitus, osteoporosis, colon cancer and anxiety and depression (Blair et al., 1995).

Regular physical activity has long been regarded as an important component of a healthy lifestyle. This impression has been reinforced by many scientific evidence linking regular physical activity to a wide array of physical and mental health benefits.

In the present study central obesity is given much importance to assess the cardio-metabolic risk factors. As per Després et. al.(2008) central obesity rather than the whole body obesity is being considered to have a greater association with metabolic health risks. Furthermore, it has been proved that central adiposity parameters are one of the appropriate tools for predicting 10 years of cardiovascular risk among men and women (Motamed et. al., 2015).

The People

Wancho are one of the most prominent tribes of Arunachal Pradesh. Formerly known for their headhunting practices, Wancho share cultural affinity with the Noctes of Arunachal Pradesh and Konyaks of Nagaland, for what they are also known to be the part of the greater Naga tribe. The Wancho are the original inhabitants of Patkai hills of Longding district, Arunachal Pradesh. According to the 2011 Census of India, the population of Wancho is 56,866. They are the third largest tribe of Arunachal Pradesh.

Unlike other tribes of Northeast India, Wancho do not have their own scripts; however, they have a very strong oral tradition of their whereabouts and historical disposition. Before the arrival of Ahom, Wanchos are said to have frequent communication with the people inhabiting the plains of present day Assam. These visits to the plains were not necessarily reckoned as very friendly by the keepers of the oral tradition. However, irrespective of their nature of mobility, soon they were found to be inhabiting in some plains of the Assam-Arunachal border and even far from it. Today in Assam, Wancho villages are found mostly in Charaideo district and a small section of them live in Dibrugarh district as well.

Since the Wanchos are living in both hills and plains, it must be having some bearing on their body composition and ultimately may put them to different health risk conditions. Wanchos living in the hills are very hard working. Just walking to and from places can be considered as vigorous intensity activity for them, which involves constant upward and downward movements of the whole body. Whereas the plains Wancho do not have to walk up and down the terrain for their day to day activities.The fact that they live in different geographical and ecological setup, it is expected that their health cannot be free of the repercussions of differing ecology.

Material and Methods

The present study was conducted among the Wanchos of Arunachal Pradesh and a small fraction of them from Assam residing in the peripheral area of the Assam-Arunachal border. The data collection was done in the two surrounding localities of Longding town; Niaunu and Zedua, RUSA village of Kanubari block, Nitong village of Tirap district, Deopani and Baregaon village of Charaideo district, Assam.

The data collection was done with the help of purposive sampling. The sample size was calculated with the help of Open Epi open-source software version 3.01, 2006. The sample size of the present study is a proportional representative of the total Wancho population of 56,886 (according to the 2011 Census of India). 400 Wancho adults, belonging to the age range from 20 to 60 years, of the present study fall under 90% confidence interval of the total population with anticipated frequency of 50% and design effect of 1.0.

A total of 400 adult Wanchos (292 hills and 108 plains) ranging from 20 to 60 years of age were measured for height, weight, waist circumference, BMR, skinfold measurements and blood pressure. The data collection on physical activity was done with the help of WHO Step-wise instrument version 3.2, 2004. The questionnaire was custom devised as a survey schedule with appropriate activity related modifications. The sample was divided into 3 physical activity levels depending on their daily activity routine, i.e., vigorously active, moderately active and sedentary. This division was made with the help of the directions given by GPAQ (Global Physical Activity Questionnaire) which was specially designed by WHO for developing countries to measure physical activity. Every subject was classified by their daily physical activities associated with work, travel and leisure time. Depending on the time invested in each of these categories, MET (Metabolic Equivalent) was calculated independently. The sum of the total MET value of the three categories was used to classify an individual in a physical activity level. Those with a MET score less than 600 in a week were considered as sedentary or physically inactive. Those who are both vigorously and moderately active throughout a week were further assessed on the basis of their independent MET for vigorous intensity and moderate intensity physical activity and put in the physical activity level according to whichever had a higher MET score. The daily household activities involving, cleaning, washing, cooking were considered as moderate intensity activity, whereas fetching water from stream, collecting firewood and daily foraging were reckoned as vigorous intensity activity. Resting time which is collected for each individual, following the guidelines of the GPAQ is exclusive of sleeping time.

Central obesity was assessed with the help of three parameters;

1. Waist circumference (WHO, 2008)

>94 cm (males)	Increased risk
>102 cm (males)	Substantially increased
>80 cm (females)	Increased risk
>88 cm (females)	Substantially increased

2. Waist-Height Ratio

$$\frac{Waist\ circumference}{Height}$$

WHO (2008) suggests that waist circumference and central adiposity indices are much more convincing and stronger in getting a clear picture of risk factor of cardiovascular diseases (CVD) and mortality caused by obesity than BMI, as these avoid the need for age, sex, and ethnic differences. The universally accepted critical value which signifies increased risk is 0.5 (Browning et al. 2010).

40 >	0.5 critical value
40 – 50	between 0.5 and 0.6
50 <	0.6 onwards

3. Conicity Index

$$\frac{Waist\ circumference\ (m)}{0.109 \times \sqrt{\frac{Weight\ (kg)}{Height\ (m)}}}$$

Different scholars have different classifications for CVD risk factor of Conicity Index. Almeida et al. (2009) has suggested a critical value of 1.25 for increased occurrence of cardiovascular risk factor. One of the sex-specific cut offs of C-Index used by Shenoy and Jagadamba (2017) in their study on influence of central obesity on Lung Age in young adults has the critical value 1.25 for males and 1.18 for females. This cut off has been used in the present study.

Blood pressure levels were categorised using classification given by "The Seventh Report of the Joint National Committee on Prevention, Detection, Evaluation and Treatment of High Blood Pressure" [JNC 7] (U.S. Department of Health and Human Services 2004). The sample was divided into four categories, normotensive, pre hypertensive, hypertensive stage 1 and hypertensive stage 2. Those with <120mm Hg systolic BP and <80 mm Hg diastolic BP were put in the normotensive category, those with 120-139 mm Hg systolic BP and 80-89 mm Hg diastolic BP were put in pre hypertensive category, those with 140-159 mm Hg systolic BP and 90-99 mm Hg diastolic BP were put in hypertensive stage 1, and finally those with ≥160mmHg systolic BP and ≥100 mm Hg diastolic BP were put in the hypertensive stage 2 category. People with prehypertension are at increased risk for progression to hypertension.

All the data analysis was done with the help of MS Excel 2007 and SPSS 16.0 software. Descriptive statistics were used to calculate the frequency of basic measurements among the participants. For the comparison of independent means of the basic measurements t-test was applied. Pearson's correlation coefficient test was applied to see the relationship among different anthropometric, physiological and behavioural variables. To test the strength of any association among variables multiple linear regression was further applied. Chi square test was used to test the significance in sex wise variance of central obesity parameters and blood pressure categories. In all the statistical analysis p-value at 0.05 level was considered to be statistically significant.

Results and Discussion

A comparison between the adult hill Wancho and adult plain Wancho on the basis of anthropometric, physiological and behavioural data are presented in Table 1. The mean stature of the sample shows that the adult plain Wancho (157.28 cm) are taller than the adult hill Wancho (155.72 cm). Both among hill and plain Wancho males fall in below medium and females fall in short stature category (Table 2) according to Martin's scale. The variances between hill and plain Wancho in their mean weight, BMI, BMR, BFP, and sum of skinfold are statistically significant at 0.05 level. Among the behavioural traits only alcohol consumption (p 0.001) has a statistically significant variance between adult hill and plain Wancho. Both among hill and plain Wancho the sex wise variance between male and female as per mean stature, weight, BMI, BFP, and in behavioural traits, physical activity level, smoking/tobacco chewing and alcohol consumption are statistically significant at 0.001 level. A total of 51.5 percent adult Wancho are vigorously active for most number of days in a week, which is the highest among the three categories of physical activity level. Adult plain Wancho are more vigorously active (54.63%) than hill Wancho in most number of days in a week (Table 1). Maximum number of adult Wancho are found to be resting less than or equal to 3 hours in most number of days in a week.

Table 1: Descriptive statistics of anthropometric, physiological and behavioural data

Variables	Hill Wanchos (N 292)	Plain Wanchos (N 108)	Total (N 400)
Stature (cm)	155.72 ± 7.27	157.28 ± 8.43	156.5 ± 7.85
Weight (kg)	55.03 ± 8.43	51.82 ± 9.86*	54.42 ± 9.15
Body Mass Index	22.73 ± 3.27	20.85 ± 2.95**	22.73 ± 3.11
Basal Metabolic Rate	1256.88 ± 164.34	1205.90 ± 203.05*	1256.88 ± 183.7
Body Fat Percent	24.37 ± 7.55	22.23 ± 6.17*	24.37 ± 6.86
Sum of Skinfold	16.52 ± 4.62	18.12 ± 3.99*	16.52 ± 4.305
Systolic Blood Pressure (mm kg)	124.1 ± 16.47	122.11 ± 13.65	124.1 ± 15.06
Diastolic Blood Pressure (mm kg)	79.03 ± 11.54	78.39 ± 9.71	79.03 ± 10.625
Physical activity level			
Vigorous	147 (50.34%)	59 (54.63%)	206 (51.5%)
Moderate	125 (42.81%)	46 (42.59%)	171 (42.75%)
Sedentary	20 (6.85%)	3 (2.78%)	23 (5.75%)
Smoking/Tobacco chewing			
Yes	106 (36.30%)	31 (28.70%)	137 (34.25%)
No	186 (63.70%)	77 (71.30%)	263 (65.75%)
Alcohol consumer*	98 (33.56%)	18 (16.67%)	116 (29%)
Non-consumer	194 (66.44%)	90 (83.33%)	284 (71%)
Resting time			
≤1 hours	34 (11.9%)	13 (11.6%)	47 (11.75%)
≤3 hours	119 (46.8%)	51 (40.5%)	170 (42.5%)
>3 hours	106 (29.4%)	32 (36.1%)	138 (34.5%)
>6 hours	33 (11%)	12 (11.2%)	45 (11.25%)

Note. Here, * $p<0.05$, ** $p<0.001$ when compared to the mean values of hill and plain. P values were obtained by independent samples t test for anthropometric and physiological variables and chi square test for behavioural data.

Table 2: Descriptive statistics of anthropometric, physiological and behavioural characteristics in both the sexes

Variables	Hill				Plain			
	Male (N 162)		Female (N 130)		Male (N 59)		Female (N 49)	
Stature (cm)	160.13±5.42		150.22±5.26**		163.19±5.59		150.15±5.06**	
Weight (kg)	57.4±7.5		52.07±8.6**		56.61±8.87		46.05±7.69**	
Body Mass Index	22.41±2.91		23.13±3.64		21.23±2.81		20.4±3.08	
Basal Metabolic Rate	1333.27±133.42		1161.69±149.15**		1322.22±165.79		1065.84±148.43**	
Body Fat Percent	19.5±4.9		30.45±5.62**		18.08±4.35		27.23±3.93**	
Sum of Skinfold	16.37±3.53		16.7±5.7		17.65±3.05		18.69±4.86	
Systolic Blood Pressure	125.44±15.85		122.42±17.14		123.68±11.72		120.22±15.58	
Diastolic Blood Pressure	79.63±11.7		78.28±11.34		78.22±8.21		78.5±11.33	
Physical activity level**								
Vigorous	107	66.05%	40	30.77%	46	77.97%	13	26.53%
Moderate	37	22.84%	88	67.69%	11	18.64%	35	71.43%
Sedentary	18	11.11%	2	1.54%	2	3.39%	1	2.04%
Smoking/ Tobacco chewing**								
Yes	100	61.73%	6	4.62%	30	50.85%	1	2.04%
No	62	38.27%	124	95.38%	29	49.15%	48	97.96%
Alcohol consumer**	97	59.88%	1	0.77%	18	30.51%	0	
Non-consumer	65	40.12%	129	99.23%	41	69.49%	49	100%
Resting time								
≤1 hours	19	11.73%	15	11.54%	4	6.78%	9	18.37%
≤3 hours	68	41.98%	51	39.23%	31	52.54%	20	40.82%
>3 hours	55	33.95%	51	39.23%	16	27.12%	16	32.65%
>6 hours	20	12.35%	13	10%	8	13.56%	4	8.16%

Note. Here, * $p<0.05$, ** $p<0.001$ when compared to the mean values of male and female. P values were obtained by independent samples t test for anthropometric and physiological variables and chi square test for behavioural data.

The three central obesity parameters are showing abdominal obesity and cardio-metabolic risk factors among the adult Wancho. According to waist circumference 3.7 percent adult plain Wancho are at increased risk and 1.85 percent are at substantially increased risk of cardio-metabolic diseases (Table 4), of which, 75 percent and 50 percent (respectively) are females and majority of them are moderately active in most number of days in a week (66.67% and 100% respectively). On the other hand, waist circumference has shown 9.93 percent adult hill Wancho at increased risk and 3.08 percent at substantially increased risk of cardio-metabolic diseases (Table 3). Among the hills, the proportion of female in these two categories is considerably much higher (82.76% and 88.89% respectively) with majority of them being moderately active in most number of days in a week (83.33% and 62.5% respectively). Among the hill Wancho 31.85 percent are at risk as per the Waist–Height Ratio of which 59.14 percent are female and 40.86 percent are male. Among the females, highest proportion of females at risk are mostly moderately active (74.55%) and among the males, highest proportion of males at risk are mostly vigorously active in maximum number of days in week. Similarly, of the total 20.55 percent adult hill Wancho at risk, according to Conicity index, 66.67 percent are female and 75 percent of them are moderately active in most days in a week. Among the plain Wancho 17.59 percent are at risk according to Waist-Height Ratio and 18.52 percent are at risk according to Conicity index. Here again, females are found to be more at risk than males. The vigorously active males (55.56% as per Waist-Height Ratio, 71.43% as per Conicity Index) are more at risk among the plain Wancho. On the other hand, moderately active females (70% as per Waist-Height Ratio, 84.62% as per Conicity Index) are more at risk among the plain Wancho. The adult hill Wancho are showing higher prevalence of central obesity across all three parameters than the adult plain Wancho. The sex wise variance in the three central obesity parameters among the hill Wancho is significant, whereas, among the plain Wancho it is not significant.

Table 3: Distribution of Physical Activity Level as per Waist Circumference, waist-Height Ratio, and Conicity Index of the hill Wanchos

Categories	Sex	Vigorous		Moderate		Sedentary		Total	
		No	%	No	%	No	%	No	%
WC status									
Normal	Male (N 162)	106	67.95	35	22.44	15	9.62	156	61.42
	Female (N 130)	35	35.71	63	64.29	0	0	98	38.58
	Total (N 292)	141	55.51	98	38.58	15	5.91	254	86.99
Increased risk	Male (N 162)	1	20	2	40	2	40	5	17.24
	Female (N 130)	3	12.5	20	83.33	1	4.17	24	82.76
	Total (N 292)	4	13.79	22	75.86	3	10.34	29	9.93
Substantially increased risk	Male (N 162)	0	0	0	0	1	100	1	11.11
	Female (N 130)	2	25	5	62.5	1	12.5	8	88.89
	Total (N 292)	2	22.22	5	55.56	2	22.22	9	3.08
WHtR status									
Normal	Male (N 162)	91	73.39	26	20.97	7	5.65	124	62.31
	Female (N 130)	28	37.33	47	62.67	0	0	75	37.69
	Total (N 292)	119	59.80	73	36.68	7	3.52	199	68.15
At risk	Male (N 162)	16	42.11	11	28.95	11	28.95	38	40.86
	Female (N 130)	12	21.82	41	74.55	2	3.64	55	59.14
	Total (N 292)	28	30.11	52	55.91	13	13.98	93	31.85
C Index status									
Normal	Male (N 162)	101	71.13	31	21.83	10	7.04	142	61.21
	Female (N 130)	31	34.44	58	64.44	1	1.11	90	38.79
	Total (N 292)	132	56.90	89	38.36	11	4.74	232	79.45
At risk	Male (N 162)	6	30	6	30	8	40	20	33.33
	Female (N 130)	9	22.5	30	75	1	2.5	40	66.67
	Total (N 292)	15	25	36	60	9	15	60	20.55

Note. All the central obesity categories are significant at 5% level between the sexes.

Table 4: Distribution of Physical Activity Level as per Waist Circumference, Waist-Height Ratio, and Conicity Index of the plain Wanchos

Categories	Sex	Vigorous		Moderate		Sedentary		Total	
		No	%	No	%	No	%	No	%
WC status									
Normal	Male (N 59)	46	80.70	9	15.79	2	3.51	57	55.88
	Female (N 49)	12	26.67	32	71.11	1	2.22	45	44.12
	Total (N 108)	58	56.86	41	40.20	3	2.94	102	94.44
Increased risk	Male (N 59)	0	0	1	100	0	0	1	25
	Female (N 49)	1	33.33	2	66.67	0	0	3	75
	Total (N 108)	1	25	3	75	0	0	4	3.70
Substantially increased risk	Male (N 59)	0	0	1	100	0	0	1	50
	Female (N 49)	0	0	1	100	0	0	1	50
	Total (N 108)	0	0	2	100	0	0	2	1.85
WHtR status									
Normal	Male (N 59)	41	82	8	16	1	2	50	56.18
	Female (N 49)	11	28.21	28	71.79	0	0	39	43.82
	Total (N 108)	52	58.43	36	40.45	1	1.12	89	82.41
At risk	Male (N 59)	5	55.56	3	33.33	1	11.11	9	47.37
	Female (N 49)	2	20	7	70	1	10	10	52.63
	Total (N 108)	7	36.84	10	52.63	2	10.53	19	17.59
C Index status									
Normal	Male (N 59)	41	78.85	9	17.31	2	3.85	52	59.09
	Female (N 49)	11	30.56	24	66.67	1	2.78	36	40.91
	Total (N 108)	52	59.09	33	37.5	3	3.41	88	81.48

At risk	Male (N 59)	5	71.43	2	28.57	0	0	7	35
	Female (N 49)	2	15.38	11	84.62	0	0	13	65
	Total (N 108)	7	35	13	65	0	0	20	18.52

Note. All the central obesity categories are not significant at 5% level between the sexes.

Table 5: Distributions of adult hill Wanchos and plains Wanchos according to blood pressure categories

Groups	Sex	Normotensive		Prehypertensive		Hypertensive				Total	
						Stage 1		Stage 2			
		N	%	N	%	N	%	N	%	N	%
Hills*	Male (N 162)	56	34.57	69	42.59	31	19.14	6	3.7	37	22.84
	Female (N 130)	69	53.08	40	30.77	14	10.77	7	5.38	21	16.15
	Total (N 292)	125	42.81	109	37.33	45	15.41	13	4.45	58	19.86
Plains	Male (N 59)	23	38.98	26	44.07	10	16.95	0	0	10	16.95
	Female (N 49)	22	44.9	19	38.78	7	14.29	1	100	8	16.33
	Total (N 108)	45	41.67	45	41.67	17	15.74	1	0.93	18	16.67

Note. Here, *$p<0.05$ in sexwise variance among the blood pressure categories.

Obesity as a risk factor of cardio-metabolic syndrome is found to be affecting more females than males. A review study about sex differences in cardiovascular risk factors also showed that CVD prevalence is higher in women than in men. Among the females, the CVD risk factors showed the association between preeclampsia, gestational diabetes and menopause onset with the occurrence of CVD (Appleman et al. 2015). Similarly, Chanak and Bose (2019) and Pohl et al. (2018) in their respective studies have found more females at risk than males. Singh et al. (2016), in their community based study, also found significantly higher prevalence of obesity among women (28.8%) as compared to men (13.3%). In their study low physical activity and increasing age were found to be the factors in higher prevalence of obesity among females. However, in present study, Wancho females cannot be put in low physical activity group, but the intensity of physical activity can be taken as factor in their showing higher prevalence of central obesity, as those who are at risk are mostly moderately active in most number of days in a week, both among hill and plain Wancho. The association of higher percentage of females at risk and higher percentage of them being mostly moderate intensity activity performers in most number of days in a week probably can be used as an indicator that vigorous activity equals to very less cardio-metabolic risk. Supporting this assumption another fact in the study is that all three central obesity parameters are showing considerably much higher percentage of males free of cardio-metabolic risk and them being mostly vigorous intensity activity performers in most days in a week. Similarly, hill Wancho are more at risk than the plain Wancho and it has been found that plain Wancho are more vigorously active than the hill Wancho (54.63% vs 50.34%). However, Waist-Height Ratio results for both hill and plain Wancho and Conicity Index results for plain Wancho, are showing that highest proportion of males at risk are actually vigorously active in most number of days in a week. If we are to consider this as an imoportant factor, then it might not be wrong to assume that Wancho are considerably very active population and in spite of that being a major factor, central obesity as a risk factor of cardio-metabolic syndrome is still present among them. Numerous studies (Dhall, 2012; Singh et al. 2016; Li et al. 2018) have shown that low physical activity leads to higher risk of metabolic syndrome, but in the present study both hill and plain Wancho are mostly vigorous to moderately active in most number of days in a week, with very few sedentary people, showing a higher proportion of those at risk being either moderately or vigorously active in most number of days in a week.

Males are found to be more hypertensive (Table 5) among both hills Wancho (19.14% at stage 1, 3.7% at stage 2) and plain Wancho (16.95% at stage 1, no one at stage 2). Among the plain Wancho, 90 percent males at stage 1 of hypertensive category are vigorously active in most number of days. In fact, highest proportions of hypertensive males are involved in vigorous intensity activity in most number of days in a week (Table 6). In comparison, (Table 5) hypertension is relatively more prevalent among the adult hill Wancho (19.86%) than the adult plain Wancho (16.67%). Among adult females, hypertension is slightly more among the plain Wancho (16.33%) than the hill Wancho (16.15%). All the females in the hypertensive category (both hill and plain Wancho) are mostly moderately active in a week. When we look into the pre hypertensive category, which depicts those with risk of hypertension, plain Wancho (41.67%) are more at risk of hypertension than the hill Wancho (37.33%), among both adult males (44.07% vs 42.59%) and females (38.78% vs 30.77%).

Table 6: Distribution of physical activity as per blood pressure of the adult hill and plain Wanchos

Groups	Sex	Blood pressure categories		Vigorous		Moderate		Sedentary		Total	
				N	%	N	%	N	%	N	%
Hills	Male (N 162)	Normotensive		43	76.79	12	21.43	1	1.79	56	34.57
		Prehypertensive		43	62.32	16	23.19	10	14.49	69	42.59
		Hypertensive	Stage 1	19	61.29	7	22.58	5	16.13	31	19.14
			Stage 2	2	33.33	2	33.33	2	33.33	6	3.70
	Female (N 130)	Normotensive		19	27.54	50	72.46	0	0	69	53.08
		Prehypertensive		16	40	23	57.5	1	2.5	40	30.77
		Hypertensive	Stage 1	3	21.43	10	71.43	1	7.14	14	10.77
			Stage 2	2	28.57	5	71.43	0	0	7	5.38
Plains	Male (N 59)	Normotensive		17	73.91	5	21.74	1	4.35	23	38.98
		Prehyperteesive		20	76.92	5	19.23	1	3.85	26	44.07
		Hypertensive	Stage 1	9	90	1	10	0	0	10	16.95
			Stage 2	0		0		0		0	0
	Female (N 49)	Normotensive		6	27.27	15	68.18	1	4.55	22	44.90
		Prehypertensive		5	26.32	14	73.68	0	0	19	38.78
		Hypertensive	Stage 1	2	28.57	5	71.43	0	0	7	14.29
			Stage 2	0	0	1	100	0	0	1	2.04

Table 7: Pearson's correlation coefficient between different variables for adult hill Wanchos Reorient

Variables	WCs	WHtRs	CIs	BMI	PHYs	BMR	BFP	SS	ST	TEE	SYS	DIA	SMK/T	ALC
WCs	1	.531"	.561"	.647"	.243"	.263"	.605"	.363"	.081	-.109	.234"	.209"	-.211"	-.193"
WHtRs		1	.617"	.660"	.302"	.226"	.584"	.363"	.053	-.210"	.262"	.288"	-.243"	-.221"
CIs			1	.402"	.275"	.031	.459"	.240"	.117"	-.184"	.189"	.214"	.-.227"	-.200"
BMI				1	.265"	.573"	-.117"	.474"	.404	-.166"	.329"	.312"	.-176"	-.121"
PHYs					1	.118"	.249"	.270"	.303"	-.667"	.096	.150"	-.244"	-.215"
BMR						1	-117"	.369"	.128"	-300"	.152"	.081	.240"	.340"
BFP							1	.271"	-.044	.059	.244"	.278"	-.476"	-.509"
SS								1	.038	-.239"	.071	.090	-.084	-.079
ST									1	-.483"	-.029	-.024	.128"	.178"
TEE										1	-.093	-.096	.002	-.048
SYS											1	.922□	.073	.052
DIA												1	.059	.007
SMK/T													1	.715"
ALC														1

Note. ** Correlation is significant at the 0.01 level, * Correlation is significant at the 0.05 level, BMR= Basal Metabolic Rate, BMI= Body Mass Index, TEE= total energy expenditure, SYS=systolic blood pressure, DIA=diastolic blood pressure, WCs= Waist Circumference status, WHtRs= Waist-Height Ratio status, CIs=Conicity Index status, PHY=physical activity levels, BFP= Body Fat Per cent, SS= sum of skinfold, ST= sedentary/resting time, SMK/T= smoking/tobacco chewing and ALC= alcohol consumption.

Table 8: Pearson's correlation coefficient between different variables for adult plain Wanchos

Variables	WCs	WHtRs	CIs	BMI	PHY	BMR	BFP	SS	ST	TEE	SYS	DIA	SMK/T	ALC
WCs	1	.493"	.478"	.449"	.162	.210"	.392"	.408"	.062	-.121	.216"	.224"	-.145	-.102
WHtRs		1	.468"	.716"	.214"	.315"	.512"	.365"	.042	-.083	.213	.256"	-.132	-.076
CIs			1	.190"	.145	-.037	.311"	.098	.001	-.045	.156	.166	-.092	-.021
BMI				1	.113	.708"	.437"	.460"	.253"	-.156	.254"	.189"	.103	.020
PHY					1	-.161	.427"	-.044	.246"	-.541"	-.063	.045	-.331"	-.165
BMR						1	-.221"	.201"	.315"	-.159	.255"	.102	.412"	.303"
BFP							1	.420"	-.089"	-.021	.055	.166	-.449"	-.410"
SS								1	-.188	.210"	.014	.010	-.099	-.144
ST									1	-456"	-.006	-.036	.016	.084
TEE										1	.081	-.0004	.073	-.050
SYS											1	.877"	.136	.108
DIA												1	.021	.057
SMK/T													1	.705"
ALC														1

Note. ** Correlation is significant at the 0.01 level, * Correlation is significant at the 0.05 level, BMR= Basal Metabolic Rate, BMI= Body Mass Index, TEE= total energy expenditure, SYS=systolic blood pressure, DIA=diastolic blood pressure, WCs= Waist Circumference status,WHtRs= Waist-Height Ratio status,CIs=Conicity Index status, PHY=physical activity levels, BFP= Body Fat Per cent, SS= sum of skinfold, ST= sedentary/ resting time, SMK/T= smoking/tobacco chewing and ALC= alcohol consumption.

Elevated blood pressure is another risk factor of cardio-metabolic syndrome. Hypertension is one of the major causes of mortality globally for the last two decades or so. Hypertension is responsible for at least 45 percent of deaths due to heart disease, and 51 percent of deaths due to stroke (WHO, 2008) studies have also shown that the risk of hypertension is high among the males than the females (Khanam et al. 2015; Chen et al. 2018; Raja et al. 2018, Khanam et al. 2015). In the present study as well the prevalance of hypertension is comapratively higher among the adult males than in females among both hill and plain adult Wancho.

Another important finding of the present study in this regard is that, highest number of those hypertensive males, both in hills and plains are mostly vigorously active in maximum number of days in a week. Similarly, the proportion of those at risk of hypertension (pre-hypertensive category) is higher among the plain Wancho males than hill Wancho males, and in general when we look at the vigorously active sample, plain Wancho are comparatively more vigorously active than the hill Wancho. A study conducted among female Filipino workers (Lu, 2008), whose work profile includes heavy lifting, prolonged standing, highly repetitive work, also showed a positive relationship between physical activity and hypertension. This study showed that excessive work was associated with poorer health, dissatisfaction with life, poor recuperation from fatigue, and hypertension. A similar pattern is visible in the present study, where the prevalence of hypertension is found to be higher among the males, who are more vigorously active than females in both hills and plains in most days of a week. Considering hypertension as a risk factor of cardio-metabolic syndrome among the Wancho, again it can be said that those who are actually relatively more active than the average population are more at cardio-metabolic risk than others.

Pearson's correlation coefficient test was applied to assess association between different variables for the adult Wancho (Table 7 and Table 8). All three central obesity parameters are showing positive, statistically significant and strong association with physical activity level among the adult hill Wancho. However, among the plain Wancho, only Waist-Height Ratio is significantly and positively associated with their physical activity level. The systolic and diastolic blood pressures are also significantly and positively associated with the three central obesity parameters among the adult hill Wancho. On the other hand, only Waist Circumference is found to be positively and significantly associated with systolic as well as diastolic blood pressure among the plain Wancho. Apart from this, Waist-Height Ratio is found to be significantly associated with only diastolic blood pressure among the plain Wancho. All three central obesity parameters are inversely correlated with smoking/tobacco chewing and alcohol consumption among both hill and plain Wancho. In both hill and plain Wancho, BMR is found to be positively and significantly associated with systolic blood pressure.

To assess the strength of these variables in predicting the variability of the three central obesity parameters, linear regression was applied (Table 9 – 11). Central obesity defined by waist circumference was found to be the strongest in association with the variables, as 49.6 percent of the variability of cardio-metabolic risk defined by Waist Circumference was predicted by the joint association of all the variables among the hill Wancho. However, among the plain Wancho, central obesity defined by Waist-Height Ratio was found to be most strongly associated with the variables, as 48.5 percent of the variability of cardio-metabolic risk defined by Waist-Height Ratio was predicted by the cumulative association of all the variables. Central obesity defined by Conicity Index was found to be having the weekest association with all the covariates among both hill and plain Wancho. Body Fat Percent was the significant predictor of the variability in all the three central obesity parameters among both hill and plains Wancho. Apart from this, Basal Metabolic Rate was found to be the significant predictor of the variability in Waist Circumference and Waist-Height Ratio among the hill Wancho and just in Waist-Height Ratio among the plain Wancho.

Table 9: Adjusted linear regression between WC and other variables for adult hill and plain Wanchos

	Variables	Standardized Coefficients	Sig.	R^2
Hill	BFP	0.628	.000	.496
	SS	0.090	.071	
	BMR	0.264	.000	
	SYS	0.197	.084	
	DIA	-0.181	.112	
	PHYs	0.025	.621	
	ST	0.062	.185	
	SMKTBC	0.0127	.840	
	ALC	0.0193	.771	
	Dependent Variable: WC			
Plain	Variables	Standardized Coefficients	Sig.	R^2
	BFP	.259	.034	.314
	SS	.265	.014	
	BMR	.206	.068	
	SYS	.101	.596	
	DIA	.067	.718	
	PHYs	.054	.602	
	ST	.056	.566	
	SMKTBC	-.127	.337	
	ALC	.058	.633	
	Dependent Variable: WC			

Note. Here, BMR= Basal Metabolic Rate, BMI= Body Mass Index, SYS= systolic blood pressure, DIA=diastolic blood pressure, BFP= Body Fat Per cent, SS= sum of skinfold, ST= sedentary/resting time, SMKTBC= smoking/tobacco chewing and ALC= alcohol consumption.

Table 10: Adjusted linear regression between WHtR and other variables for adult hill and plain Wanchos

	Variables	Standardized Coefficients	Sig.	R^2
Hill	BFP	.532	.000	.462
	SS	.095	.064	
	BMR	.237	.000	
	SYS	-.077	.514	
	DIA	.172	.145	
	PHYs	.082	.113	
	ST	.023	.629	
	SMKTBC	-.041	.534	
	ALC	.020	.773	
	Dependent Variable: WHtR			
Plain	**Variables**	**Standardized Coefficients**	**Sig.**	**R^2**
	BFP	.539	.000	.485
	SS	.032	.731	
	BMR	.488	.000	
	SYS	-.124	.455	
	DIA	.217	.183	
	PHYs	.033	.713	
	ST	-.067	.436	
	SMKTBC	-.146	.204	
	ALC	.116	.273	
	Dependent Variable: WHtR			

Note. Here, BMR= Basal Metabolic Rate, BMI= Body Mass Index, SYS= systolic blood pressure, DIA=diastolic blood pressure, BFP= Body Fat Per cent, SS= sum of skinfold, ST= sedentary/resting time, SMKTBC= smoking/tobacco chewing and ALC= alcohol consumption.

Table 11: Adjusted linear regression between C-Index and other variables for adult hill Wanchos

	Variables	Standardized Coefficients	**Sig.**	**R^2**
Hill	BFP	.387	.000	.265
	SS	.091	.128	
	BMR	.006	.928	
	SYS	.000	.999	
	DIA	.087	.529	
	PHYs	.101	.094	
	ST	.103	.068	
	SMKTBC	-.066	.384	
	ALC	.051	.524	
	Dependent Variable: C Index			
Plain	**Variables**	**Standardized Coefficients**	**Sig.**	**R^2**
	BFP	.352	.011	.129
	SS	-.028	.817	
	BMR	-.024	.848	
	SYS	.191	.375	
	DIA	-.064	.762	
	PHYs	.006	.957	
	ST	.021	.851	
	SMKTBC	-.051	.730	
	ALC	.145	.293	
	Dependent Variable: C Index			

Note. Here, BMR= Basal Metabolic Rate, BMI= Body Mass Index, SYS= systolic blood pressure, DIA=diastolic blood pressure, BFP= Body Fat Per cent, SS= sum of skinfold, ST= sedentary/resting time, SMKTBC= smoking/tobacco chewing and ALC= alcohol consumption.

Studies have proved that only leisure time vigorous to moderate physical activity (or intentional exercise) can act as a preventive measure of CVD risk. Huai et al. (2013) suggested an inverse relationship between levels of recreational physical activity and risk of hypertension. Holtermann et al. (2011) in their study talked about the difference between occupational and leisure time physical activity. When describing about the level of physical activity and its impact on health, the importance of looking it from different dimensions is of great emphasis. They found that high level of occupational physical active increases the risk of Long Term Sickness Absence (LTSA) among the employees in both males and females. However, even low level of leisure-time physical activity decreases the risk of LTSA. Hu et al. (2002) have found in their study that doing more than 60 minutes of commuting physical activity or combined commuting and leisure time physical activity was related to the highest mean blood pressure and the highest prevalence of hypertension among both genders compared with going to and from work by bus. However, 31 – 60 minutes of commuting or combined commuting and leisure-time physical activity is related with lowest level of hypertension. In the present study, all the central obesity parameters are showing positive association with physical activity level, suggesting that as the level of physical activity increases their cardio-metabolic risk also increases. This association is much stronger among the adult hill Wancho than the adult plain Wancho. The Wancho in general have very little differences in their economic or educational status and are mostly farmers or wage labourers, and especially those living in hills are involved in labour-intensive bodily movements right after waking up in the morning. Their farming lands are always far from their place of living and in a relatively obscure edge of a hill surrounded by thick greenery. As male folks are basically more involved in cultivation and other related works, perhaps that is why vigorously active males are more at risk than the rest. In the plains even though the occupation does not vary from the hill Wancho, but the people are subjected to less labour-intensive daily body movement because of the terrain they are living. Therefore, a level of high physical activity may be to an extent beneficial for their overall health, as they are found to be considerably much less at risk.

Conclusion

Prevalence of cardio-metabolic risk as defined by the central obesity was found to be considerably more among the adult females than the adult male Wancho in both hills and plains. Majority of them were found to be doing moderate intensity physical activity in most days of a week. The prevalence of hypertension is found to be higher among the males, who are more vigorously active than females in both hills and plains in most days of a week. Waist Circumference and BMR is found to be positively and significantly associated with systolic as well as diastolic blood pressure among the plain Wancho. As the level of physical activity increases their cardio-metabolic risk also increases. Waist circumference and Waist-Height Ratio were found to be the strongest in association with variables. The physical activity level is positively associated at a significant level with central obesity. The hill Wancho are more at risk than the plain Wancho. The plains Wancho despite sharing the same ethnicity and culture are geographically and ecologically living in a less challenging environment.

Acknowledgment

This study is a part of the doctoral research of the researcher which is funded by the Indian Council of Medical Research under the scheme of ICMR-JRF 2017.

References

Almeida RT, Almeida MM, Araujo TM. 2009. Abdominal obesity and cardiovascular risk: performance of anthropometric in women. *Arquivos Brasileiros De Cardiologia*. 92: 345-350.

Appleman Y, Rijn BB, Haaf ME, Boersma E, Peters SAE. 2015. Sex differences in cardiovascular risk factors and disease prevention. *Atherosclerosis*. 241(1): 211-218.

Blair SN, Russell RP, Michael P, William LH, Caroline AM, Claude B, David B, Walter E, Gregory WH, Abby CK, Andrea K, Arthur SL, Bess H M, Jeremy M, Ralph SP, Kevin P, Micheal LP, James S, Jack W. 1995. Physical Activity and Public Health. *Journal of American Medical Association*. 273: 402-407.

Browning LM, Hsieh SD, Ashwell M. 2010. A systematic review of waist-to-height ratio as a screening tool for the prediction of cardiovascular disease and diabetes: 0.5 could be suitable global boundary value. *Nutrition Research Reviews*. 23: 247-269.

Chanak M, Bose K. 2019. Central obesity and hypertesion among rural adults of Pachim Medinipur, West Bengal, India. *Anthropological Review*. 82(3): 239-252.

Chen X, Liu Y, Sun X, Yin Z, Li H, Deng K, Cheng C, Liu L, Luo X, Zhang R, Liu F, Zhou Q, Wang C, Li L, Zhang L, Wang B, Zhou Y, Zhou J, Han C, Zhang H, Yang X, Pang C, Yin L, Feng T, Zhou J, Zhang M, Hu D. 2018.

Comparison of body mass index, waist circumference, conicity index, and waist to height ratio for predicting incidence of hypertension: the rural Chinese cohort study. *Journal of Human Hypertension*. 32: 228-235.

Dhall Meenal. 2012. Physical Activity Pattern and Metabolic Syndrome among Adult Punjabi Males and Females. PhD dissertation, University of Delhi (unpublished).

Després JP, Lemieux I, Bergeron J, Pibarot P, Mathieu P, Larose E. 2008. Abdominal obesity and the metabolic syndrome: Contribution to global cardiometabolic risk. *Arteriosclerosis, Thrombosis, and Vascular Biology*. 28: 1039-1049.

Holtermann A, Hansen J V, Burr H, Sogaard K, Sjogaard G. 2011. The health paradox of occupational and leisure time physical activity. *British Journal of Sports Medicine*. 46: 291-295.

Hu G, Pekkarinen H, Hanninen O, Tian H, Guo Z. 2002. Commuting, leisure time physical activity and cardiovascular risk factors in China. *Medicine & Science in Sports & Exercise*. 34: 234–238.

Huai P, Xun H, Reilly H K, Wang Y, Ma W, Xi B. 2013. Physical activity and risk of hypertension: A meta-analysis of prospective cohort studies. *Hypertension*. 62: 1021-1026.

Khanam M A, Lindeboom W, Razzaque A, Niessen L, Milton A H. 2015. Prevalence and determinants of pre-hypertension and hypertension among the adults in rural Bangladesh: findings from a community-based study. BMC Public Health. 15:203.

Li Y, Zhao L, Yu D, Wang Z, Ding G. 2018. Metabolic syndrome prvalence and its risk factors among adults in China: A nationally representative cross-sectional study. *PloS ONE*. 13: 6.

Lu J L. 2008. Occupational hazards and illiness of Filipino women workers in export processing zones. *International Journal of Occupational Safety and Ergonomics*. 14: 333-342.

Mittelmark M B. 1994. *The epidemiology of aging*. In: Hazzard W.R., Bierman E.L., Blass J.P., Ettinger Jr. W.H., Halter J.B. (Eds.), Principles of Geriatric Medicine and Gerontology, ed. 3. McGraw-Hill Book Company, New York.

Motamed N, Perumal D, Zamani F, Ashrafi H, Haghjoo M, Saeedian FS. 2015. Conicity index and waist-to-hip ratio are superior obesity indices in predicting 10-year cardiovascular risk among men and women. *Clinical Cardiology*. 38: 527-534.

Paul PJ, Samson R, William A, Akila B, Purty AJ, Bazroy J. 2017. Prevalence and factors associated with hypertension: a commu- nity based cross-sectional study among adults in an urban area of Puducherry, South India. *Indian Journal of Community Medicine and Public Health*. 4:

1620–1626.

Pohl HH, Arnold EF, Dummel KL, Cerentini TM, Reuter EM, Reckziegel M B. 2018. Anthropometric indicators and cardiovascular risk factors in rural workers, *Revista Brasileira De Medicina Do Esporte*. 24:: 64-68.

Raja TK, Muthukumar T, Mohan Anisha P. 2018. A cross-sectional study on prevalence of hypertension and its associated risk factors among rural adults in Kanchipuram, district, Tamil Nadu. *Indian Journal of Community Medicine and Public Health*. 5: 249-253.

Shenoy U, Jagadamba. 2017. Influence of central obesity assessed by conicity index on lung age in young adults. *Journal of Clinical and Diagnostic Research*. 11: CC09-CC12.

Singh S, Issac R, Benjamin A I, Kaushal S. 2016. Prevalence and association of physical activity with oobesity: An urban, community-based, cross-sectional study. *Indian Journal of Community Medicine*. 41:77.

U.S. Department of Health and Human Services. 2004. *The Seventh Report of the Joint National Committee on Prevention, Detection, Evaluation and Treatment of High Blood Pressure*.

World Health Organization. 2003. *Diet, nutrition and the prevention of chronic diseases*. Geneva.

World Health Organization. 2008a. Causes of Death [online database]. Geneva. (Accessed September 12 2019). (http://www.who.int/healthinfo/global_burden_disease/cod_2008_sources_methods.pdf)

World Health Organization. 2008b. *Waist Circumference and Waist-Hip Ratio: Report of a WHO Expert Consultation*. Geneva.

World Health Organization. 2009. *Global Recommendations on Physical Activity for health*. Geneva.

Chapter Ninteen

VARIATION AND ASSOCIATION OF BODY PHYSIQUE WITH NUTRITIONAL STATUS IN ADULT MISING POPULATION OF ASSAM

Nutsolu Lohe and Sudipta Ghosh

Abstract

The present study aims to determine the association between somatotype characteristics and nutritional status among the adult Mising males and females. A cross sectional sample of 250 adult Mising aged 18-40 years comprising of 125 males and 125 females were collected from two villages of Dhemaji district, Assam. In order to examine the nutritional status, body mass index (BMI) was calculated for each subject and categorized according to WHO classification. Further, anthropometric somatotyping was rated using Heath and Carter's method, to evaluate somatotype characteristics of adult Mising. It was observed that in somatotype characteristic mesomorphy dominates over the other two somatotype components in males, whereas mesomorphy and endomorphy were found to be co-dominant in females. The results of multivariate multiple regression analysis suggests gender as one of the most influential determinants ($p<0.001$) of all the three components of physique in both males and females. Further, age group significantly ($p<0.05$) influenced nutritional status and mesomorphic component of physique in adult Mising. Over all, Missing males were muscular, whereas Mising females were mostly muscular-fatty in their physique with both showing overweight and/ or obesity in their nutritional status.

Keywords: *Body Physique, Nutritional Status, Mising Population, Assam*

Introduction

In developing countries like India, which are typically known for high prevalence of under nutrition, significant proportions of overweight and obese now coexist with the undernourished (Popkin, 2002). Interestingly even Northeast India, which is mostly comprised of a number of tribal states accommodating hundreds of ethnically and genetically varied tribal populations, is no exception to this scenario. For example, over nutrition and obesity among tribal populations like Tankhul Naga (Mungreiphy, 2011), Ao Naga (Longkumer, 2013) and others have been reported by previous investigators. Thus, the metabolic syndromes and the resultant cardio-vascular diseases including overweight and obesity are one of the growing public health burdens in Northeast India (Gupta and Misra, 2007; Shah and Afzal, 2013; Zaman and Borang, 2014; Meshram et al., 2015). Rural-urban comparisons and migration studies indicate that effect of reduced levels of physical activity and the dietary changes that occur with effective urbanisation (Anjana et al., 2004; Das et al., 2008) could be few important reasons behind this.

Most of the tribal populations in India belong to low socio-economic status, where they need to put in lots of physical labour to sustain their livelihood. As a result, they are mostly muscular in their physique (Roy and Pal, 1997; Ghosh and Malik, 2010; Ghosh et al., 2017) and underweight in their nutritional status (Ghosh et al., 2017). Tribes living in the Northeast part of India also survive similar subsistence pattern. However, the geographical topography of this region is mostly hilly terrain and the climatic condition is cool and chilly in most of the states of this region. Consequently, tribes of this region are generally muscular-fatty (Ghosh and Dawhuo, 2016) in their physique and overweight and/or obese in their nutritional status (Longkumer, 2013; Ghosh and Dawhuo, 2016). Further, with the influence of urbanization and economic transition, many tribal populations with their traditional protein-fat rich dietary intake become susceptible to metabolic syndromes like obesity, which is known as 'epidemiological transition' (Yusuf et al., 2001). With this information, the present paper aims to examine the variations and association between anthropometric somatotype and nutritional status in adult Mising tribal population from Assam, Northeast India with special emphasis on the role of gender (if any) in such association.

Materials and Methods

A cross-sectional study of the body physique and nutritional status of the adult Mising was conducted in two villages of Dhemaji district, Assam. A sample of 250 adult Mising age ranged between 18-40 years, comprising of 125 males and 125 females was collected. Careful selection was done to include only those subjects who are apparently normal and healthy. Anthropometric measurements were taken on the right side of the subject and measurement of bone diameter, girth measurement and skin-fold measurement were taken on the left side of the subject. With the help of structured schedule, data on socio-economic profile such as occupation, education, health related activities such as smoking, drinking and chewing tobacco, work related physical activities and self reported morbidity pattern were also collected.

Anthropometric somatotyping

In accordance with internationally accepted standards ten body measurements were taken on each subject (Martin and Saller, 1957 ; Heath and Carter, 1967; Tanner et al., 1969). These were: 1) Height vertex; 2) Body weight, 3) Bicondylar humerus, 4) Bicondylar femur, 5) Mid upper arm circumference, 6) Calf circumference, 7) Skinfold at triceps, 8) Skinfold at subscapula, 9) Skinfold at suprailliac and 10) Skinfold at calf. Anthropometric measurements were taken following standardised protocols and all the measurements were taken using anthropometric Rod and Sliding Caliper. Circumferences were measured with the help of Steel Tape. All the skinfold measurements were taken on the left side of the subject, following Tanner (1969). Skinfold measurement in the present study was taken with the Holtain skinfold caliper in mm, with the dial marked in division of 0.2 mm.

Anthropometric somatotyping was calculated using Heath and Carter's method (1967). Three somatotype components, i.e. Endomorphy, Mesomorphy and Ectomorphy were then plotted on somatocharts, after calculating 'X' and 'Y'. Individual somatotypes of Mising adults were classified into thirteen categories following Carter (2002). A One-way Analysis of Variance (ANOVA) was computed to examine the association between the somatotype components and body mass index (BMI).

Body mass index (BMI)

In order to assess nutritional status, anthropometric measurements like height and weight were taken on each participant following internationally accepted standards (Martin and Saller, 1957). BMI was calculated by the formula, body mass (kg)/stature (m^2).

The World Health Organisation (WHO) regional office for Western Pacific Region, along with the International Association for the study of Obesity (IASO) and the International Task Force (IOTF), has recommended a BMI of 23.0 kg/m^2 as the cut-off point for defining overweight in Asian populations. This BMI classification was used in the present study. Chi-square test was calculated to analyse age and sex differences in nutritional status. In addition, T-test was computed to examine sex difference in anthropometric measures, anthropometric somatotype and BMI.

All the statistical computations were done using SPSS 15.0 for Windows. Multivariate multiple regression analysis was used to assess the effect of selected socio-demographic factors on somatotype characteristics and BMI for Mising adults.

Results

Background information in terms of descriptive statistics of anthropometric measurements showed significantly higher values in males ($p<0.001$), except for skinfold thicknesses that are significantly greater ($p<0.001$) in females (Table 1). Interestingly, no sex difference ($p=0.402$) was observed in the nutritional status, where both male and female Mising were normal (Table 1).

Table 1. Comparative differences in anthropometric features and body composition variables between adult Mising males and females

Mising	Males (N=125)		Females(N=125)		T-test	
Variable	Mean	SD	Mean	SD	t	p-value
Age (yr.)	28.17	6.83	28.01	6.80	0.19	0.853
Height vertex (cm)	162.47	6.00	151.82	5.21	14.99	<0.001
Body weight (kg)	58.66	8.92	50.50	7.76	7.72	<0.001
Bicondylarhumerus (cm)	6.77	0.58	5.82	0.43	14.70	<0.001
Bicondylarfemur (cm)	8.92	0.64	8.01	0.69	10.82	<0.001
Skinfold at triceps (mm)	6.17	2.79	9.26	3.82	-7.32	<0.001
Skinfold at sub-scapular (mm)	10.80	5.58	12.25	4.51	-2.26	0.025
Skinfold at supra-iliac (mm)	7.53	4.58	10.82	4.50	-5.74	<0.001
Skinfold at calf (mm)	6.56	3.60	11.11	3.94	-9.54	<0.001
Mid-upper arm circumference(cm)	25.01	1.97	23.77	2.38	4.49	<0.001

Mid- calf circumference(cm)	32.66	2.79	31.07	2.56	4.67	<0.001
Body mass Index (kg/m²)	22.17	2.75	21.87	2.86	0.84	0.402
Endomorphy	2.41	1.28	3.52	1.24	-6.98	<0.001
Mesomorphy	4.14	0.93	3.53	0.98	5.06	<0.001
Ectomorphy	2.20	1.12	1.75	1.09	3.29	0.001

In somatotype characteristics Mising males were found to be predominately mesomorphic over endomorphic and ectomorphic components, which were found to be co-dominant (Table 1). On the other hand, females showed co-dominance of both mesomorphic and endomorphic components of physique over ectomorphy (Figure 1).Dominance of the mesomorphic component among Mising was also apparent from the somatochart (Figure 2). Distribution of Mising in various somatotype categories indicated a substantial concentration around mesomorphic components, irrespective of sex difference (Table 2). A considerable percentage of Mising males (29%) and females (34%) were found to be Endomorphic-Mesomorph. This indicates towards a fatty-muscular type of physique in both males and females (Figure 3).

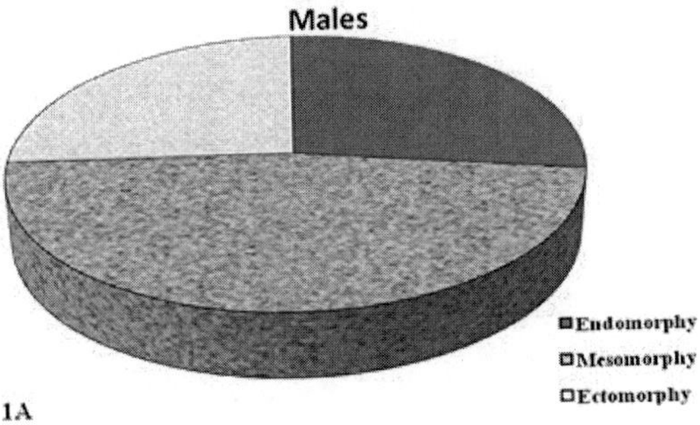

1A

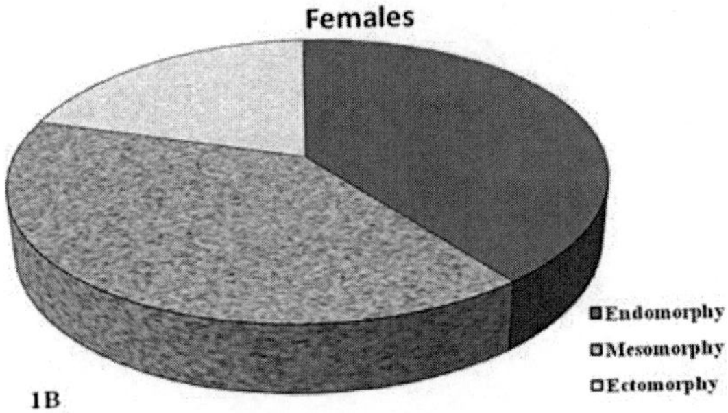

1B

Figure 1. Somatotype components among adult Mising males (1A) and females (1B)

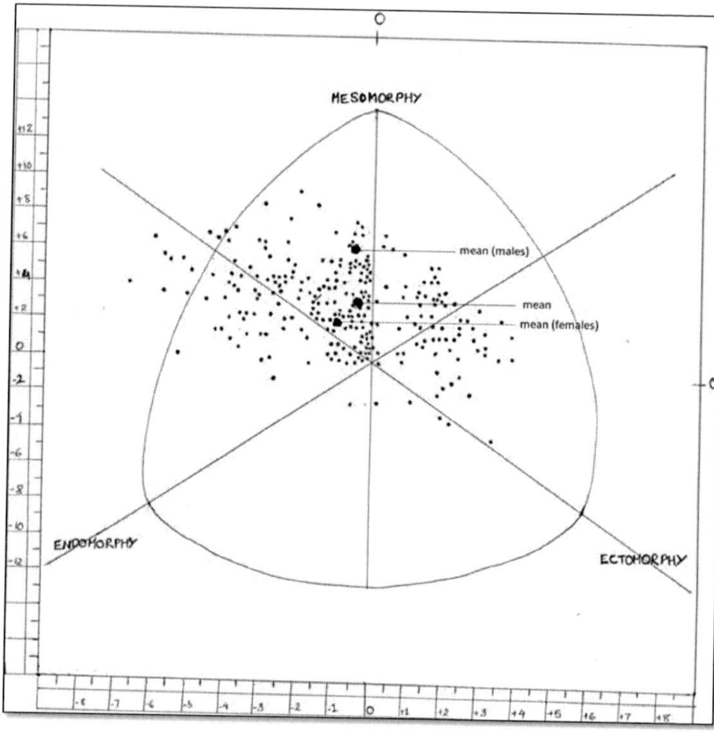

Figure 2. Somatochart of the adult Mising males and females

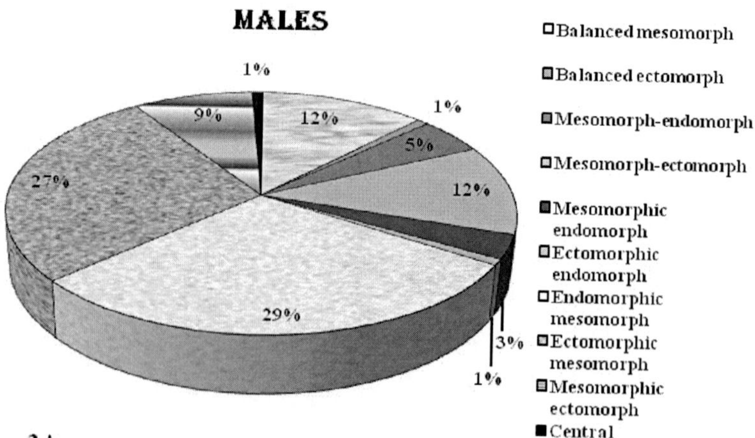

3A

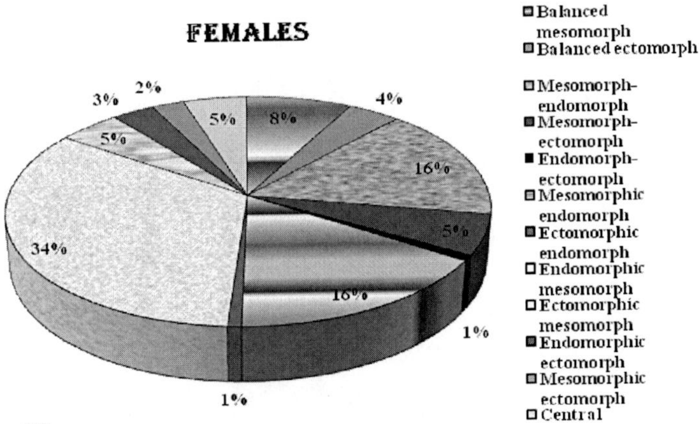

3B

Figure 3. Occurrence of various somatotype categories in Mising males (3A) and females (3B)

Table 2. Comparative differences in somatotype categories between adult Mising males and females

Somatotype category	Males		Females	
	Frequency	Percentage	Frequency	Percentage
Balanced mesomorph	15	12.00	10	8.00
Balanced ectomorph	1	0.80	5	4.00
Mesomorph-endomorph	6	4.80	20	16.00
Mesomorph-ectomorph	15	12.00	7	5.60
Endomorph-ectomorph	0	0.00	1	0.80
Mesomorphic endomorph	4	3.20	20	16.00
Ectomorphic endomorph	1	0.80	1	0.80
Endomorphic mesomorph	37	29.60	42	33.60
Ectomorphic mesomorph	34	27.20	6	4.80
Endomorphic ectomorph	0	0.00	4	3.20
Mesomorphic ectomorph	11	8.80	3	2.40
Central	1	0.80	6	4.80
Total	125	100.00	125	100.00

Table 3. Nutritional status amongst the adult Mising, by age group and sex

	Younger Adult (18-26 yrs.)						Older Adult (27-40 yrs.)					
BMI Categories	Males		Females		Total		Males		Females		Total	
	N	%	N	%	N	%	N	%	N	%	N	%
Underweight	2	3.23	5	7.81	7	5.56	4	6.35	6	9.84	10	8.06
Normal weight	39	62.90	44	68.75	83	65.87	34	53.97	31	50.82	65	52.42
Overweight	18	29.03	5	7.81	23	18.25	11	17.46	14	22.95	25	20.16
Obesity	3	4.84	10	15.63	13	10.32	14	22.22	10	16.39	24	19.35
Total	62	100.00	64	100.00	126	100.00	63	100.00	61	100.00	124	100.00
χ^2 Test (Sex difference)	12.68						1.53					
p-value	0.0054						0.6746					

Nutritional status, as evaluated from body mass index (BMI), suggested that a high percentage of Mising were found to be overweight and/or obese despite the fact whether they were young adults, i.e.18-26 years (28.6%) or older adults, i.e. 27-40 years (39.5%) (Table 3). Interestingly, significant sex difference was observed in the nutritional status of the younger adults (p=0.0054) but not the older adults (p=0.6746), suggesting that with the advancement of aging both males and females tend to become overweight and/or obese in this population (Table 3). On the other side, age difference was found to be apparent in males (p=0.020) than in females (p=0.088), mainly because a good percentage of young adult males are overweight as compared to their counterpart females (Figure 4).

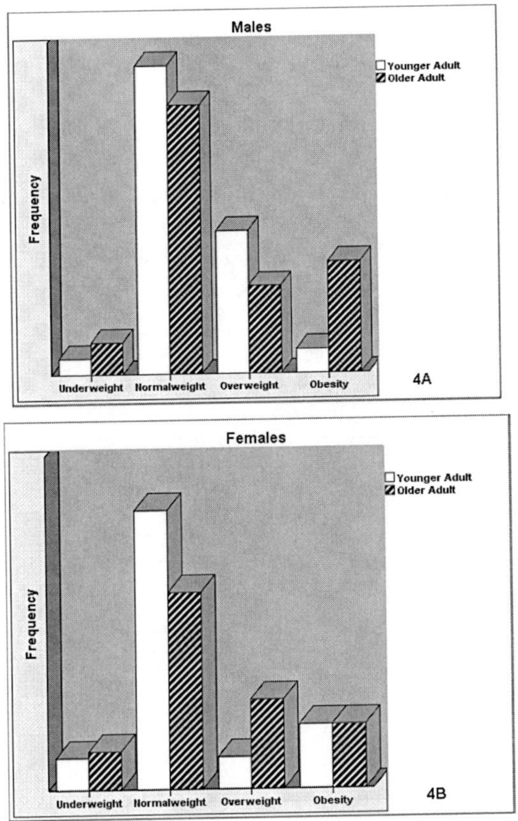

(χ^2 test (Age difference): Males: 9.809 (p-value: 0.020); Females: 6.539 (p-value: 0.088)

Figure 4. *Nutritional status amongst the adult Mising males (4A) and females (4B), by age group*

Table 4 displayed the relation between nutritional status and somatotype components in Mising adults. Significant ($p<0.001$) association was noticed between nutritional status and all the three somatotype components, further confirming the fact that nutritional status indeed influence and shape the body physique of an individual. Considerably greater endomorphic and mesomorphic with negligible ectomorphic components of physique were found in overweight and/or obese Mising, irrespective of the sex (Table 4).Further it was found that overweight and/or obese Mising showed greater mesomorphic component over endomorphic component, especially in males. This is perhaps in contradiction with the general notion that overweight and obese people should be fattier or endomorphic in their somatotype components. Our results suggest that on average adult Mising possess higher muscle mass and less fat mass, at least in males. Consequently, when they show high BMI that is due to the possession of higher fat-free mass. This is possible mainly because BMI depicts both fat-mass and fat-free mass (Durnin and Womersley, 1974).

Table 4. Somatotype characteristics (mean±SD) according to nutritional status in Mising males and females

BMI Categories§	Endomorphy	Mesomorphy	Ectomorphy
Males			
Underweight (6)	1.11±0.12	3.31±0.46	4.29±0.43
Normal weight (73)	1.81±0.61	3.81±0.81	2.74±0.71
Overweight (29)	3.05±1.14	4.52±0.74	1.39±0.37
Obesity (17)	4.35±1.31	5.21±0.70	0.56±0.38
ANOVA	49.86(p<0.001)	20.29(p<0.001)	102.60(p<0.001)
Females			
Underweight (11)	2.42±0.41	2.50±0.80	3.84±0.60
Normal weight (75)	3.03±0.85	3.29±0.76	2.05±0.60
Overweight (19)	4.48±1.05	4.16±0.86	0.89±0.37
Obesity (20)	5.06±1.01	4.38±0.96	0.27±0.21
ANOVA	41.44(p<0.001)	19.21(p<0.001)	135.63(p<0.001)

§ Number of subjects in each category is given in parenthesis

Table 5. Main results of multivariate multiple regression analysis of endomorphy, mesomorphy, ectomorphy and BMI variation in adult Mising population. Effects of variables: General model including all tested variables and most parsimonious model including only statistically significant parameter estimates (β coefficientand p-values* for each variable with multiple R^2)

Dependent variables	Confounding Variables	General model (GM)		Most parsimonious model (MP)	
		β coefficient	p-values	β coefficient	p-values
Endomorphy	Age group Young vs. Old	0.363931	0.034515		
	Sex Male vs. Female	1.318944	0.000000	1.140968	0.000000
	Income	0.000020	0.079787	0.000022	0.051647
	Physical activity Light vs. Heavy	-0.586392	0.245930		
	Occupation	-0.187632	0.258554		
	Morbidity pattern	-0.066761	0.746770		
	Drinking habit	-0.179656	0.307231		
Multiple R^2		19.4%		18.5%	
Mesomorphy	Age group Young vs. Old	0.355357	0.006399	0.310578	0.010598
	Sex Male vs. Female	-0.584204	0.001260	-0.597501	0.000001
	Income	0.000007	0.430396		
	Physical activity Light vs. Heavy	-0.111869	0.769007		
	Occupation	-0.069620	0.578206		
	Morbidity pattern	0.043816	0.778860		
	Drinking habit	-0.242443	0.068549		
Multiple R^2		13.1%		11.8%	
Ectomorphy	Age group Young vs. Old	-0.244927	0.106173		
	Sex Male vs. Female	-0.664783	0.001684	-0.469290	0.000930
	Income	-0.000005	0.609878		
	Physical activity Light vs. Heavy	0.602298	0.176990		
	Occupation	0.187929	0.199817		
	Morbidity pattern	0.132646	0.467330		
	Drinking habit	0.112508	0.468387		
Multiple R^2		6.2%		5.0%	
Body mass index (Nutritional status)	Age group Young vs. Old	0.837657	0.029359	0.750990	0.043474
	Sex Male vs. Female	0.223931	0.672751		
	Income	0.000022	0.391593		
	Physical activity Light vs. Heavy	-1.639496	0.144540		
	Occupation	-0.448116	0.225164		
	Morbidity pattern	-0.304866	0.509662		
	Drinking habit	-0.313204	0.425690		
Multiple R^2		3.4%		1.9%	

* Significant p values are highlighted in bold

The results of multivariate multiple regression (MMR) analysis of selected socio-demographic confounders on somatotype components and nutritional status is presented in Table 5. The variation of somatotype components and nutritional status that can be explained through these predictor variables were 19.4% in endomorphy, 13.1% in mesomorphy, 6.2% in ectomorphy and 3.4% in BMI. Income ($p<0.05$) and gender ($p<0.001$) found to be the most crucial confounding factors of endomorphic component of somatotype, which explains 18.5% of the total variation in endomorphy, as evident from the most parsimonious model (MPM). Similarly, gender was found to be an influential determinant($p<0.001$) in both mesomorphic and ectomorphic components of physique in Mising population, where females showed lesser rating of these two components than males, as evident from the significant yet negative β coefficient values. On the other hand age group, i.e. being young or old, significantly ($p<0.05$) impacted the nutritional status and mesomorphic component of physique in adult Mising (Table 5).

Discussion

The present paper is one of the very few researches that have aimed to understand the association between nutritional status and body composition in terms of somatotype components. In addition, the paper emphasises on if such association is gender specific or common across genders. In line with the broader literature, significant ($p<0.001$) gender differences were evident in all the anthropometric measurements and somatotype components, except for the nutritional status ($p=0.402$).

Mising males were predominantly mesomorphic in their physique. One of the important factors behind this could be physical hard work, necessary for survival in harsh conditions. Mising people use primitive technology for cultivation in a land that requires more physical labour than cultivation with modern technology. As a consequence, these compel them to do a lot of physical hard work to sustain their livelihood, resulting into muscular body physique, as also reported by the author elsewhere (Ghosh and Malik, 2010; Ghosh et al., 2017).On the other hand, endomorphic and mesomorphic components were found to be co-dominantly present in Mising females. The reason for such physique of Mising females indicates toward their more sedentary life than their counterpart males. For example, it was observed during data collection that almost all the females generally engaged themselves all through the day in weaving other than household chores. In fact, Mising females are well known for their weaving skills. They do not buy clothes from the market instead weave all the clothes for the entire family at home.

Our results have revealed significant body size and shape differences between Mising males and females, except for their nutritional status where both showed tendency to develop overweight and obesity with age. High percentages of overweight and obese individuals in this community, irrespective of their sex could be because of their high consumption of fat and protein. Mising are known for their voracious pork consumption, where their daily diet is generally comprised of pork meat and pork fat. As a consequence, despite their requirement to put in a lot of physical labor everyday due to their practice of primitive technology based agriculture, they tend to develop obesity after 27-30 years of their age.

It is perhaps interesting to observe here that numerous populations, e.g. Santhal, Oraon, Bhoi and Mising, that are all engaged in similar primitive technology based agriculture, develop muscular body structure and hence a predominance of mesomorphic component in physique, irrespective of their different ethnic and/or genetic background (Roy and Pal, 1997; Ghosh and Malik, 2010; Ghosh and Dawhuo, 2016; Ghosh et al., 2017). Thus, predominance of mesomorphic component in one's physique can be considered as a universal phenomenon in response to a hard and laborious lifestyle that requires severe physical activity, irrespective of one's ethnic and/or genetic background, as reported by the author elsewhere (Ghosh et al., 2017). Hence, micro-evolutionary forces like natural selection might have played an imperative role in the protection of predominantly muscular physique amongst geographically and ethnically diverse populations as a process of adaptation to similar harsh and laborious environments during the course of evolution.

On the other side, development of other two somatotype components and the degree of fat accumulation in these tribal populations varies, perhaps due to the differences in their climatic condition and dietary intake. For example, Santhal live under hot and dry climatic condition, where larger body surface area with little fat in the body is more adaptive for efficient heat dissipation. As a result, they have greater ectomorphic component over endomorphic component. Moreover, they normally have a dietary intake with very less consumption of protein and/or fat, which led them to develop a nutritional status that is mostly underweight and almost never obese (Ghosh, 2017). On the other hand, Mising and Bhoi populations live under comparatively cooler climatic conditions, which have compelled them to develop greater endomorphic component over ectomorphic component in their physique as a better adaptive strategy. Further, probably because of such environmental conditions, they generally have a protein and fat rich daily dietary intake, more so in case of the Mising. Resultantly, they have a nutritional status with higher percentages of overweight and obese individuals in their communities.

Conclusion

To conclude, we observed that Mising males are muscular built, whereas Mising females are muscular-fatty built as their adaptive mechanism to cope with their subsistence pattern. Gender is one of the most crucial determining factors of their physique, while age is the most important parameter to influence the nutritional status of this population. Overall, subsistence pattern influences body composition or physique of an individual much in a similar pattern across ethnically and genetically diverse populations. However, nutritional status is directly impacted by the dietary intake of the individuals, irrespective of their subsistence pattern.

Acknowledgements

We gratefully acknowledge the Mising participants for this investigation. Our sincere thanks to the Headman and all the people of Borola and Uriamguri villages, for their co-operation, hospitability and willingness to help, without which, the present study would have been impossible.

This work was funded by the Department of Anthropology, North-Eastern Hill University, Shillong.

References

Anjana M, Sandeep S, Deepa R, Vimaleswaran KS, Farooq S, Mohan V. 2004. Visceral and central abdominal fat and anthropometry in relation to diabetes in Asian Indians. *Diabetes Care*. 27: 2948-2953.

Carter JEL. 2002. *The Heath–Carter anthropometric somatotype:instructions manual*. USA.

Das M, Pal S. Ghosh A. 2008. Rural urban differences of cardiovascular disease risk factors in adult Asian Indians. *American Journal of Human Biology*. 20: 440-445.

Durnin JVGA, Womersley J. 1974. Body fat assessed from total body density and its estimation from skinfold thickness: measurements on 481 men and women aged from 62 to 72 years. *British Journal of Nutrition*. 32: 77-97.

Ghosh S, Dawhuo T. 2016. *Somatotype Components and Body Mass Index: A case study of the adult Bhoi males*: In Khongsdier R, Sarthak S. (eds.). People of North East India : Bio-cultural Dimensions, pp. 135-147.

Ghosh S, Malik SL. 2010. Variations of body physique in Santhals:an Indian tribe. *Collegium Antropolegicum*. 34: 467-472.

Ghosh S, Dosaev T, Prakash J, Livshits G. 2017. Quantitative genetic analysis of the body composition and blood pressure association in two ethnically diverse populations. *American Journal of Physical Anthropology*. 162: 701–714.

Gupta R, Misra A. 2007. Type 2 diabetes in India: regional disparities. *The British Journal of Diabetes and Vascular Disease*. 7: 12-16.

Heath BH, Carter JEL. 1967. A modified somatotype method. *American Journal of Physical Anthropology*. 27: 57-74.

Longkumer T. 2013. Physical growth and nutritional status among Ao Naga children of Nagaland, Northeast India. *Journal of Anthropology*. Article ID 291239.

Martin R, Saller K. 1957. *Lerbuch der Athropologie*. Stuttgart. Gustav Fischer Verlag.

Meshram II, Rao MVV, Rao VS, Laxmaiah A, Polasa K. 2016. Regional variation in the prevalence of overweight/obesity, hypertension and diabetes and their correlates among the adult rural population in India. *British Journal of Nutrition*. 115: 1265-1272.

Mungreiphy NK, Kapoor S, Sinha R. 2011. Association between BMI, blood pressure, and age: study among Tangkhul Naga tribal males of Northeast India. *Journal of Anthropology*. Article ID 748147.

Popkin BM, Monteiro C, Wang Y. 2002. Trends of obesity and underweight in older children and adolescents in the United States, Brazil, China, and Russia. *The American Journal of Clinical Nutrition*. 75: 971-977.

Roy SK, Pal B. 1997. Comparison of somatotype of Oraon occupational groups of Jalpaiguri district, Northern West Bengal. *Journal of Human Ecology*. 8: 179-183.

Shah A, Afzal M. 2013. Prevalence of diabetes and hypertension and association with various risk factors among different Muslim populations of Manipur, India. *Journal of Diabetes and Metabolic Disorders*. 12: 52.

Tanner JM, Hiernaux J, Jarnan S. 1969. *Growth and physique studies*. In: Weiner JS and Lourie JA (eds.), Human Biology- A Guide to Field Methods. Oxford: Blackwell Scientific Publication, pp. 315-340.

Yusuf S, Reddy S, Ounpuu S, Anand S. 2001. Global burden of cardiovascular diseases: part I: general considerations, the epidemiologic transition, risk factors, and impact of urbanization. *Circulation*.104: 2746-2753.

Zaman FA, Borang A. 2014. Prevalence of diabetes mellitus amongst rural hilly population of North Eastern India and its relationship with associated risk factors and related co-morbidities. *Journal of Natural Science, Biology and Medicine*. 5: 383.

Chapter Twenty

NUTRITIONAL STATUS AND AGE AT MENARCHE OF CHAKMA TRIBAL GIRLS OF TRIPURA, NORTHEAST INDIA

SHILPI SAHA, SATYAPRIYA ROY AND SAMIR KUMAR SIL

ABSTRACT

Background: Menarche is the first onset of menstrual bleeding and considered as an indicator of attaining reproductive maturity in girls. Various factors may influence age at menarche such as genetic, nutritional status, environment, socio-economic status and education. The main objective of this study is to determine mean age at menarche and whatever nutritional status affects it.Method: This cross sectional study was carried out on 591 school going Chakma tribal girls aged 10-18 years from North, Unokoti, Dhalai and South District of Tripura. The subjects were selected using stratified multistage clustered random sampling method. Data on age at menarche have been collected by using retrospective method of recall from adolescent Chakma girls of different schools of Tripura. To study the effect of nutrition on age at menarche, different anthropometric measurements like height, weight, triceps and subscapular skinfold were recorded. The body mass index (BMI) was also calculated. The measurements were used to estimate percent body fat (PBF) and fat-free mass (FFM) from skinfold thickness. Result: Among studied sample 382 girls had experienced menarche, their mean age at menarche is 12.30 year (1.66). At age 10 mean height of premenarche girls is 133.27 cm, postmenarcheal girls is 142.53 cm. From 13 to 18 years of age BMI had increased gradually where overall increase was found (4.3 kg/m^2)

from 10 to 18 years which is statistically significant with age (p<0.001). Percent body fat is also statistically significant with age (p<0.001). The mean age at menarche of study population was also influenced by their socio-economic and demographic condition. Conclusion: Nutritional status is better in postmenarcheal girls than premenarcheal girls. Socio-economic condition and family size had influence age at menarche. This study characterizes typical differential rates of positive change in different measurements of body composition after attaining menarche.

Keywords: *Nutritional status, menarche, percent body fat, Chakma girls, Tripura*

INTRODUCTION

Menarche is the first onset of menstrual bleeding and considered as an indicator of attaining reproductive maturity in girls. It is considers as one of the distinct milestones in women's lives. Various factors may affect age at menarche like nutritional status, environmental condition, socio-economic status, diet, sibling-ship, genetics, physical activity and level of education (Gaudineau et al., 2010). Physical growth and nutritional status in adolescents are greatly influenced by the process of sexual maturation and hence cannot be exactly assess without information of the level of sexual maturation (Sizonenko and Himes, 1993). Though nutrition influences growth, development and maturation during infancy, childhood and adolescence but at the period of adolescence nutrients requirements are the highest (Heitmann, 1990). Research showed that girls with malnutrition would experience menarche delay in compared to girls with good nutritional condition (Lifshitz et al., 1993). The main reason of such delay is due to insufficient intake of proteins, calories, fats and other nutrients required for the synthesis of gonadotropin hormone. The energy needs for the girls of age between 10-12 years were 2050 kcal, while those who were age between 13-15 years old requires 2350 kcal. Adolescent girls comprise a vulnerable group, mainly in India where female child is neglected one. In female menarche is a part of intricate process of growing up. Anthropometry is a sensitive indicator for health, physical growth and development in children and adolescent so it has been used in many contexts associated with nutritional status (Chumlea et al., 2003). The age of onset of menarche varies from 9 to 18 years with the average age in USA being about 12.8 years, whereas in India it is lower to some extent and has been reported to be around 12 years (Chumlea et al., 2003; Khadilkar et al., 2006). Some studies in North East India have been reported varying mean age at menarche in different population variation (Saha and Sil, 2015; Deb, 2011, 2009; Das and Das, 1967) and in different parts of India, ranging from 12.3 years in Bengali girls (Banerjee et al., 2007) to 15.4 years in lower socio-economic group of western India (Rao et al., 1998). Though age at menarche has been reported in many Indian subpopulations, but no information is available on the Chakma tribal population of Tripura.

Materials and Methods

This cross-sectional study was carried out among 591 school going rural Chakma tribal girls aged 10 to 18 years residing in North, Dhalai, Unokoti and South districts of Tripura. Tripura is one of the Northeast states of India which is the main homeland of 19 different tribes. Geographically, it locates between 22°56′ and 24°32′, North longitude and between 91°10′ and 92°21′, East longitude with a total area of 10,491 Sq.km. According to 2011 census, in Tripura, out of the territories' total population of 36,71,032, Scheduled tribes numbered 11,66,813, which constitute 31.78 percent of the total population. The subjects were chosen from rural areas (villages) of the state of Tripura, which is the habitat of the Chakma tribal people. The school going Chakma girls were selected using a stratified multistage clustered random sampling method. Initially 605 Chakma girls aged 10-18 years were identified and approached to participate in the study. The age of each subject was recorded from their birth certificates and school register. Mothers of every child were included as respondents. Apart from the different anthropometric measurements of children, information on various factors that directly or indirectly affect the nutritional outcome was also obtained. A semi-structured questionnaire was prepared which included some baseline information of the children and their parents in regard to nutrition. The questionnaire was finalized by pretest and discussion prior to beginning of the study. All the data were collected after receiving the consent from school authorities and their parents. Decimal age calendar is mainly used to find out the student's decimal age by subtracting the date of birth from the date of data collected. The subjects in different age groups were classified by following the same principle. Children who had undergone any major surgical operation or suffering from any systemic disease were excluded from the study. Of these 605 Chakma tribal girls, 14 of them were excluded from the study as their birth certificate were either not valid or they were not belongs to the age group 10-18 years. This study was carried out in accordance with the ethical guidelines for human experiments, as laid down by the Helsinki Declaration of 2000 (Touitou et al., 2004). The data were collected during the period from August 2018 through April 2019. Other general information regarding their socio-economic and demographic condition, parent's education and occupation, family income, size, structure and property etc., was also recorded. According to the modified Kuppusswamy scale, the socio-economic status of all the Chakma girls was low (Mishra and Singh, 2003).

The anthropometric measurements like standing height, body weight, triceps skinfold thickness (TRSF) and subscapular skinfold thickness (SBSF) of each girl were measured using standard technique (Weiner and Lourie, 1969). Standing height was measured by an anthropometer rod (GPM Swiss made) with the head held in the Frankfort horizontal plane and recorded to the nearest 0.1 cm. Body weight of the subject, with bare feet and wearing minimum clothing, was taken in the early morning (empty stomach) using a portable weighing machine (Libra) to the nearest 0.5 kg. Body mass index (BMI) was calculated by dividing body weight with standing height (kg/m^2). Skinfold thickness was measured using the Holtain skinfold caliper with a constant spring pressure of 10 g mm^{-2} on the right side of the body. Mean of the three measurements in single location was accepted. The intra-observer technical error of measurement (TEM) was also calculated to determine the accuracy of the anthropometric measurements. Double measurements from the same number of subjects (n = 10) had been taken by the same measurer (SS) with six hours of difference. The corresponding calculated values of intra observer showed that, all the anthropometric measurements were within the normal range of errors reported in literatures (Uijaszek and Kerr, 1999; Frisancho, 1990; Malina,1987). Skinfold equation for estimating percentage of body fat (%BF) of Chakma tribal girls was used from the method developed by Slaughter et al. (1988) by using multicomponent model reference measures. This equation uses the sum of triceps and subscapular skinfold thickness (mm) to predict body fat.

$$\%\text{Body fat} = 1.33(\text{TRSF} + \text{SBSF}) - 0.013(\text{TRSF} + \text{SBSF})^2 - 2.5$$

$$\text{Fat mass (kg)} = \text{Body weight (kg)} \times \%\text{BF}/100$$

Fat-free mass (FFM) was calculated by subtracting fat mass (FM) from weight. FM and FFM each were then divided by height-squared to generate the fat-mass index (FMI) and fat free mass index (FFMI), respectively. Pearson's correlation coefficient was used to evaluate the relationship between the anthropometric variables and menarcheal age. An effect of socio-economic condition on age at menarche was calculated by using Cox's proportional hazards regression model (Cox, 1972). Descriptive statistics and ANOVA has been used to calculate the level of significance. The statistical analysis was performed using Microsoft excel 2007 and statistical package for social science (SPSS 17.0) software.

Results

The present study had shown age wise variation in different anthropometric variable from10-18 years of age in adolescence period i.e. highest growing stage and entering into puberty, girls experience menarche at this stage. This study shows that girls with high BMI experience early menarche. Body fat calculated from skinfolds gives a direct estimate of body fat mass (Pramanik et al., 2014) especially on children and adolescents (Sharma and Mondal, 2018) and may be used in field studies. In this cross-sectional study it was shown that girls with higher body mass and body fat mass experience early onset of menarche than the other girls prior to menarche or whether these differences were constituted partially or completely after menarche. The retrospective data on age at menarche are available from 382 Chakma girls. Accordingly, age distribution with frequencies and percentage of the menstruating girls derived from this data set are shown in Table 1. Mean age at menarche, calculated from the retrospective data is found to be in the order of 12.30 year ± 0.50 with the standard deviation of 1.66 year. Table 2 shows age wise change in Body Mass index and percent body fat. In this study 10.65 % of Body Fat is increasing with age advancement. In one way ANOVA result indicate body mass Index increased progressively from 13 years to 18 years of age where overall increase was (4.3 kg/m^2) from 10 to 18 years which is statistically significant ($p<0.001$).

Table 1. Age distribution of menarcheal status of Chakma girls of Tripura (Retrospective data)

Age range(Years)	Frequency	% of menstruating girls	CumulativePercentage
9.6-10.0	13	3.40	3.4
10.1-10.5	14	3.66	7.06
10.6-11.0	20	5.24	12.3
11.1-11.5	42	10.99	23.29
11.6-12.0	68	19.11	42.4
12.1-12.5	102	25.39	67.79
12.6-13.0	63	16.49	84.28
13.1-13.5	30	7.85	92.14
13.6-14.0	17	4.45	96.59
14.1-14.5	8	2.09	98.69
14.6-15.0	5	1.31	100
Total	382	100	

Table 2. Age specific increase in Anthropometric variables of Adolescents

Variable	10 years	11 years	12 years	13 years	14 years	15 years	16 years	17 years	18 years	p
	Mean Sd	Mean Sd	Mean Sd	Mean Sd	Mean Sd	Mean Sd	Mean Sd	Mean Sd	Mean Sd	
BMI (kg/m^2)	16.4 1.74	17.53 1.62	17.69 1.47	18.03 1.84	18.95 1.65	19.82 1.46	20.39 1.01	20.57 1.07	20.7 1.57	*
Percent body fat	15.21 3.74	16.32 3.46	18.39 2.56	19.42 4.13	20.89 3.66	23.11 3.46	24.5 3	25.38 2.19	25.86 2.74	*
Significant difference p<0.001										

Table 3 represents age wise comparison of premenarcheal and postmenarcheal anthropometric characters of Chakma tribal girls. It has shown that postmenarcheal girls were significantly higher anthropometric variables (height, weight and BMI) than premenarcheal girls. Correlation studies show mean age at menarche were highly correlated ($p < 0.01$) with percent body fat, fat mass and fat free mass (Table 4).

Table 3.Age wise comparison of anthropometric variables between premenarcheal and postmenarcheal Chakma girls of Tripura

	Height (cm)			Weight (kg)			BMI (kg/m^2)		
Age	Pre-menarche	Post-menarche	p	Pre-menarche	Post-menarche	p	**Pre-menarche**	**Post-menarche**	**p**
10	133.27 (4.85)	142.53 (2.51)	0.01	28.94 (4.20)	42.22 (4.45)	*	16.23 (1.54)	20.76 (1.46)	*
11	136.18 (5.75)	144.67 (3.30)	*	31.54 (3.74)	40.95 (2.94)	*	16.96 (1.21)	19.57 (1.35)	*
12	138.24 (4.60)	148.05 (3.82)	*	32.33 (2.91)	40.73 (4.08)	*	16.90 (1.07)	18.55 (1.39)	*
13	143.24 (6.51)	149.63 (6.71)	0.005	32.47 (1.99)	41.83 (4.98)	*	15.86 (1.04)	18.65 (1.55)	*
14	144.25 (5.02)	154.18 (6.11)	0.008	33.50 (1.01)	45.52 (5.24)	*	16.12 (0.64)	19.12 (1.55)	0.002

Significant difference $p<0.001$

Table 4. Pearson's correlation between anthropometric measurements of tribal girls of Tripura

Variables	Mean age at menarche	Percent body fat (%)	Fat Mass (Kg)	Fat free mass (kg)	Fat mass index (kg/ sqm)	Fat free mass index (kg/sqm)
Mean age at menarche	-	0.993	0.99	0.963	0.992	0.919
Percent body fat (%)	0.993	-	0.998	0.979	0.999	0.931
Fat Mass (Kg)	0.99	0.99	-	0.982	0.999	0.94
Fat free mass (kg)	0.963	0.979	0.982	-	0.976	0.959
Fat mass index (kg/sqm)	0.992	0.999	0.999	0.976	-	0.94
Fat free mass index (kg/sqm)	0.919	0.931	0.94	0.992	0.94	-
Significant at $p < 0.01$ level						

In respect of recall data, the effects of socio-economic factors have been investigated through Cox's proportional hazards regression model (Cox, 1972), after excluding the cases when the date has not been recalled or only a range of data has been recalled (i.e., retaining only those cases where menarche has not occurred or the exact date of menarche has been recalled). The statistical significance of the binary variable described in Table 5, taken one at a time along with age as predictors in the Cox regression model for age at menarche, is examined [FSH-1 if father has passed higher secondary and above and 0 for others, MHS-1 mother has passed higher secondary and above and 0 for others, FMWR- if father is manual worker and 0 for others, Affluent-1 if per capita monthly family expenditure is >5000 and above (INR) and 0 for <5000 (INR), Small family-1 if family size is ≤3 and 0 for others, Sibling-1 if the number of sib is ≤1 and 0 for others, Parity-1 if first born and 0 for others].

Table 5. Effects of different socio-economic factors on age at menarche of Chakma tribal girls of Tripura

Socio-economic variables	**Estimated multiplier for baseline hazard of menarche (with standard error of regression coefficient)**	***p*-value**
FSH	exp[-0.12340*FSH]- 0.95408	0.897
MSH	exp[1.53054*MSH]- 0.61806	*
FMWR	exp[0.58191*FMWR]- 0.11318	*
Affluent	exp[-0.27597*Affluent]- 0.83310	0.740
Sibling	exp[0.34980*Sibling]- 0.16888	*
Parity	exp[-0.05572 *Parity]- 0.09864	0.572

*p value <0.05

This study shows none of these variables was significant when more than one of them was included in the model. It shows that mothers' education, fathers' occupation and size of sibship was significant at 5 % level. Further, girls having mother at least secondary level, fathers' are manual worker and having no sibling are more likely to have earlier onset of menarche than others.

Discussion

This is the first time such type of study has been carried out and reported from the state of Tripura. For the past 50 years, the mean age at menarche in different Indian populations has varied from 11.5 years to 15.2 years. (Arora et al., 1989; Singh 1986; Sengupta et al., 1996; Banerjee et al., 2007). The first menstrual period or age at menarche is an important maturity indicator for assessing the developmental stage of pubertal female (Rokade and Mane, 2009). More subcutaneous fat and high BMI of a pre-pubertal age (5-9 years) are associated with an increased possibility of early menarche (>11 years) (Freedman et al., 2002). At present it is found that age specific mean value of anthropometric variables are increasing which shows growth spurt in adolescence stage. After age 12 years BMI had gradually increased with mean age at menarche which was influenced by height and weight. Although BMI was increased progressively from age 13 years to 18 years, but overall BMI was rising by age (4.3 kg/m^2) in between 10 to 18 years. Mean age at menarche has positive correlation with percent body fat.

When mean age at menarche of Chakma girls (12.30 year ± 0.50) is compared with other tribes of in North East India show a similar trend of higher mean menarcheal age: 12.45 years in Assamese (Deb,

2009) and 13.22 years in Khasi girls of Meghalaya (Deb, 2011). However, some of the studies of other Indian girls it is found that adolescent girls of Kerala, Andhra Pradesh (Reddy and Radhika, 2003) and Jammu (Sharma et al., 2006) have higher mean age at menarche 12.11, 13.88 and 13.85 respectively. Age at menarche in most females ranges between 10-16 years. General improvement in nutritional status and health condition has been suggested to explain the downward trend.

In our study the trend of higher mean age at menarche was well marked of lower socio-economic groups. The lower socio-economic status is usually associated with large family norms, poor living conditions, improper nutrition, could be the reason for growth retardation and poor physical and psychosexual maturity in them explaining the late onset of menarche. Higher mean age at menarche was observed in families with more children when comparing family with one or two children. The effect of family size and birth order on menarcheal age may be indirectly due to socio-economic influences (Dewhurst et al., 1984).

Different socio-economic factors influence the onset of menarche in this population. Mothers' education, fathers' occupation and family size influence the age at menarche in Chakma population. Association between various socio-economic factors with age at menarche differs according to ethnicity in India (Singh 1986; Arora et al., 1989; Sengupta et al., 1996; Reddy et al., 1997; Khatoon et al., 2011; Saxena 2014; Tarannum et al., 2018).

Conclusion

In conclusion, age at menarche was found to be delayed (12.30 year) in Chakma tribal girls of Tripura. Present study also gives information on the health and nutritional status of adolescent girls of Tripura which influences the female reproductive and child health conditions. There is scarcity on such data from this state of India; hence further study needs to be done among girls from other areas of the state before the data can be extrapolated to the Indian statistics. Present study sample experiences their late menarche is comparing to other tribes of north eastern region and to rest Indians. In global perspective the age at menarche in this study is less than European and North American countries most but closer to most African and Asian studies.

Acknowledgements

The researchers acknowledge all the school authorities for providing permission to carry out this work. We would like to thank all participating subjects of the present study for their cooperation. We also thank Dr Parasmani Dasgupta, Professor, Indian Statistical Institute, Kolkata and Mr. Samrat Hore, Assistant Professor (Stage-II), Department of Statistics, Tripura University, for their guidance and valuable suggestions during the work.

References

Arora R, Rajaram P, Gowri. 1989. Population based study of menstrual disorders in Pondicherry: A preliminary study. *The Journal of Obstetrics and Gynecology of India*. 39: 492-497.

Banerjee I, Chakraborty S, Bhattacharyya NG, Bandyopadhyay S, Saiyed HN, Mukherjee D. 2007. A cohort study of correlation between body mass index and age at menarche in healthy Bengali girls. *Journal of Indian Medical Association*. 105: 75-78.

Chumlea WC, Schubert CM, Roche AF, Kulin HE, Lee PA. 2003. Age at menarche and racial comparison in US girls. *Pediatrics*. 111: 110-113.

Cox DR. 1972. Regression models and life tables (with discussion). *Journal of Royal Statistical Society*. 34: 187-220.

Das PB, Das BM.1967. Age at menarche of Kalita girls in Assam. *Man in India*. 47: 113-117.

Deb R. 2009. Variation in the age at menarche of the Assamese and Bengali girls of Guwahati, Assam. *Anthropologist*.11: 259-264.

Deb R. 2011. Age at menarche in adolescent Khasi girls, Meghalaya. *Indian Pediatrics*. 48: 69.

Freedman DS, Khan LK, Serdula MK, Dietz WH, Srinivasan SR. 2002. Relation to age at menarche to race, time period and anthropometric dimensions: the Bogalusa Heart Study. *Paediatrics*. 110: e43.

Frisancho AR. 1990. *Anthropometric standardization for the assessment of growth and nutritional status*. Michigan: The University of Michigan Press Ann Arbor; 1990.

Gaudineau A, Ehlinger V, Emmanuelle G. 2010. Factors associated with early menarche: results from the French Health Behaviour in School aged Children (HBSC) study. *BMC Public Health*. 10: 175.

Heitmann BL. 1990. Evaluation of body fat estimated from body mass index, skinfolds and impedance. A comparative study. *European Journal of Clinical Nutrition*. 44: 831-837.

Khadilkar VV, Stanhope RG, Khadilkar V. 2006. Secular trends in puberty. *Indian Pediatrics*. 43: 475-478.

Khatoon T, Verma AK, Kumar IR, Rupani R, Singh M, Rizvi A. 2011. Age at menarche and affecting Bio-Social factors among the girls of Lucknow, Uttar Pradesh. *Journal of Indian Academy of Forensic Medicine*. 33: 221-

223.

Lifshitz F, Tarim O, Smith MM. 1993. Nutrition in adolescence. *Endocrinology & Metabolism Clinics of North America*. 22: 673-683.

Malina RM, Brown KH, Zavaleta AN. 1987. Relative lower extremity length in Mexican American and in American black and white youth. *American Journal of Physical Anthropology*. 72: 84–94.

Mishra D, Singh HP. 2003. Kuppuswami's socio-economic status scale –A revision. *Indian Journal of Pediatrics*. 70: 273–274.

Pramanik P, Chowdhury R, Das A. 2014. Reference values of body fat indices for semi urban children and adolescent of Bengali ethnicity. *Global Journal of Biology, Agriculture and Health Sciences*. 3: 19–29.

Rao S, Joshi S, Kanade A, 1998. Height velocity, body fat and menarcheal age of Indian girls. *Indian Pediatrics*. 35: 619-628.

Reddy PH, Modell B. 1997. The biagas of Madhya Pradesh: a demographic study. *Journal of Biosocial Science*. 29: 19-31.

Reddy BKC, Radhika P. 2003. Age at menarche and some biosocial factors among the girls of Nellore, Andhra Pradesh. *Anthropologist*. 5: 215-216.

Rokade SA, Mane AK. 2009. A study of age at menarche, the secular trend and factors associated with it. *The Internet Journal of Biological Anthropology*. 3: 1939-4594.

Saha S, Sil SK. 2015. Age at menarche in adolescent Chakma Girls of Tripura. *International Journal of Sciences and Applied Research*. 2: 51-53.

Saxena R. 2014. Impact of socio-economic status on age at menarche. *International Journal of Multidisciplinary Approach & Studies*. 1: 76-82.

Sengupta S, Gogoi G, Chetry HB. 1996. Variation in menarcheal age of Assamese girls. *Journal of Indian Medical Association*. 94: 88-90.

Singh GM. 1986. Onset of menarche in girls of Ludhina. *Indian Pediatrics*. 23: 263-265.

Sharma N, Vaid S, Manhas A. 2006. Age at menarche in two caste groups (Brahmins and Rajputs) from rural areas of Jammu. *Anthropologist*. 8: 55-57.

Sharma J, Mondal N. 2018. Physical growth and body composition assessment among rural adolescent girls (10-16 years) of Karbi Anglong, Assam, Northeast India. *Journal of Life Sciences*. 10: 16–28.

Sizonenko PC, Himes JH. 1993. Introduction to the use and interpretation of anthropometry in adolescence. *Hormone Research*. 39: 7-8.

Slaughter MH, Lohman TG, Boileau R. 1988. Skinfold equation for estimation of body fatness in children and youth. *Human Biology*. 60: 709–723.

Tarannum F, Khalique N, Eram U. 2018. A community based study on age of menarche among adolescent girls in Aligarh. *International Journal of Community Medicine and Public Health*. 5: 395-400.

Touitou Y, Portaluppi F, Smolensky MH, Rensing L. 2004. Ethical principles and standards for the conduct of human and animal biological rhythm research. *Chronobiology International*. 21: 161–170.

Ulyasek SA, Kerr DA. 1999. Anthropometric measurement error and the assessment of nutritional status. *British Journal of Nutrition*. 82:165–177.

Weiner JS, Lourie JA. 1969. *Human biology: aguide to field methods*. International Biological Programme, Handbook no. 9. Oxford, UK: Blackwell Scientific Publications.

LIST OF CONTRIBUTORS

John Basumatary

ICMR-SRF, Department of Anthropology, Gauhati University

Gulrukh Begum

Associate Professor, Department of Anthropology, Gauhati University. E-mail: gulrukhbegum@yahoo.co.in

Nitamoni Bharali

Research Scholar, Department of Anthropology, Assam University (Diphu Campus), Karbi Anglong-782462, Assam, India. E-mail: nmbharali@gmail.com

Antara Bose

Research Fellow, Department of Anthropology, University of North Bengal, District: Darjeeling, Pin-734013, West Bengal, India. E- mail: abose1202@gmail.com

Sumitabha Chakraborty

Sumitabha Chakraborty, Anthropological Survey of India, Eastern Regional Centre, Kolkata, E-mail: chakrabortysumitabha@gmail.com

Dipankar Chatterjee

Assistant Professor, Division of Rural and Tribal Development, RKM Vivekananda Educational and Research Institute (Deemed University), Ranchi Campus, E-mail: dipcha123@gmail.com

Sudipta Dey

Research Scholar, Department of Anthropology and Tribal studies, Sidho-Kanho-Birsha University, Purulia

Abhijit Ghosal

Assistant Professor in Anthropology, Subarnarekha Mahavidyalaya, Gopiballavpur, Jhargram E-mail: anth.abhijit@gmail.com

Sudipta Ghosh

Assistant Professor, Department of Anthropology, North-Eastern Hill University, Mawkynroh-Umshing, Shillong- 793022, Meghalaya. E-mail: ghosh.sudiptaa@gmail.com

Gangaina Kameih

Department of Anthropology, University of Delhi, Delhi 110 007, India.

Gautam K. Kshatriya

Professor (Retired) Department of Anthropology, University of Delhi, Delhi-110007, India. E-mail: g26_51@yahoo.co.in

Nutsolu Lohe

Research scholar, Department of Anthropology, North-Eastern Hill University, Mawkynroh-Umshing, Shillong- 793022, Meghalaya. E-mail: nutsolul@gmail.com

Prasenjit Mahato

Department of Anthropology and Tribal Studies, Sidho-Kanho-Birsha University, Purulia

Sudhanshu Shekhar Mahato

Assistant Professor, Department of Sociology, A.S. College, Deoghar (Jharkhand), E-mail: mahatosssocio@gmail.com

Koustab Majumdar

Teaching Assistant, Division of Rural and Tribal Development, RKM Vivekananda Educational and Research Institute (Deemed University), Ranchi Campus, E-mail: koustab3662@gmail.com

Gopal Chandra Mandal

Associate Professor and Head, Department of Anthropology, Bangabasi College, Kolkata. (M) 09433773205, E-mail: golmal_anth@rediffmail.com

Jayanty Mitra

M. Sc. Student, Indira Gandhi National Open University, Bhubaneswar.

Nitish Mondal

Associate Professor, Department of Anthropology, Sikkim University, Gangtok 737102, Sikkim, India. E-mail: nitishanth@gmail.com

M. Siva Durga Prasad Nayak

Assistant Professor, Department of Community Medicine, RIMS Medical Colleges, Ongole, Andhra Pradesh. E-mail: sivadurgaprasadnayak@gmail.com

Manoj Raul

Research Scholar, Ramakrishna Mission Vivekananda Educational and Research Institute, Faculty of IRTDM, Division of Rural and Tribal development, School of Agriculture and Rural Development, Morabadi, Ranchi, Jharkhand-834008. E-mail: manojraul0999@gmail.com

Satyapriya Roy

Research Scholar, Department of Human Physiology, Tripura University. E-mail: satyapriya_roy123@yahoo.com

Shilpi Saha

Department of Human Physiology, Tripura University. (A Central University), Suryamaninagar 799022, Tripura. E-mail: shilpisaha_07@yahoo.com

Jaydip Sen

Professor, Department of Anthropology, University of North Bengal, District: Darjeeling, Pin-734013, West Bengal, India. E-mail: jaydipsen@rediffmail.com

Jaydeep Sengupta

Assistant Professor, Department of Anthropology and Tribal Studies, Sidho-Kanho-Birsha University, Purulia. E-mail: senjaydeep@gmail.com

Maitreyee Sharma

Assistant Professor, Department of Anthropology, Dibrugarh University. E-mail: maitreyeesharma@dibru.ac.in

P Dash Sharma

Retired Professor, Department of Anthropology, Ranchi University, Ranchi 834008, Jharkhand.Mailing address: Diganta Apartment, A-3, 3rd Floor, 11-New Santoshpur Main Road, Kolkata 700075, West Bengal. E-mail: pdashsharma@rediffmail.com

Samir Kumar Sil

Professor, Department of Human Physiology, Tripura University. (A Central University). E-mail: s_k_sil@yahoo.com

Kh. Narendra Singh

Professor, Department of Anthropology, Assam University (Diphu Campus), Karbi Anglong-782462, Assam, India. E-mail: kh.singh@rediffmail.com

Sunita Sreegiri

Associate Professor, Department of Community Medicine, Andhra Medical College, Visakhapatnam, Andhra Pradesh.

Jenny Jami

Assistant Professor, Department of Anthropology, Saint Claret College, Ziro, Arunachal Pradesh, India - 91120. E-mail: jennyjami77@gmail.com

D K Limbu

Professor, Department of Anthropology, North-Eastern Hill University, Shillong, India - 793022. E-mail: dhruba_limbu@yahoo.co.in

Nilakantha Panigrahi

Associate Professor, Department of Anthropology and Tribal Development, Guru Ghasidas Viushwavidyalaya, Bilaspur, Chhattisgarh, E-mail: nilakantha.panigrahi@gmail.com

Sephali Mohanta

Research Scholar, COATS, Koraput, Berhampur University, Bhanja Vihar Berhampur. E-mail:sephalimohanta2015@gmail.com

Bidyut Krishna Goswami

Professor, Department of Pathology,North Bengal Medical College, Sushrutanagar, Darjeeling, West Bengal. E-mail: drbkg61@gmail.com

Sreeparna Banerjee

Research scholar, Department of Anthropology, West Bengal State University, Berunanpukuria, PO-Malikapur, Barasat, West Bengal, India 700126. E-mail: banerjeesree15@gmail.com

Shimul Roy

Assistant Professor, Department of Anthropology, Vidyasagar University, Midnapore 721102, West Bengal, India.E-mail: shimulroy888@gmail.com

Subir Biswas

Professor, Department of Anthropology, West Bengal State University, Berunanpukuria, PO-Malikapur, Barasat, West Bengal, India 700126. E-mail: gargisubir@gmail.com

Manoranjan Pal

Retired Professor, Economic Research Unit, Indian Statistical Institute, 203 BT Road, Kolkata 700 108, West Bengal, India.E-mail: manoranjan.pal@gmail.com

Premananda Bharati

Retired Professor, Biological Anthropology, Indian Statistical Institute, 203 BT Road,Kolkata 700 108, West Bengal, India. E-mail: pbharati@gmail.com